The Flowers of Evil

volume 2

Shuzo Oshimi

VERTICAL.

Contents

Chapter 7: Madness

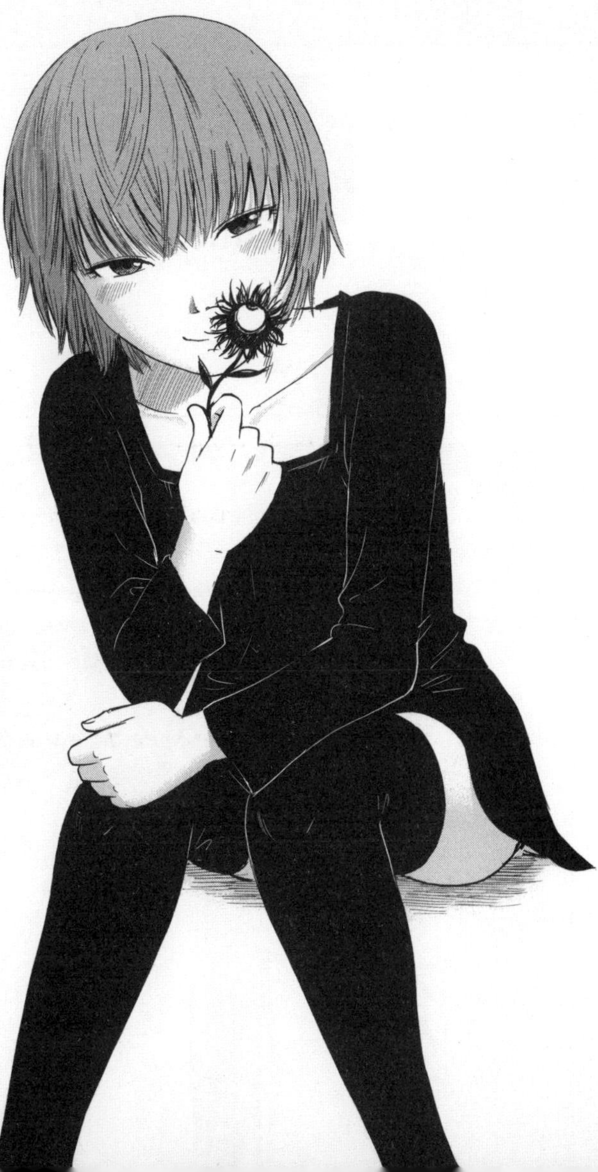

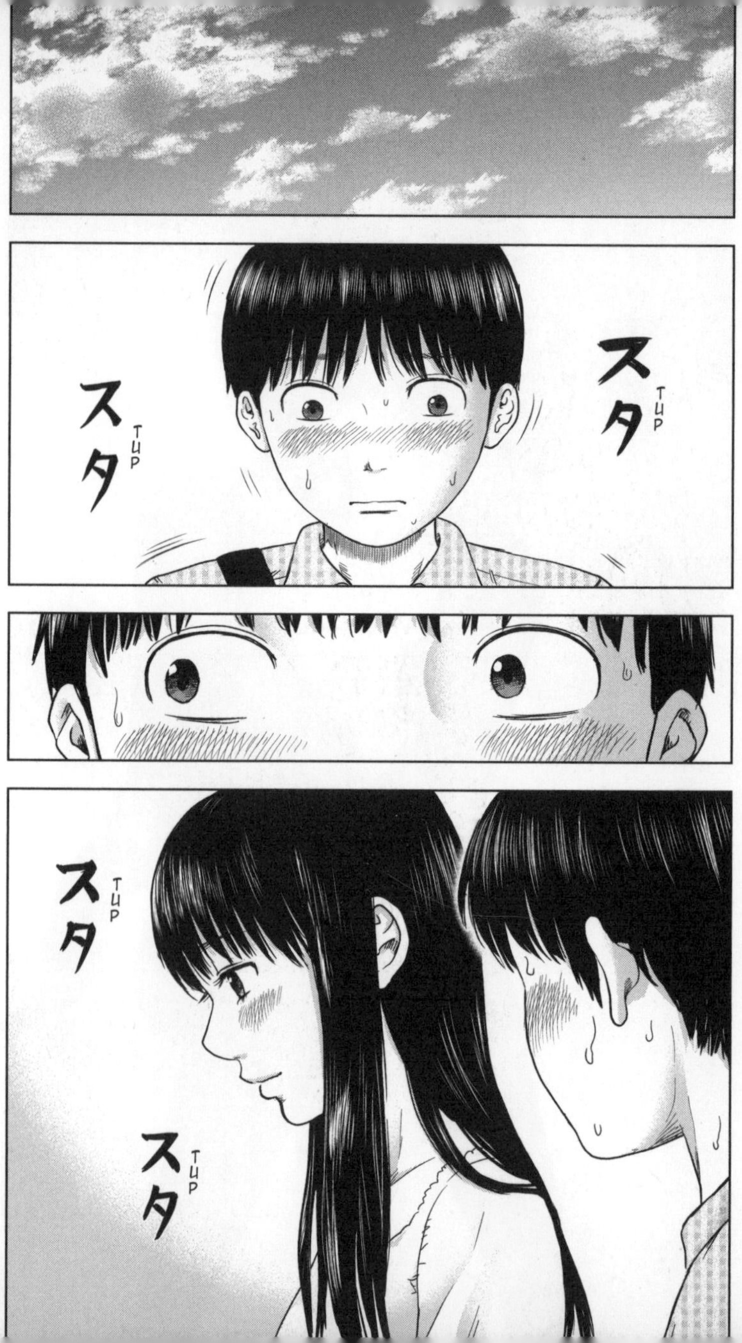

スタ TUP
スタ TUP
スタ TUP
スタ TUP

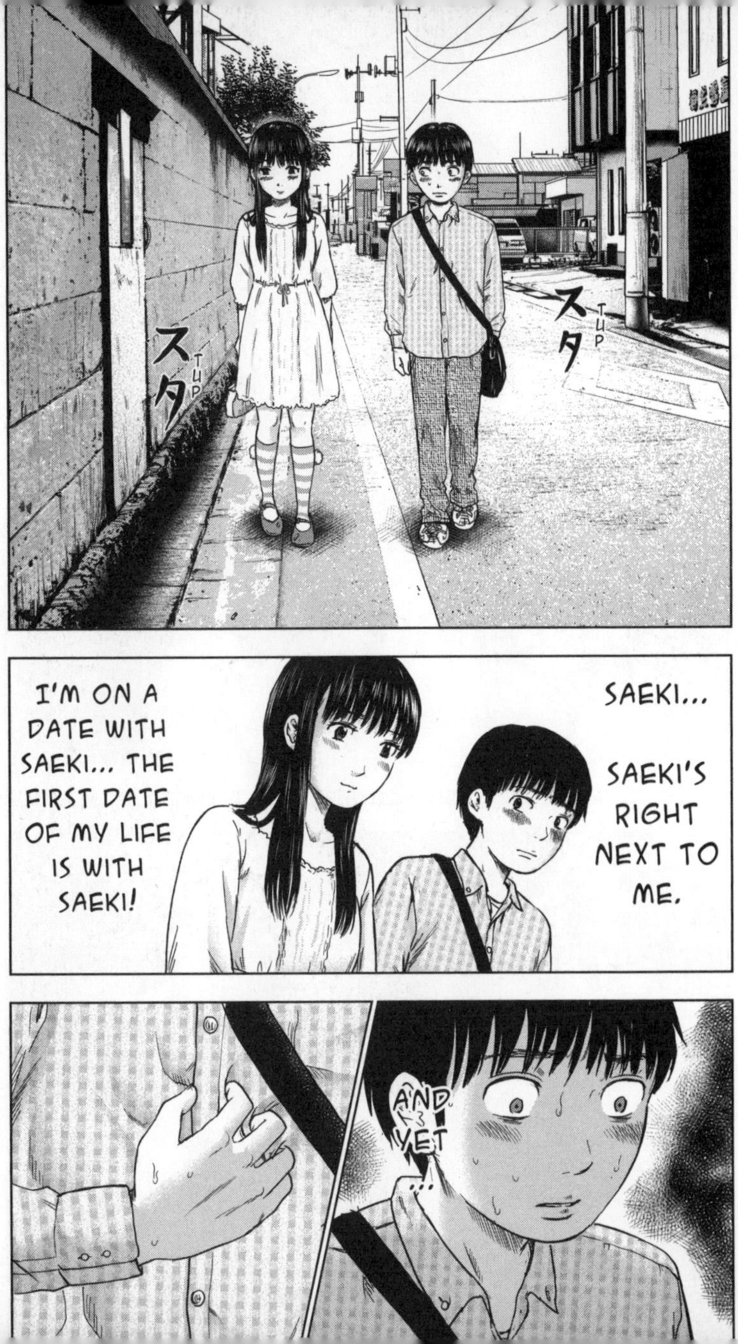
スタ
TUP
スタ
TUP
SAEKI...
SAEKI'S RIGHT NEXT TO ME.
I'M ON A DATE WITH SAEKI... THE FIRST DATE OF MY LIFE IS WITH SAEKI!
AND YET...

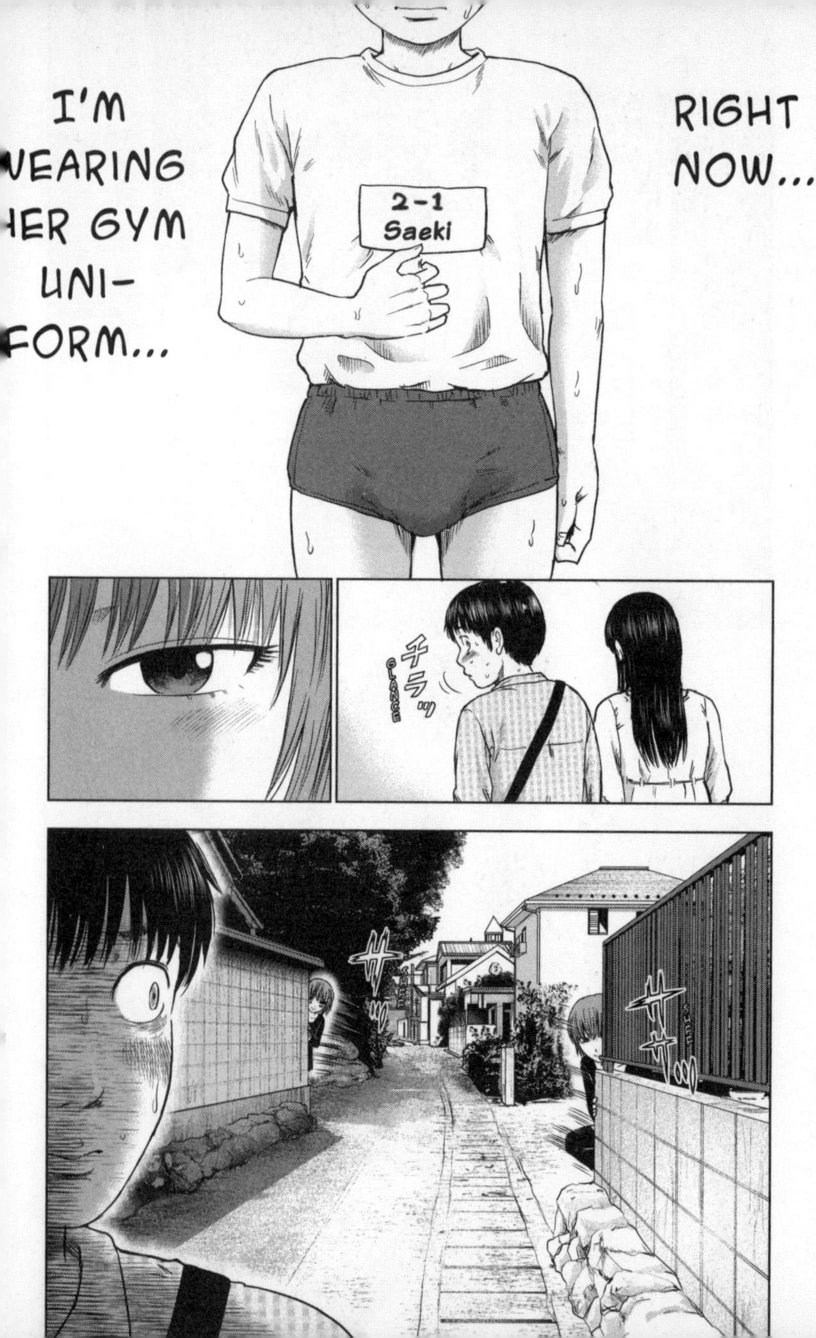
RIGHT NOW...
2-1
Saeki
I'M WEARING HER GYM UNI-FORM...
チラッ
GLANCE
ササッ
SHFF
ササッ
SHFF

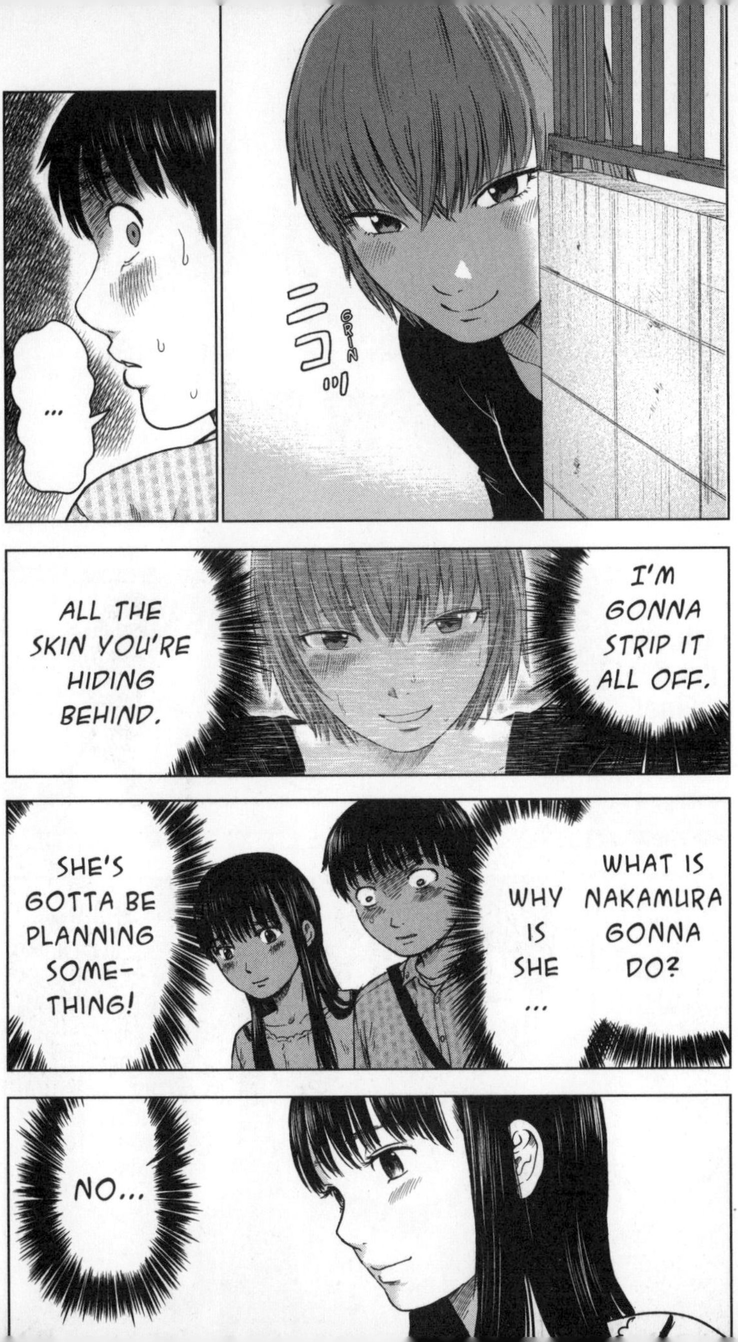
ニコッ
GRIN
...
I'M GONNA STRIP IT ALL OFF.
ALL THE SKIN YOU'RE HIDING BEHIND.
WHAT IS NAKAMURA GONNA DO?
WHY IS SHE ...
SHE'S GOTTA BE PLANNING SOME-THING!
NO...

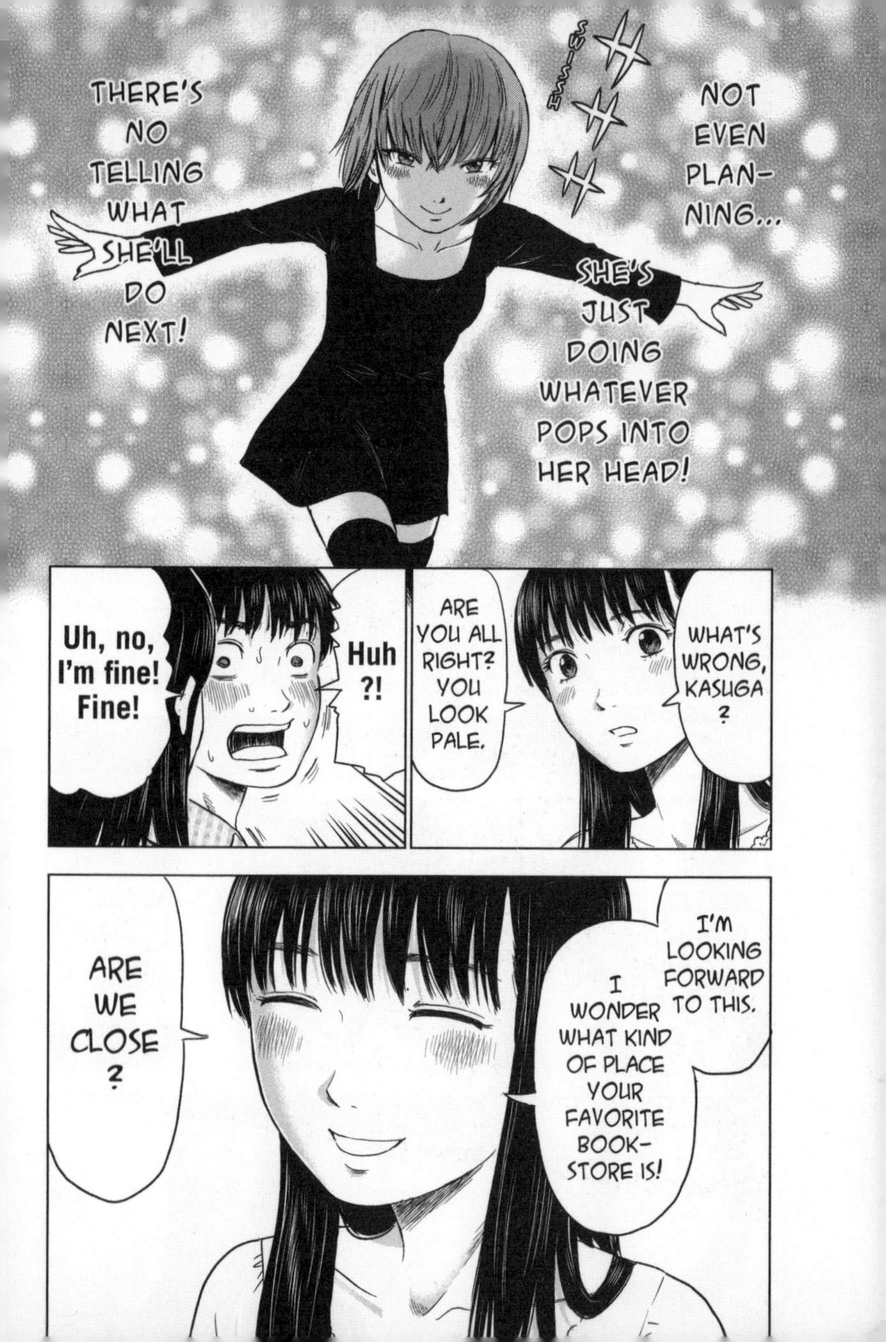
NOT EVEN PLAN-NING...
SHE'S JUST DOING WHATEVER POPS INTO HER HEAD!
THERE'S NO TELLING WHAT SHE'LL DO NEXT!
WHAT'S WRONG, KASUGA?
ARE YOU ALL RIGHT? YOU LOOK PALE.
Huh ?!
Uh, no, I'm fine! Fine!
I'M LOOKING FORWARD TO THIS.
I WONDER WHAT KIND OF PLACE YOUR FAVORITE BOOK-STORE IS!
ARE WE CLOSE?

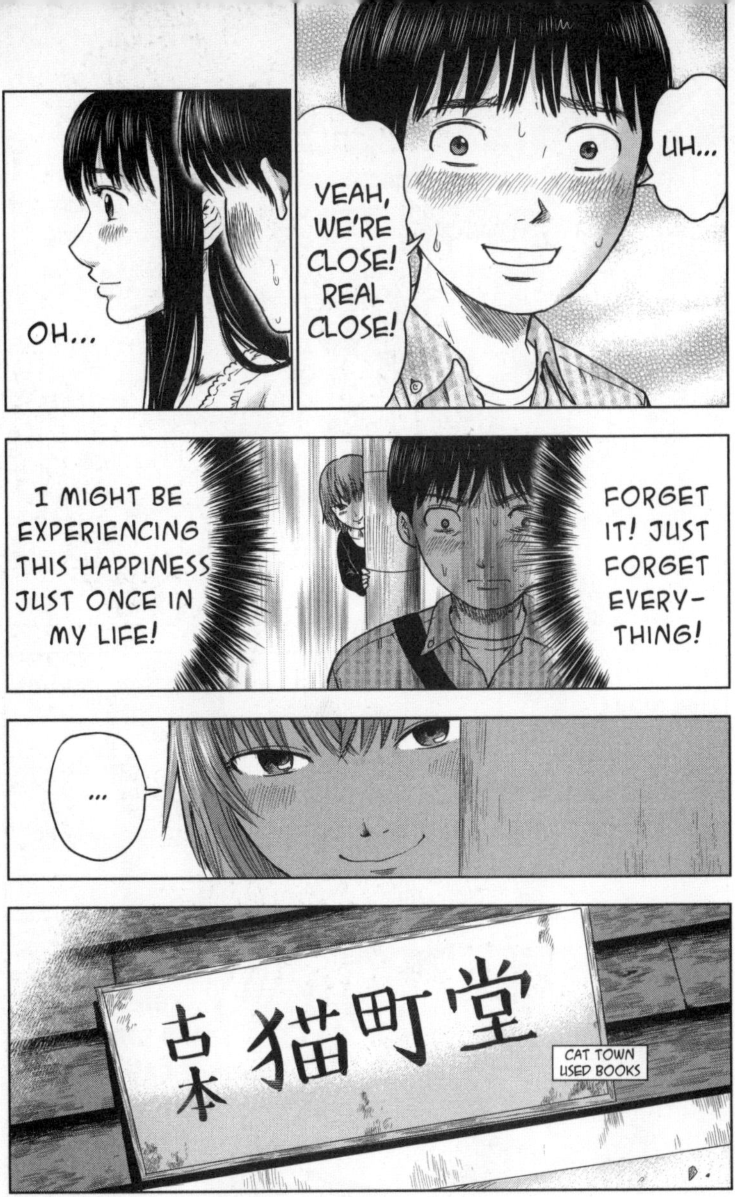
UH...
YEAH, WE'RE CLOSE! REAL CLOSE!
OH...
FORGET IT! JUST FORGET EVERY-THING!
I MIGHT BE EXPERIENCING THIS HAPPINESS JUST ONCE IN MY LIFE!
...
古本 猫町堂
CAT TOWN USED BOOKS

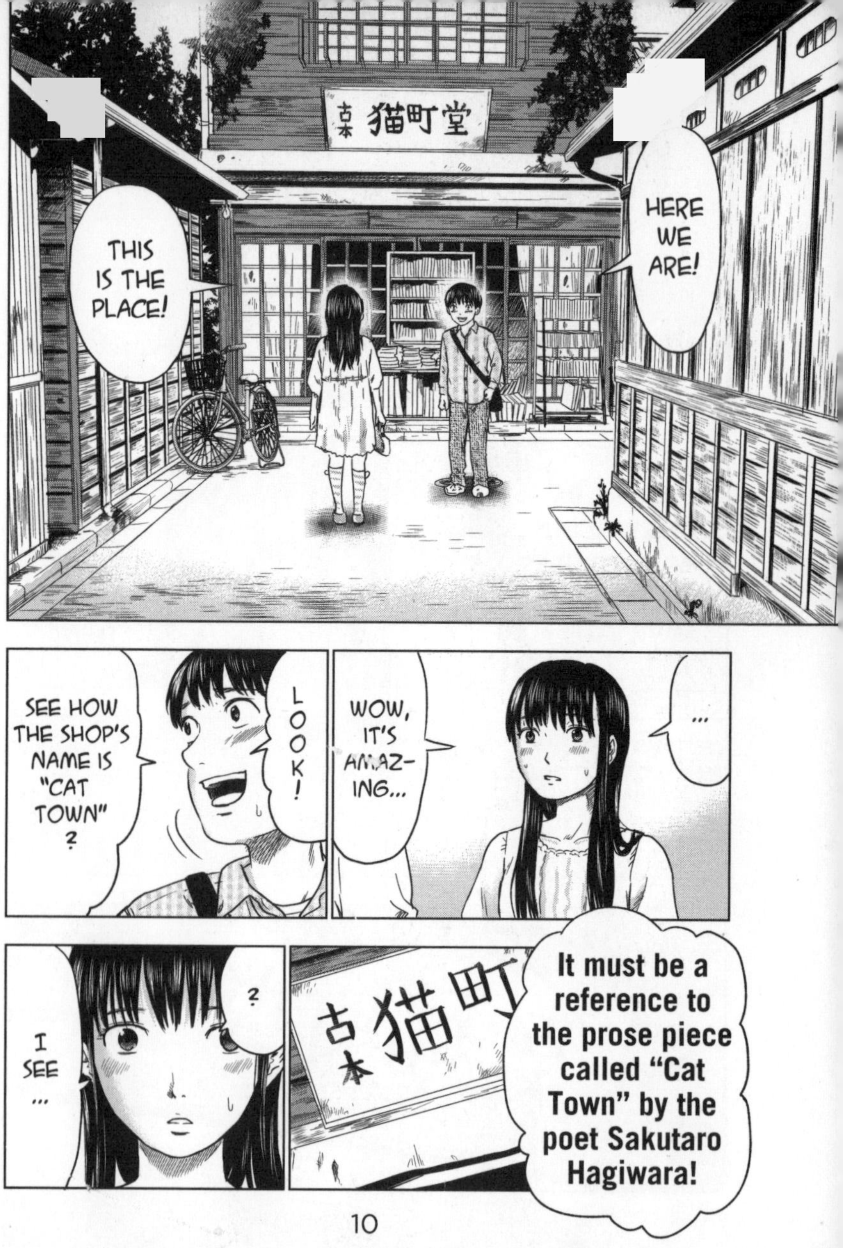
HERE WE ARE!
THIS IS THE PLACE!
...
WOW, IT'S AMAZ-ING...
LOOK!
SEE HOW THE SHOP'S NAME IS "CAT TOWN"?
It must be a reference to the prose piece called "Cat Town" by the poet Sakutaro Hagiwara!
?
I SEE ...

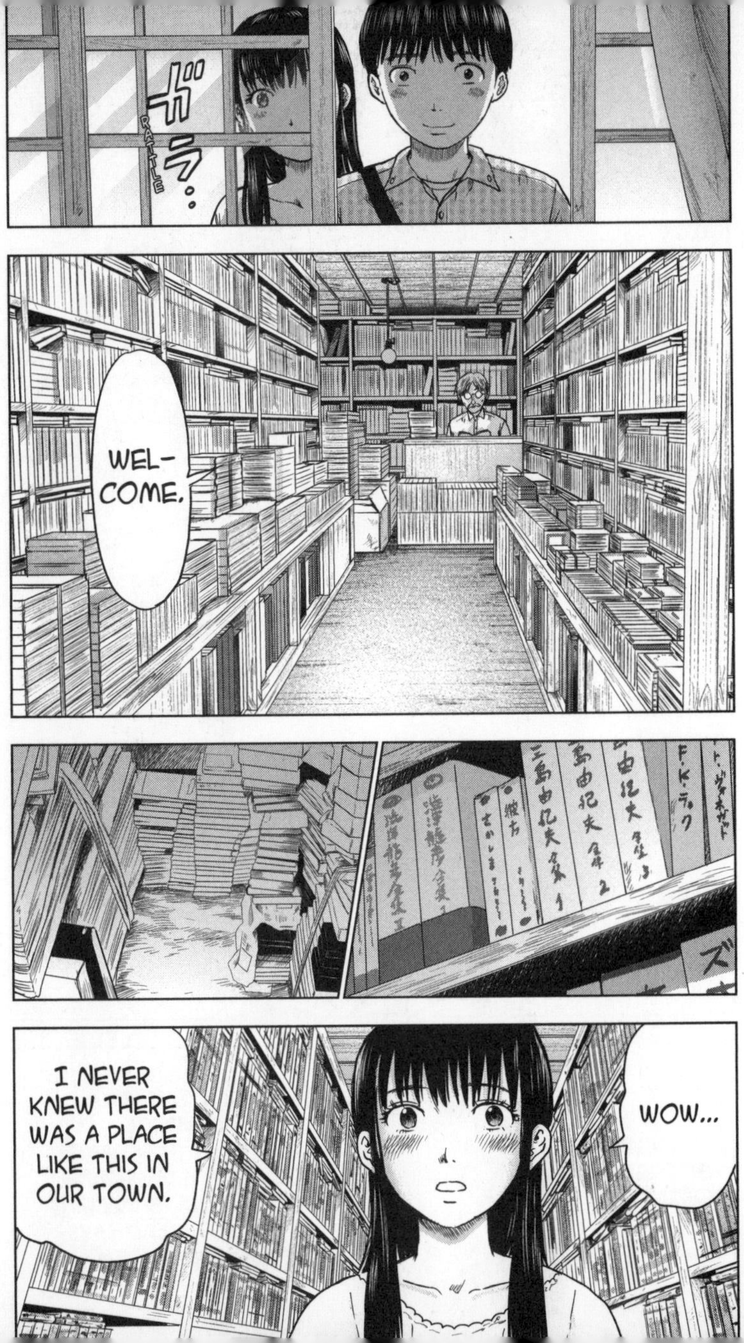
ガラ
RATTLE
WEL-COME.
WOW...
I NEVER KNEW THERE WAS A PLACE LIKE THIS IN OUR TOWN.

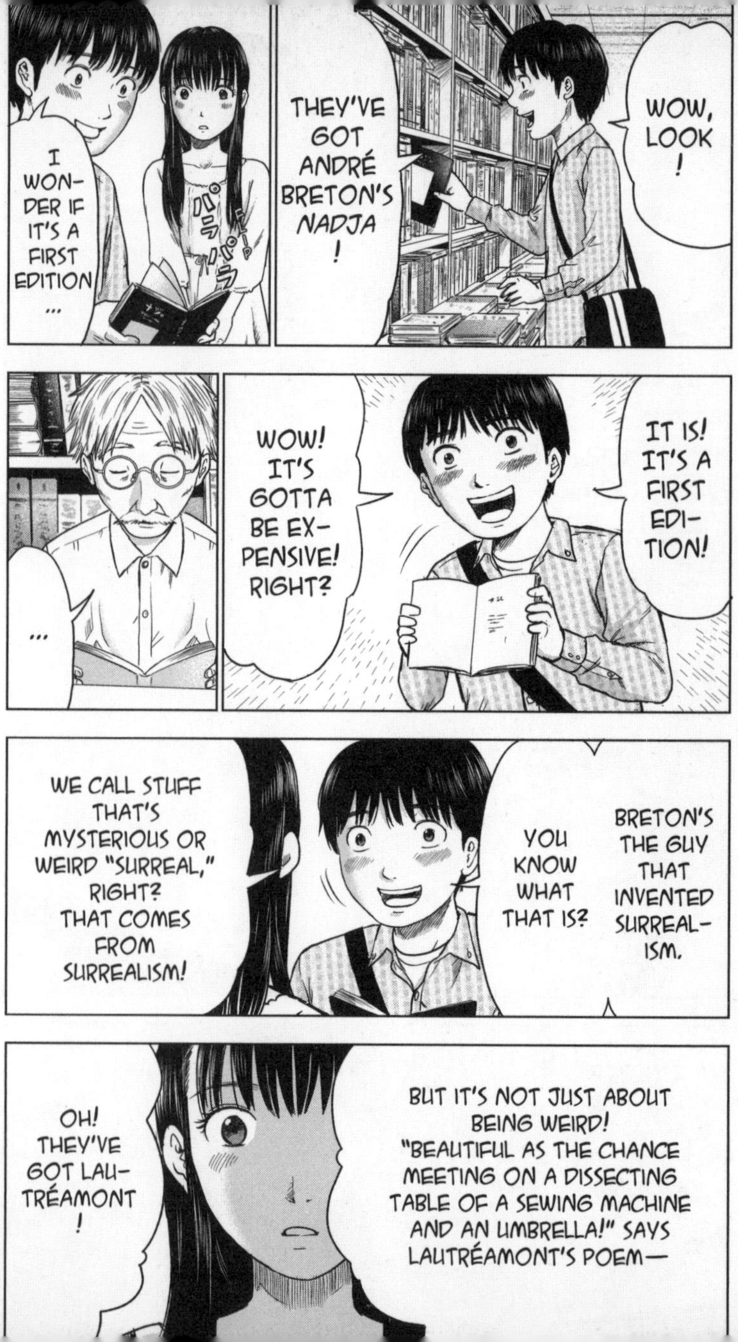
WOW, LOOK!
THEY'VE GOT ANDRÉ BRETON'S NADJA!
FLIP
I WONDER IF IT'S A FIRST EDITION...
IT IS! IT'S A FIRST EDITION!
WOW! IT'S GOTTA BE EXPENSIVE! RIGHT?
...
BRETON'S THE GUY THAT INVENTED SURREALISM.
YOU KNOW WHAT THAT IS?
WE CALL STUFF THAT'S MYSTERIOUS OR WEIRD "SURREAL," RIGHT? THAT COMES FROM SURREALISM!
BUT IT'S NOT JUST ABOUT BEING WEIRD! "BEAUTIFUL AS THE CHANCE MEETING ON A DISSECTING TABLE OF A SEWING MACHINE AND AN UMBRELLA!" SAYS LAUTRÉAMONT'S POEM—
OH! THEY'VE GOT LAUTRÉAMONT!

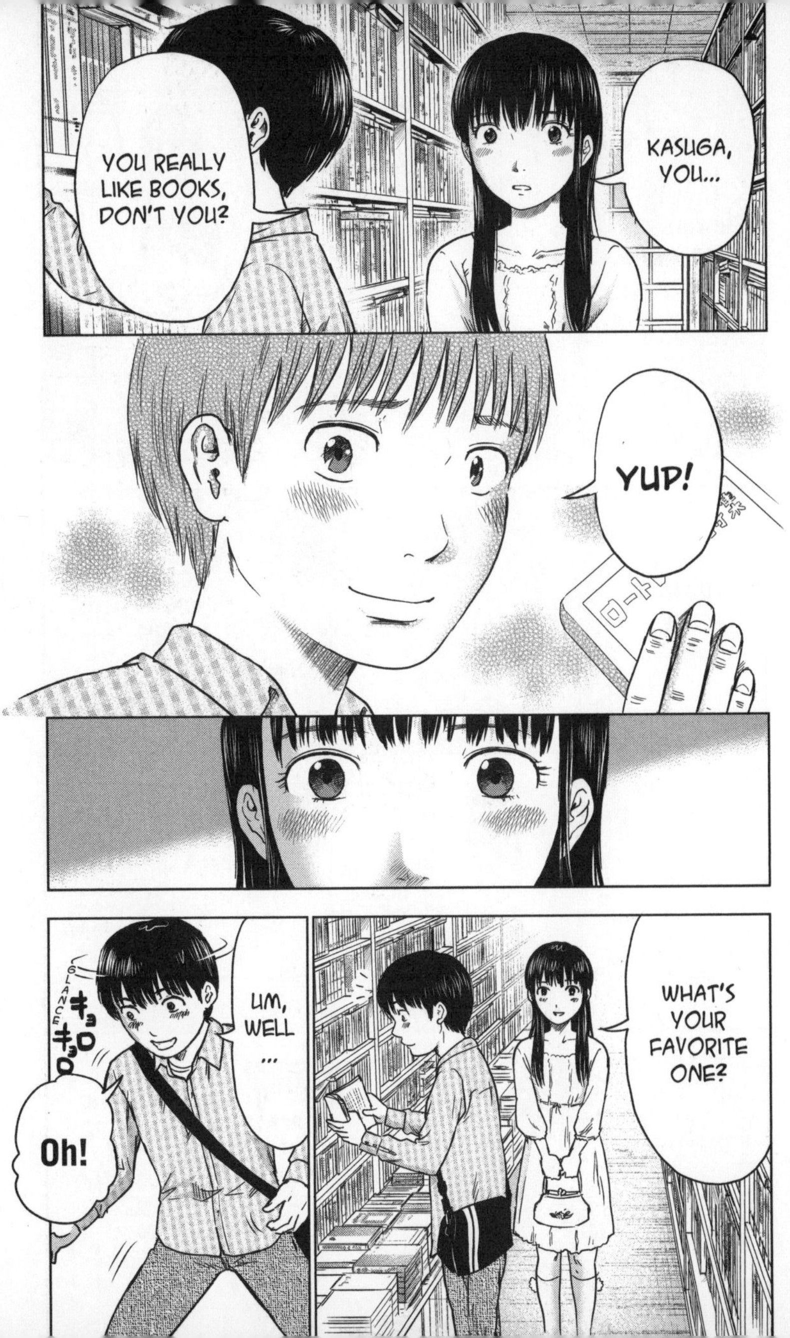
KASUGA, YOU...
YOU REALLY LIKE BOOKS, DON'T YOU?
YUP!
WHAT'S YOUR FAVORITE ONE?
UM, WELL ...
GLANCE キョロキョロ
Oh!

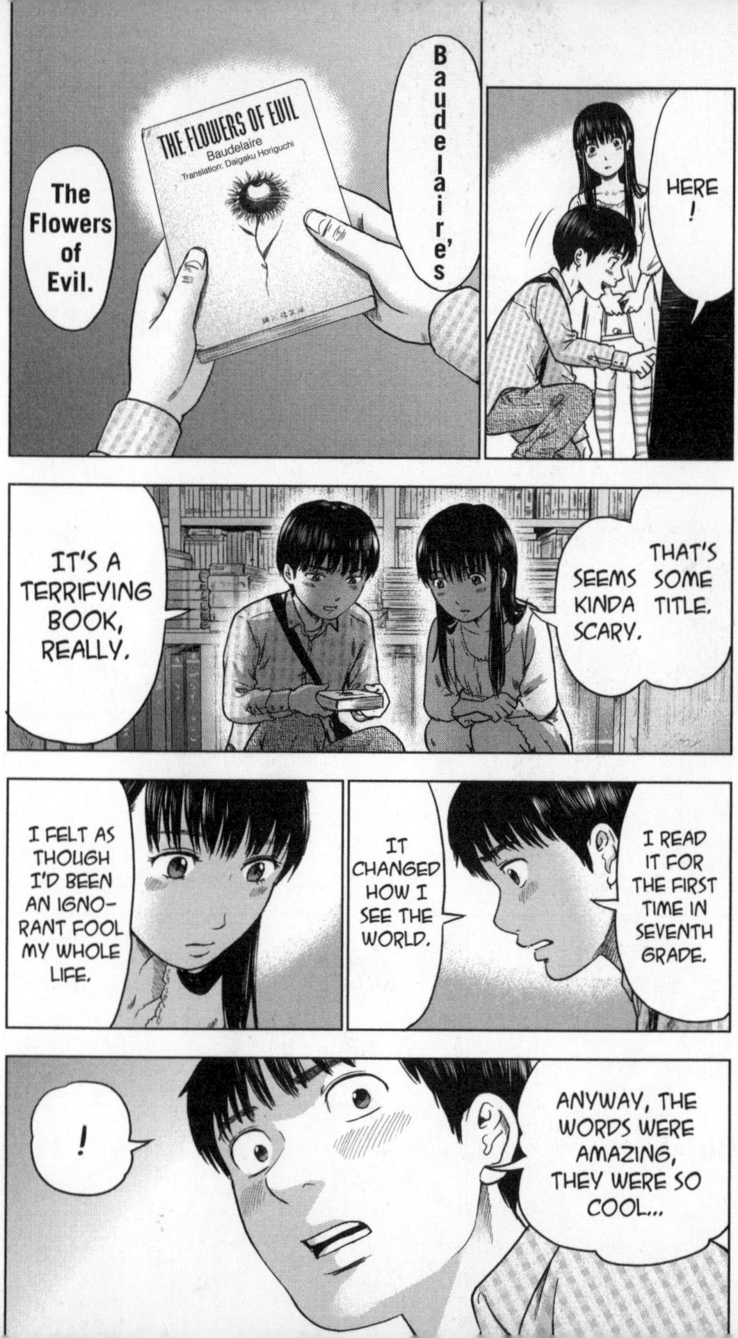
HERE!
Baudelaire's
THE FLOWERS OF EVIL
Baudelaire
Translation: Daigaku Horiguchi
The Flowers of Evil.
THAT'S SOME TITLE. SEEMS KINDA SCARY.
IT'S A TERRIFYING BOOK, REALLY.
I READ IT FOR THE FIRST TIME IN SEVENTH GRADE.
IT CHANGED HOW I SEE THE WORLD.
I FELT AS THOUGH I'D BEEN AN IGNORANT FOOL MY WHOLE LIFE.
ANYWAY, THE WORDS WERE AMAZING, THEY WERE SO COOL...
!

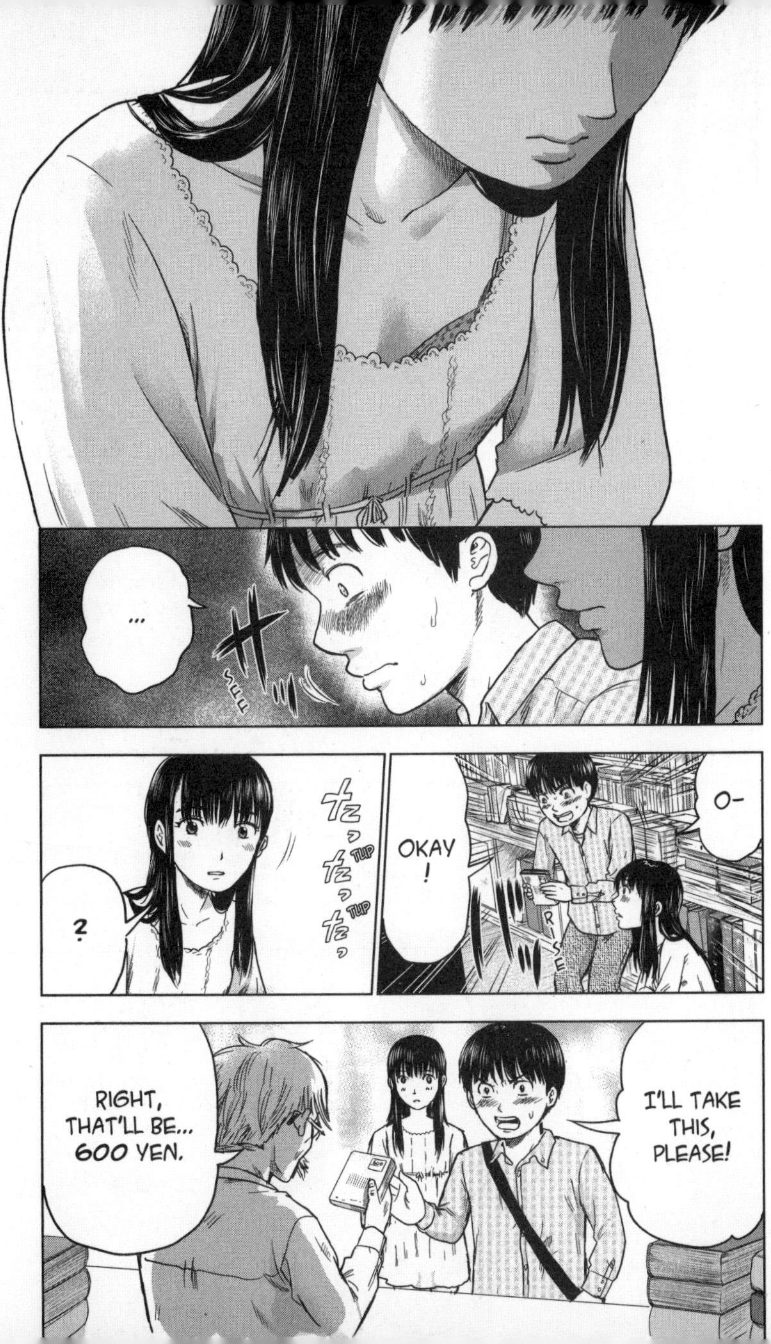
...
O-
OKAY!
RISE
TUP
TUP
?
I'LL TAKE THIS, PLEASE!
RIGHT, THAT'LL BE... 600 YEN.

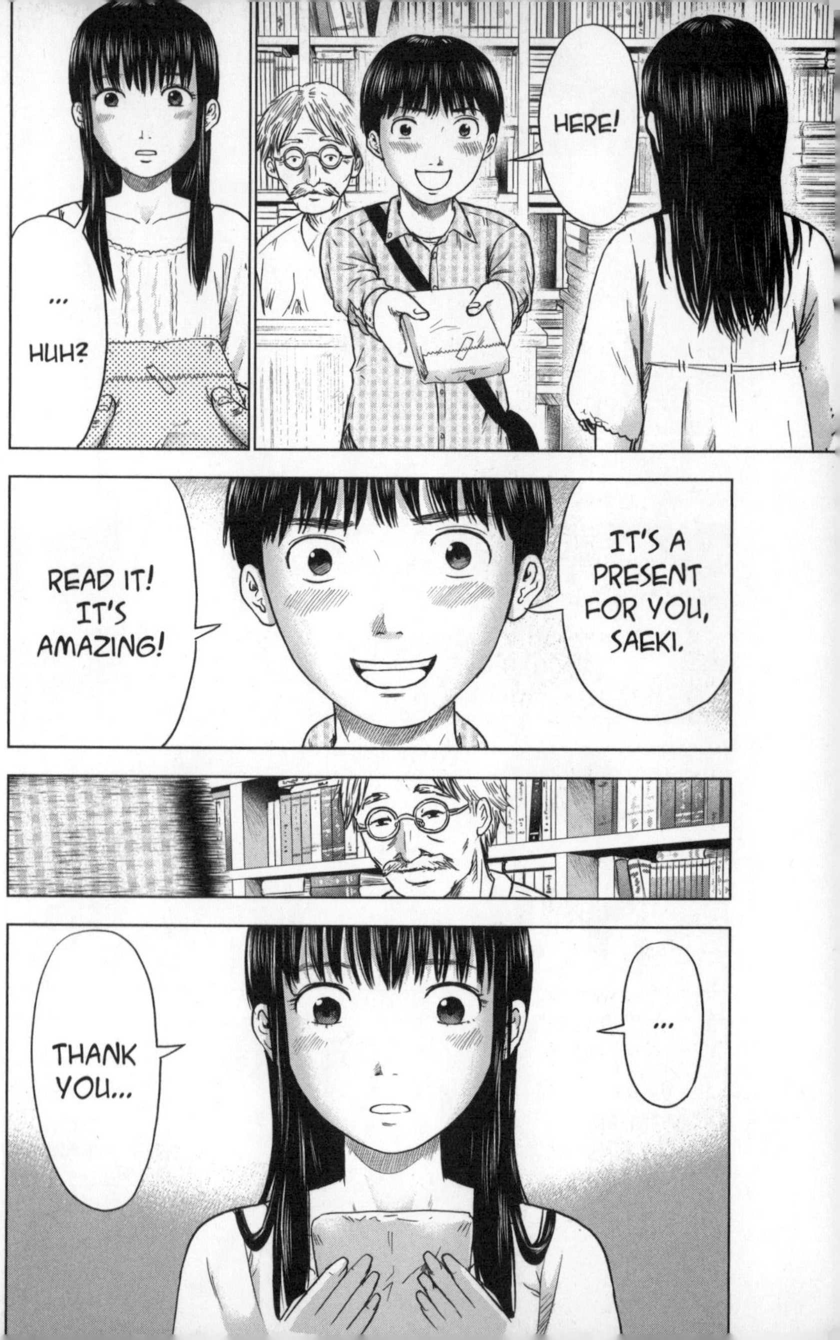
HERE!
...
HUH?
IT'S A PRESENT FOR YOU, SAEKI.
READ IT! IT'S AMAZING!
...
THANK YOU...

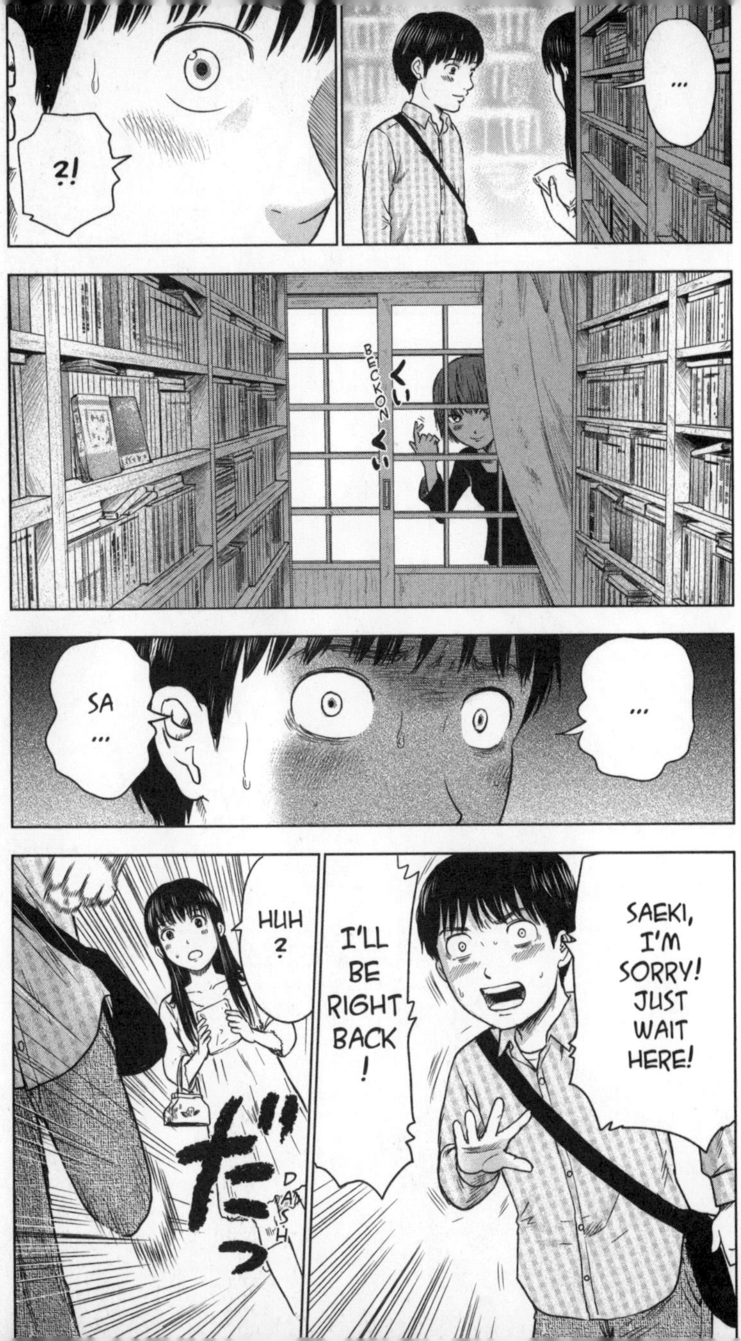
...
?!
くい
BECKON
くい
...
SA ...
SAEKI, I'M SORRY! JUST WAIT HERE!
I'LL BE RIGHT BACK!
HUH?
ダッ
DASH

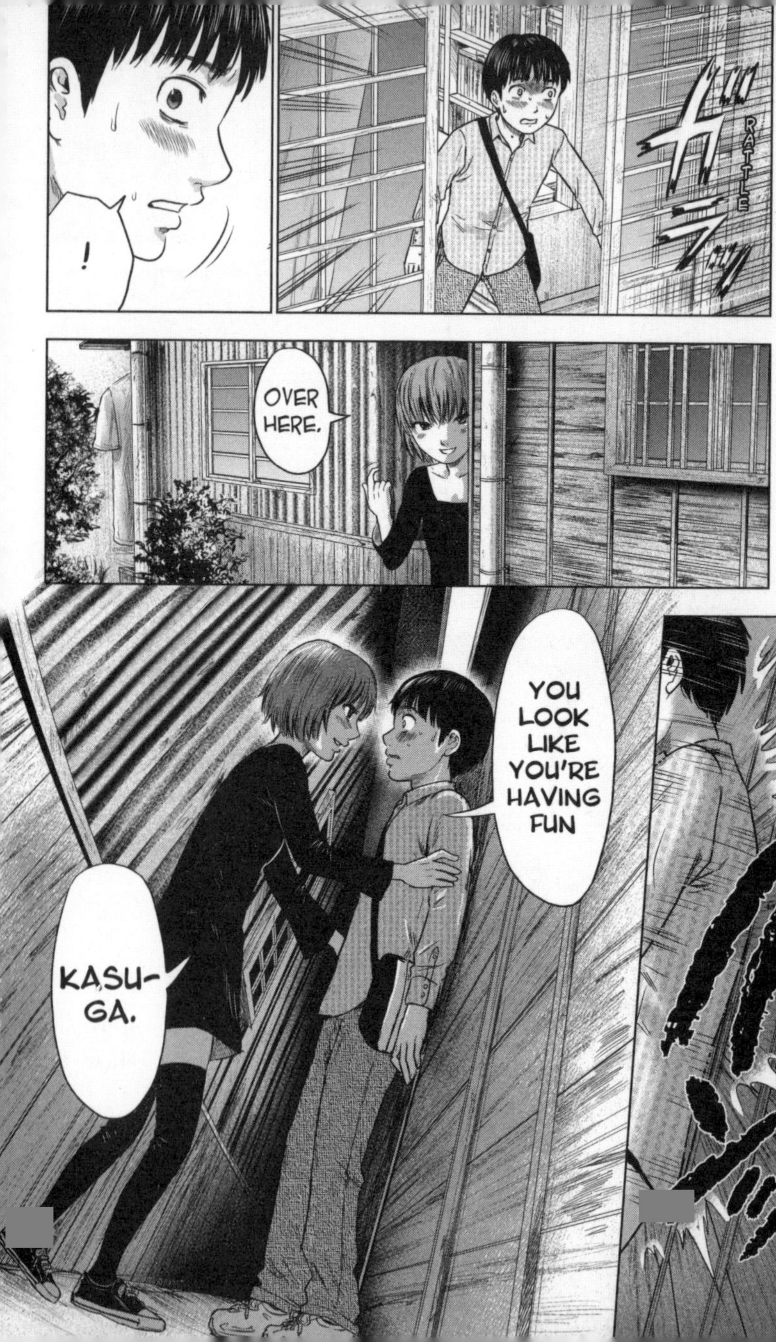
RATTLE
!
OVER HERE.
WHAM
YOU LOOK LIKE YOU'RE HAVING FUN
KASU-GA.

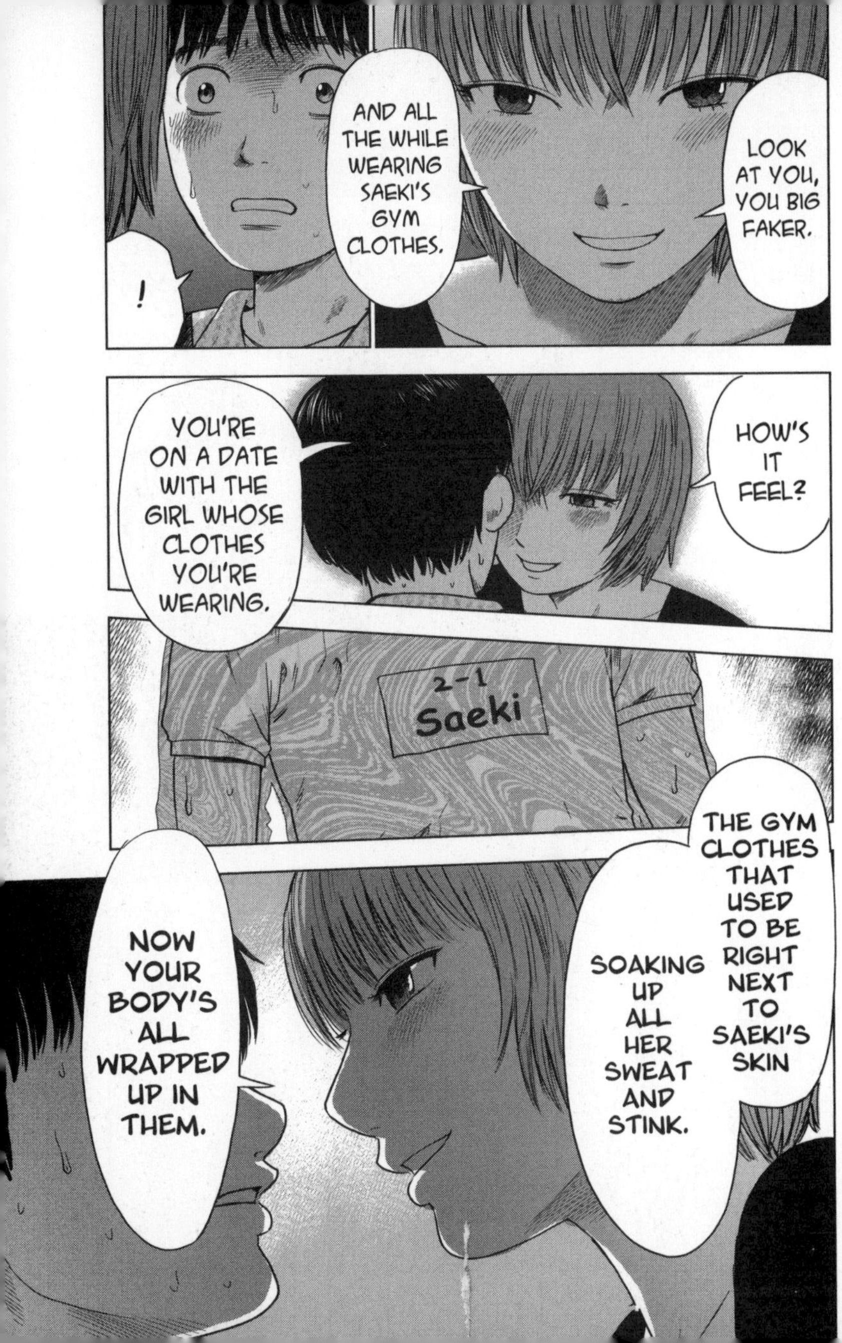
LOOK AT YOU, YOU BIG FAKER.
AND ALL THE WHILE WEARING SAEKI'S GYM CLOTHES.
!
HOW'S IT FEEL?
YOU'RE ON A DATE WITH THE GIRL WHOSE CLOTHES YOU'RE WEARING.
2-1 Saeki
THE GYM CLOTHES THAT USED TO BE RIGHT NEXT TO SAEKI'S SKIN
SOAKING UP ALL HER SWEAT AND STINK.
NOW YOUR BODY'S ALL WRAPPED UP IN THEM.

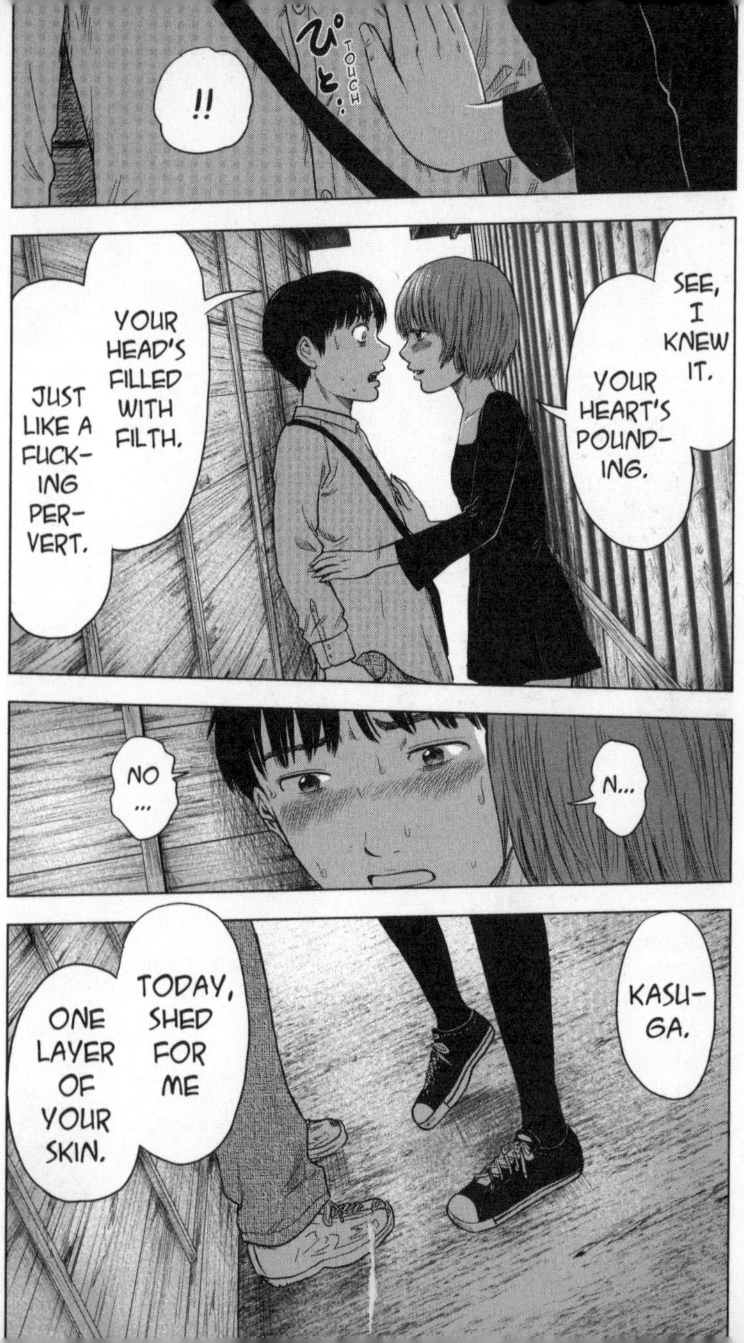
ぴと…
TOUCH
!!
SEE, I KNEW IT.
YOUR HEART'S POUNDING.
YOUR HEAD'S FILLED WITH FILTH.
JUST LIKE A FUCKING PERVERT.
N...
NO ...
KASUGA.
TODAY, SHED FOR ME
ONE LAYER OF YOUR SKIN.

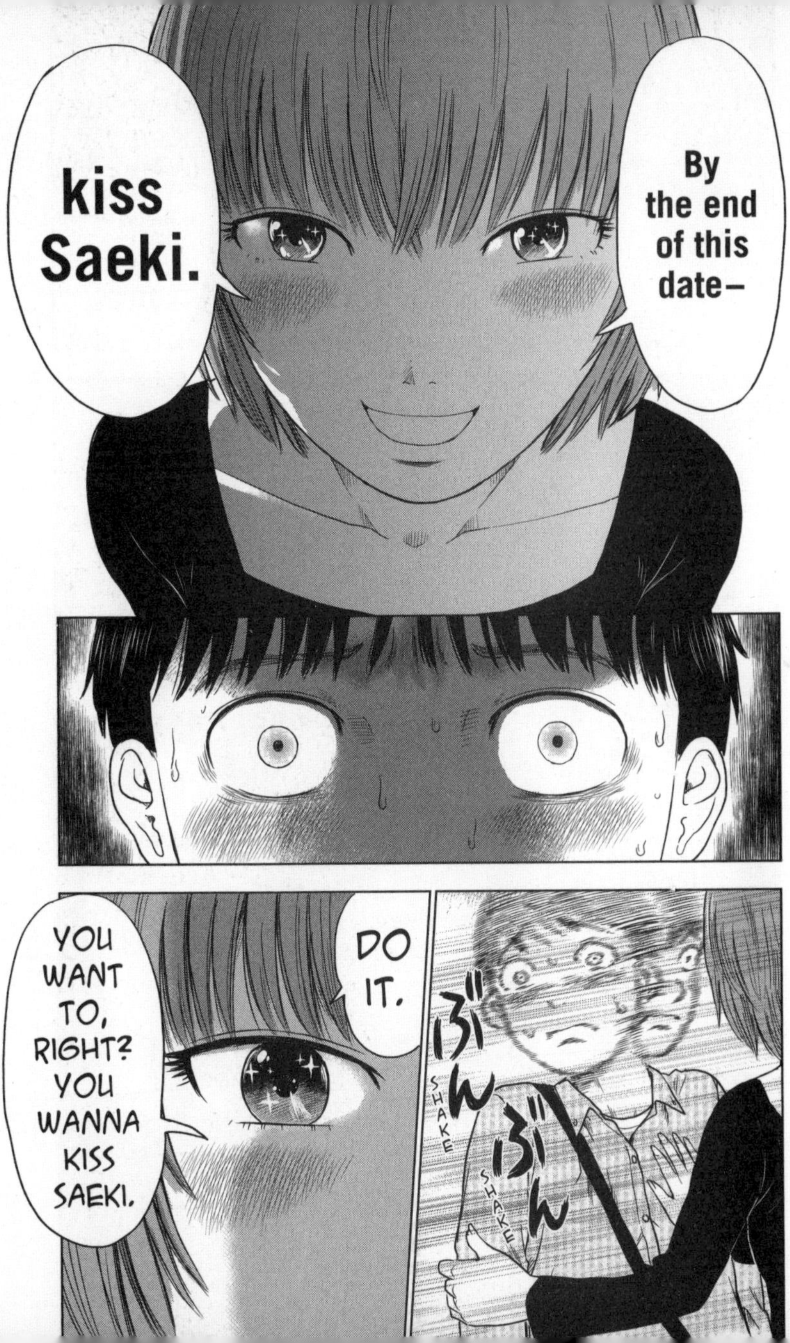
By the end of this date–
kiss Saeki.
SHAKE
SHAKE
DO IT.
YOU WANT TO, RIGHT? YOU WANNA KISS SAEKI.

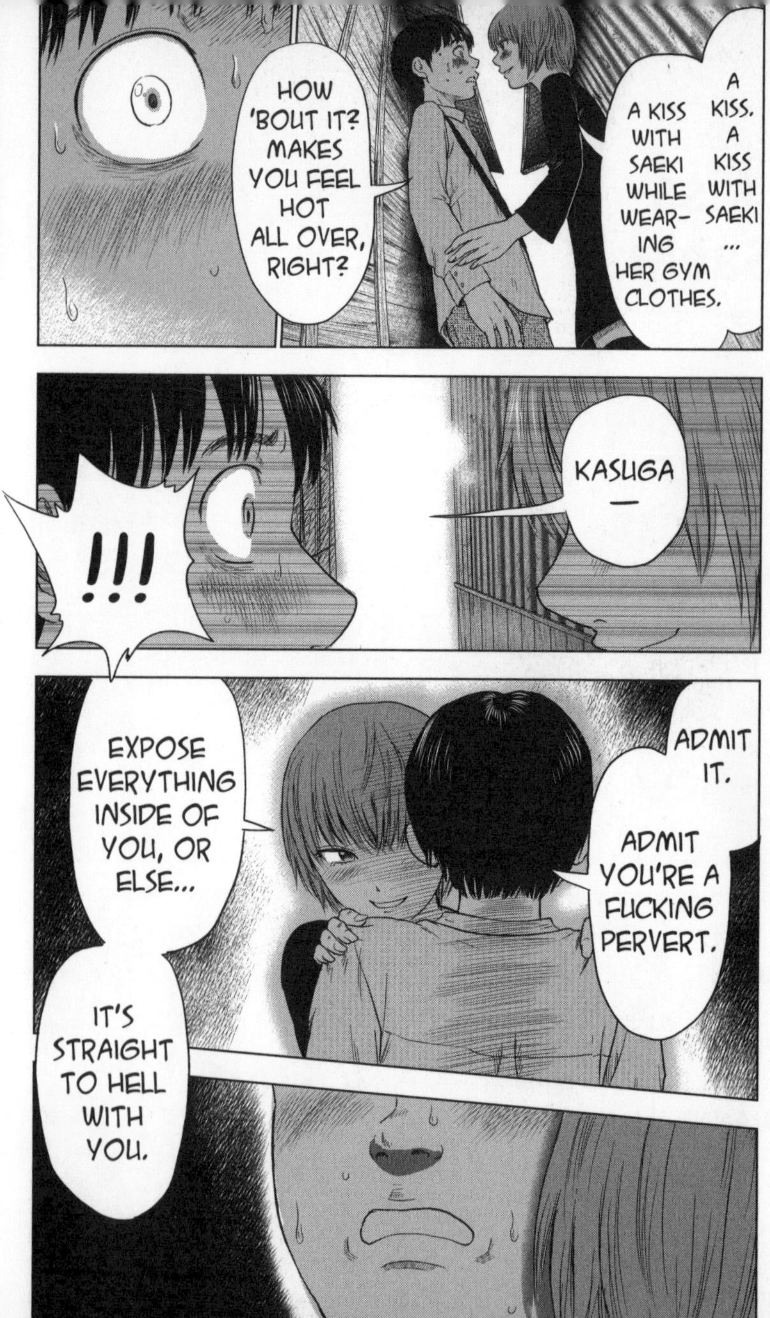
A KISS. A KISS WITH SAEKI...
A KISS WITH SAEKI WHILE WEARING HER GYM CLOTHES.
HOW 'BOUT IT? MAKES YOU FEEL HOT ALL OVER, RIGHT?
KASUGA —
!!!
ADMIT IT.
ADMIT YOU'RE A FUCKING PERVERT.
EXPOSE EVERYTHING INSIDE OF YOU, OR ELSE...
IT'S STRAIGHT TO HELL WITH YOU.

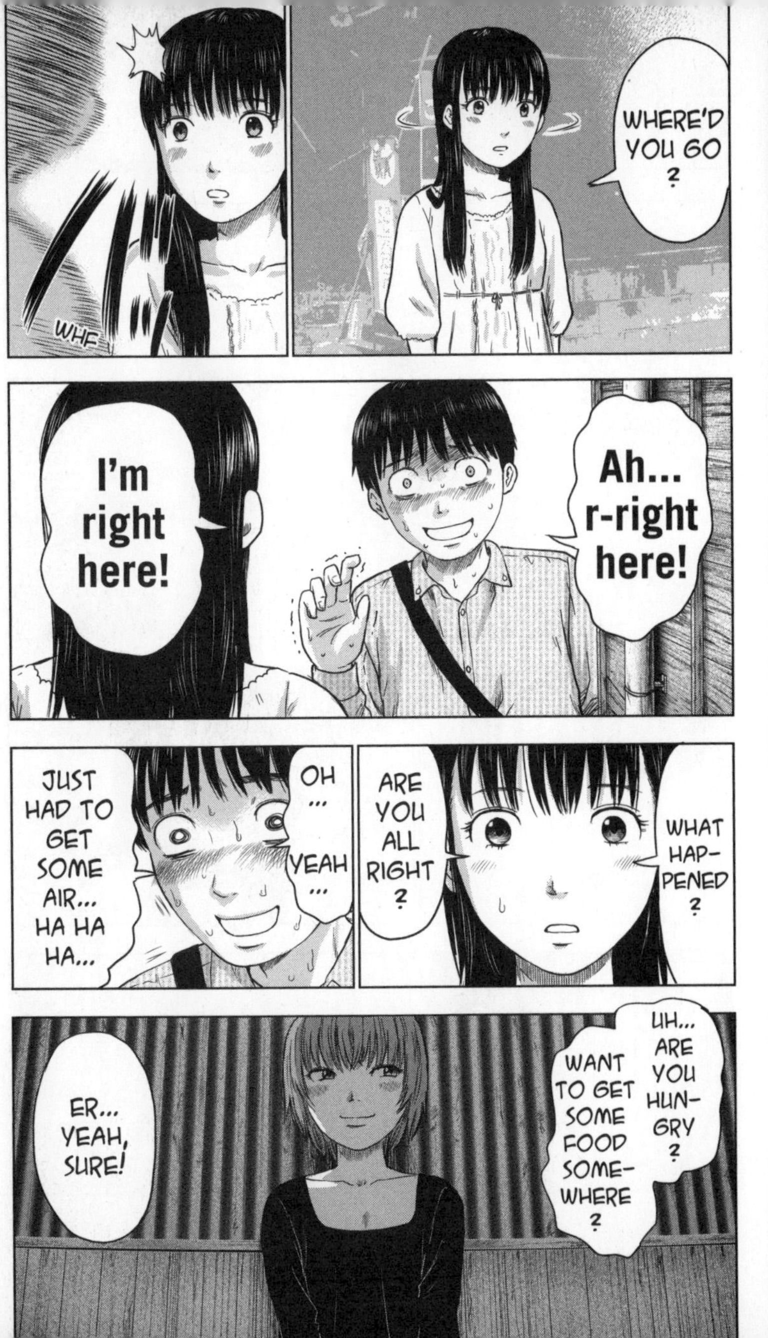
WHERE'D YOU GO?
WHF
Ah... r-right here!
I'm right here!
WHAT HAP-PENED?
ARE YOU ALL RIGHT?
OH... YEAH...
JUST HAD TO GET SOME AIR... HA HA HA...
UH... ARE YOU HUN-GRY?
WANT TO GET SOME FOOD SOME-WHERE?
ER... YEAH, SURE!

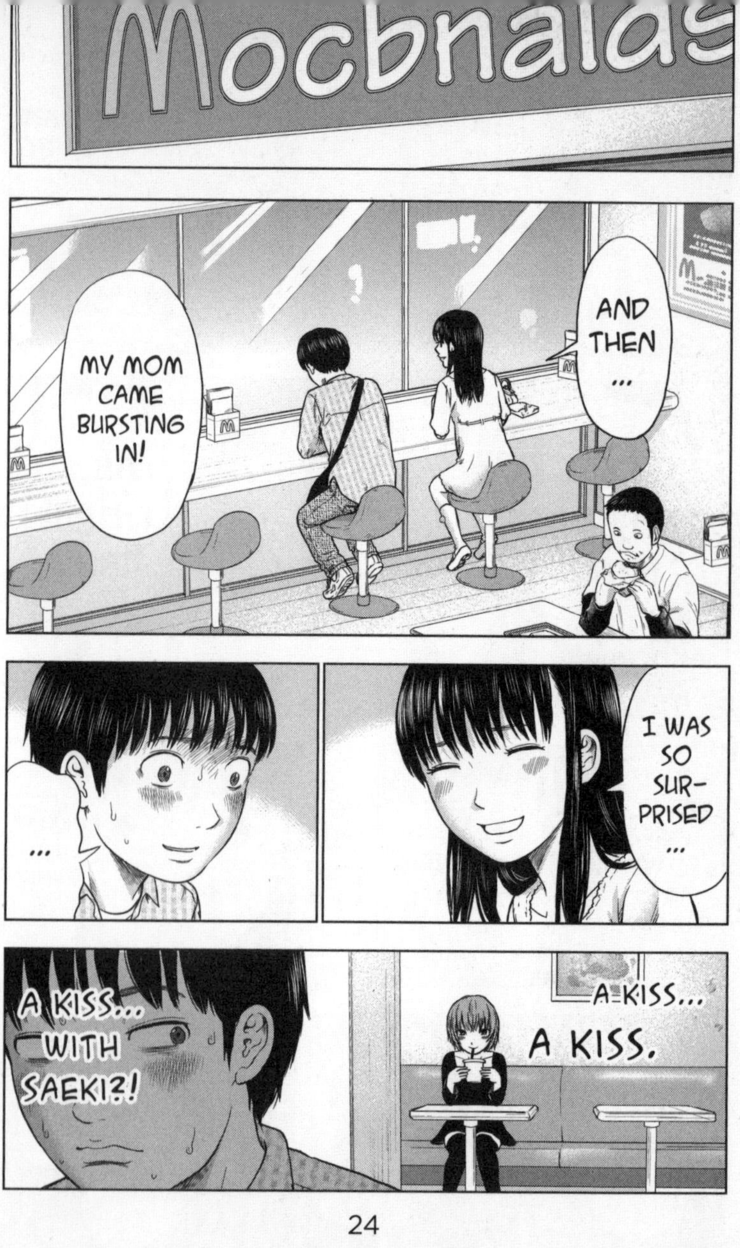
Mocbnalds
AND THEN ...
MY MOM CAME BURSTING IN!
I WAS SO SUR-PRISED ...
...
A KISS...
A KISS.
A KISS... WITH SAEKI?!

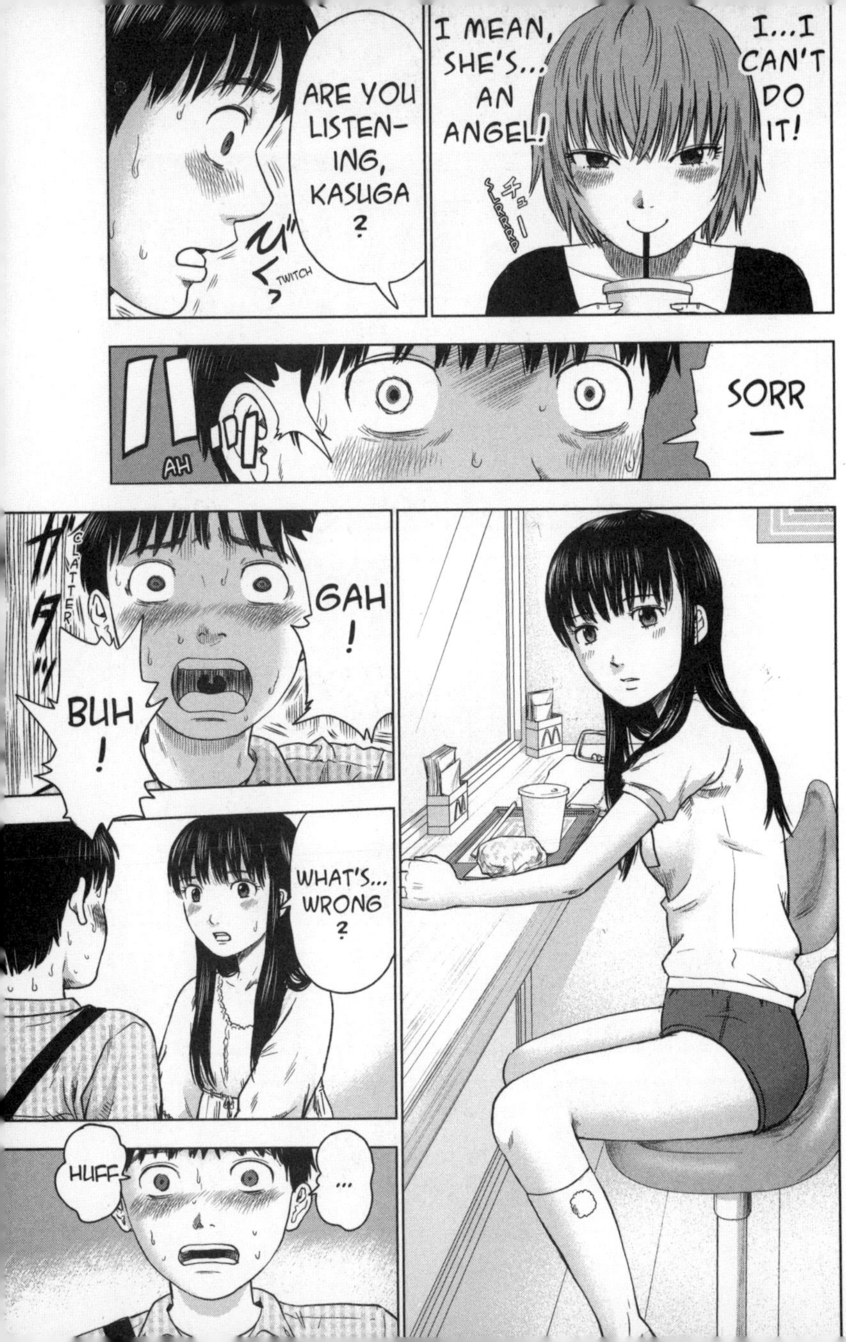
I...I CAN'T DO IT!
I MEAN, SHE'S... AN ANGEL!
SLURRRP
ARE YOU LISTENING, KASUGA?
TWITCH
SORR—
AH
GAH!
BUH!
CLATTER
WHAT'S... WRONG?
...
HUFF

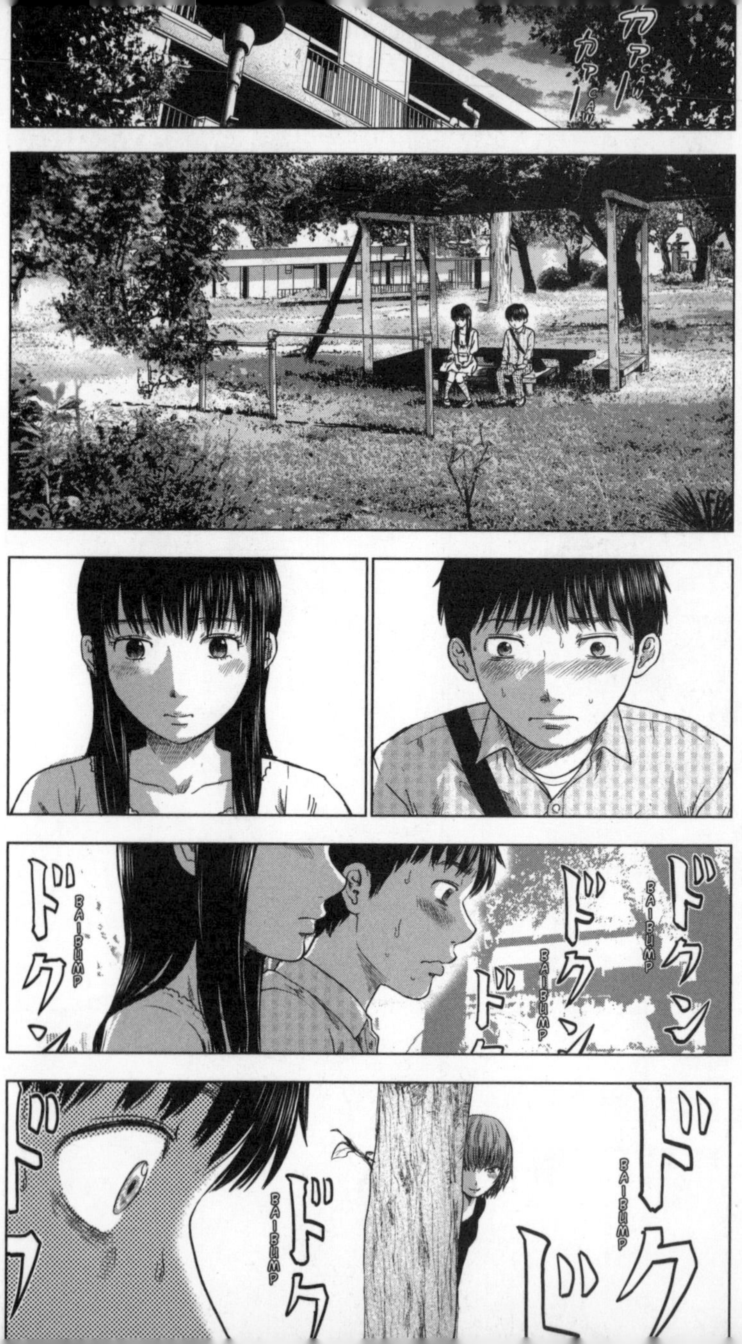

カァー
CAW
カァー
CAW
ドクン
BA-BUMP
ドクン
BA-BUMP
ド
ドク
BA-BUMP
ドク
BA-BUMP
ドク
BA-BUMP
ド

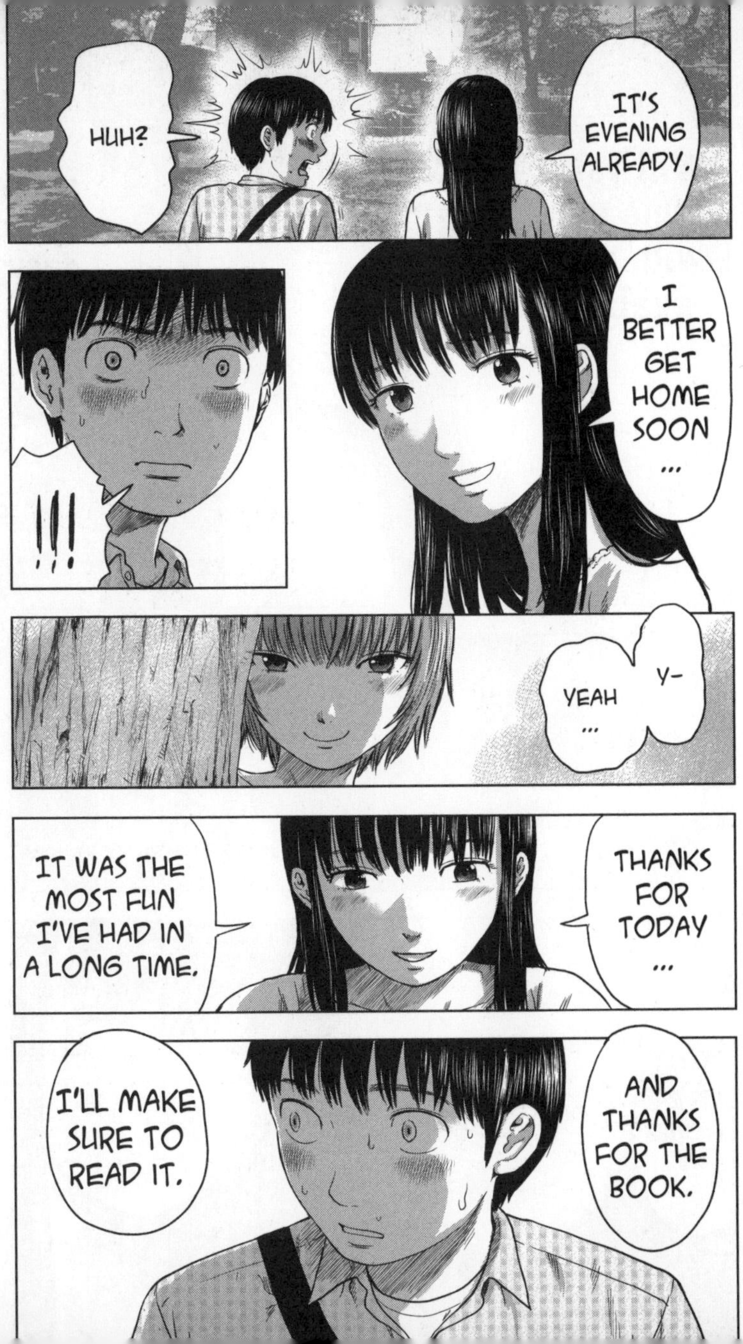
IT'S EVENING ALREADY.
HUH?
I BETTER GET HOME SOON ...
!!!
Y- YEAH ...
THANKS FOR TODAY ...
IT WAS THE MOST FUN I'VE HAD IN A LONG TIME.
AND THANKS FOR THE BOOK.
I'LL MAKE SURE TO READ IT.

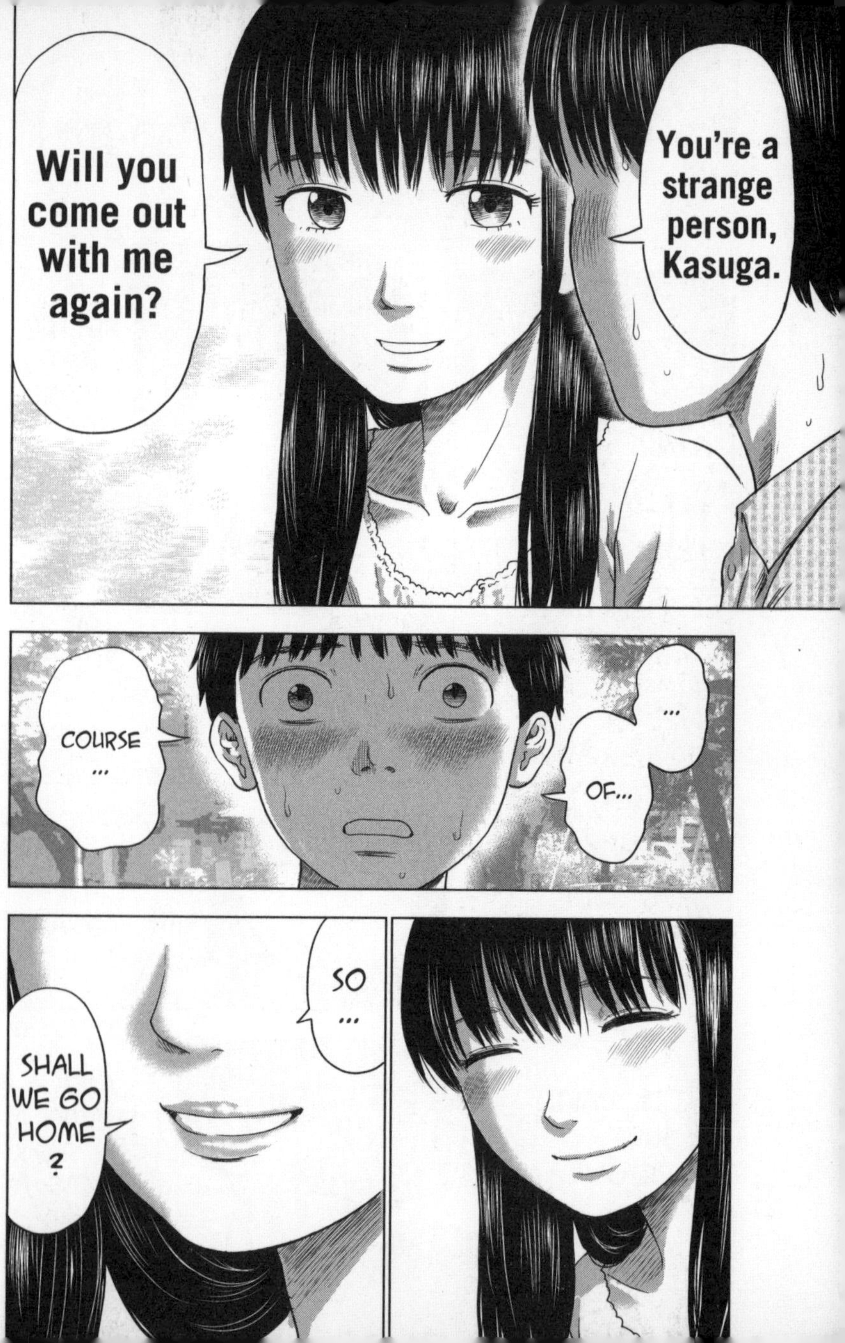
You're a strange person, Kasuga.
Will you come out with me again?
... OF...
COURSE ...
SO ...
SHALL WE GO HOME ?

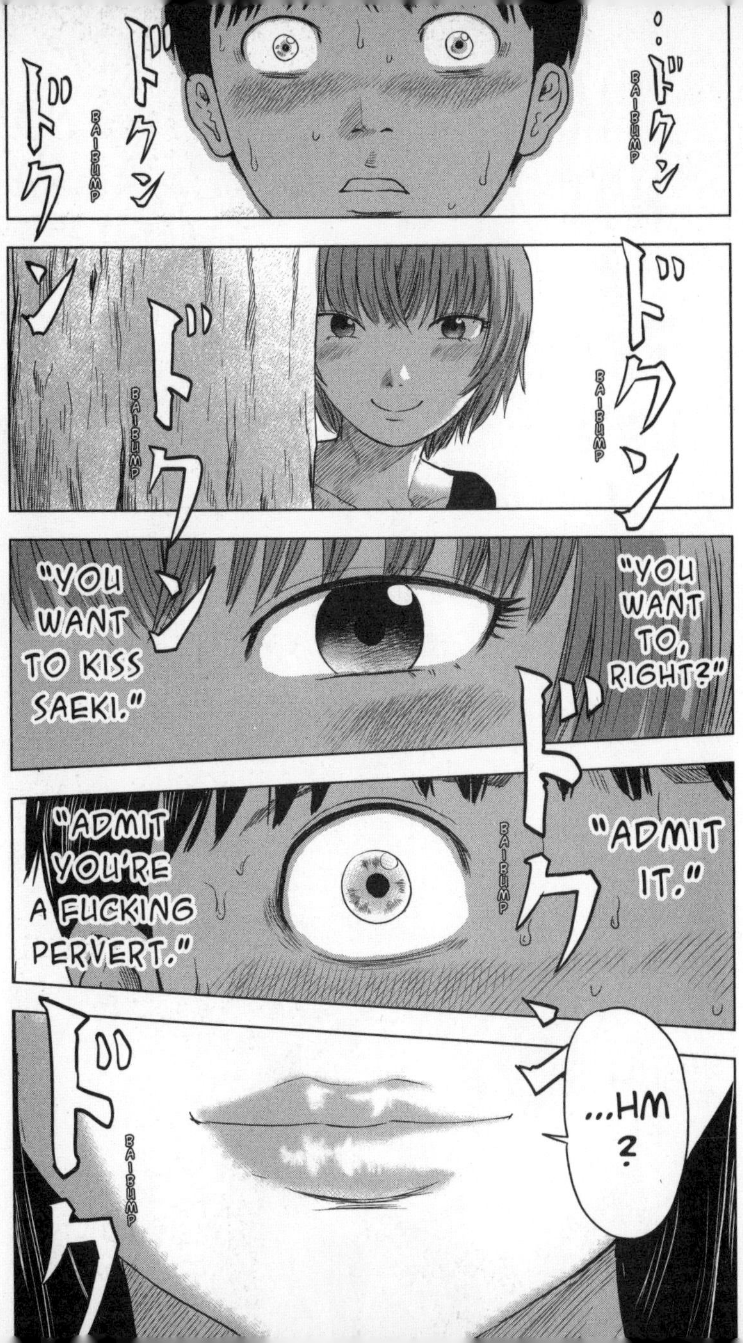
..ドクン
BA-BUMP
ドクン
BA-BUMP
ドクン
ドクン
BA-BUMP
ドクン
BA-BUMP
"YOU WANT TO, RIGHT?"
"YOU WANT TO KISS SAEKI."
"ADMIT IT."
ドクン
BA-BUMP
"ADMIT YOU'RE A FUCKING PERVERT."
...HM?
ドク
BA-BUMP

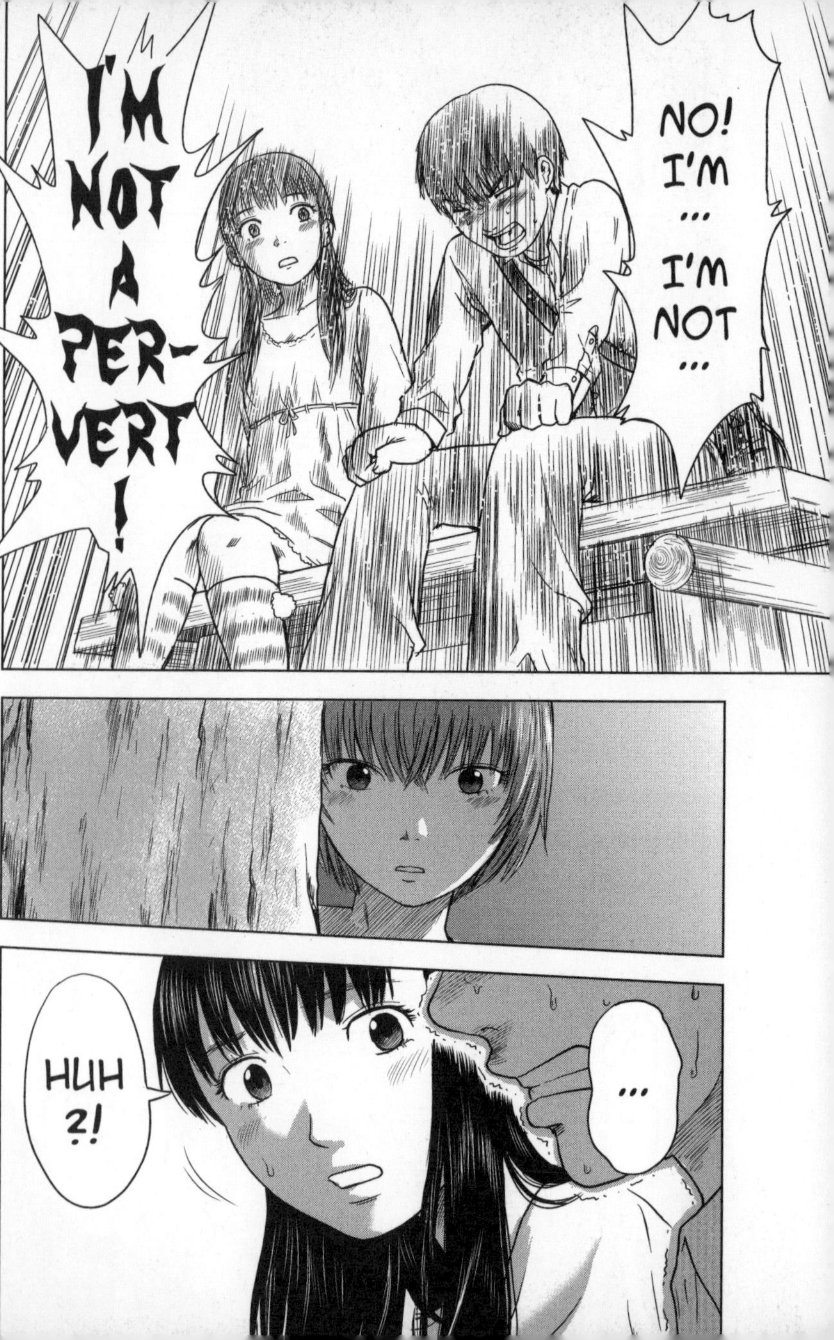
NO! I'M ... I'M NOT ...
I'M NOT A PER-VERT!
...
HUH?!

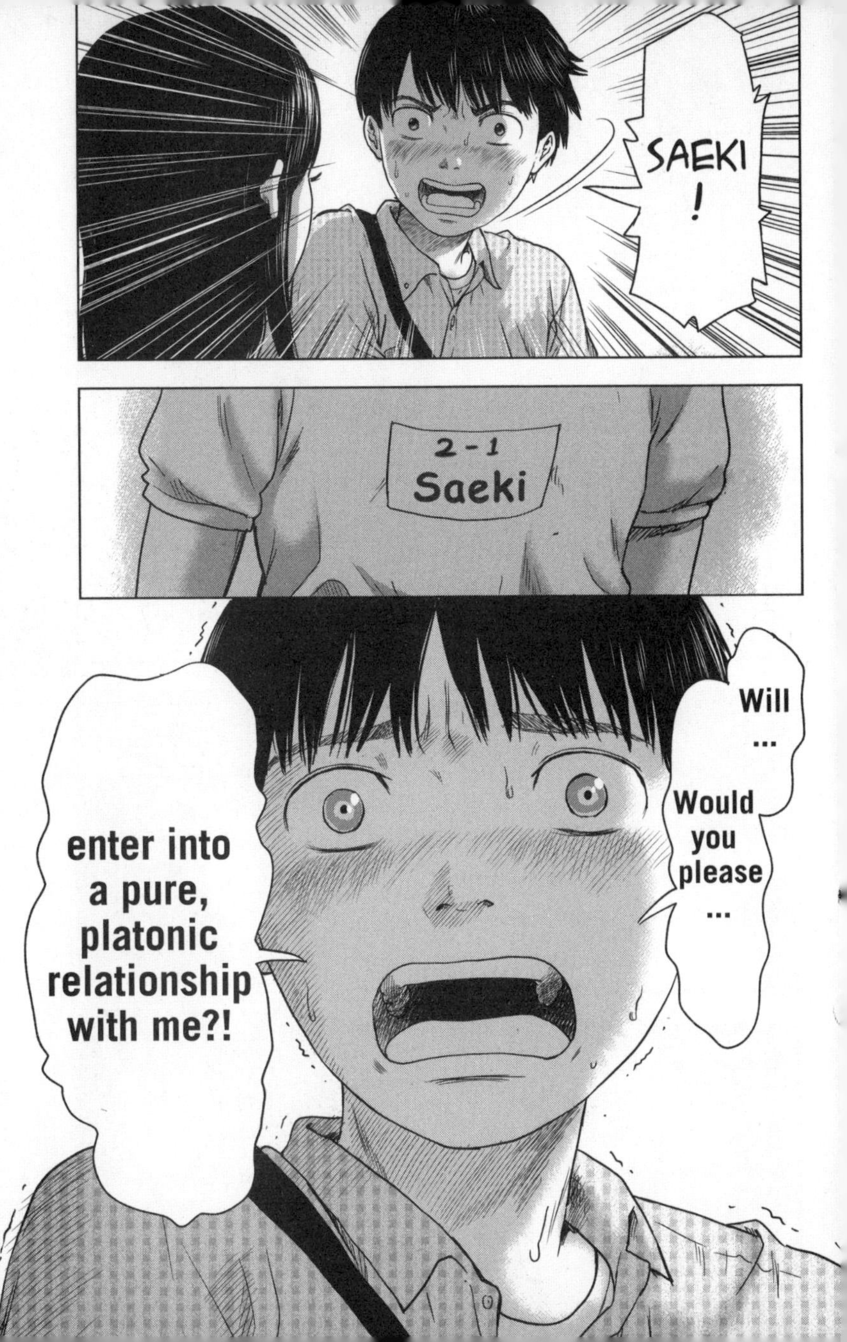
SAEKI!
2-1
Saeki
Will... Would you please...
enter into a pure, platonic relationship with me?!

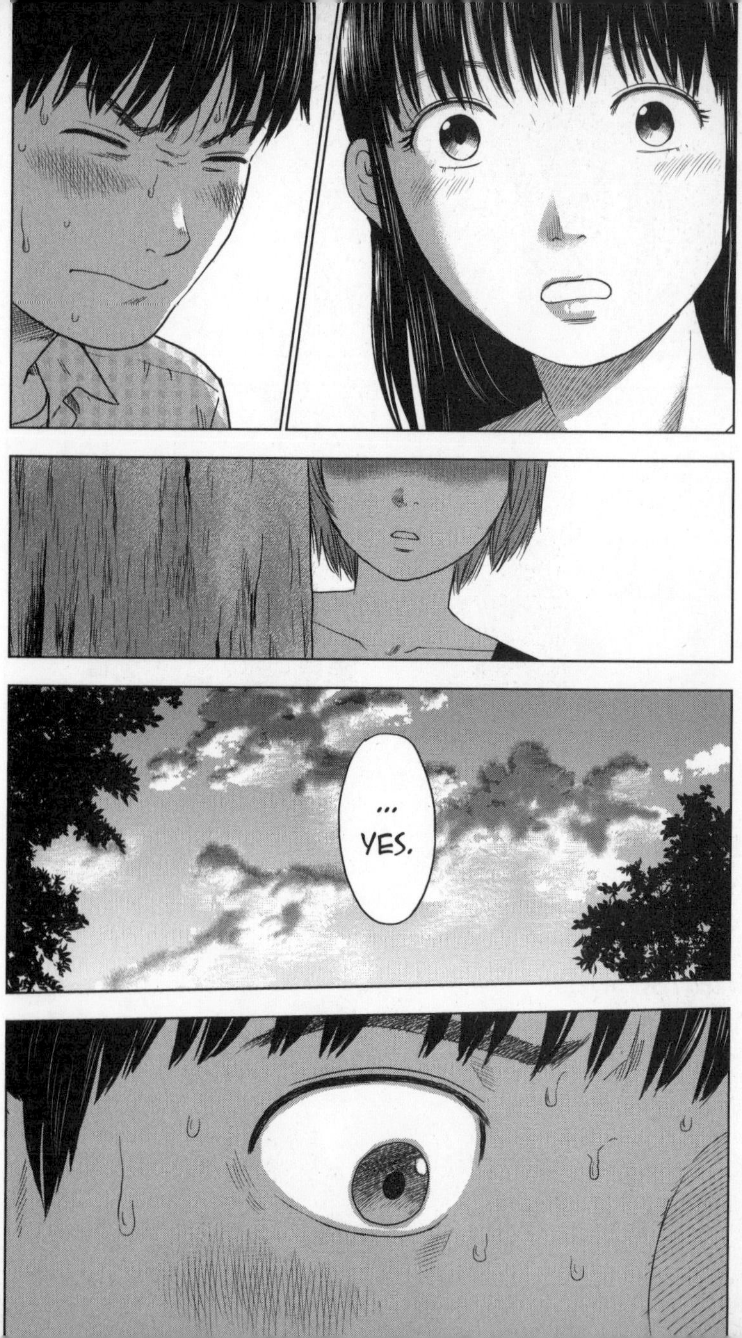
...
YES.

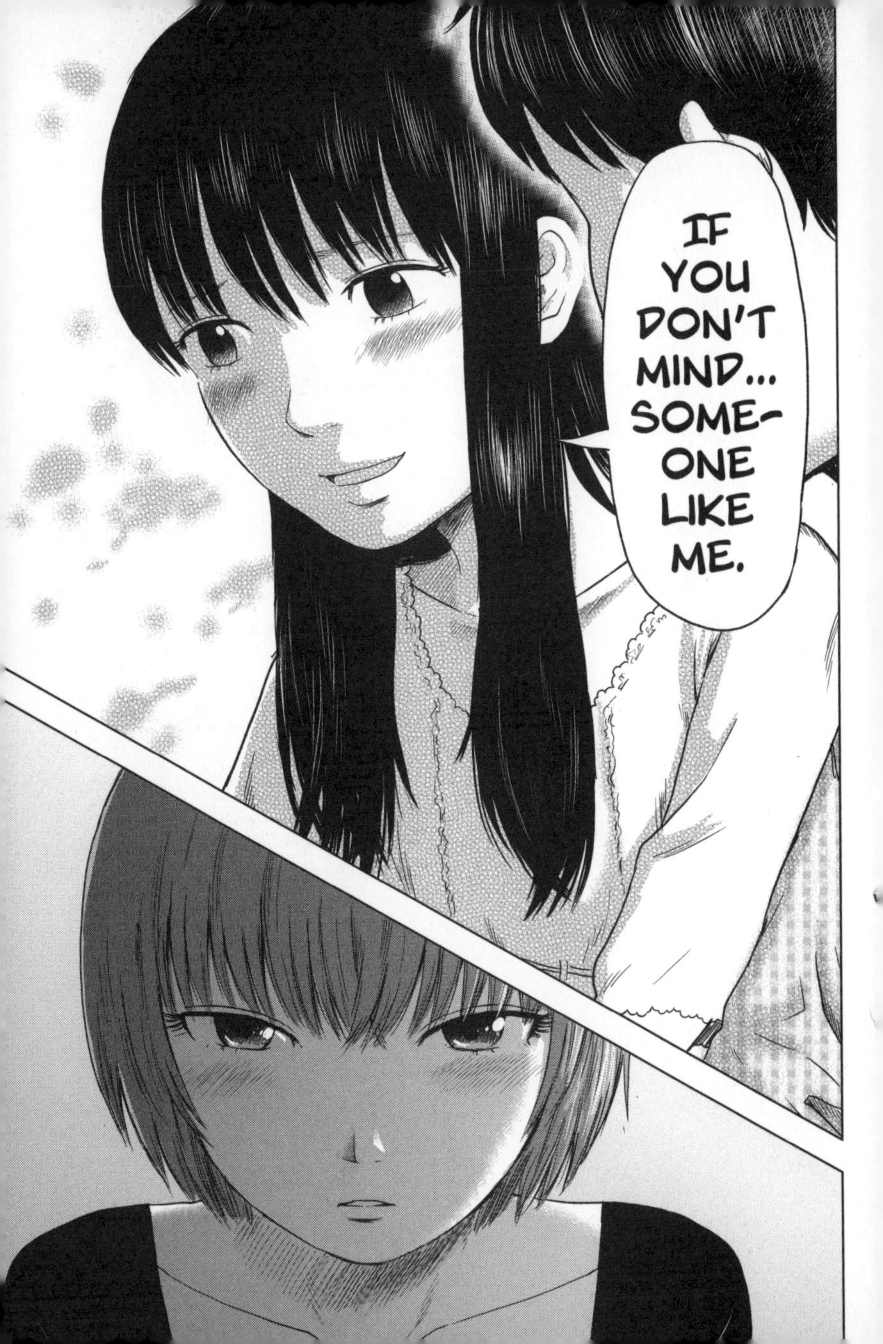
IF YOU DON'T MIND... SOME-ONE LIKE ME.

Afterword

Chapter 7

Regarding the surrealism that Kasuga unsolicitedly explained in the bookstore: André Breton was a Frenchman. In 1924, he published the "Principles of Surrealism."

He gathered like-minded artists around him and established a group. When my middle-school-aged self looked at photographs of the group, I was blown away by how cool they all were.

Gazing at the illustrations of people like Max Ernst and Paul Delvaux made me pant.

Chapter 8: Confession

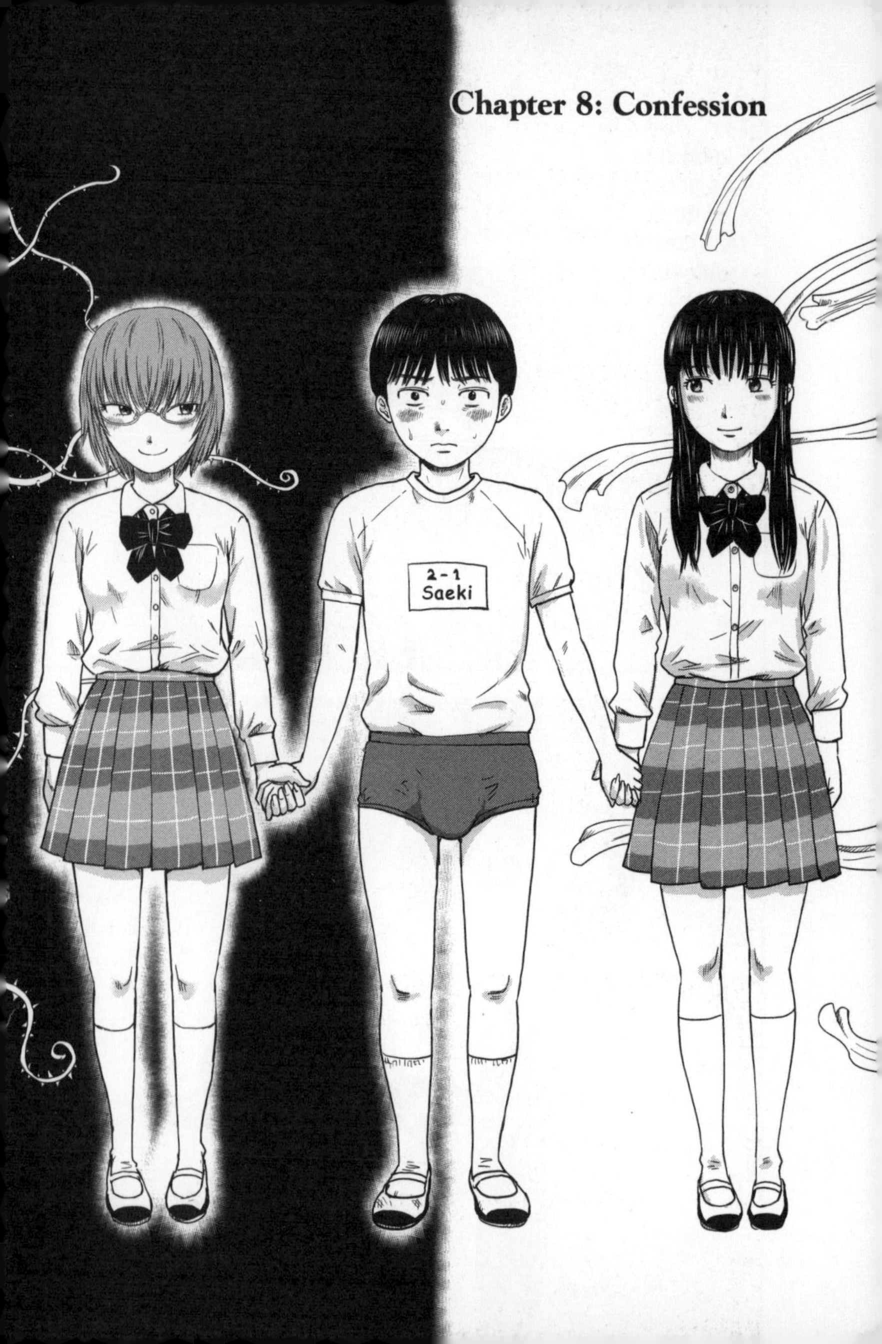
2-1
Saeki

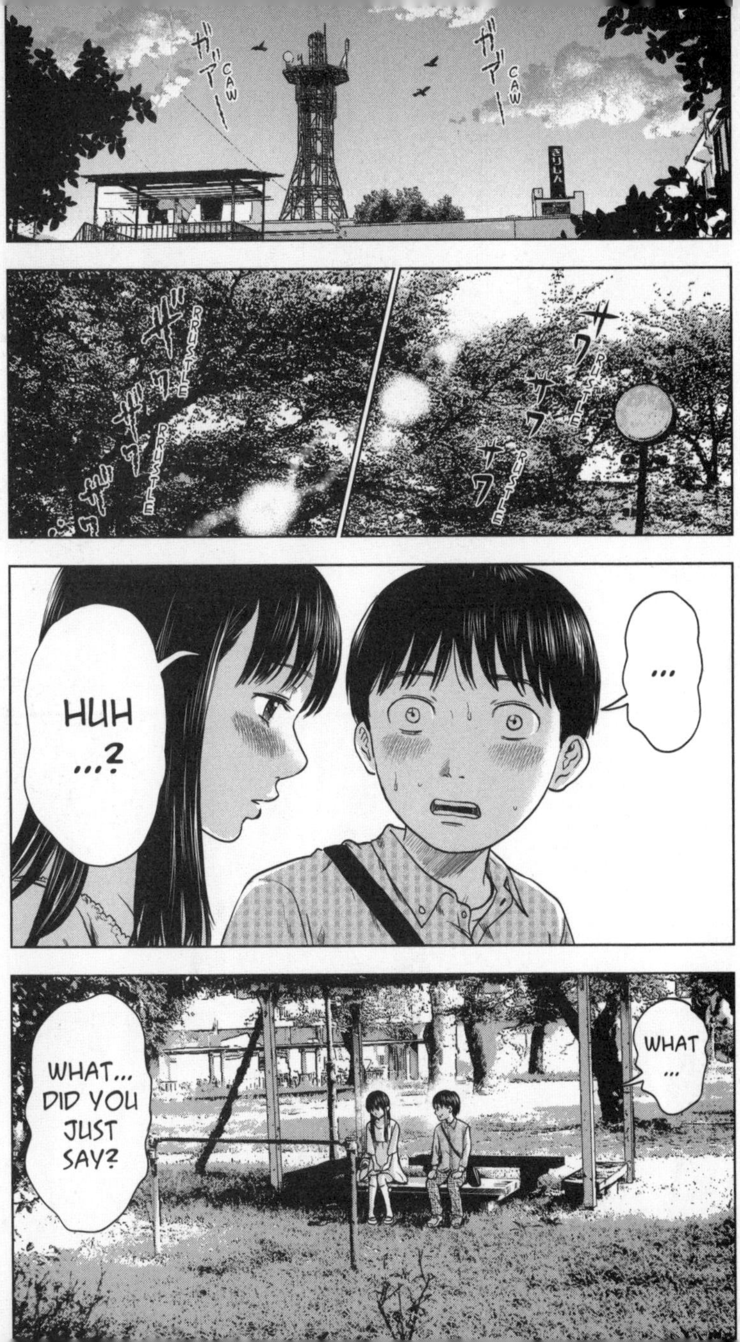
ガァーー
CAW
ガァーー
CAW
サワ サワ サワ
RUSTLE
RUSTLE
ザワ ザワ ザワ
RRUSTLE
RRUSTLE
...
HUH ...?
WHAT ...
WHAT... DID YOU JUST SAY?

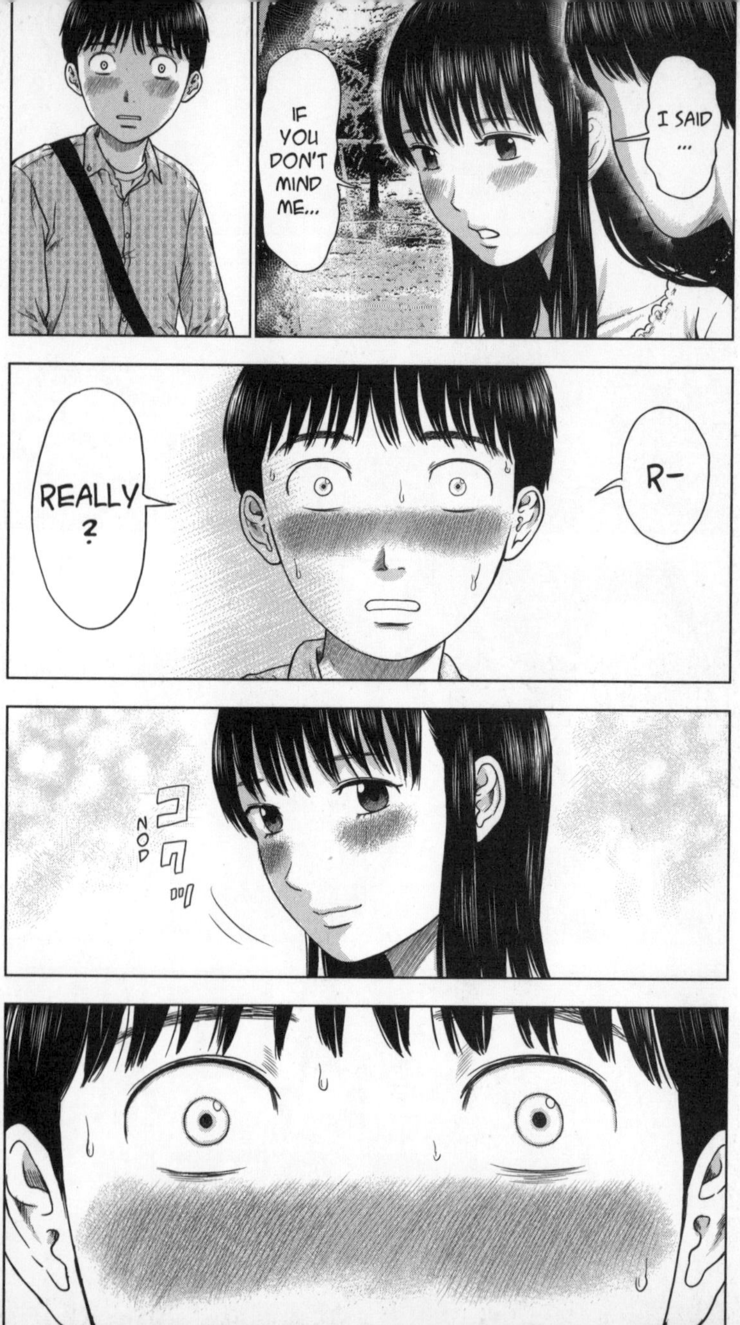
I SAID ...
IF YOU DON'T MIND ME...
R-
REALLY ?
NOD
コクッ

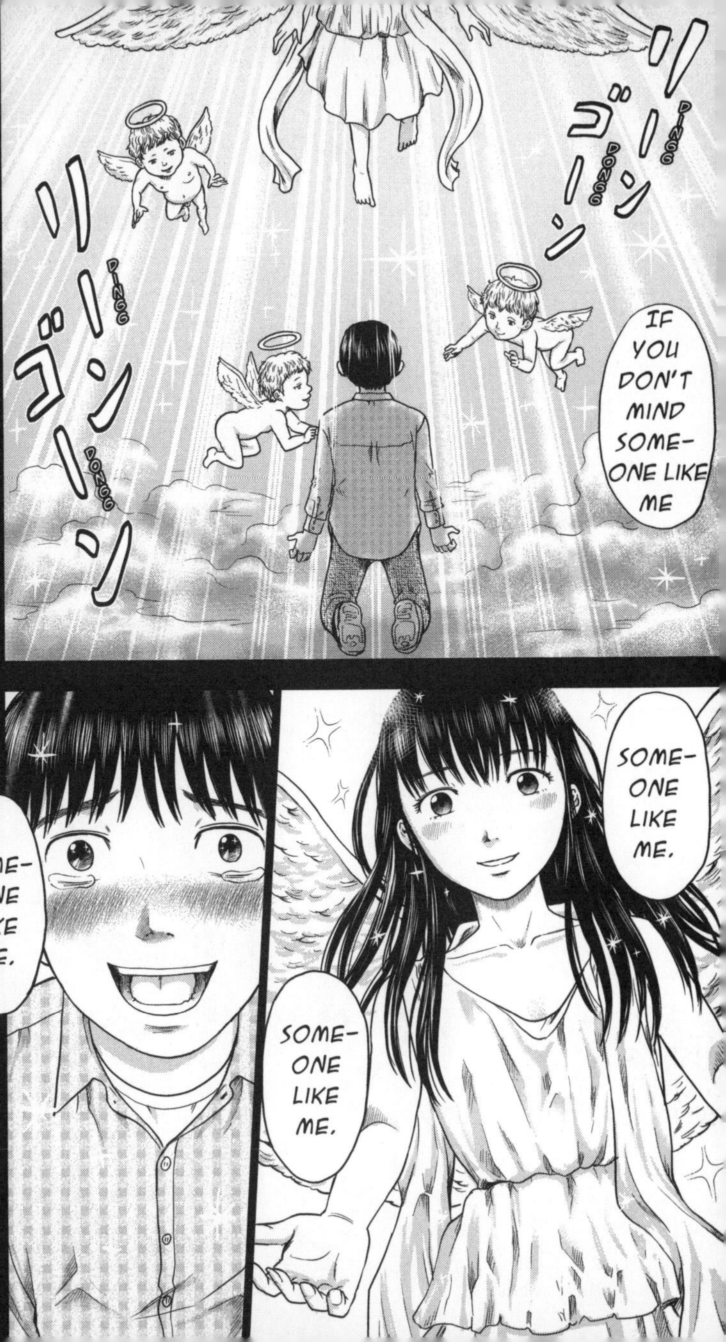

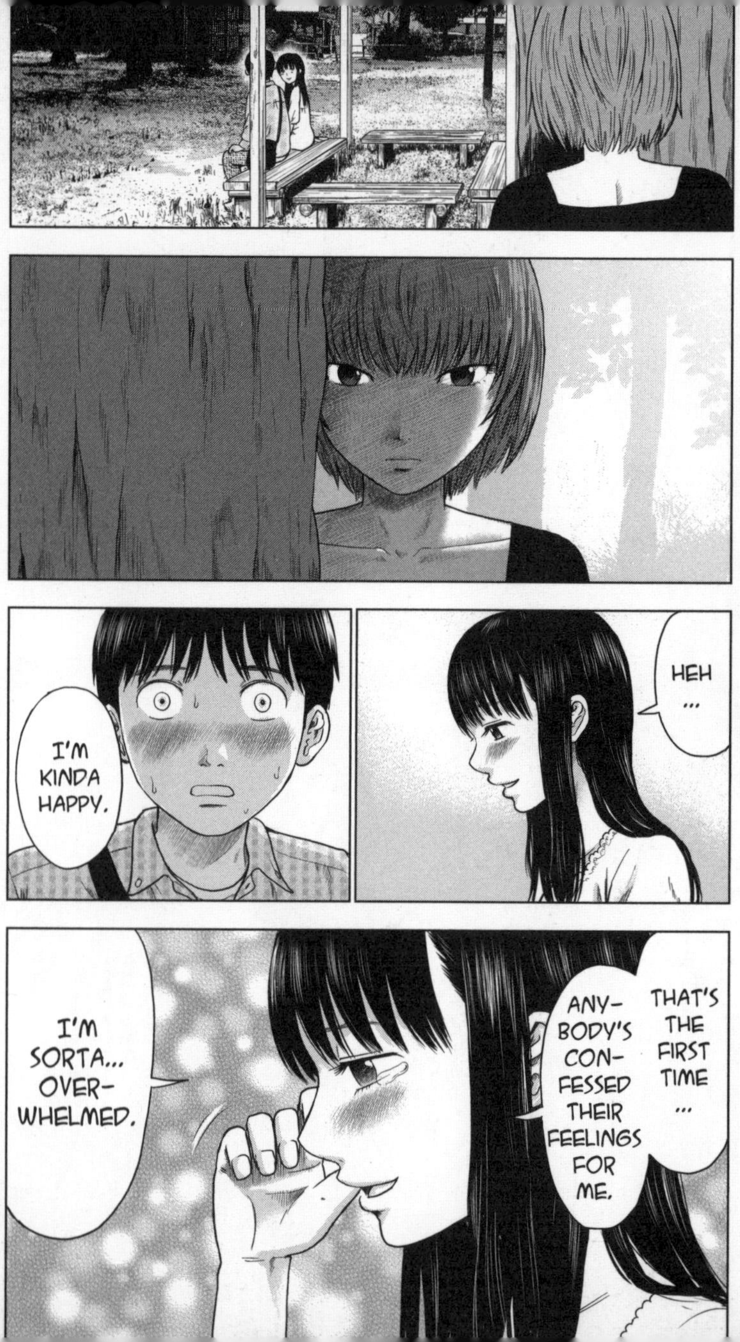
HEH ...
I'M KINDA HAPPY.
THAT'S THE FIRST TIME ...
ANY-BODY'S CON-FESSED THEIR FEELINGS FOR ME.
I'M SORTA... OVER-WHELMED.

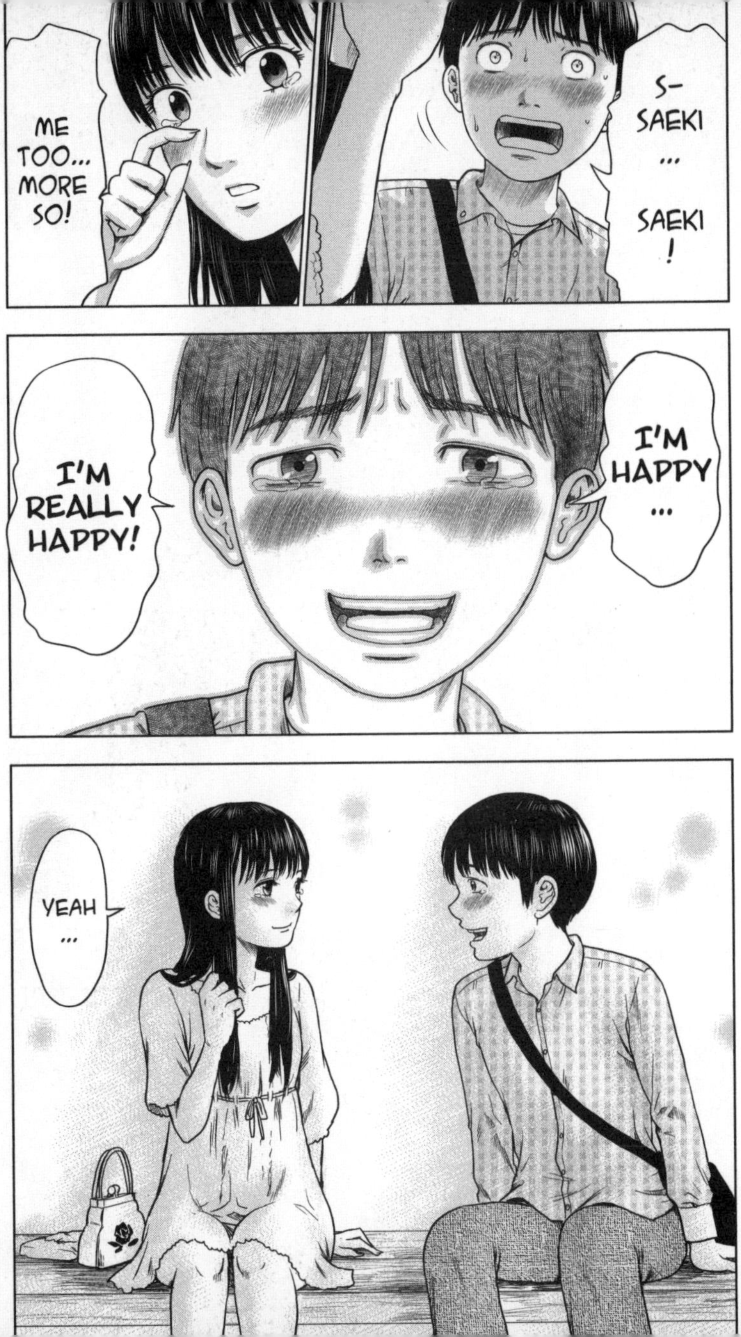
S-SAEKI... SAEKI!
ME TOO... MORE SO!
I'M HAPPY...
I'M REALLY HAPPY!
YEAH...

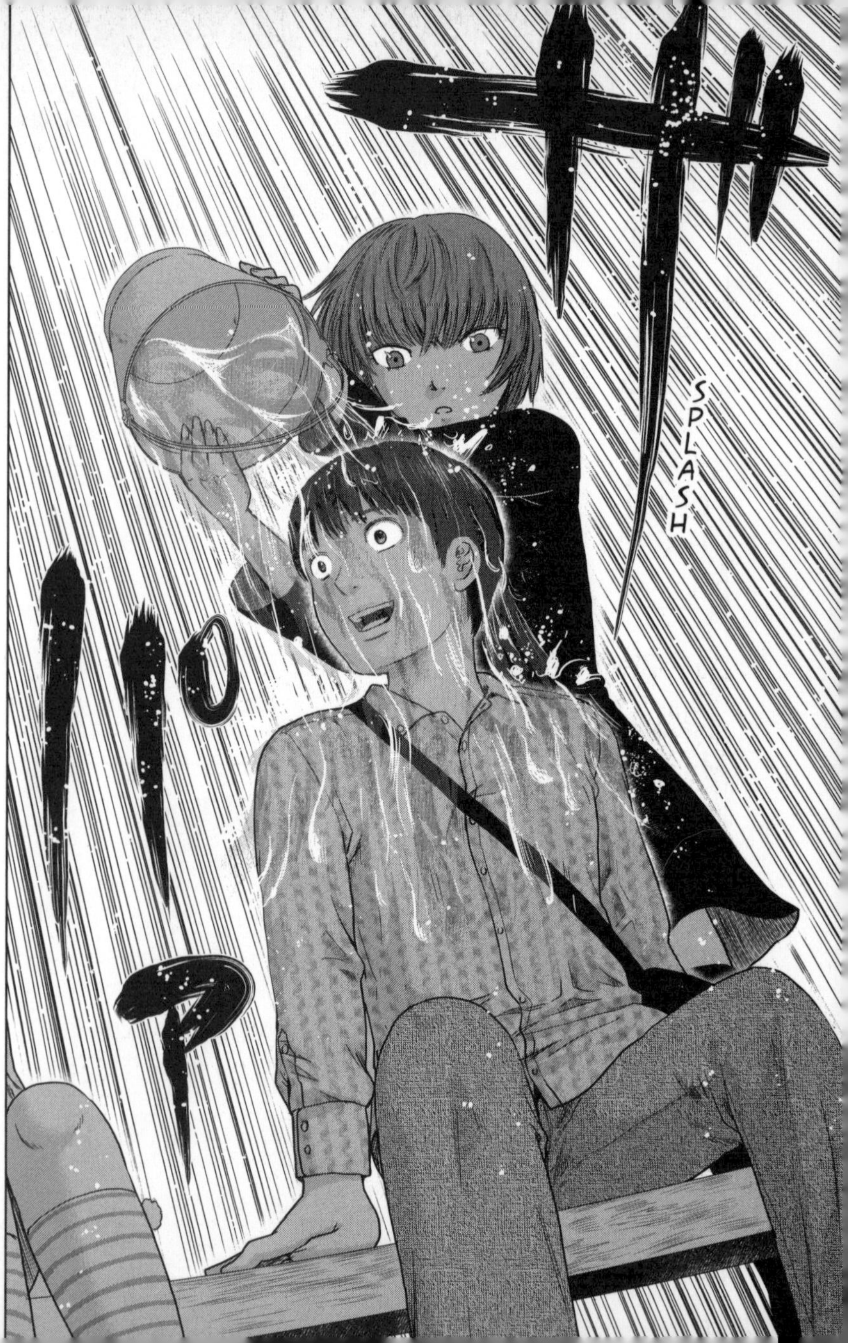
SPLASH

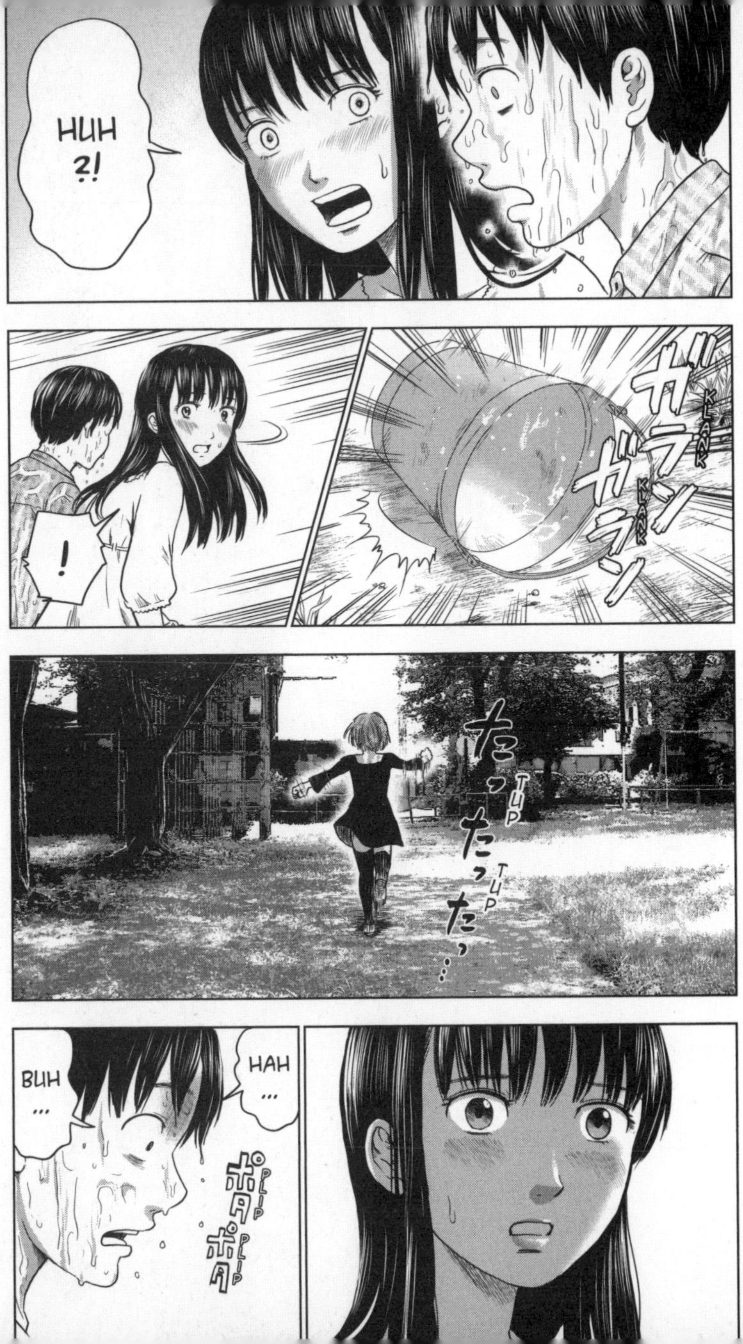
HUH ?!
ガラン
KLANK
ガラン
KLANK
!
たったった…
TUP
TUP
HAH ...
BUH ...
ポタポタ
PLIP
PLIP

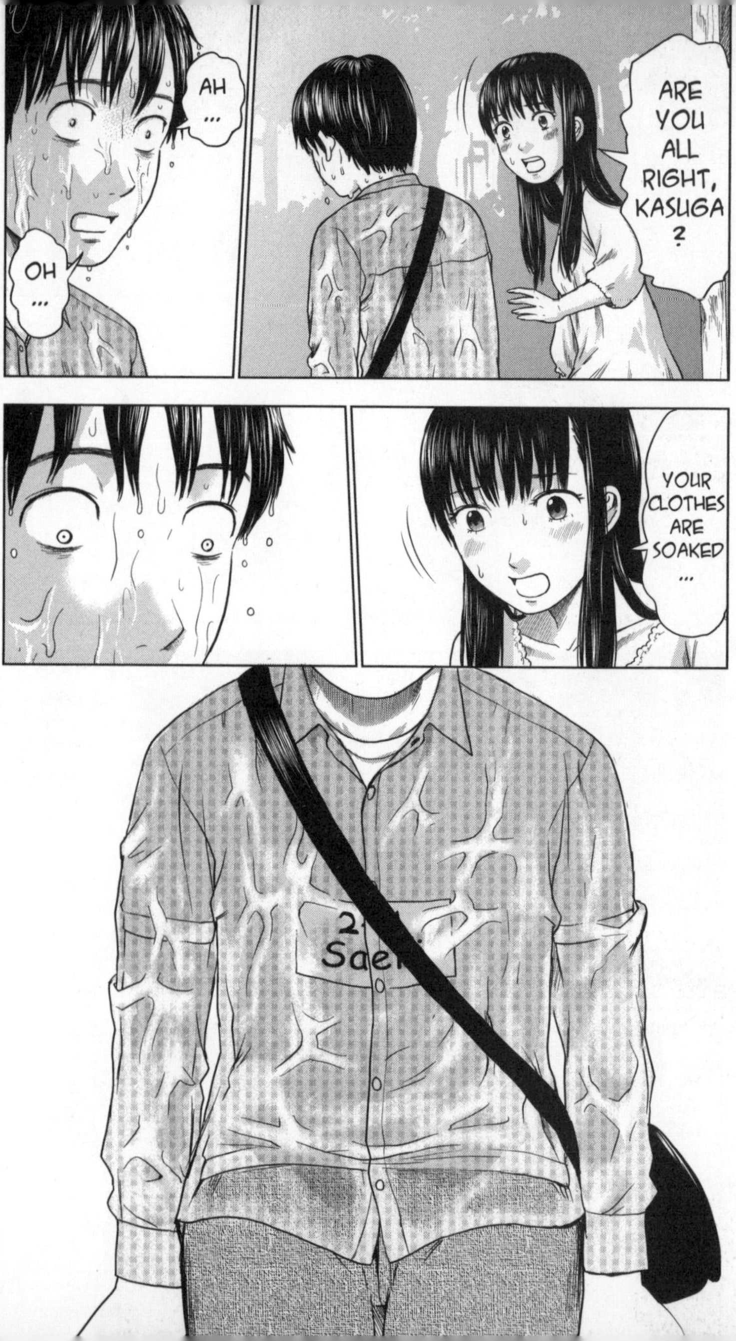
ARE YOU ALL RIGHT, KASUGA?
AH ...
OH ...
YOUR CLOTHES ARE SOAKED ...

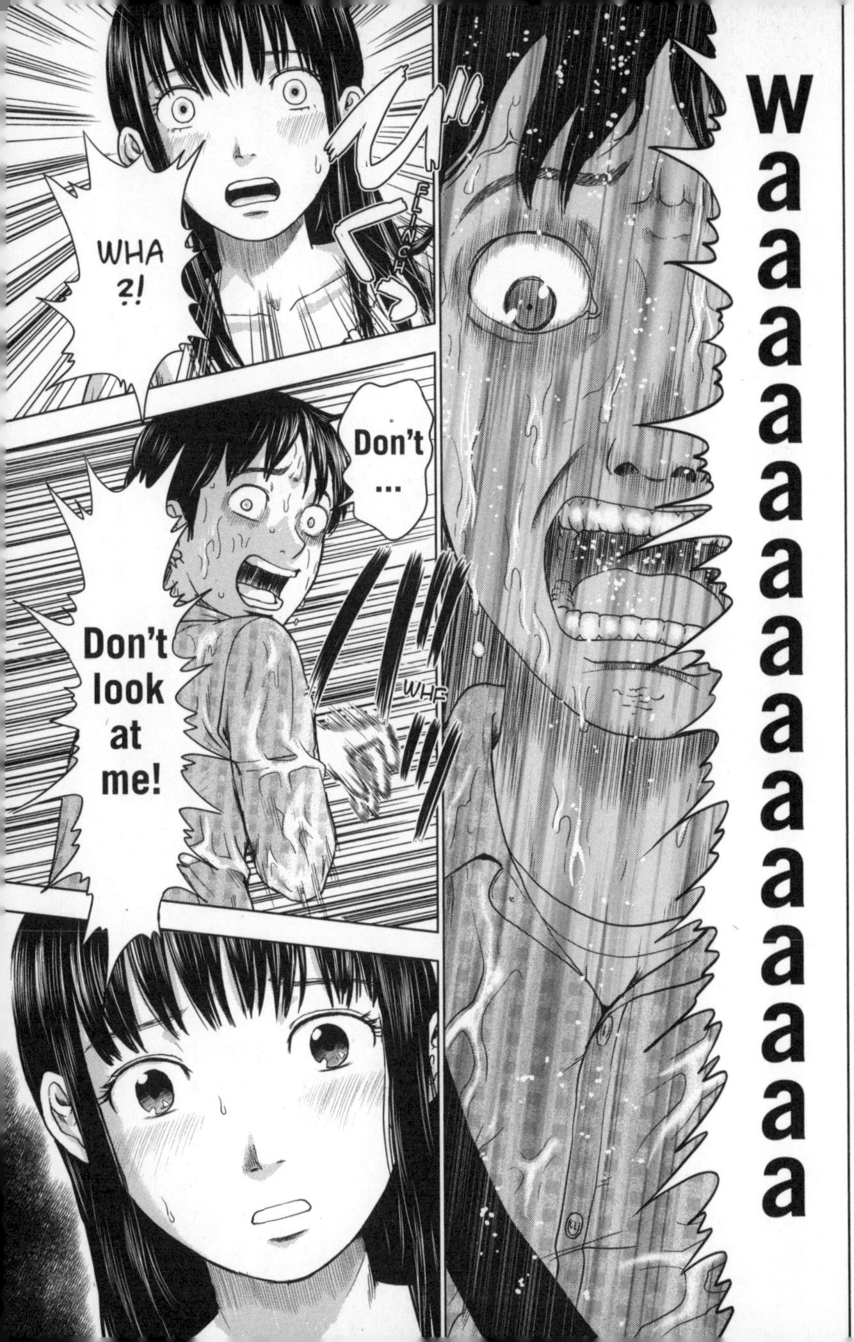
Waaaaaaaaaaaaaaaa
WHA ?!
FLINCH
Don't ...
Don't look at me!
WHF

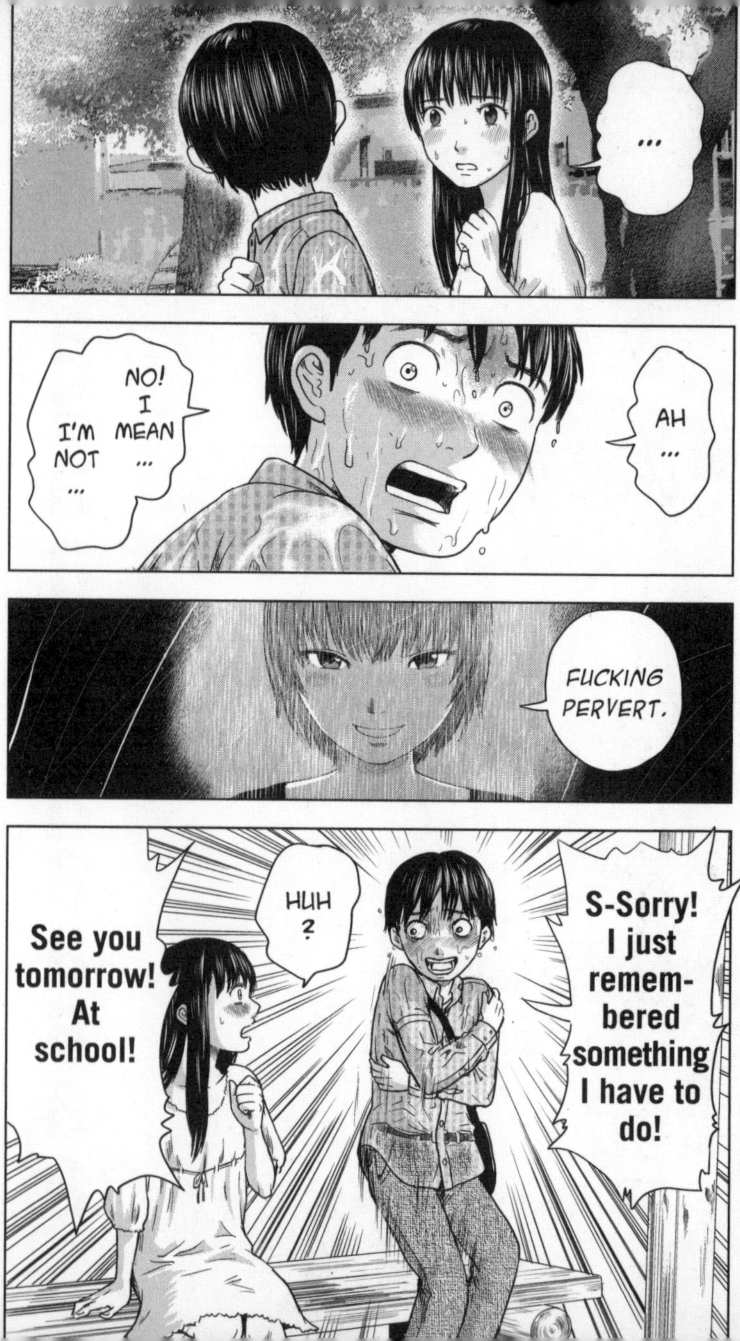
...
AH ...
NO! I MEAN ...
I'M NOT ...
FUCKING PERVERT.
S-Sorry! I just remembered something I have to do!
HUH?
See you tomorrow! At school!

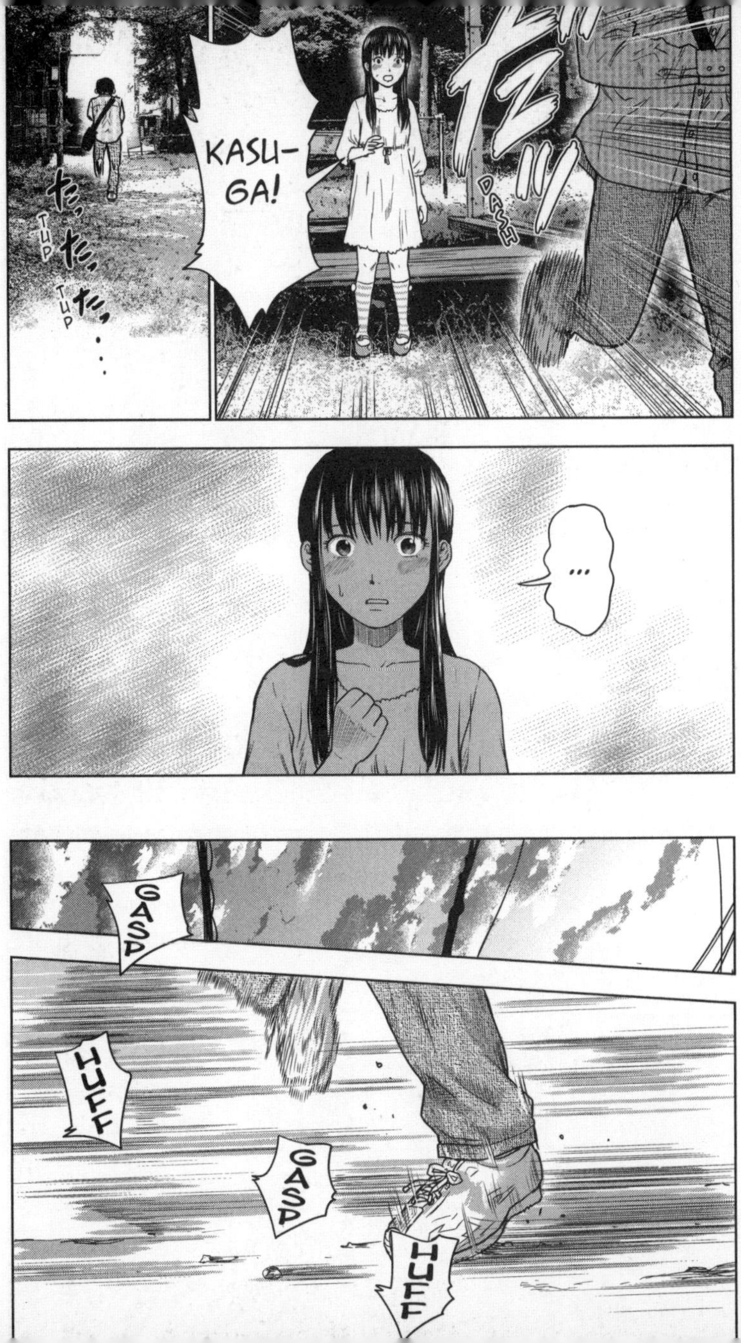
DASH
KASU-GA!
TUP
TUP
...
...
GASP
HUFF
GASP
HUFF

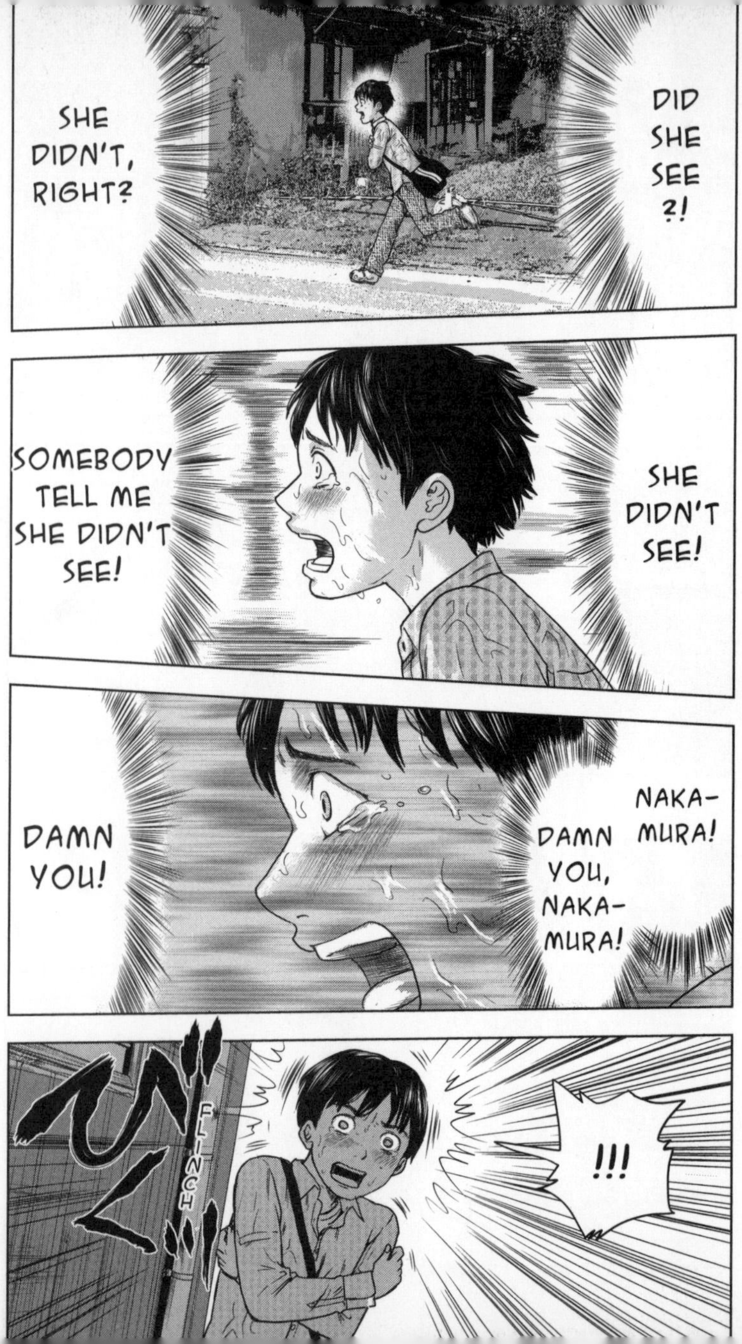
DID SHE SEE?!
SHE DIDN'T, RIGHT?
SHE DIDN'T SEE!
SOMEBODY TELL ME SHE DIDN'T SEE!
NAKA-MURA!
DAMN YOU, NAKA-MURA!
DAMN YOU!
!!!
FLINCH

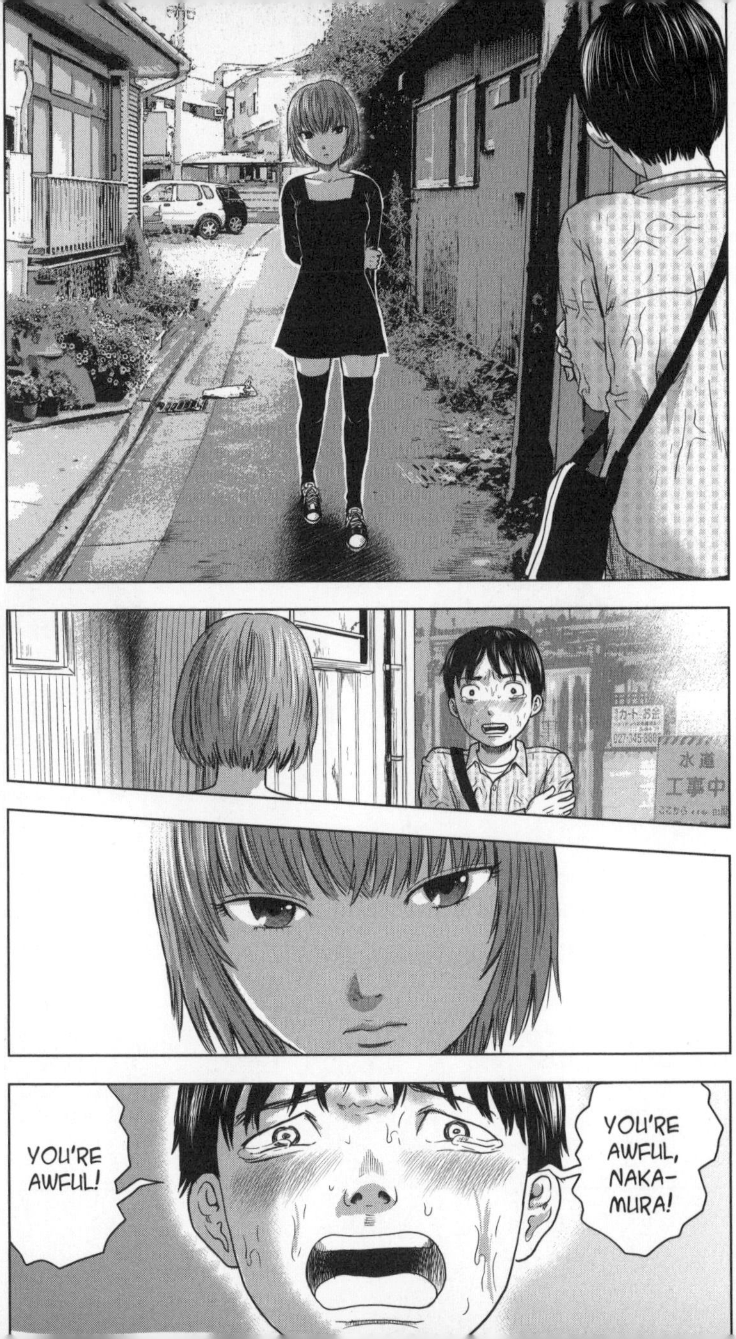
水道
工事中
YOU'RE AWFUL, NAKA-MURA!
YOU'RE AWFUL!

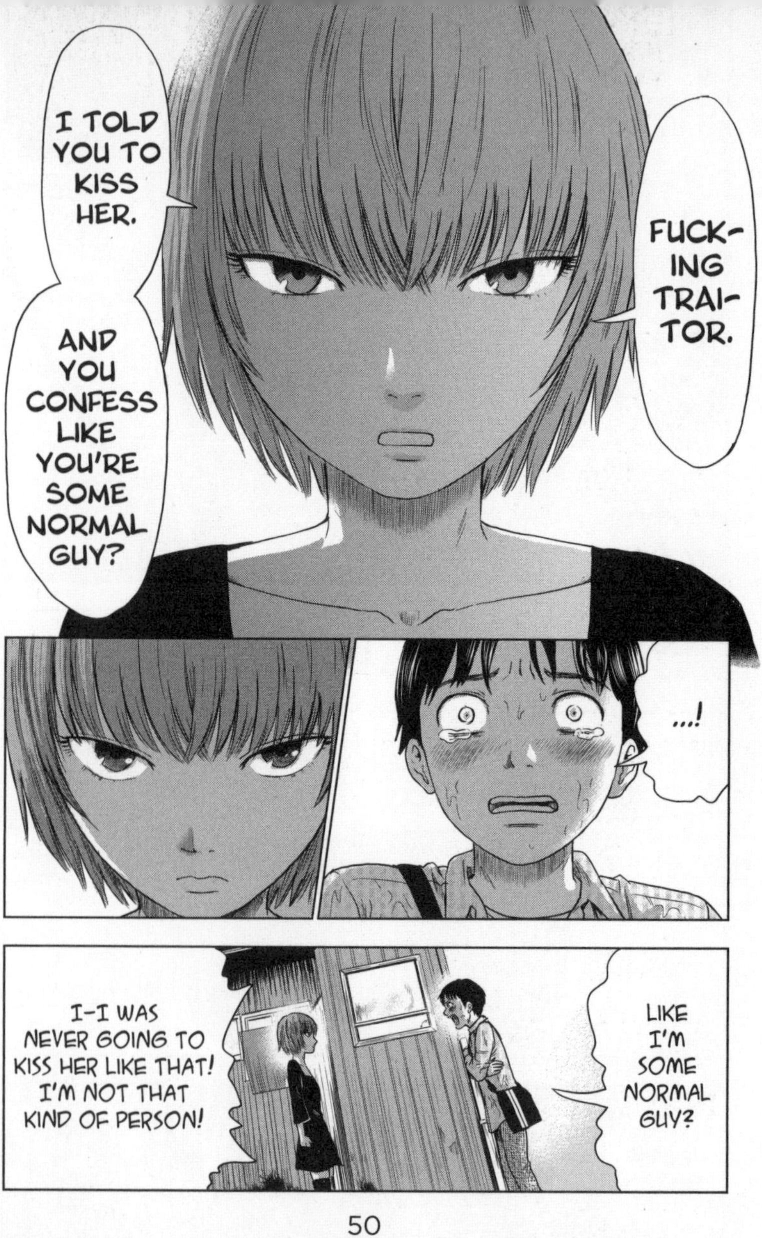
FUCK-ING TRAI-TOR.
I TOLD YOU TO KISS HER.
AND YOU CONFESS LIKE YOU'RE SOME NORMAL GUY?
...!
LIKE I'M SOME NORMAL GUY?
I-I WAS NEVER GOING TO KISS HER LIKE THAT! I'M NOT THAT KIND OF PERSON!

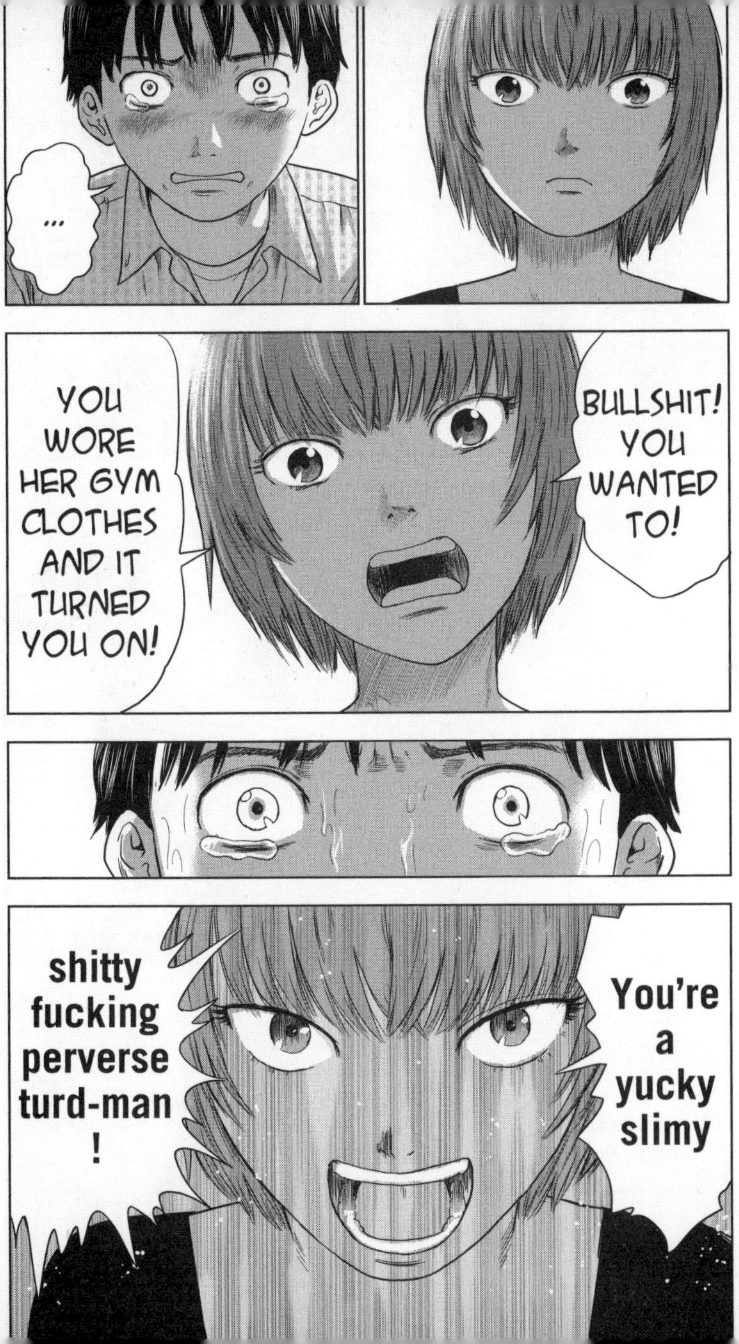
...
BULLSHIT! YOU WANTED TO!
YOU WORE HER GYM CLOTHES AND IT TURNED YOU ON!
You're a yucky slimy
shitty fucking perverse turd-man !

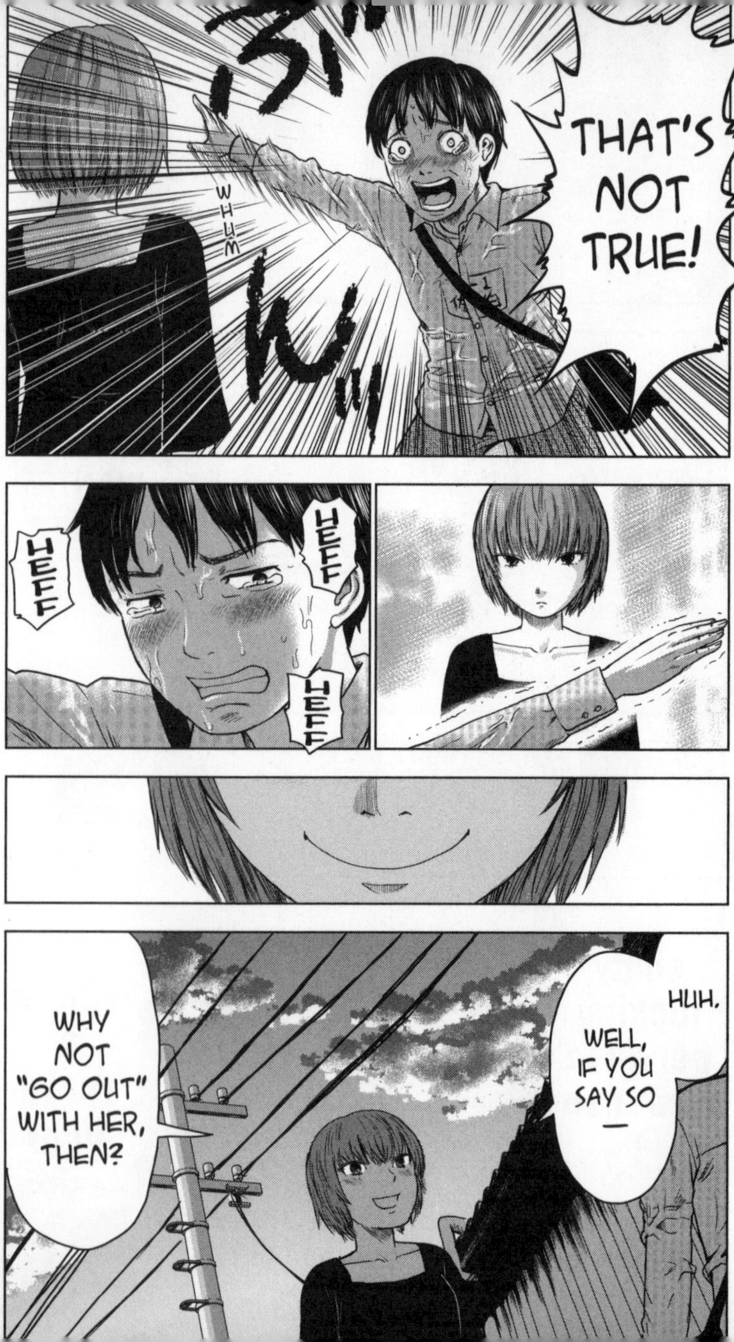
THAT'S NOT TRUE!
WHUM
HEFF HEFF
HEFF HEFF
HUH.
WELL, IF YOU SAY SO —
WHY NOT "GO OUT" WITH HER, THEN?

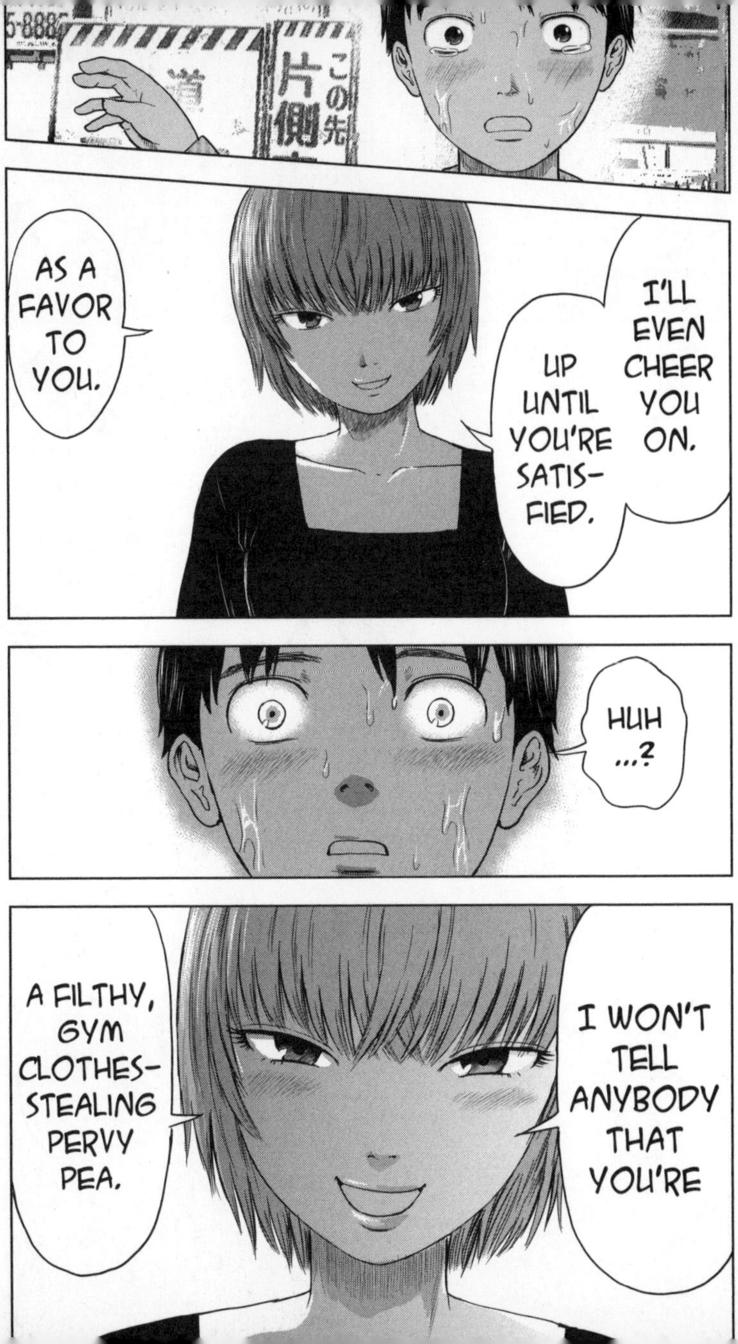
この先
片側
I'LL EVEN CHEER YOU ON.
UP UNTIL YOU'RE SATIS-FIED.
AS A FAVOR TO YOU.
HUH ...?
I WON'T TELL ANYBODY THAT YOU'RE
A FILTHY, GYM CLOTHES-STEALING PERVY PEA.

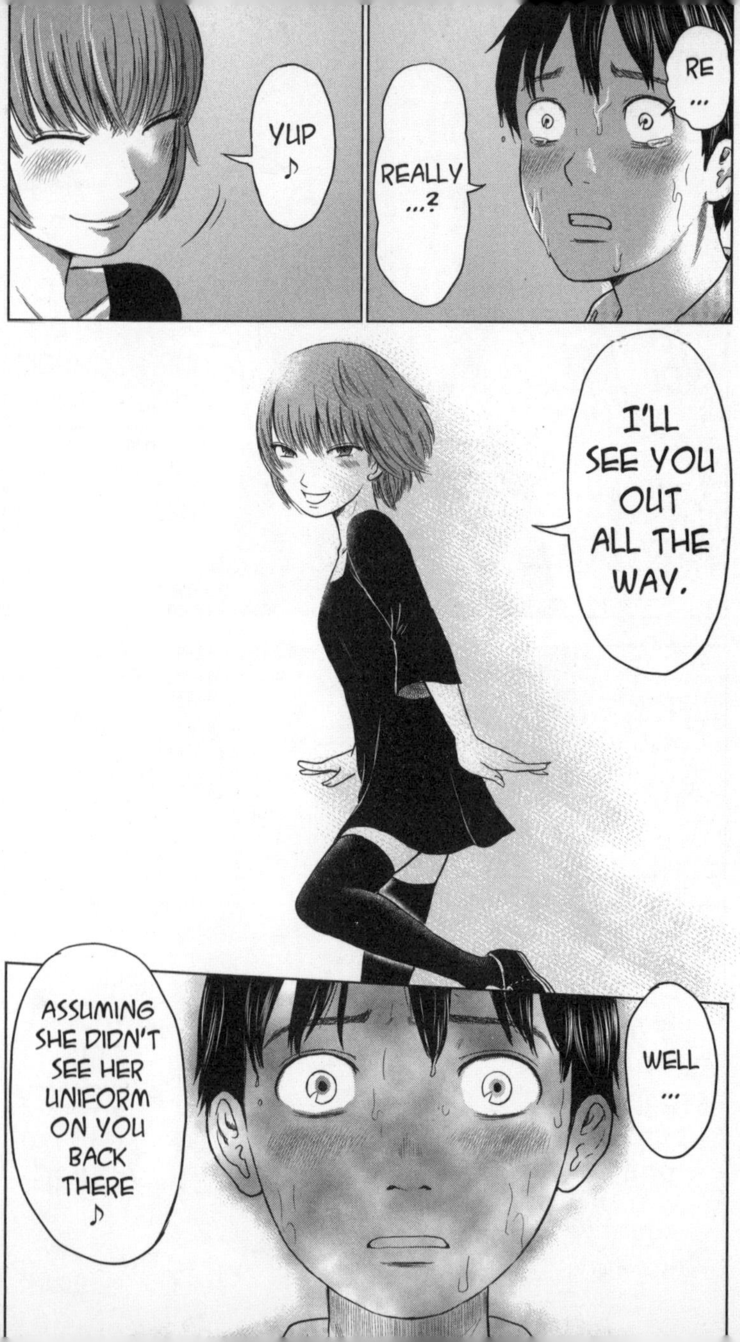
RE ...
REALLY ...?
YUP ♪
I'LL SEE YOU OUT ALL THE WAY.
WELL ...
ASSUMING SHE DIDN'T SEE HER UNIFORM ON YOU BACK THERE ♪

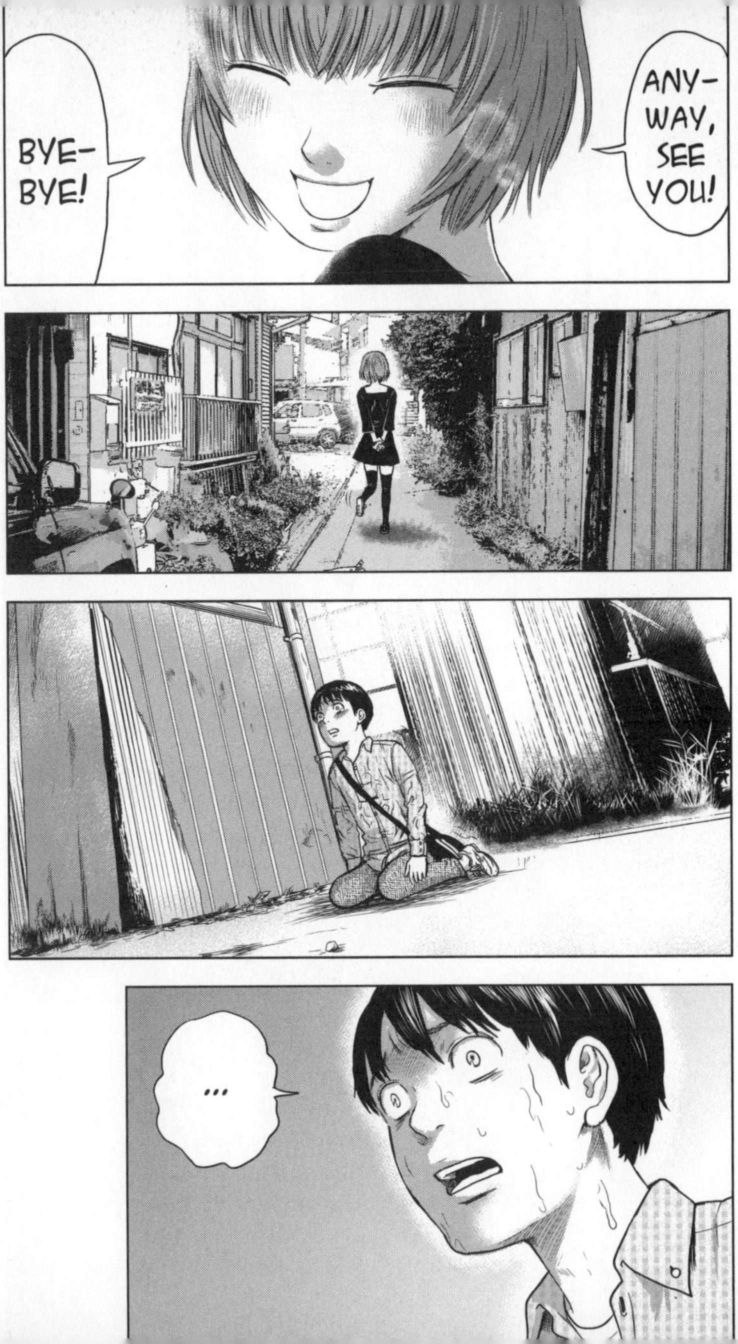
ANY-WAY, SEE YOU!
BYE-BYE!
...

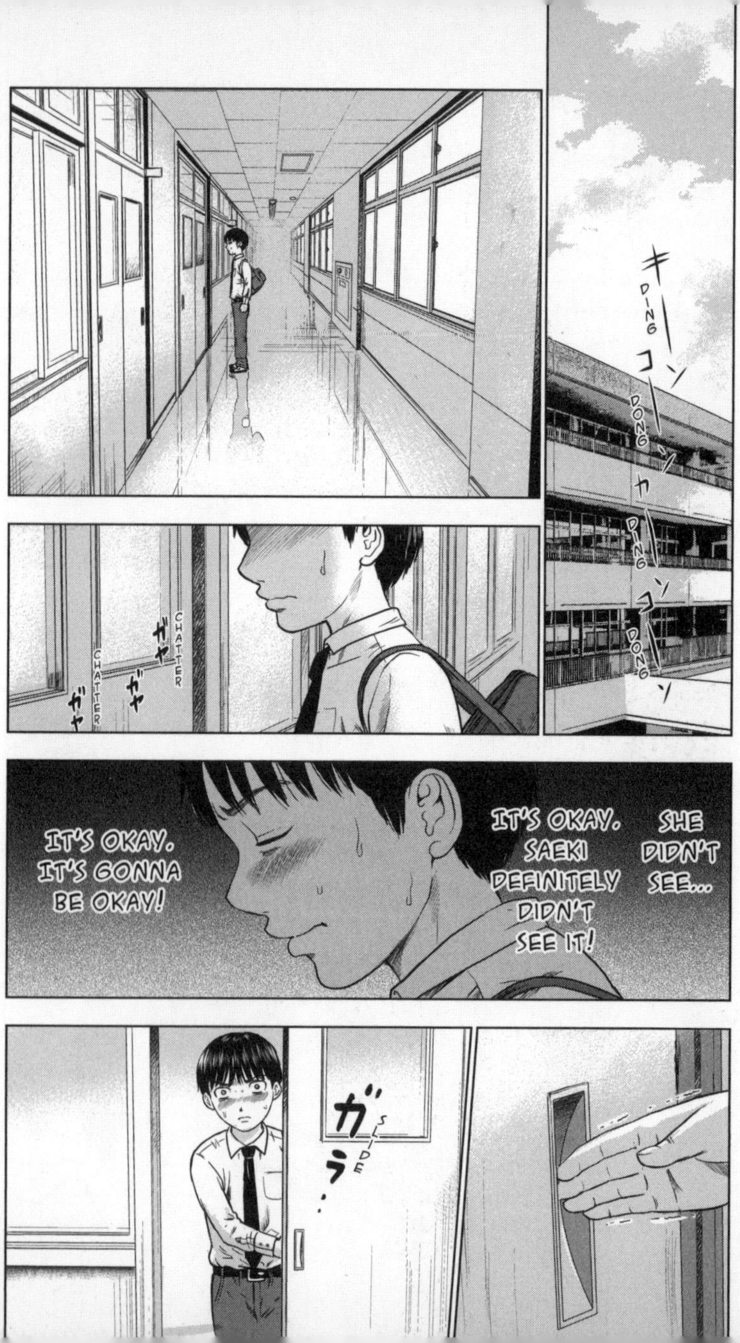
キーンコーンカーンコーン
DING DONG DING DONG
ガヤガヤガヤ
CHATTER CHATTER
SHE DIDN'T SEE...
IT'S OKAY. SAEKI DEFINITELY DIDN'T SEE IT!
IT'S OKAY. IT'S GONNA BE OKAY!
ガラ..
SLIDE

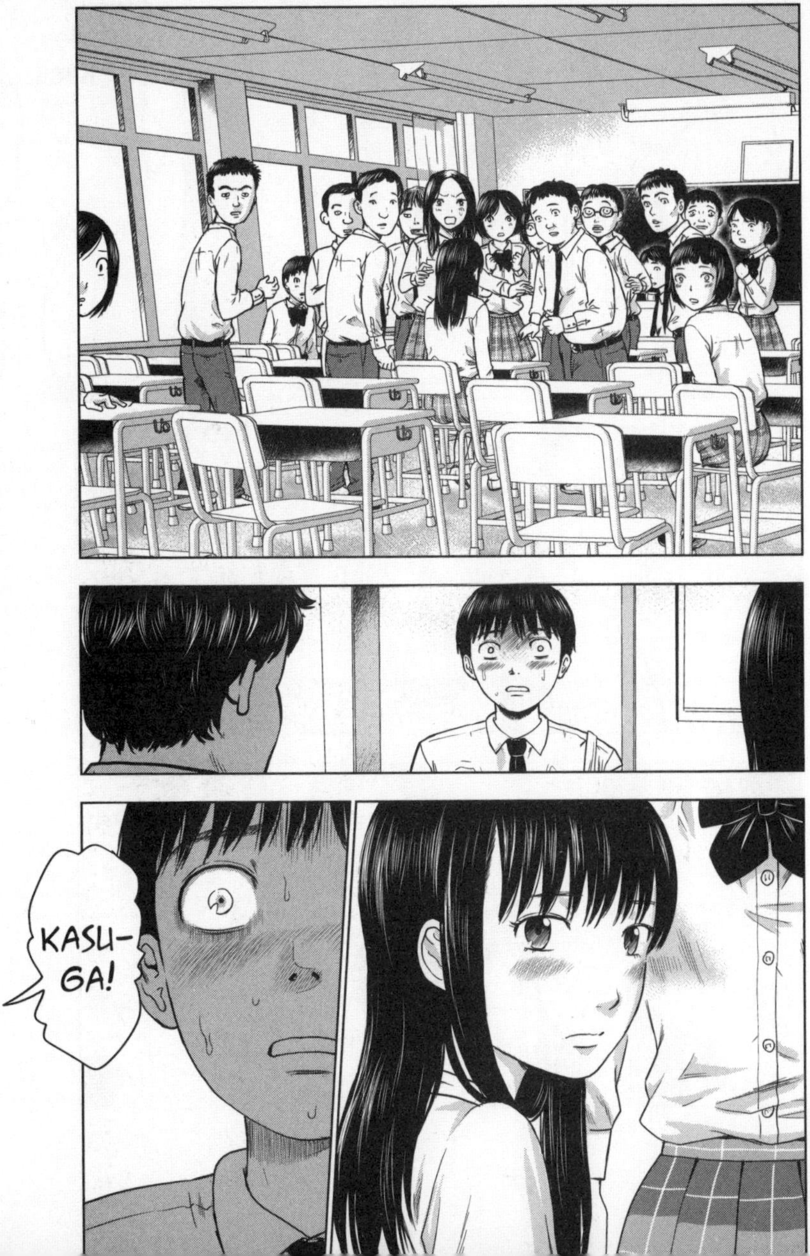
KASU-GA!

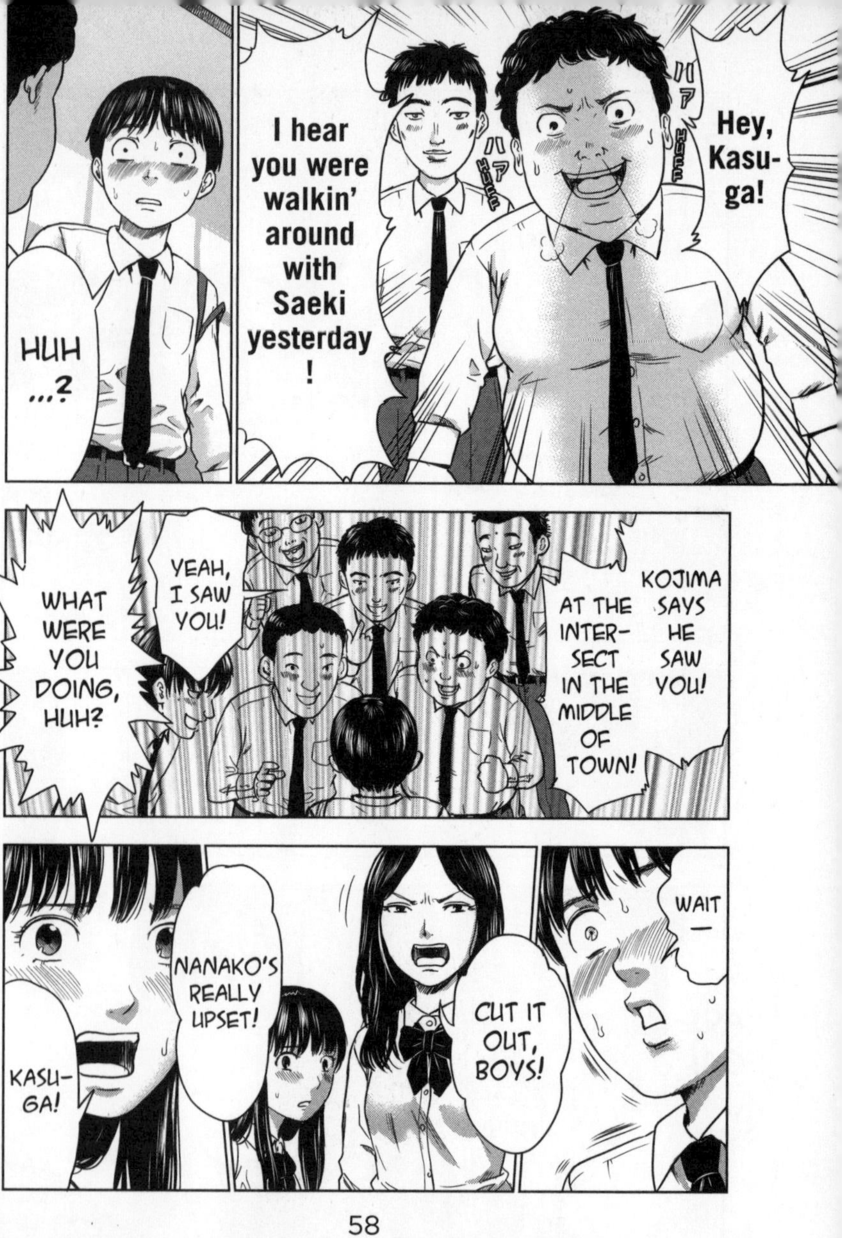
Hey, Kasu-ga!
ハァ HUFF
ハァ HUFF
I hear you were walkin' around with Saeki yesterday!
HUH ...?
KOJIMA SAYS HE SAW YOU!
AT THE INTER-SECT IN THE MIDDLE OF TOWN!
YEAH, I SAW YOU!
WHAT WERE YOU DOING, HUH?
WAIT —
CUT IT OUT, BOYS!
NANAKO'S REALLY UPSET!
KASU-GA!

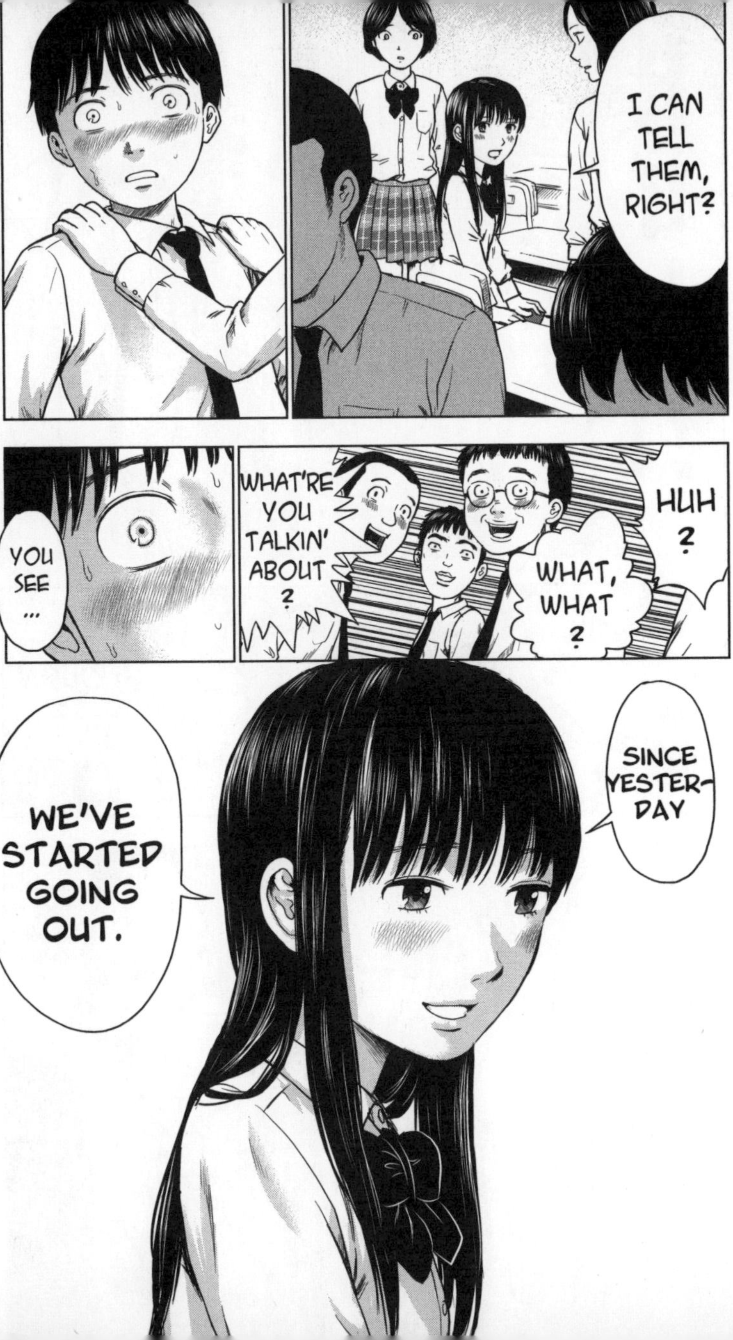
I CAN TELL THEM, RIGHT?
HUH?
WHAT, WHAT?
WHAT'RE YOU TALKIN' ABOUT?
YOU SEE ...
SINCE YESTER-DAY
WE'VE STARTED GOING OUT.

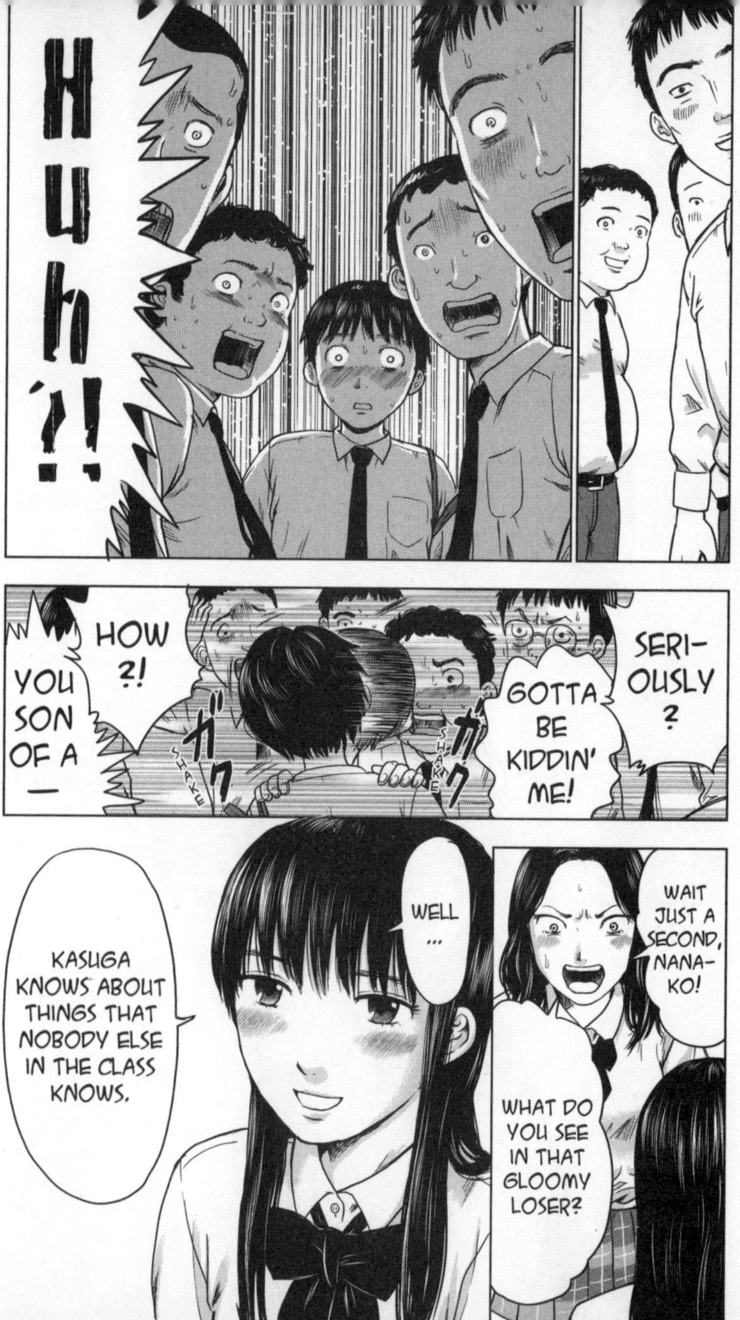
HUH?!
SERIOUSLY?
GOTTA BE KIDDIN' ME!
SHAKE
SHAKE
HOW?!
YOU SON OF A—
WAIT JUST A SECOND, NANAKO!
WHAT DO YOU SEE IN THAT GLOOMY LOSER?
WELL...
KASUGA KNOWS ABOUT THINGS THAT NOBODY ELSE IN THE CLASS KNOWS.

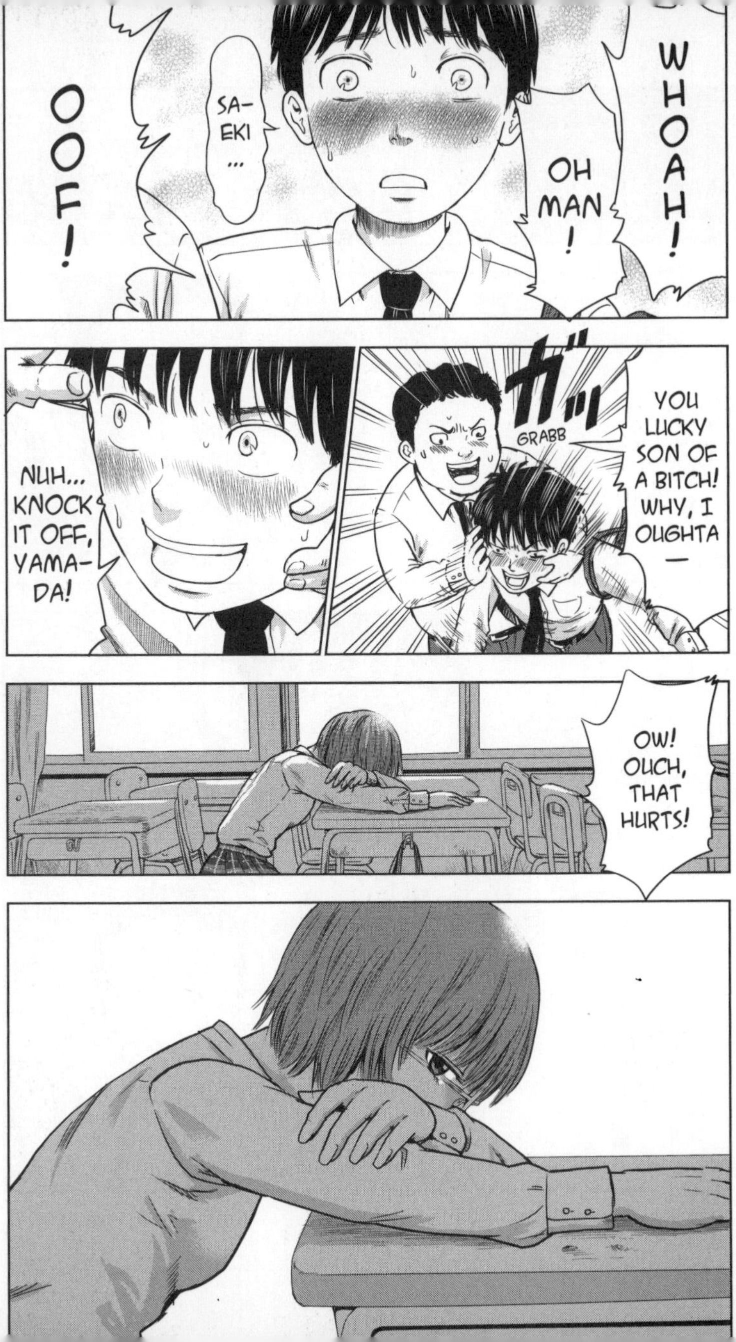
WHOAH!
OH MAN!
SA-EKI...
OOF!
ガッ
GRABB
YOU LUCKY SON OF A BITCH! WHY, I OUGHTA—
NUH... KNOCK IT OFF, YAMADA!
OW! OUCH, THAT HURTS!

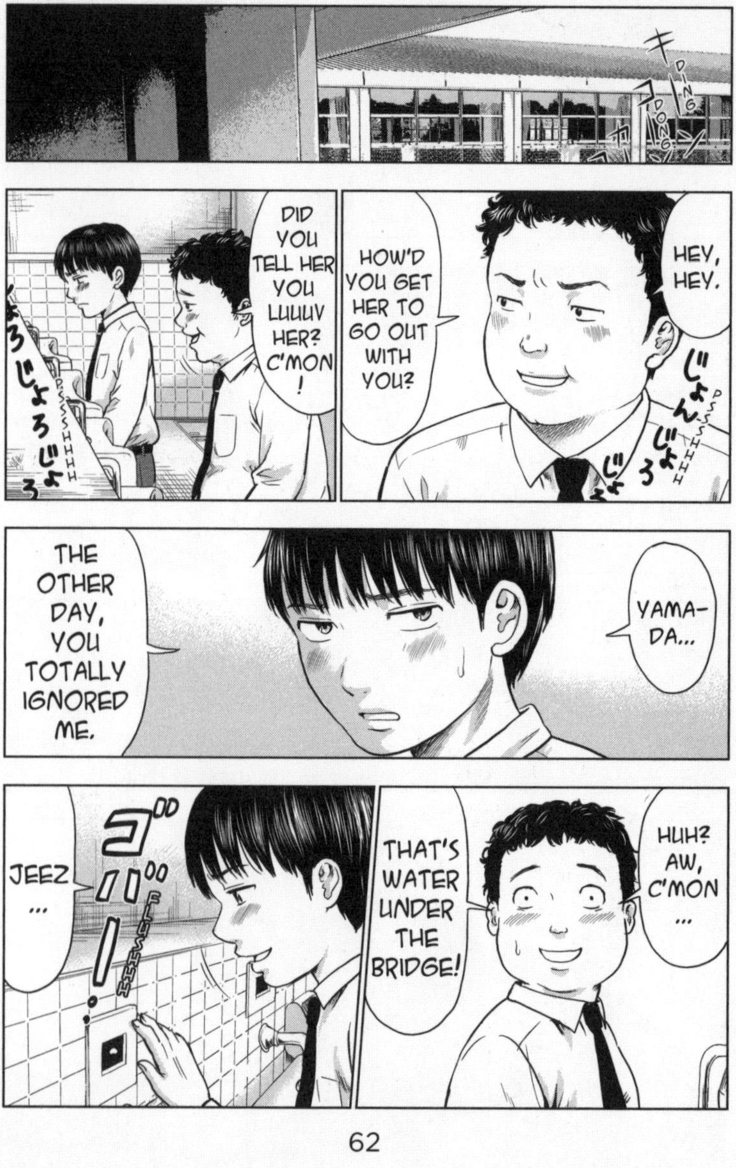
DING
DONG
HEY, HEY.
HOW'D YOU GET HER TO GO OUT WITH YOU?
PSSSHHHH
DID YOU TELL HER YOU LUUUV HER? C'MON!
PSSSHHHH
YAMA-DA...
THE OTHER DAY, YOU TOTALLY IGNORED ME.
HUH? AW, C'MON...
THAT'S WATER UNDER THE BRIDGE!
JEEZ...

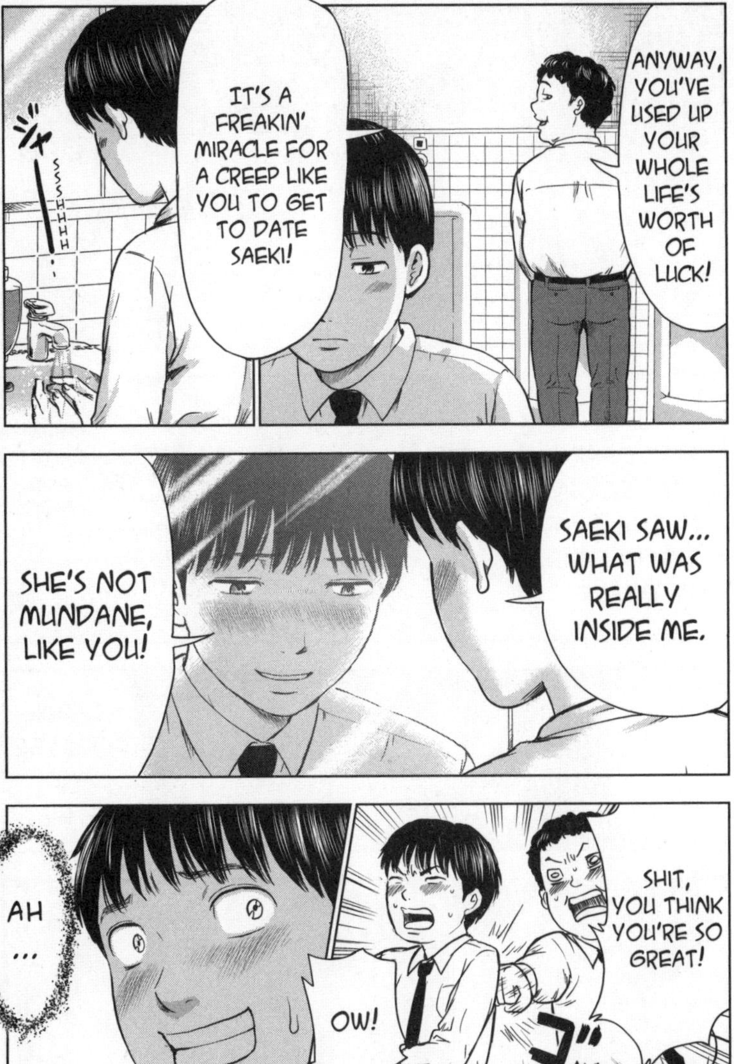
ANYWAY, YOU'VE USED UP YOUR WHOLE LIFE'S WORTH OF LUCK!
IT'S A FREAKIN' MIRACLE FOR A CREEP LIKE YOU TO GET TO DATE SAEKI!
SSSHHHH...
SAEKI SAW... WHAT WAS REALLY INSIDE ME.
SHE'S NOT MUNDANE, LIKE YOU!
SHIT, YOU THINK YOU'RE SO GREAT!
WHOK
OW!
AH ...

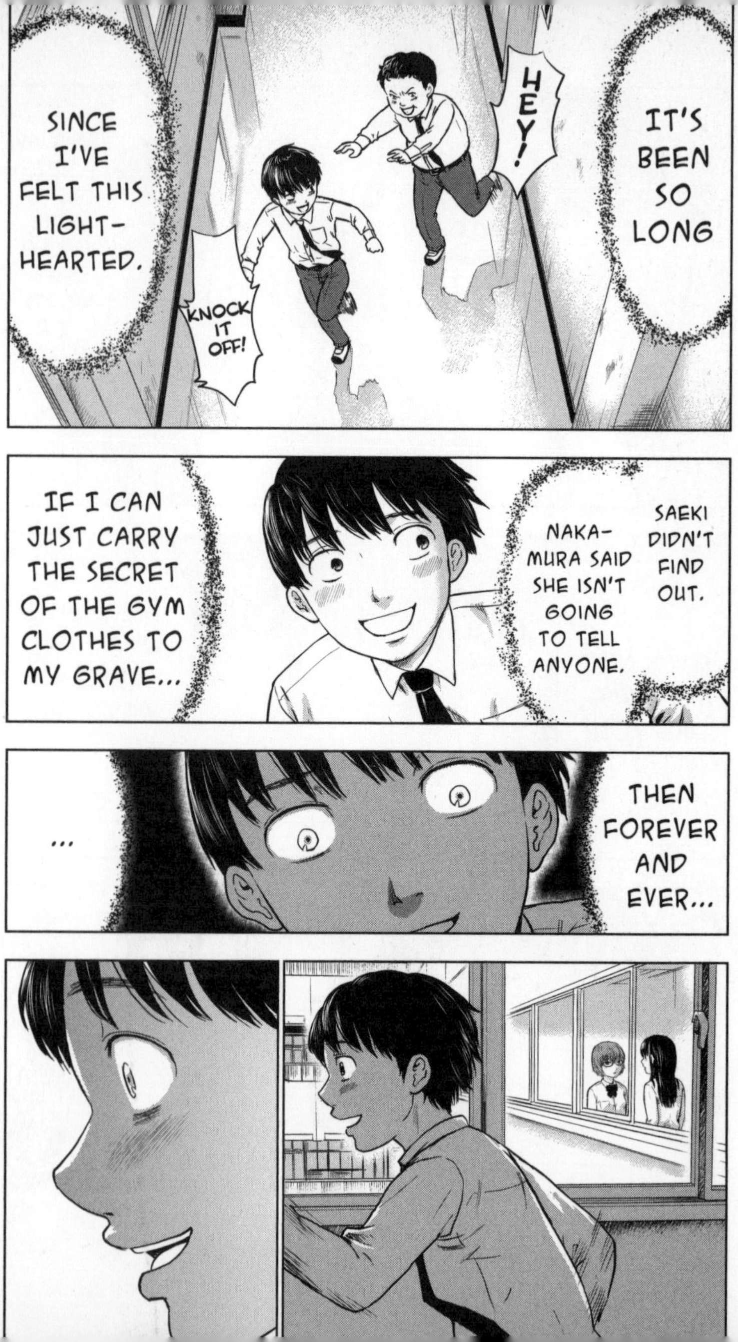
IT'S BEEN SO LONG
HEY!
SINCE I'VE FELT THIS LIGHT-HEARTED.
KNOCK IT OFF!
SAEKI DIDN'T FIND OUT.
NAKA-MURA SAID SHE ISN'T GOING TO TELL ANYONE.
IF I CAN JUST CARRY THE SECRET OF THE GYM CLOTHES TO MY GRAVE...
THEN FOREVER AND EVER...
...

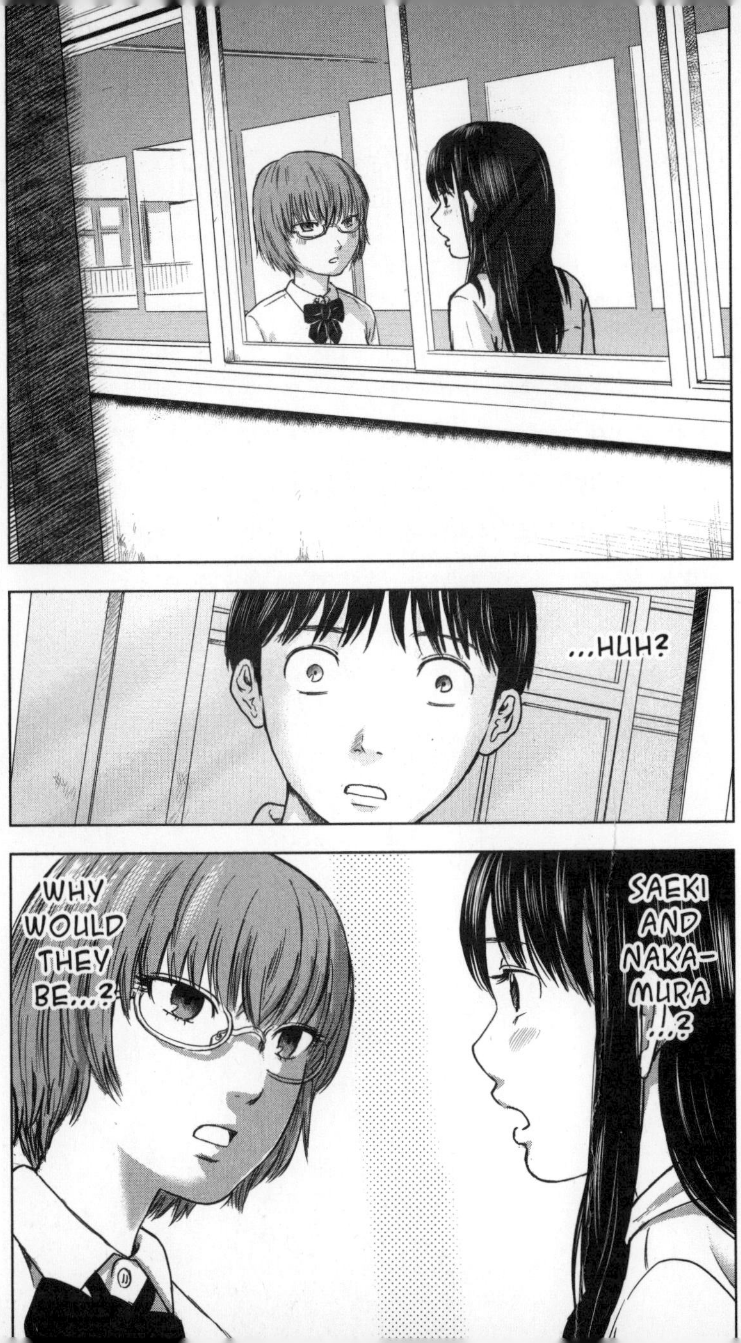
...HUH?
SAEKI AND NAKAMURA ...?
WHY WOULD THEY BE...?

Afterword

Chapter 8

The park where Kasuga confesses his feelings to Saeki is a
park about a minute's walk from the house where I grew up.
I played there as a kid all the time. Now it's full of weeds,
only the frame of the swingset remains, the slide has been
removed, and it's nothing more than an empty lot.
While the areas flanking the bypass highway thrive,
the central part of my countryside hometown is fading fast.

Chapter 9: The Fraying String

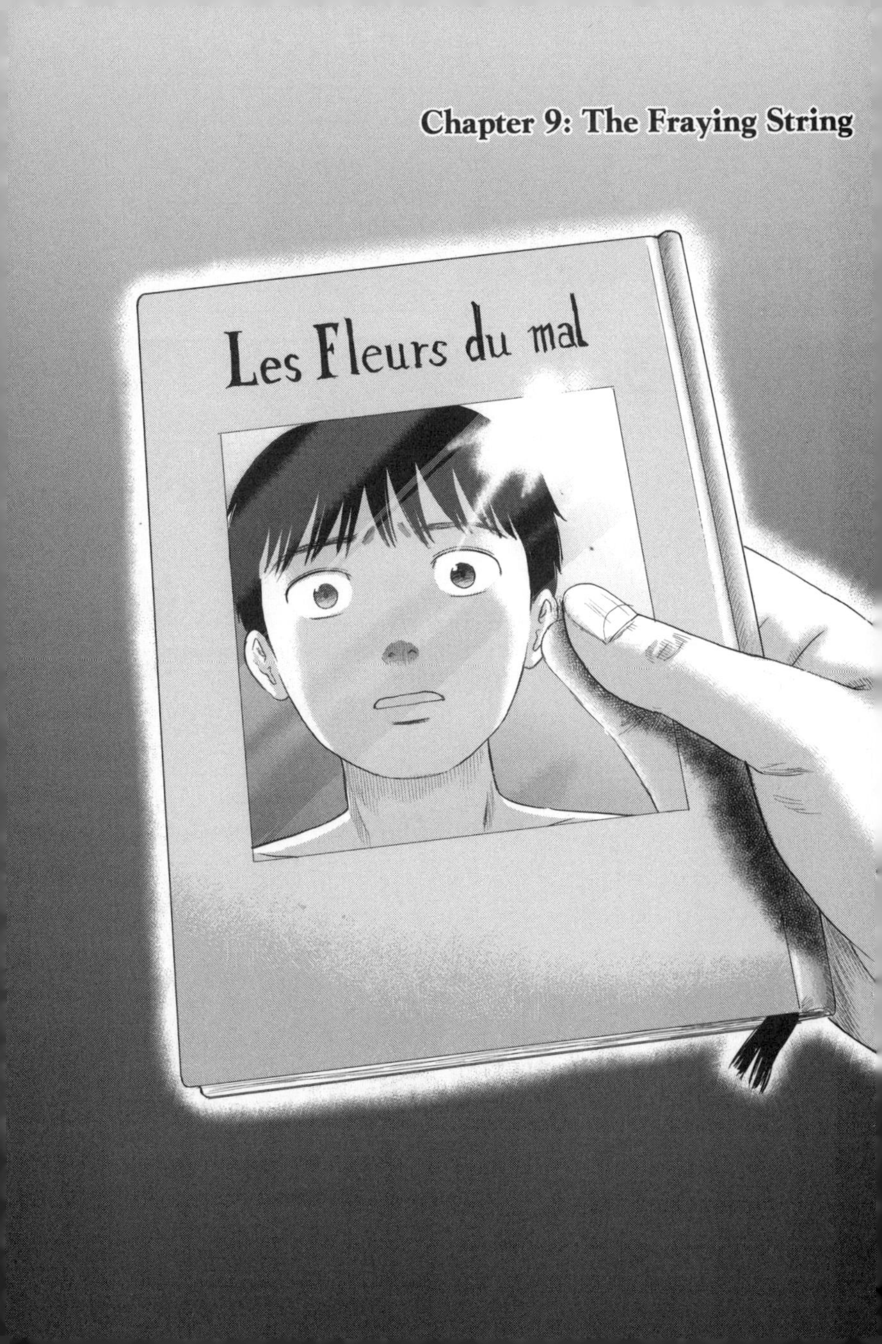
Les Fleurs du mal

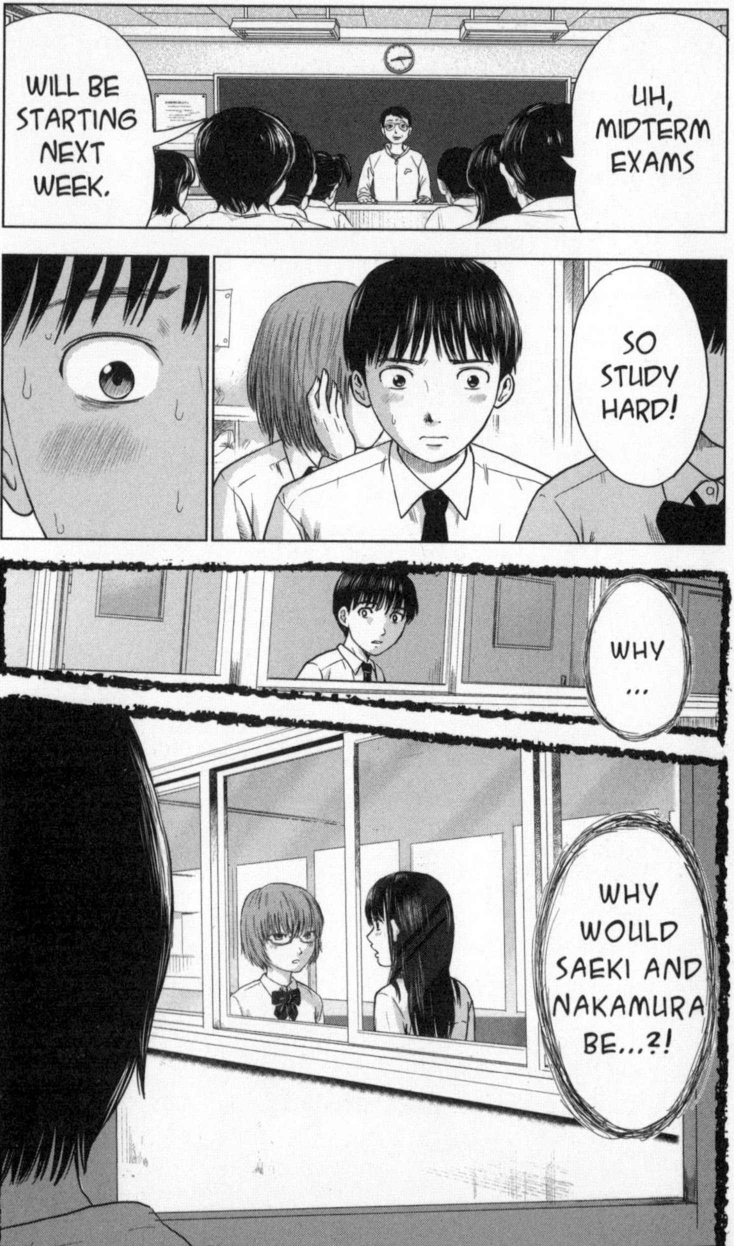
UH, MIDTERM EXAMS
WILL BE STARTING NEXT WEEK.
SO STUDY HARD!
WHY ...
WHY WOULD SAEKI AND NAKAMURA BE...?!

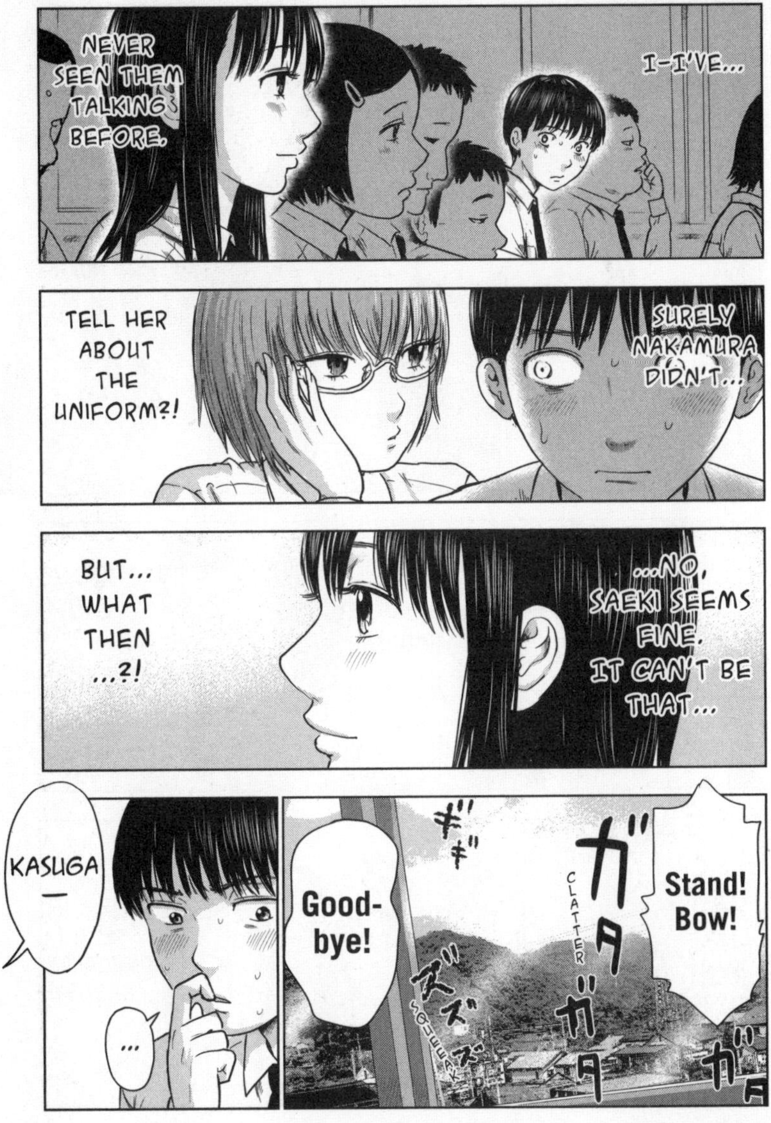
I-I'VE...
NEVER SEEN THEM TALKING BEFORE.
SURELY NAKAMURA DIDN'T...
TELL HER ABOUT THE UNIFORM?!
...NO, SAEKI SEEMS FINE. IT CAN'T BE THAT...
BUT... WHAT THEN ...?!
Stand! Bow!
CLATTER
SQUEEEAK
Good-bye!
KASUGA—
...

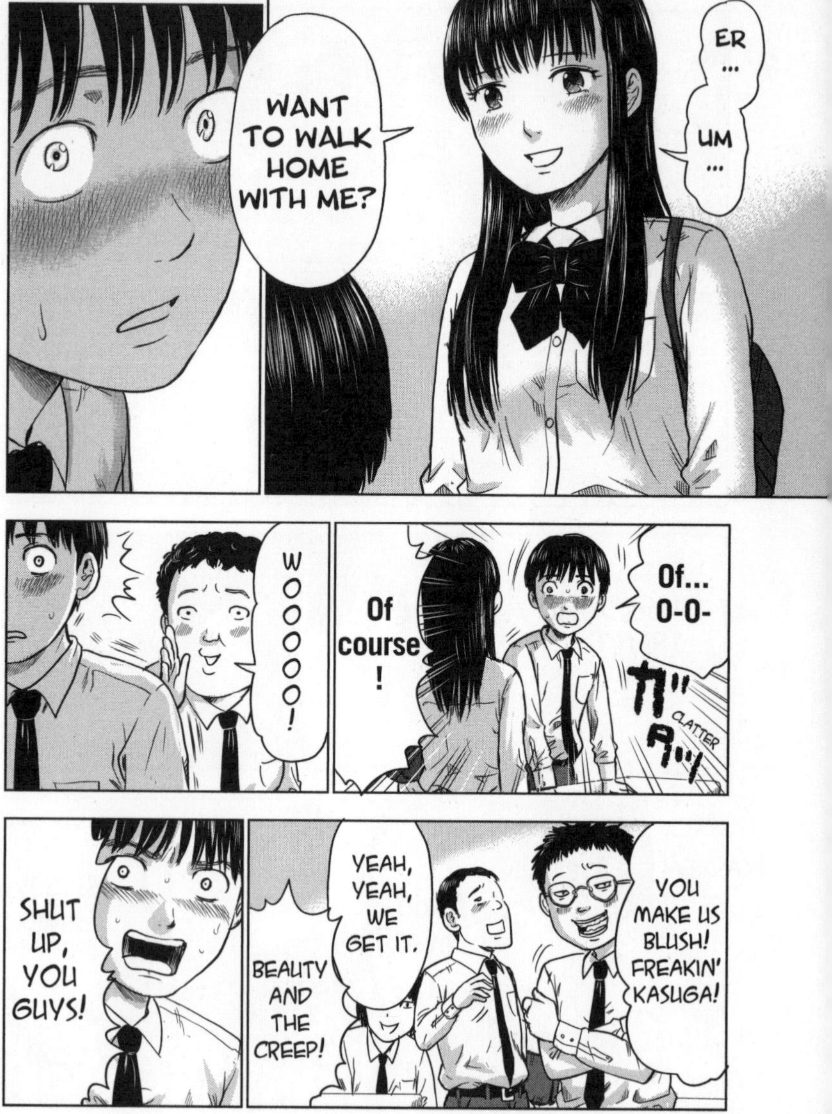
ER ... UM ...
WANT TO WALK HOME WITH ME?
Of... O-O-
Of course!
CLATTER
WOOOOOO!
YOU MAKE US BLUSH! FREAKIN' KASUGA!
YEAH, YEAH, WE GET IT.
BEAUTY AND THE CREEP!
SHUT UP, YOU GUYS!

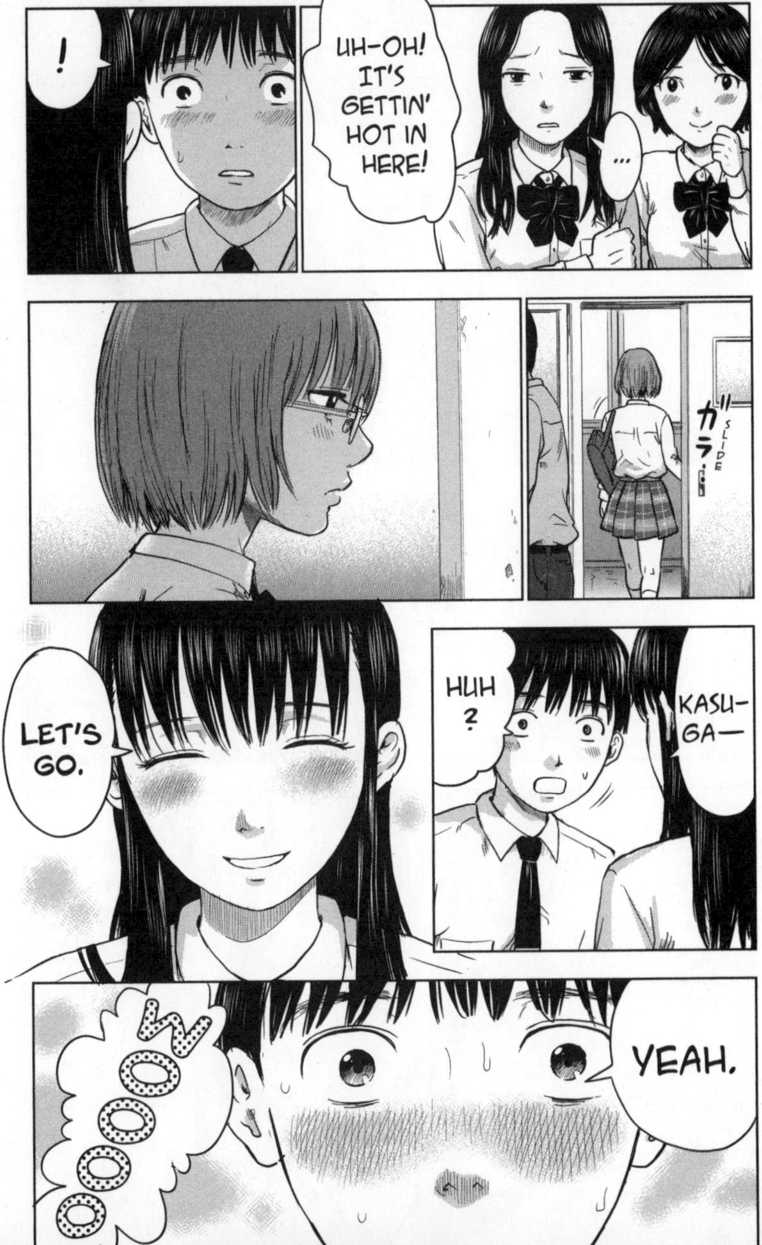
UH-OH! IT'S GETTIN' HOT IN HERE!
...
!
ガラ SLIDE
KASU-GA—
HUH ?
LET'S GO.
YEAH.
WOOOOOO

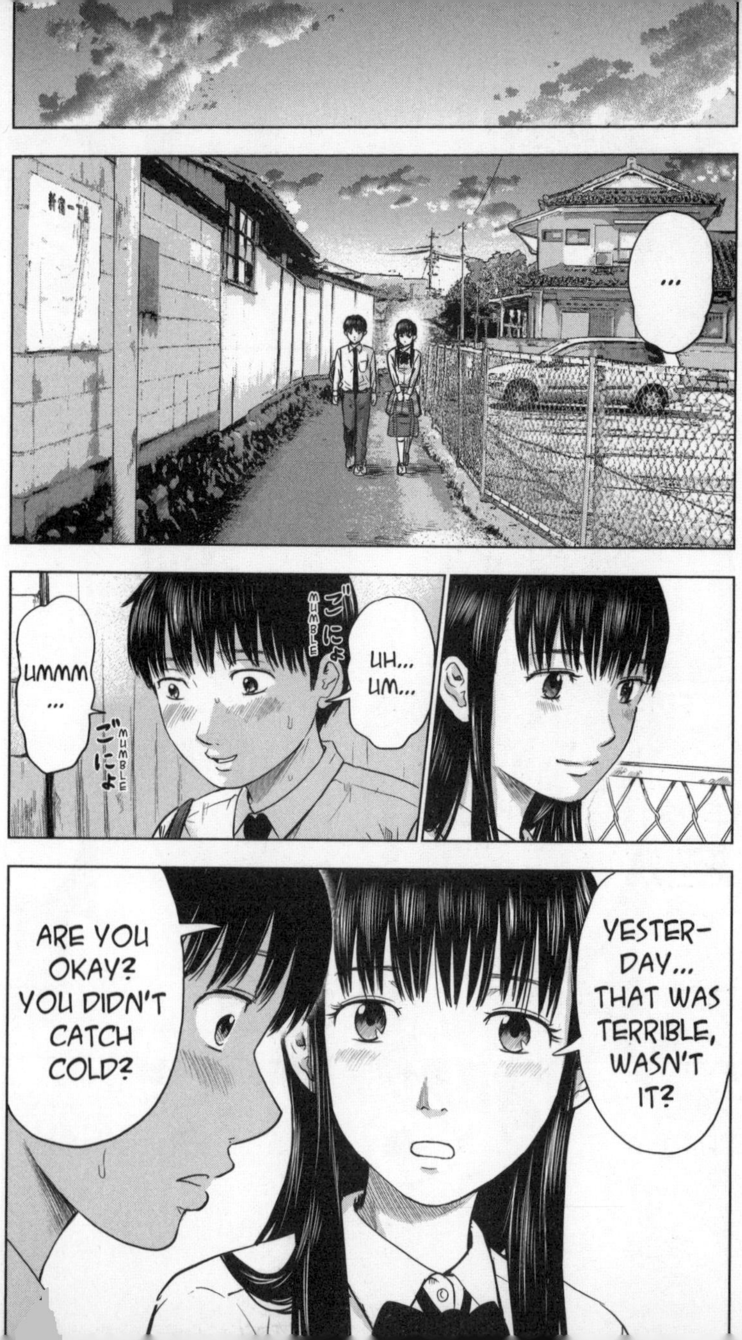
...
ごにょ MUMBLE
UH... UM...
UMMM ...
ごにょ MUMBLE
YESTER-DAY... THAT WAS TERRIBLE, WASN'T IT?
ARE YOU OKAY? YOU DIDN'T CATCH COLD?

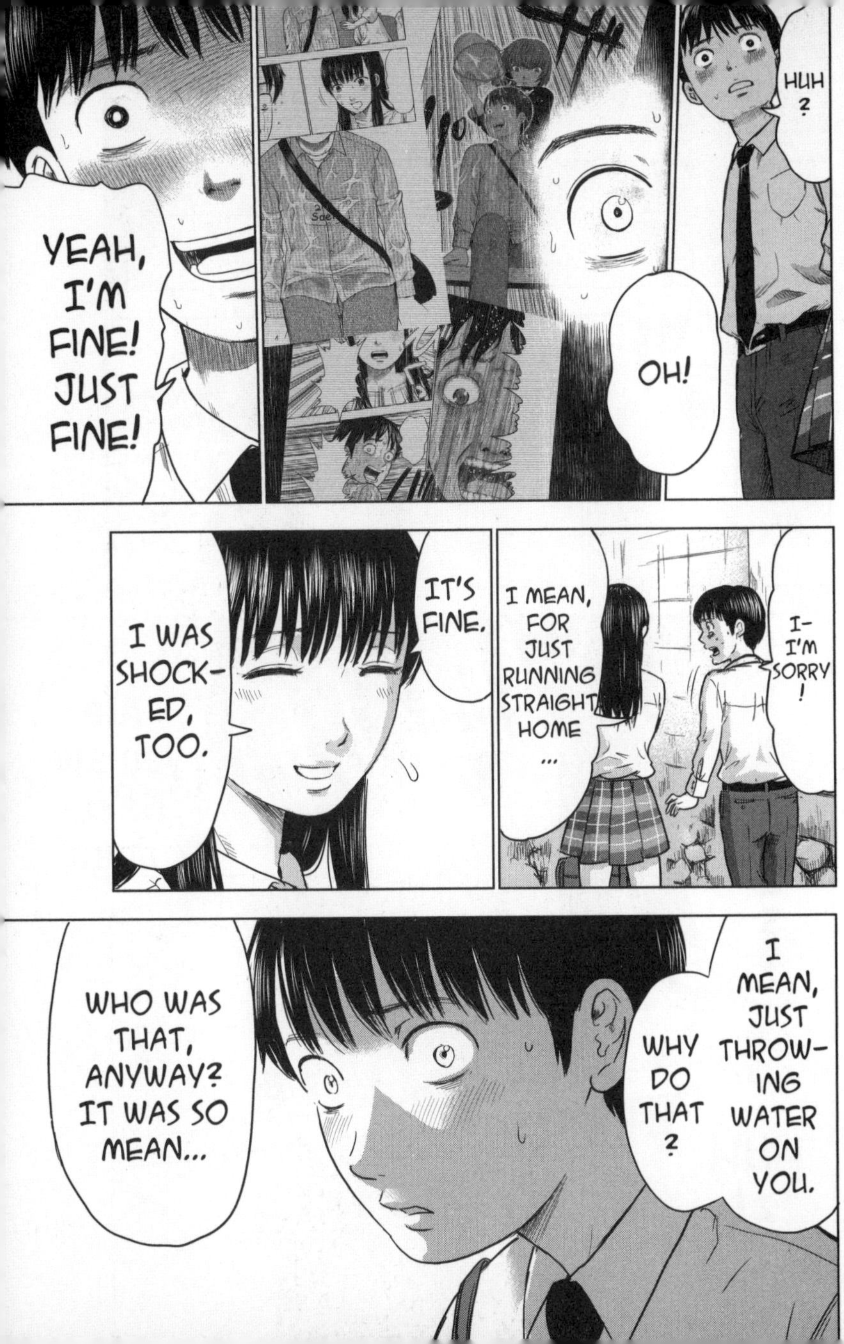
HUH?
OH!
YEAH, I'M FINE! JUST FINE!
I- I'M SORRY!
I MEAN, FOR JUST RUNNING STRAIGHT HOME ...
IT'S FINE.
I WAS SHOCKED, TOO.
I MEAN, JUST THROWING WATER ON YOU.
WHY DO THAT?
WHO WAS THAT, ANYWAY? IT WAS SO MEAN...

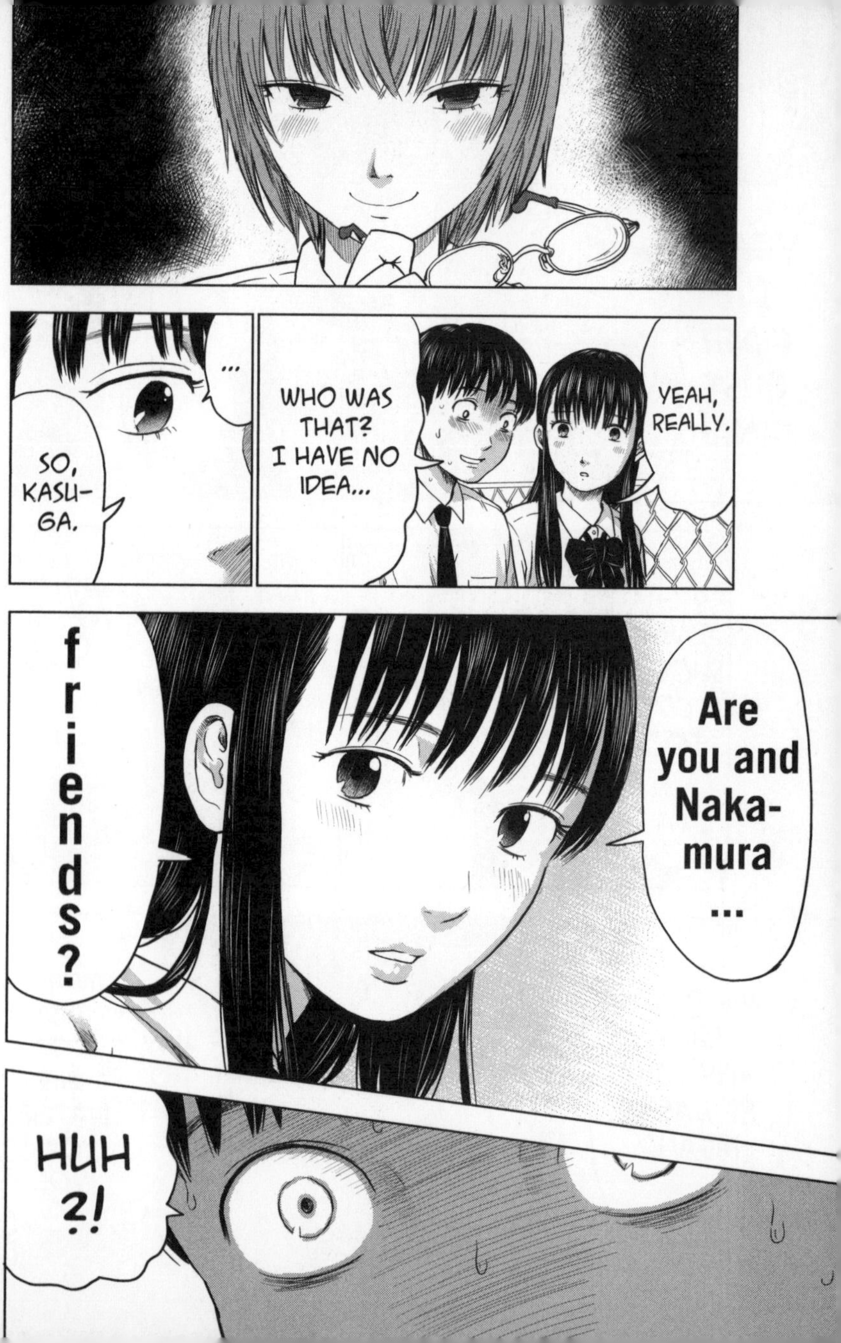
YEAH, REALLY.
WHO WAS THAT? I HAVE NO IDEA...
...
SO, KASUGA.
Are you and Naka-mura ...
friends?
HUH ?!

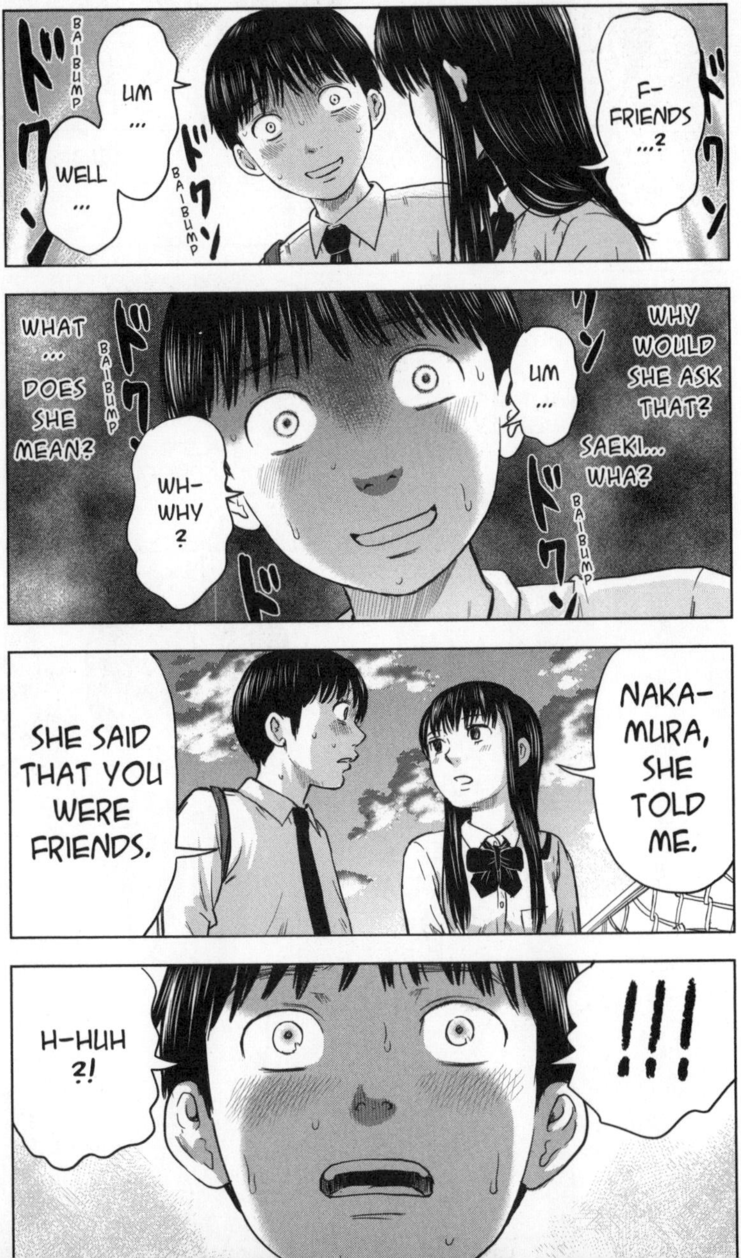
F-FRIENDS ...?
BAIBUMP
UM ...
WELL ...
BAIBUMP
WHY WOULD SHE ASK THAT?
SAEKI... WHA?
BAIBUMP
UM ...
WH-WHY?
BAIBUMP
WHAT ... DOES SHE MEAN?
NAKA-MURA, SHE TOLD ME.
SHE SAID THAT YOU WERE FRIENDS.
!!!
H-HUH?!

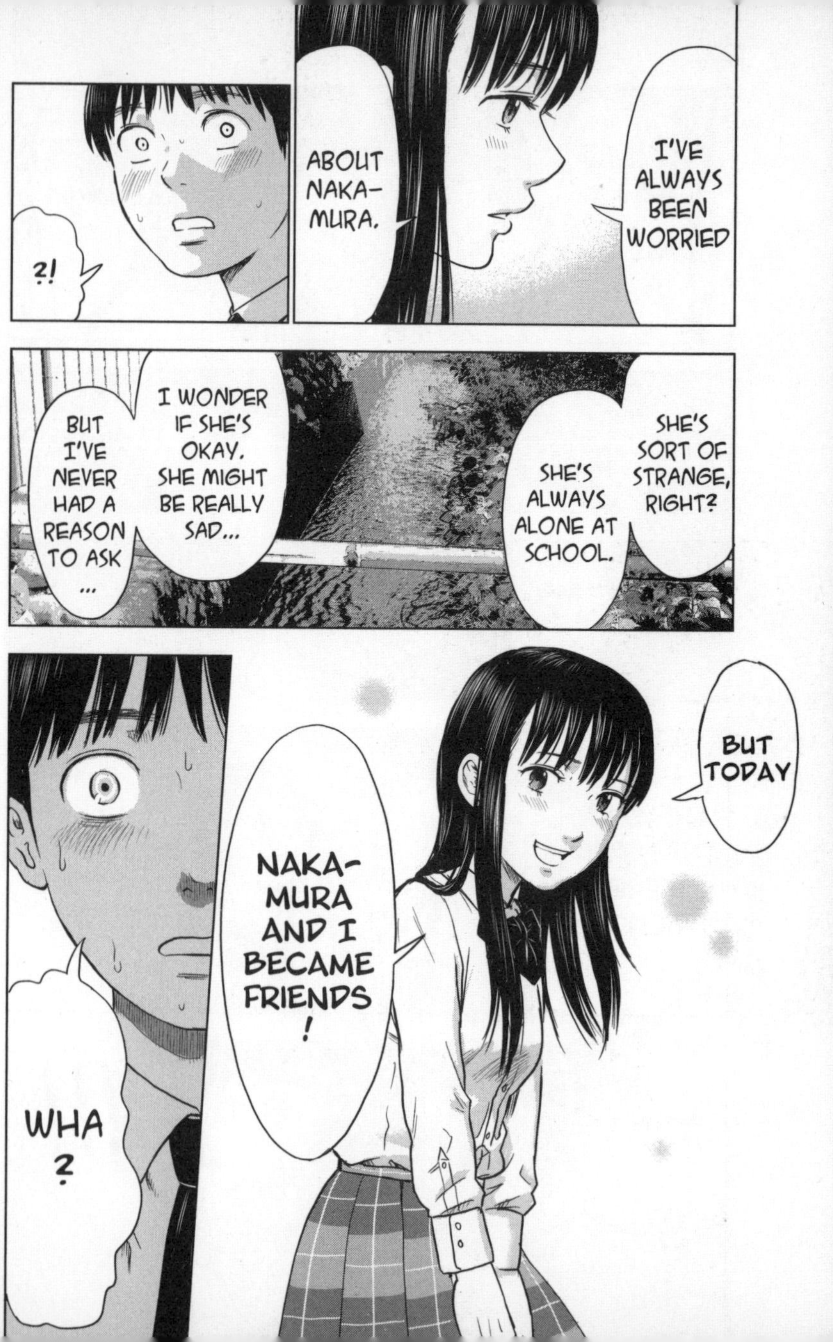
I'VE ALWAYS BEEN WORRIED
ABOUT NAKA-MURA.
?!
SHE'S SORT OF STRANGE, RIGHT?
SHE'S ALWAYS ALONE AT SCHOOL.
I WONDER IF SHE'S OKAY. SHE MIGHT BE REALLY SAD...
BUT I'VE NEVER HAD A REASON TO ASK ...
BUT TODAY
NAKA-MURA AND I BECAME FRIENDS!
WHA?

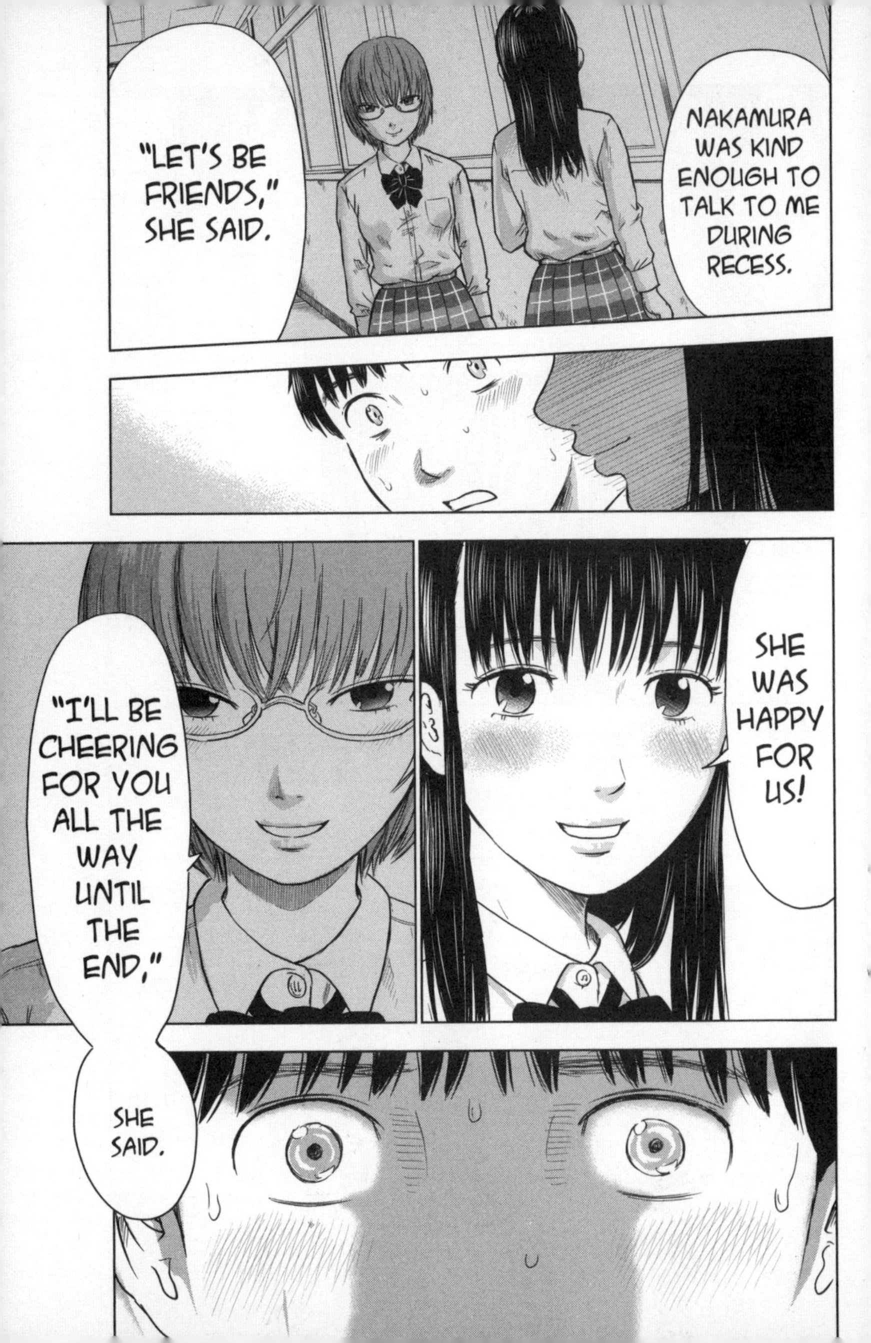
NAKAMURA WAS KIND ENOUGH TO TALK TO ME DURING RECESS.
"LET'S BE FRIENDS," SHE SAID.
SHE WAS HAPPY FOR US!
"I'LL BE CHEERING FOR YOU ALL THE WAY UNTIL THE END,"
SHE SAID.

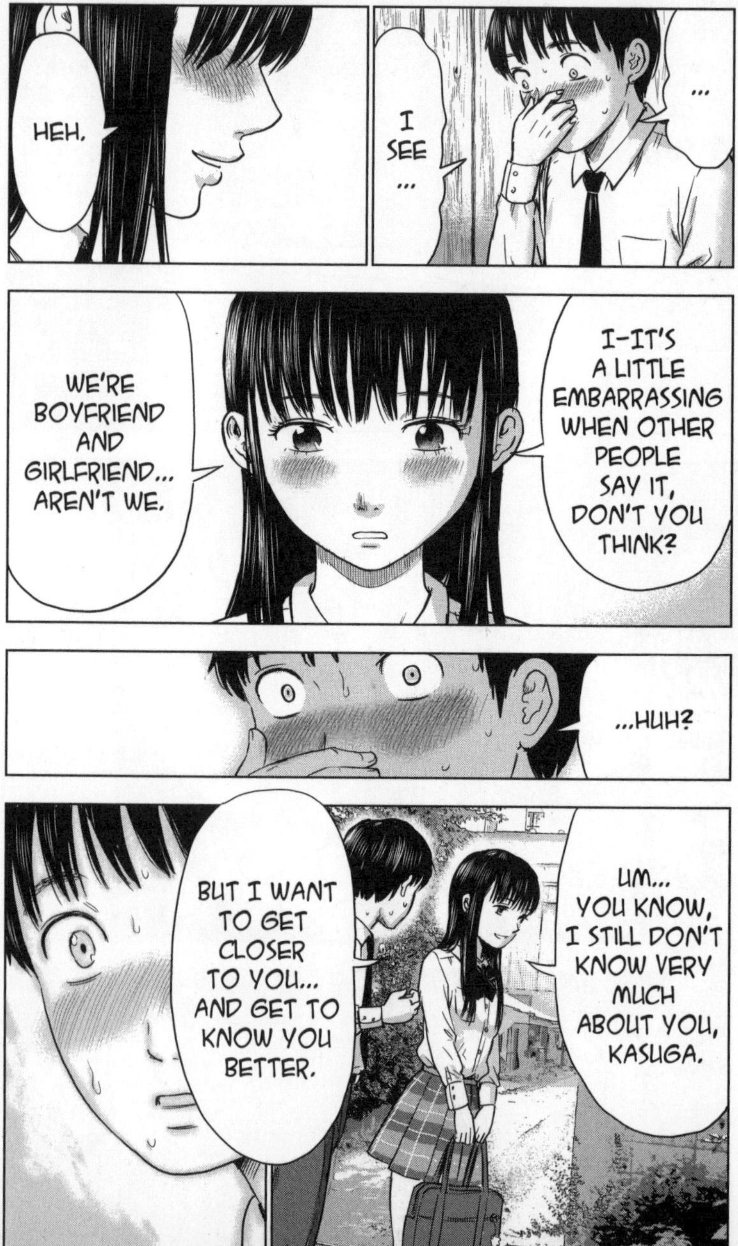
...
I SEE ...
HEH.
I-IT'S A LITTLE EMBARRASSING WHEN OTHER PEOPLE SAY IT, DON'T YOU THINK?
WE'RE BOYFRIEND AND GIRLFRIEND... AREN'T WE.
...HUH?
UM... YOU KNOW, I STILL DON'T KNOW VERY MUCH ABOUT YOU, KASUGA.
BUT I WANT TO GET CLOSER TO YOU... AND GET TO KNOW YOU BETTER.

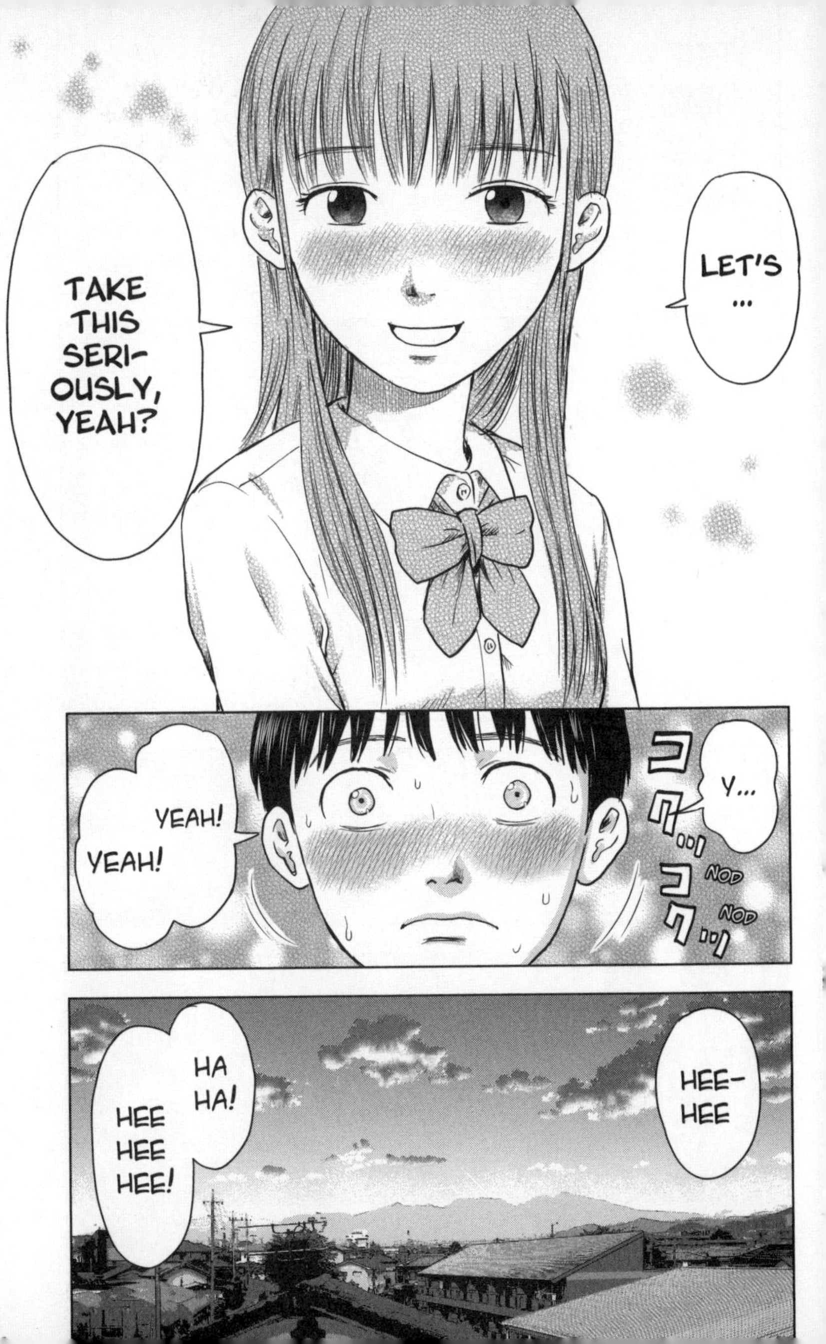
LET'S ...
TAKE THIS SERI- OUSLY, YEAH?
Y...
コクッ
NOD
コクッ
NOD
YEAH! YEAH!
HEE- HEE
HA HA! HEE HEE HEE!

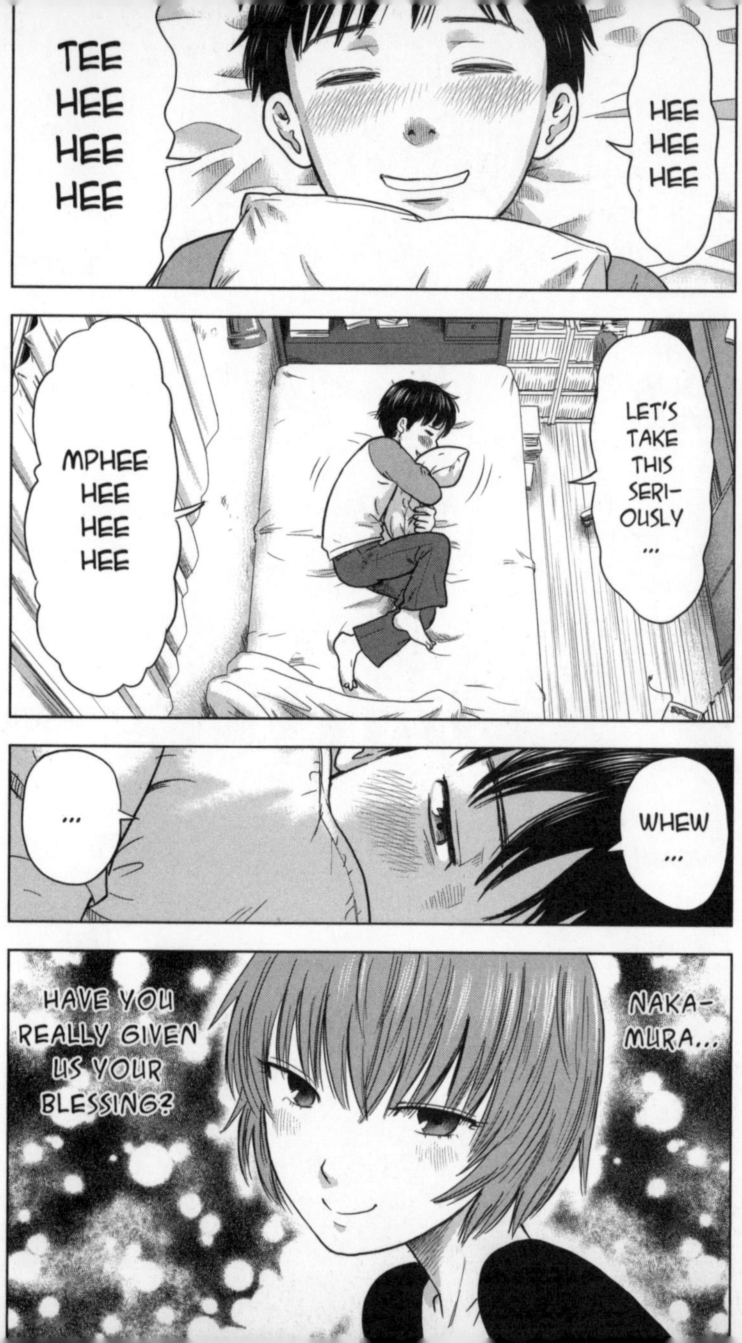
HEE HEE HEE
TEE HEE HEE HEE
LET'S TAKE THIS SERI-OUSLY ...
MPHEE HEE HEE HEE
WHEW ...
...
NAKA-MURA...
HAVE YOU REALLY GIVEN US YOUR BLESSING?

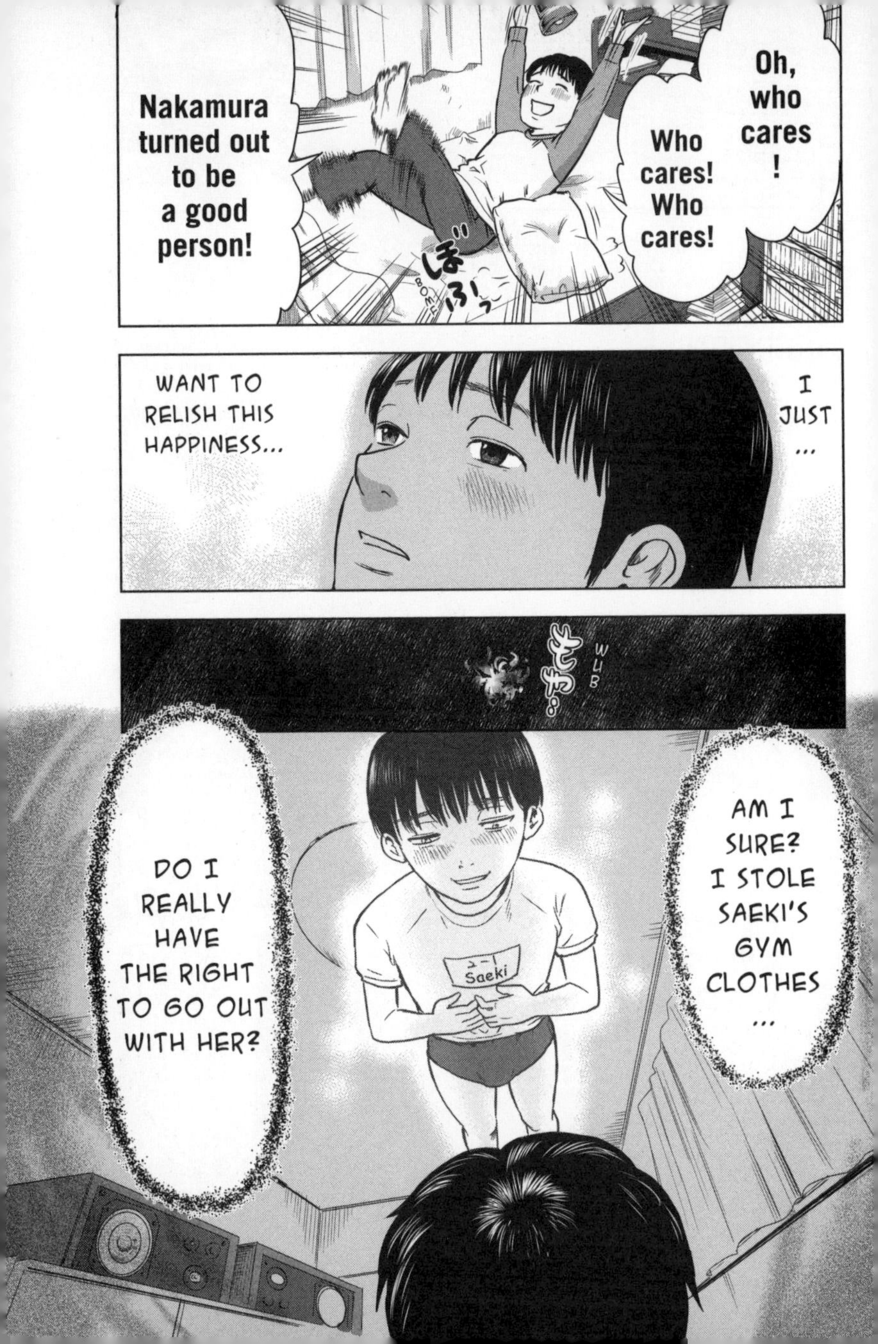
Oh, who cares!
Who cares! Who cares!
Nakamura turned out to be a good person!
ぼふっ
BOMF
I just...
want to relish this happiness...
もわ。
WUB
Am I sure? I stole Saeki's gym clothes...
Saeki
Do I really have the right to go out with her?

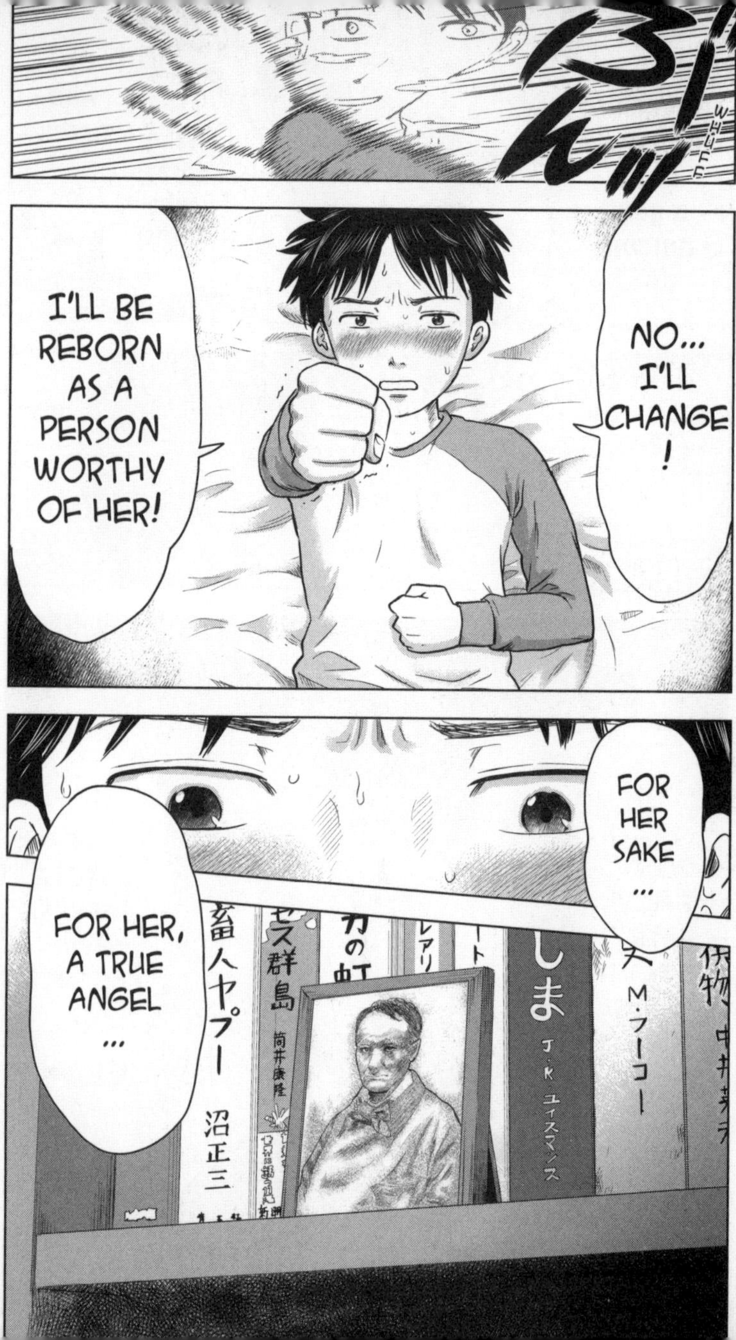
WHUFF
NO... I'LL CHANGE!
I'LL BE REBORN AS A PERSON WORTHY OF HER!
FOR HER SAKE...
FOR HER, A TRUE ANGEL...
畜人ヤプー
沼正三
M・フーコー
J・K・ユイスマンス

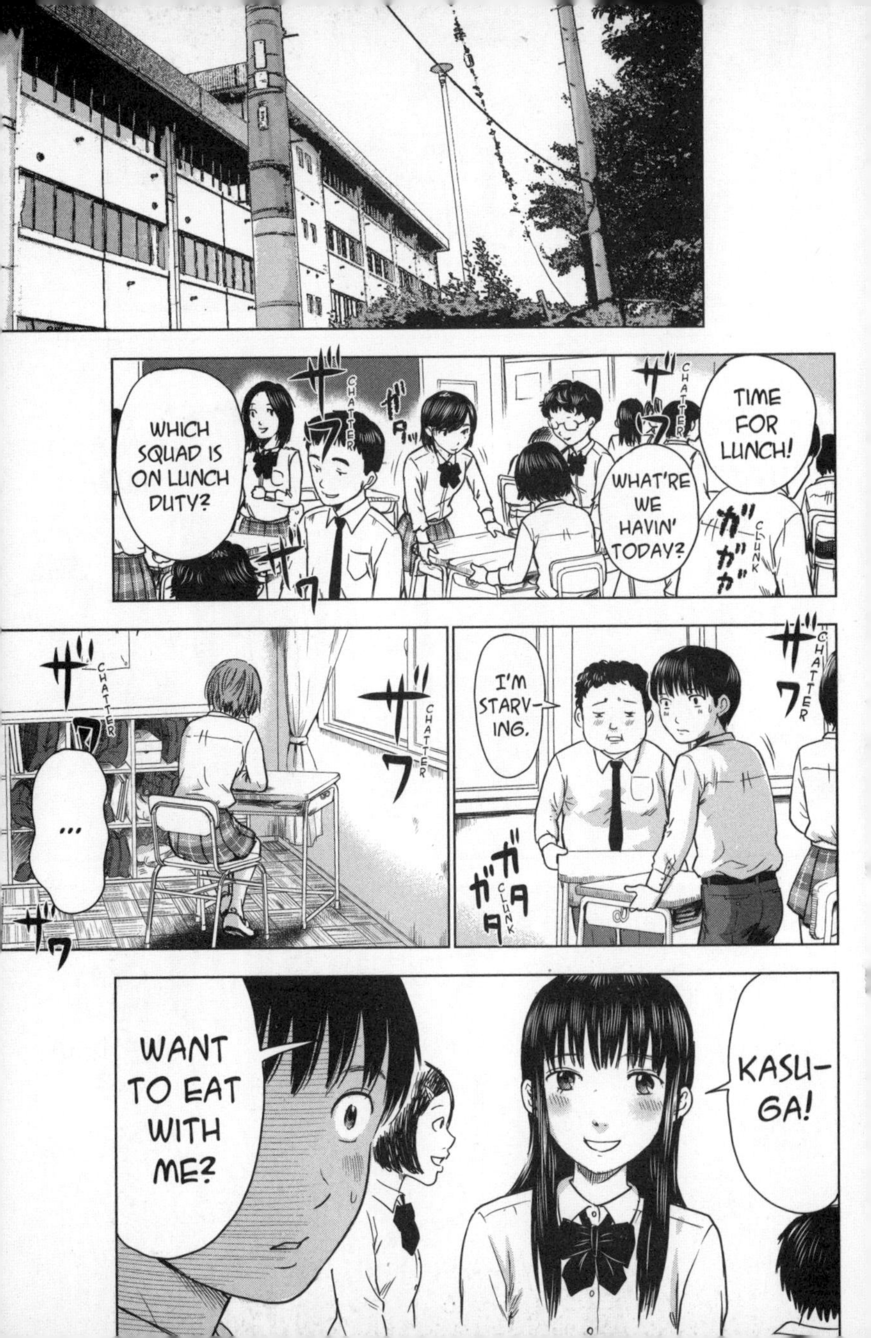

CHATTER
TIME FOR LUNCH!
WHAT'RE WE HAVIN' TODAY?
CLUNK
CHATTER
WHICH SQUAD IS ON LUNCH DUTY?
CHATTER
I'M STARV-ING.
CLUNK
CHATTER
CHATTER
...
KASU-GA!
WANT TO EAT WITH ME?

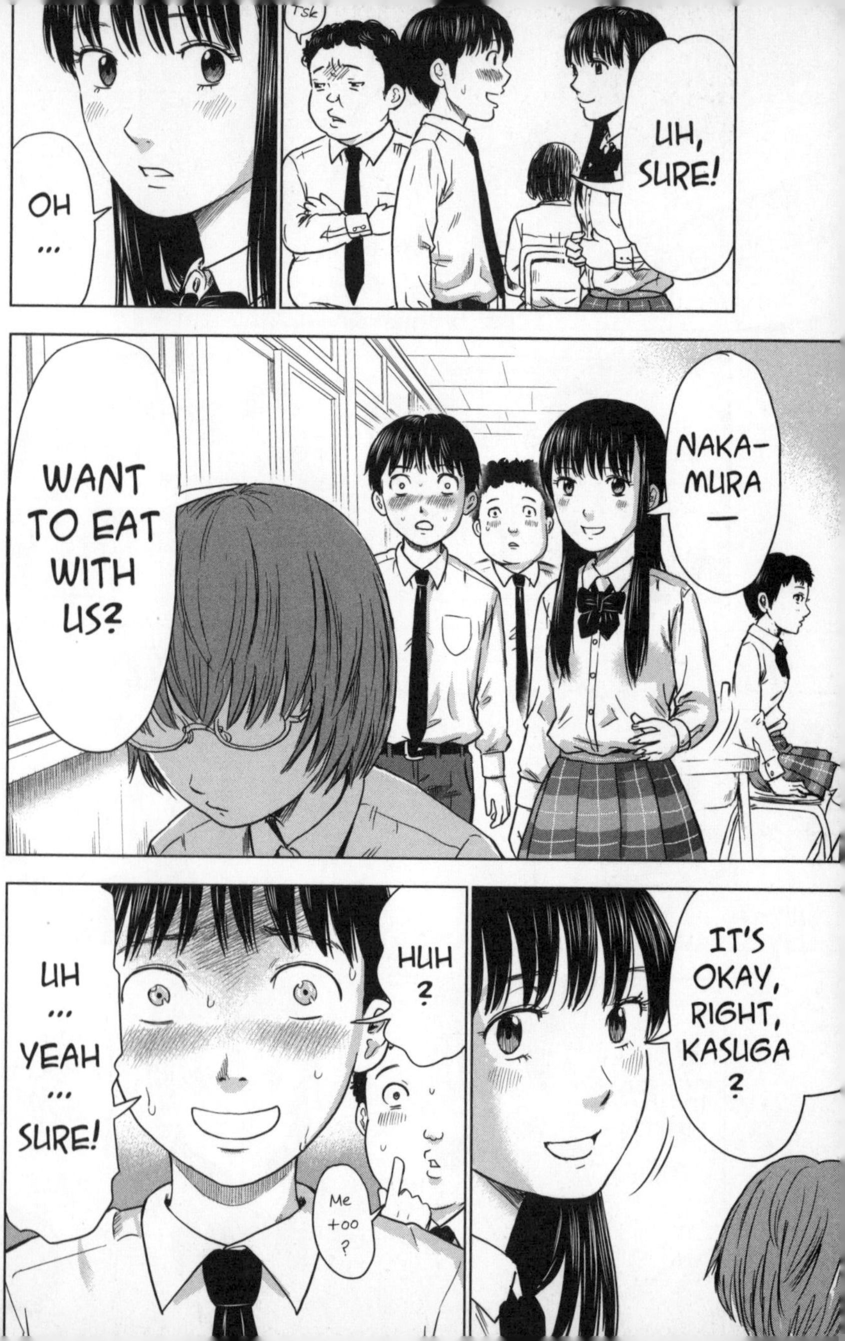
UH, SURE!
Tsk
OH ...
NAKA-MURA —
WANT TO EAT WITH US?
IT'S OKAY, RIGHT, KASUGA ?
HUH ?
UH ... YEAH ... SURE!
Me too ?

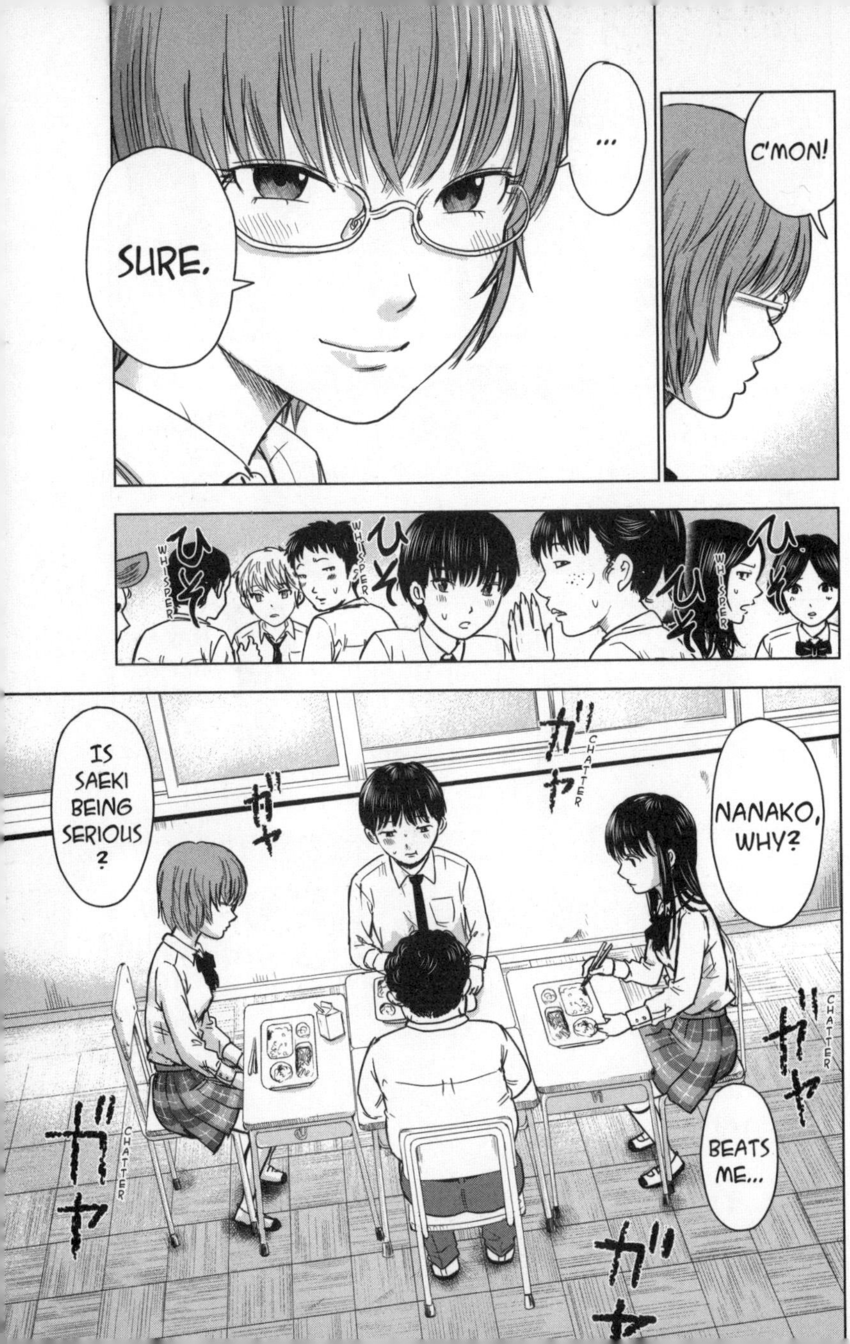
C'MON!
...
SURE.
ひそ WHISPER
ひそ WHISPER
ひそ WHISPER
ひそ WHISPER
NANAKO, WHY?
ガヤ CHATTER
ガヤ
IS SAEKI BEING SERIOUS?
ガヤ CHATTER
BEATS ME...
ガヤ CHATTER
ガヤ

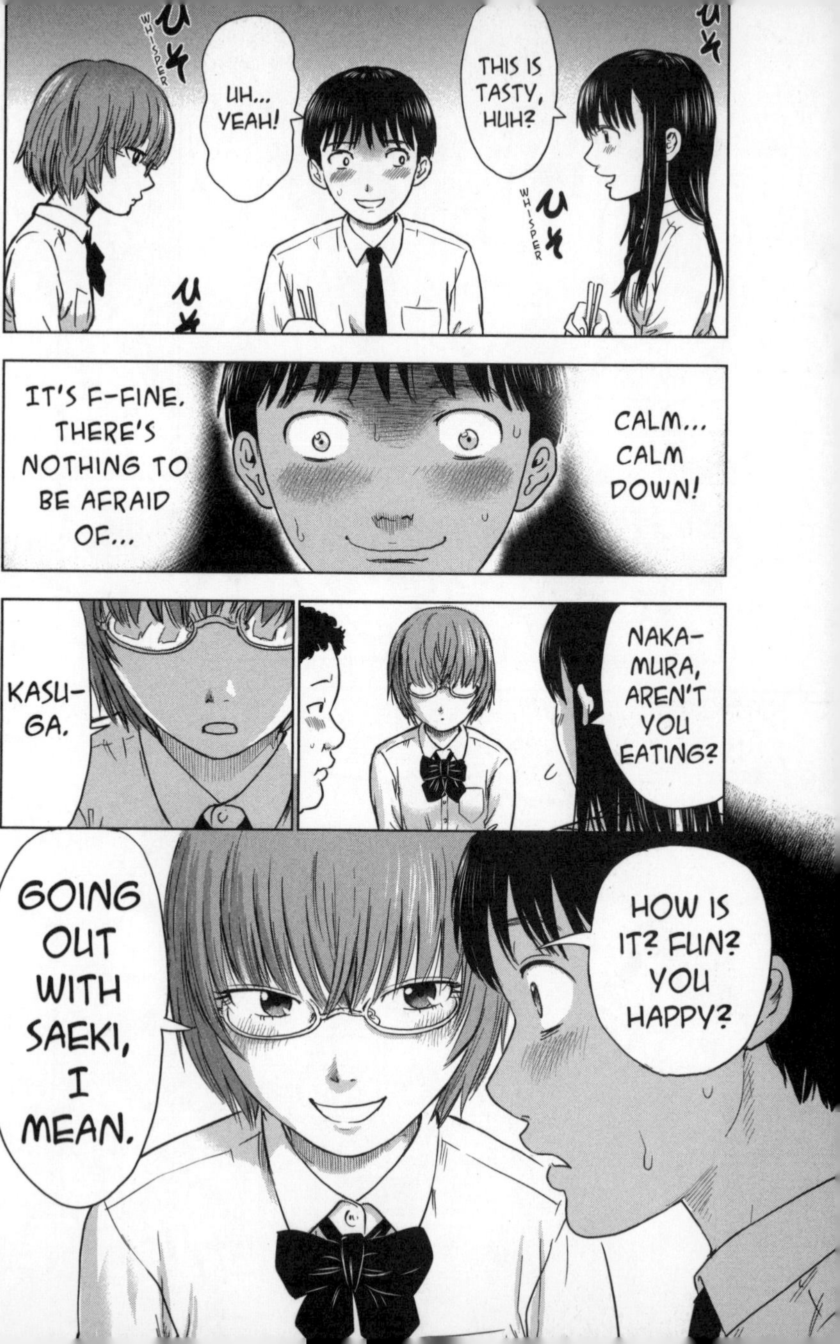
WHISPER
THIS IS TASTY, HUH?
UH... YEAH!
WHISPER
CALM... CALM DOWN!
IT'S F-FINE. THERE'S NOTHING TO BE AFRAID OF...
NAKA-MURA, AREN'T YOU EATING?
KASU-GA.
HOW IS IT? FUN? YOU HAPPY?
GOING OUT WITH SAEKI, I MEAN.

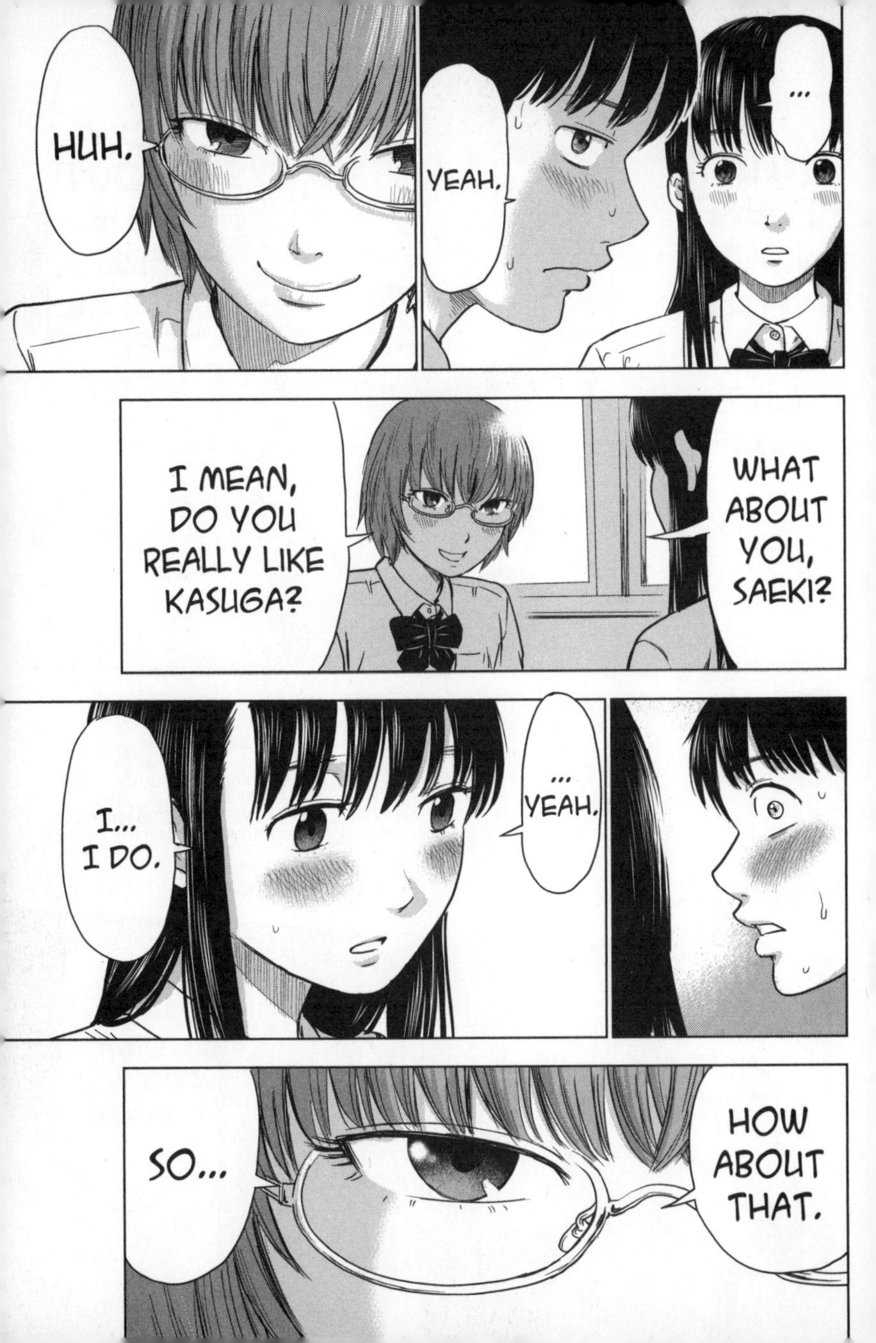
...
YEAH.
HUH.
WHAT ABOUT YOU, SAEKI?
I MEAN, DO YOU REALLY LIKE KASUGA?
... YEAH.
I... I DO.
HOW ABOUT THAT.
SO...

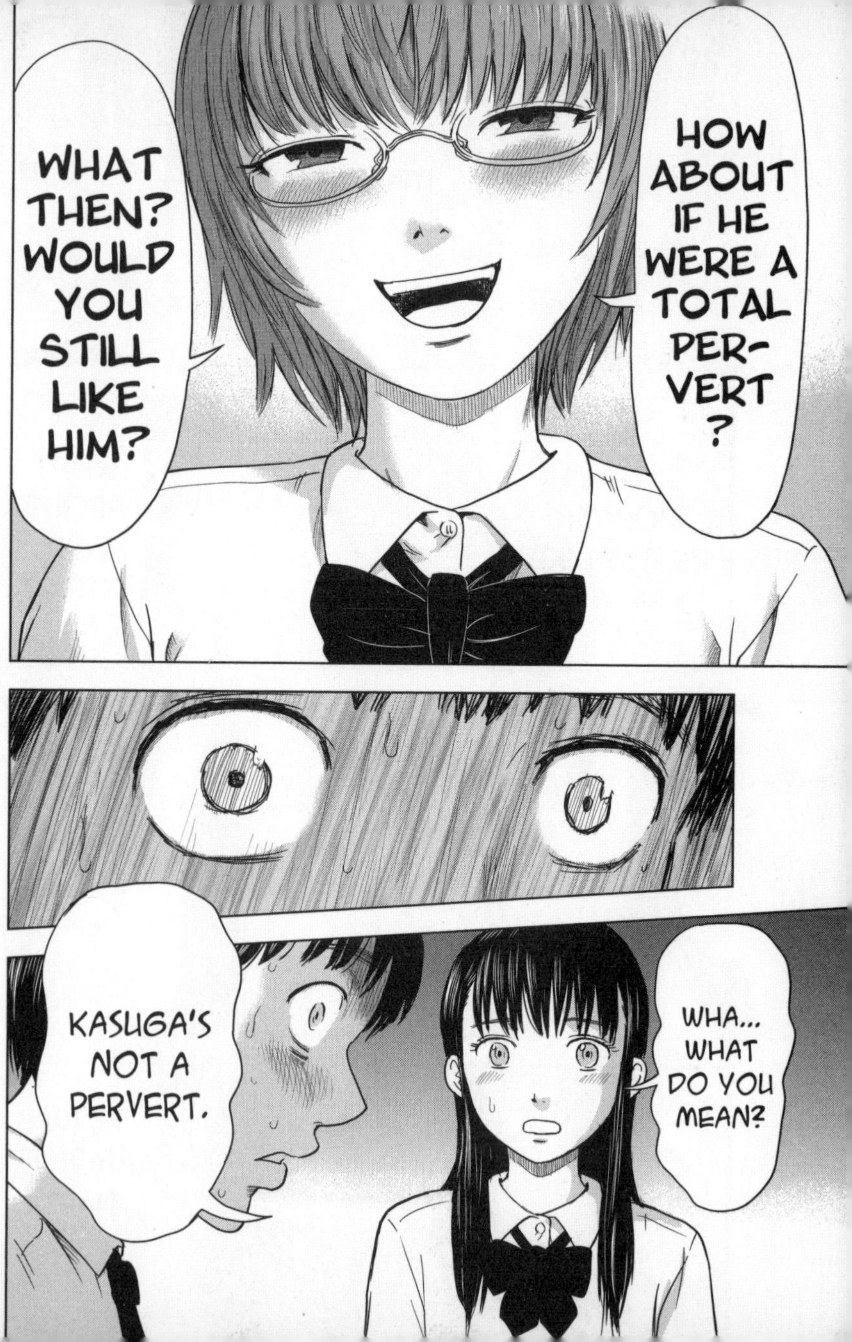
HOW ABOUT IF HE WERE A TOTAL PER-VERT?
WHAT THEN? WOULD YOU STILL LIKE HIM?
WHA... WHAT DO YOU MEAN?
KASUGA'S NOT A PERVERT.

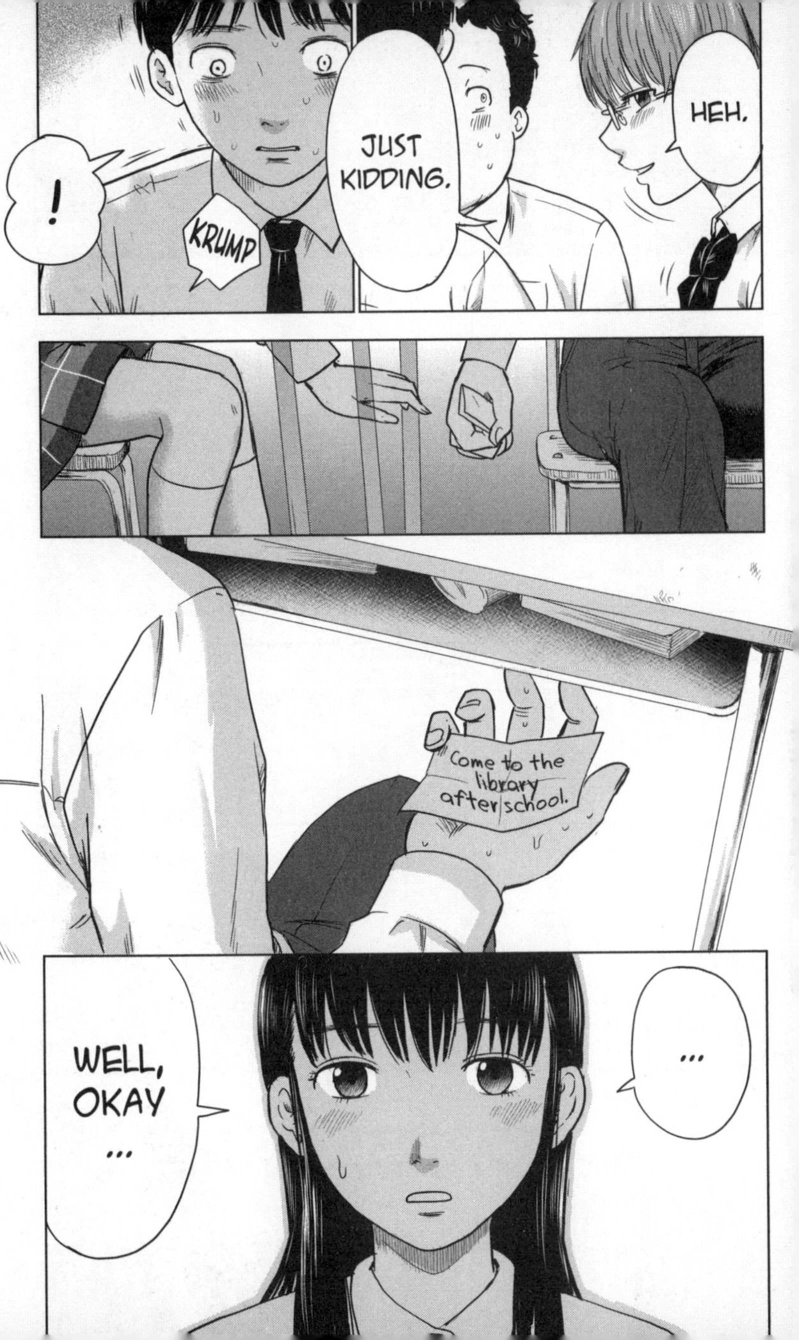
HEH.
JUST KIDDING.
KRUMP
!
Come to the library after school.
...
WELL, OKAY ...

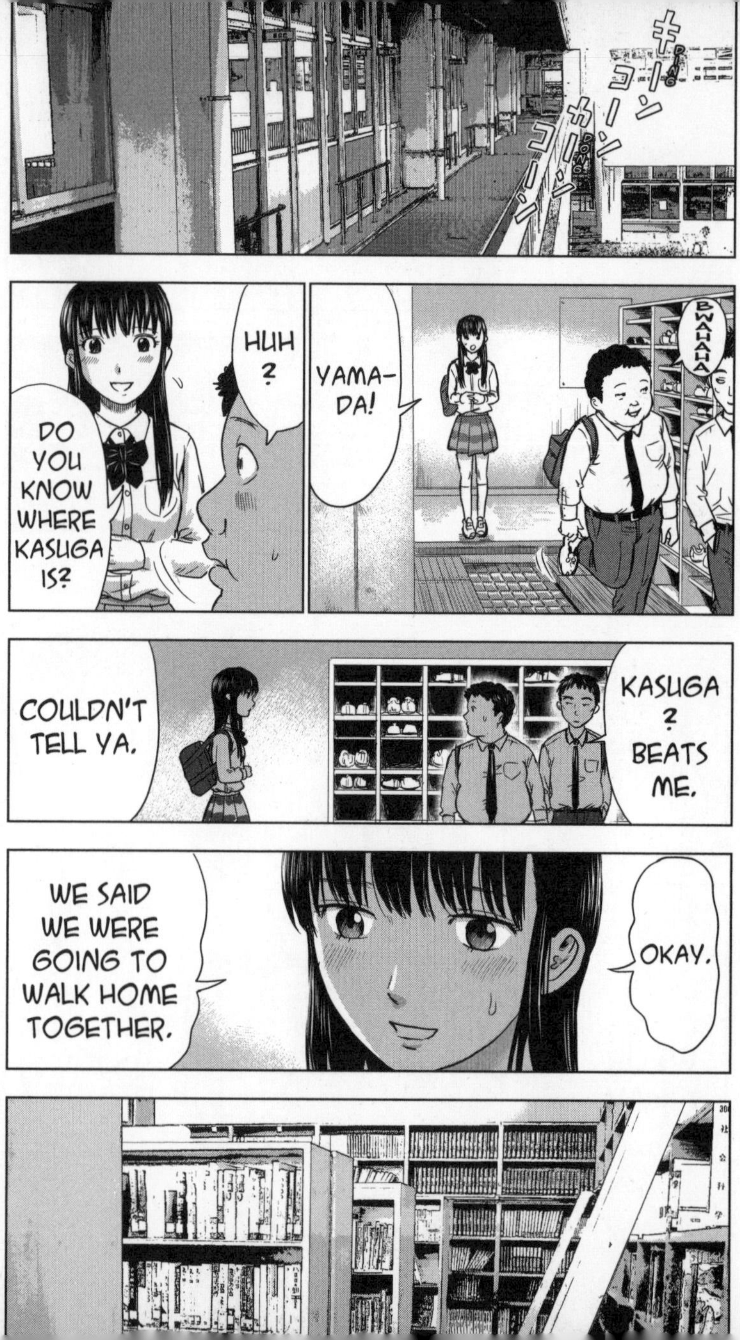
キーンコーン
DING
カーンコーン
DONG
BWAHAHA
YAMA-DA!
HUH?
DO YOU KNOW WHERE KASUGA IS?
KASUGA? BEATS ME.
COULDN'T TELL YA.
OKAY.
WE SAID WE WERE GOING TO WALK HOME TOGETHER.

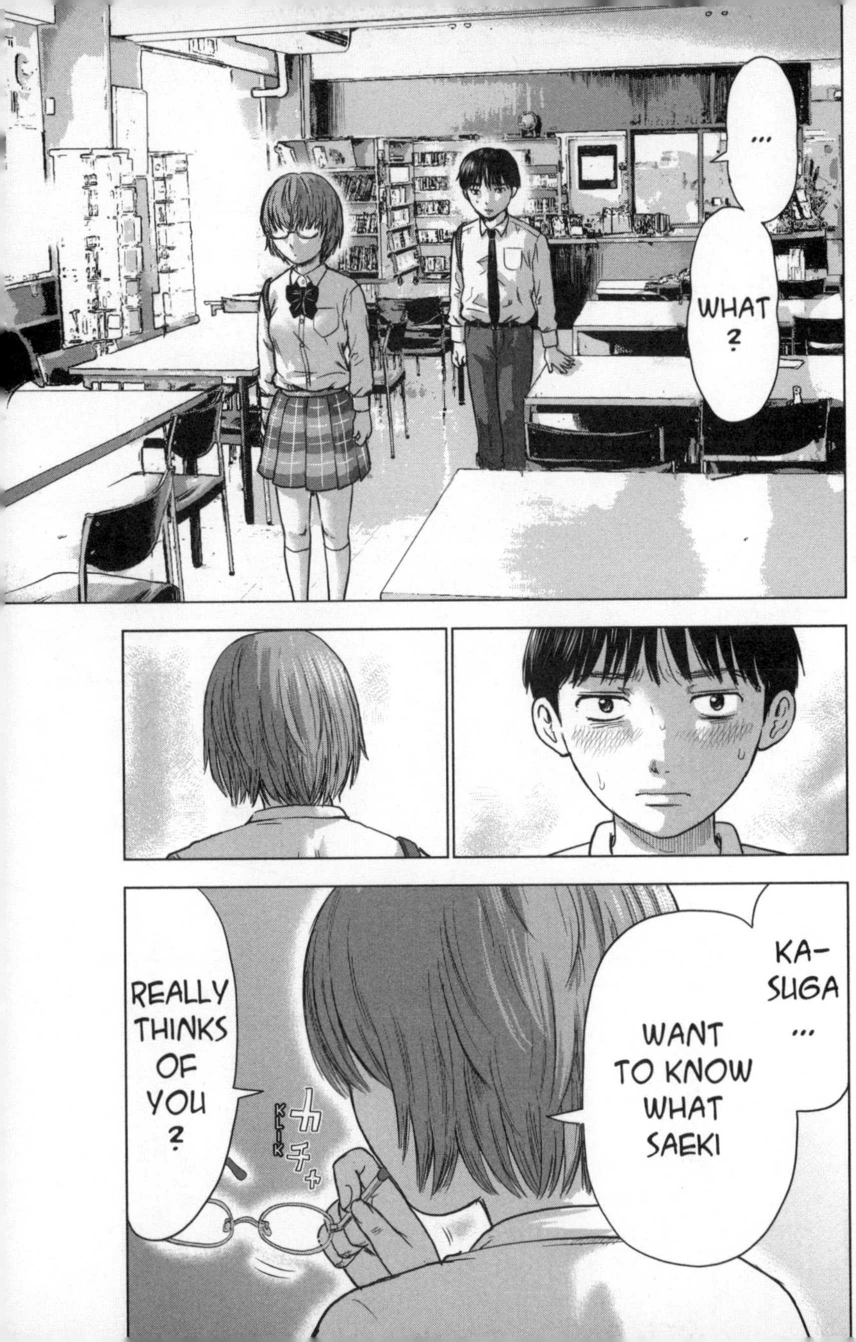
...
WHAT?
KA-SUGA...
WANT TO KNOW WHAT SAEKI
KLIK
カチャ
REALLY THINKS OF YOU?

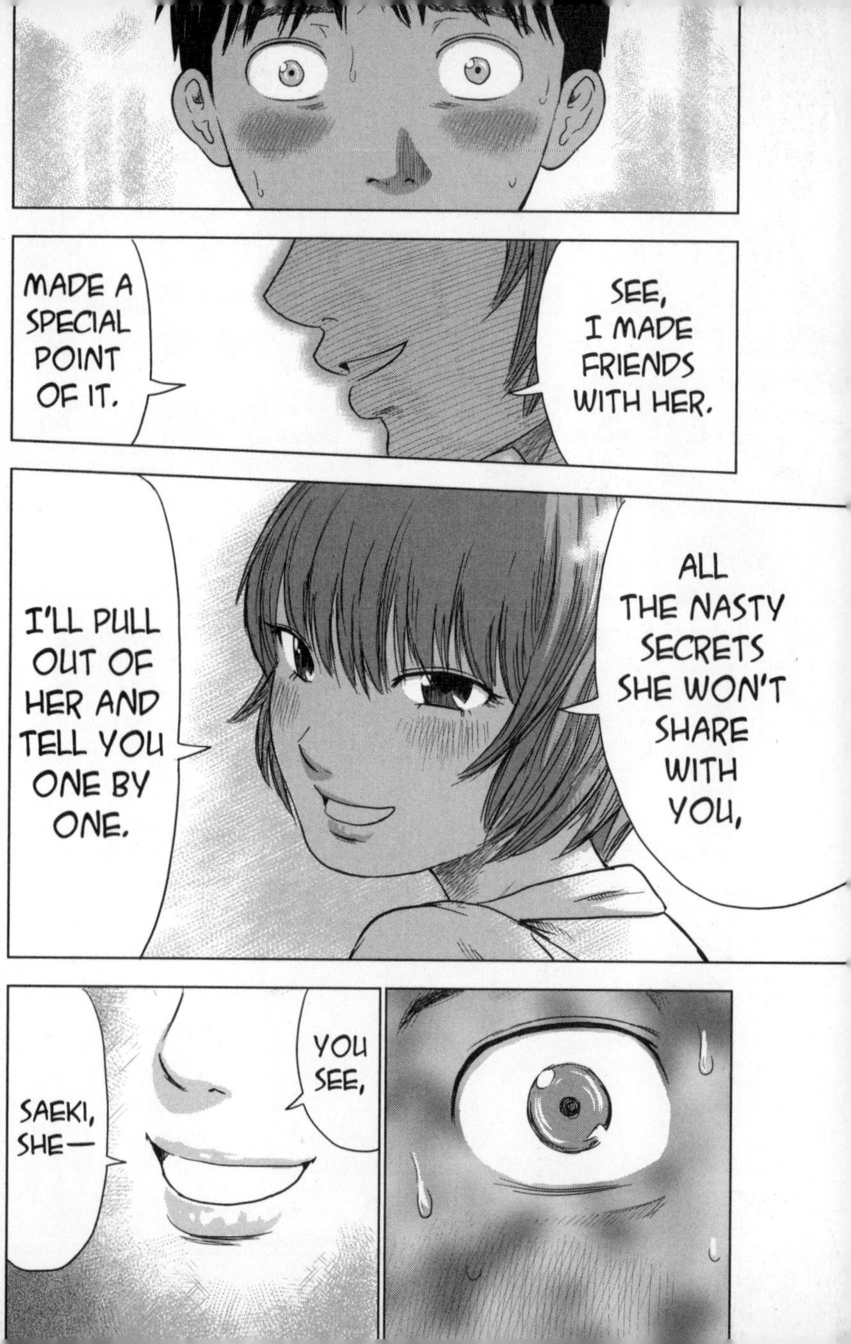
SEE, I MADE FRIENDS WITH HER.
MADE A SPECIAL POINT OF IT.
ALL THE NASTY SECRETS SHE WON'T SHARE WITH YOU,
I'LL PULL OUT OF HER AND TELL YOU ONE BY ONE.
YOU SEE,
SAEKI, SHE—

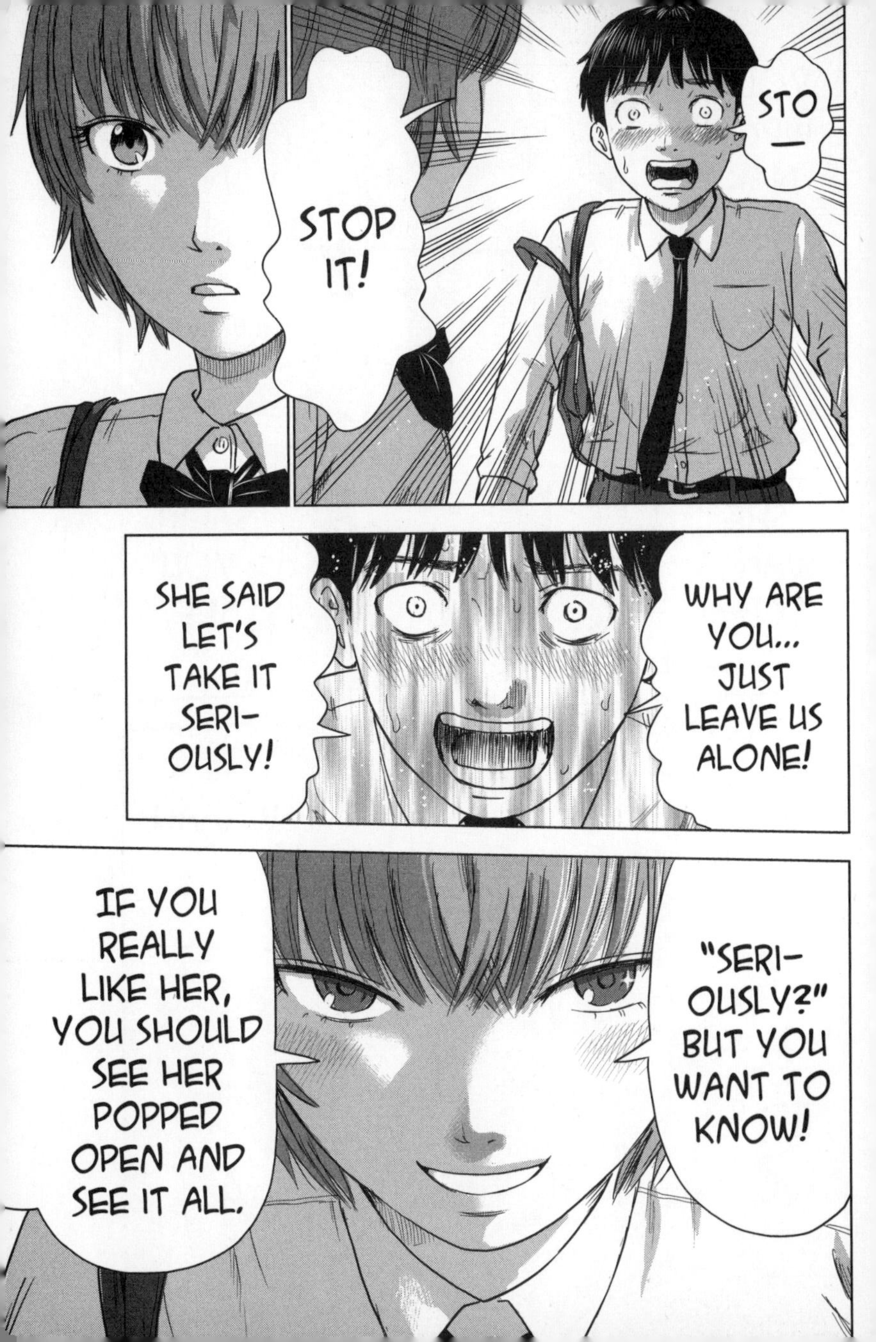
STO —
STOP IT!
WHY ARE YOU... JUST LEAVE US ALONE!
SHE SAID LET'S TAKE IT SERIOUSLY!
"SERIOUSLY?" BUT YOU WANT TO KNOW!
IF YOU REALLY LIKE HER, YOU SHOULD SEE HER POPPED OPEN AND SEE IT ALL.

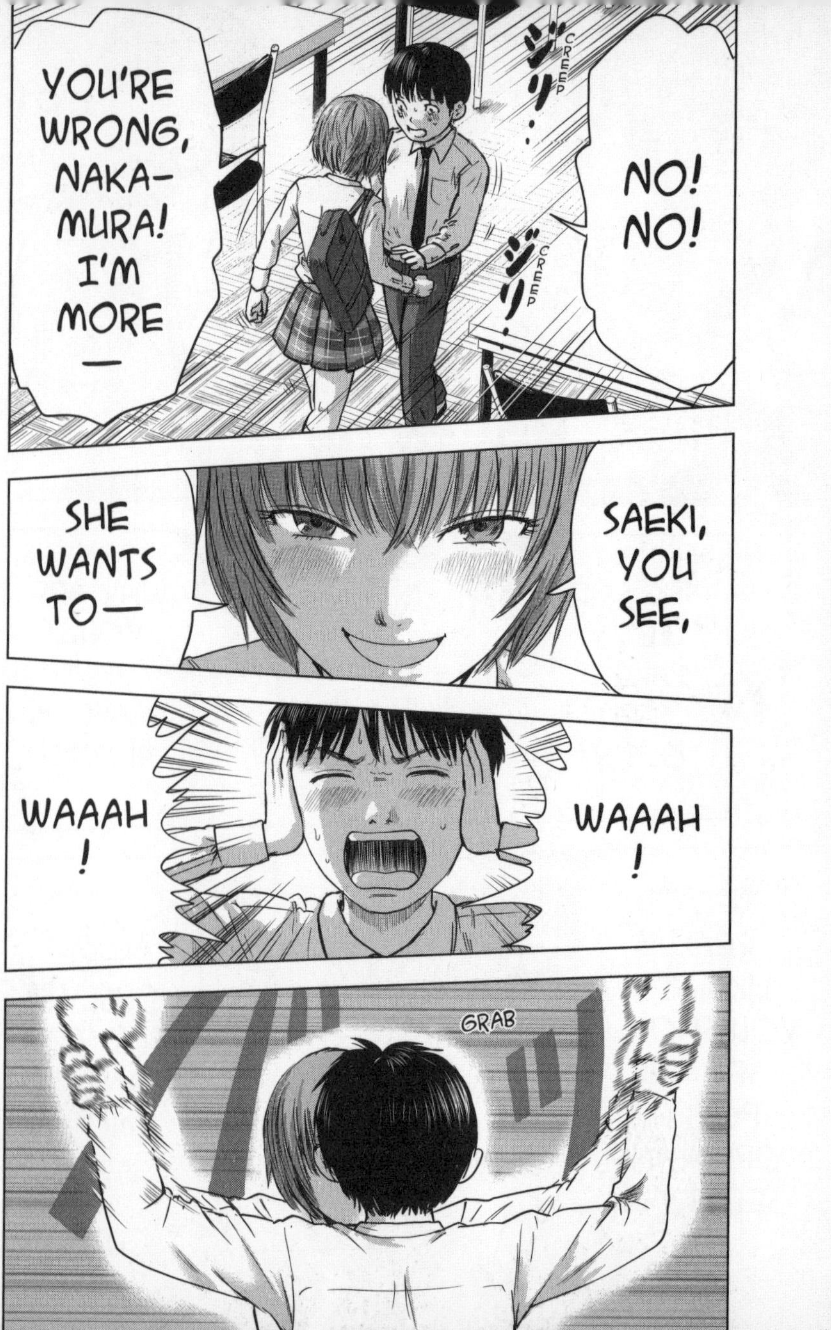
NO! NO!
ジリ・・ CREEP
ジリ・ CREEP
YOU'RE WRONG, NAKA-MURA! I'M MORE —
SAEKI, YOU SEE,
SHE WANTS TO—
WAAAH!
WAAAH!
GRAB

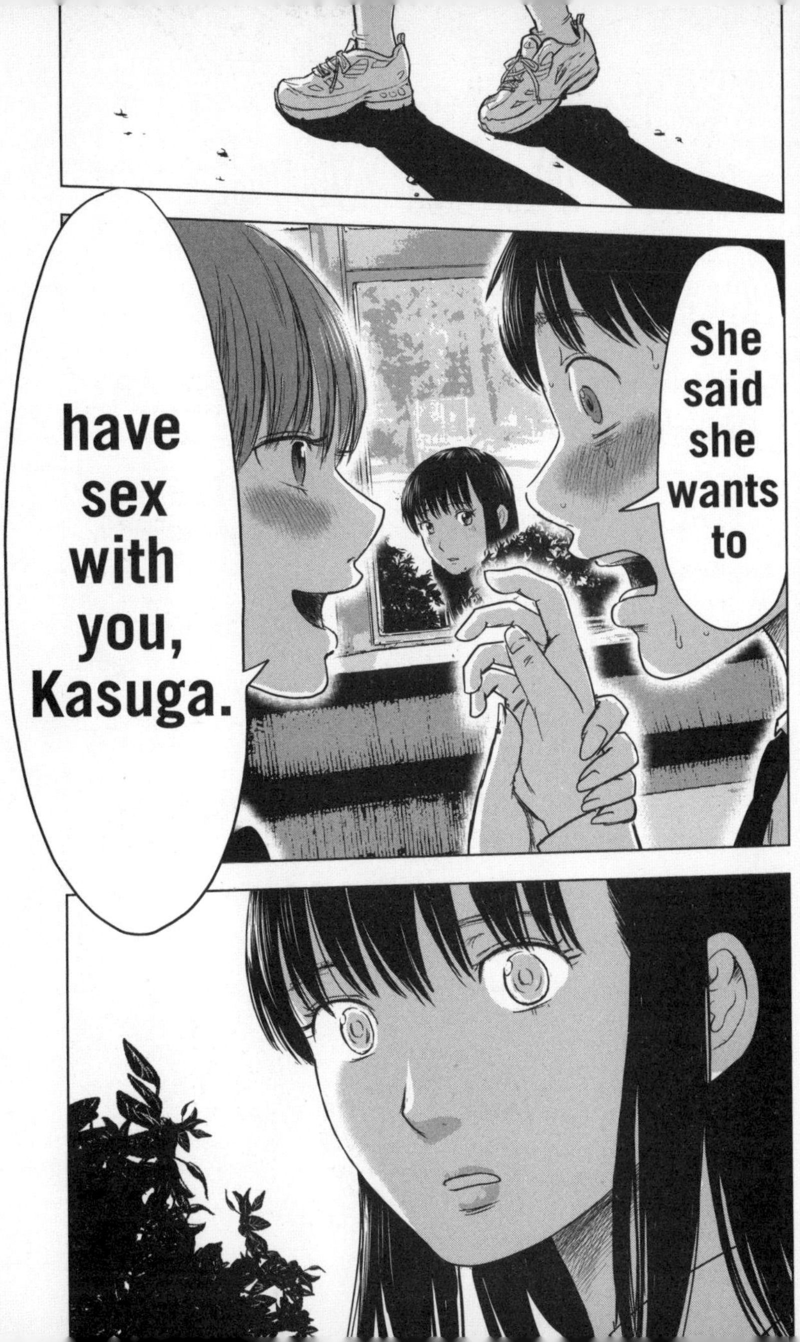
She said she wants to
have sex with you, Kasuga.

Afterword

Chapter 9

I casually hid a character from Yoneko Takamoto's manga *Koishinobu* (also serialized in *Monthly Shonen Magazine*) into this chapter. It's payback for her constantly parodying *The Flowers of Evil*. If you're interested, you should definitely check out *Koishinobu* volume 1!

Chapter 10

The frontispiece of this chapter is a parody of Francisco Goya's painting "The Naked Maja." There are two versions of this painting: one with a clothed Maja, and one where she is nude. In middle school it shocked me: "They can do that?" Goya's another artist I like.

Chapter 10: Spleen and Ideal

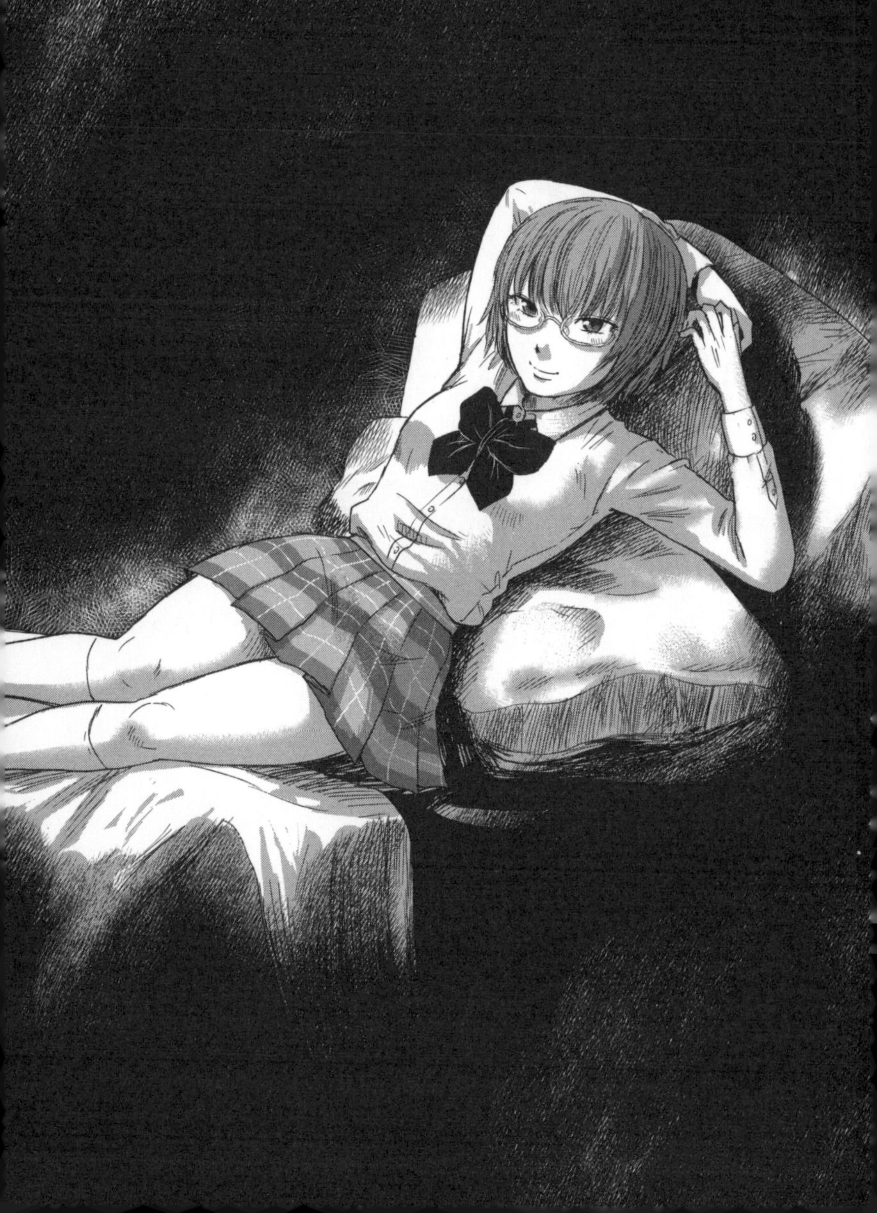

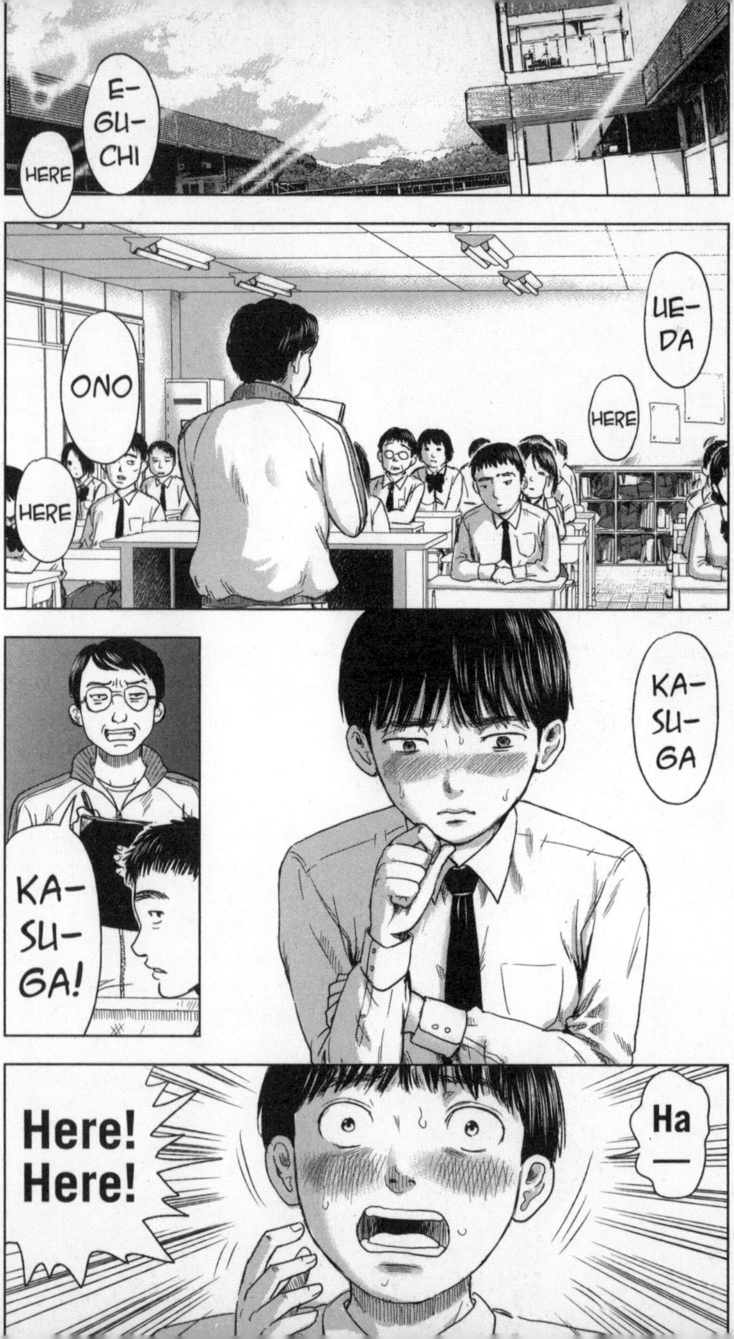
E-GU-CHI
HERE
UE-DA
HERE
ONO
HERE
KA-SU-GA
KA-SU-GA!
Ha —
Here! Here!

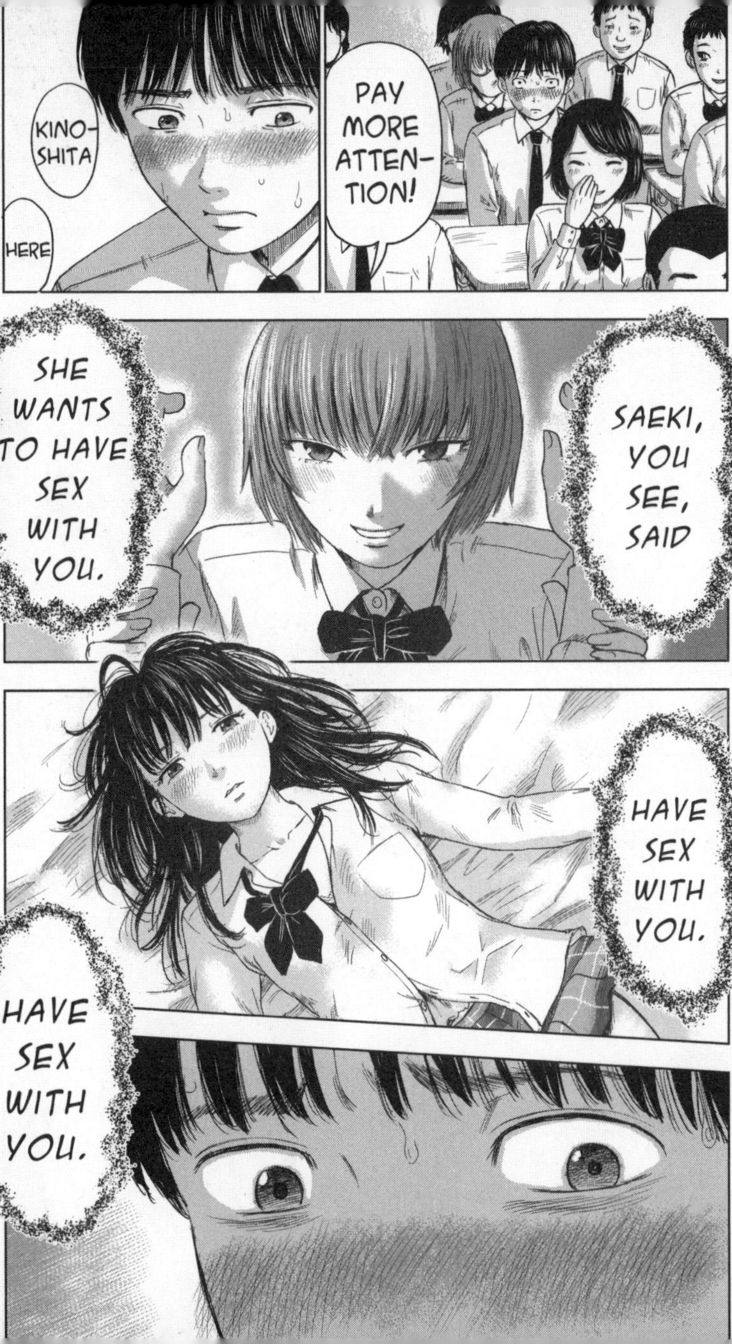
PAY MORE ATTEN-TION!
KINO-SHITA
HERE
SAEKI, YOU SEE, SAID
SHE WANTS TO HAVE SEX WITH YOU.
HAVE SEX WITH YOU.
HAVE SEX WITH YOU.

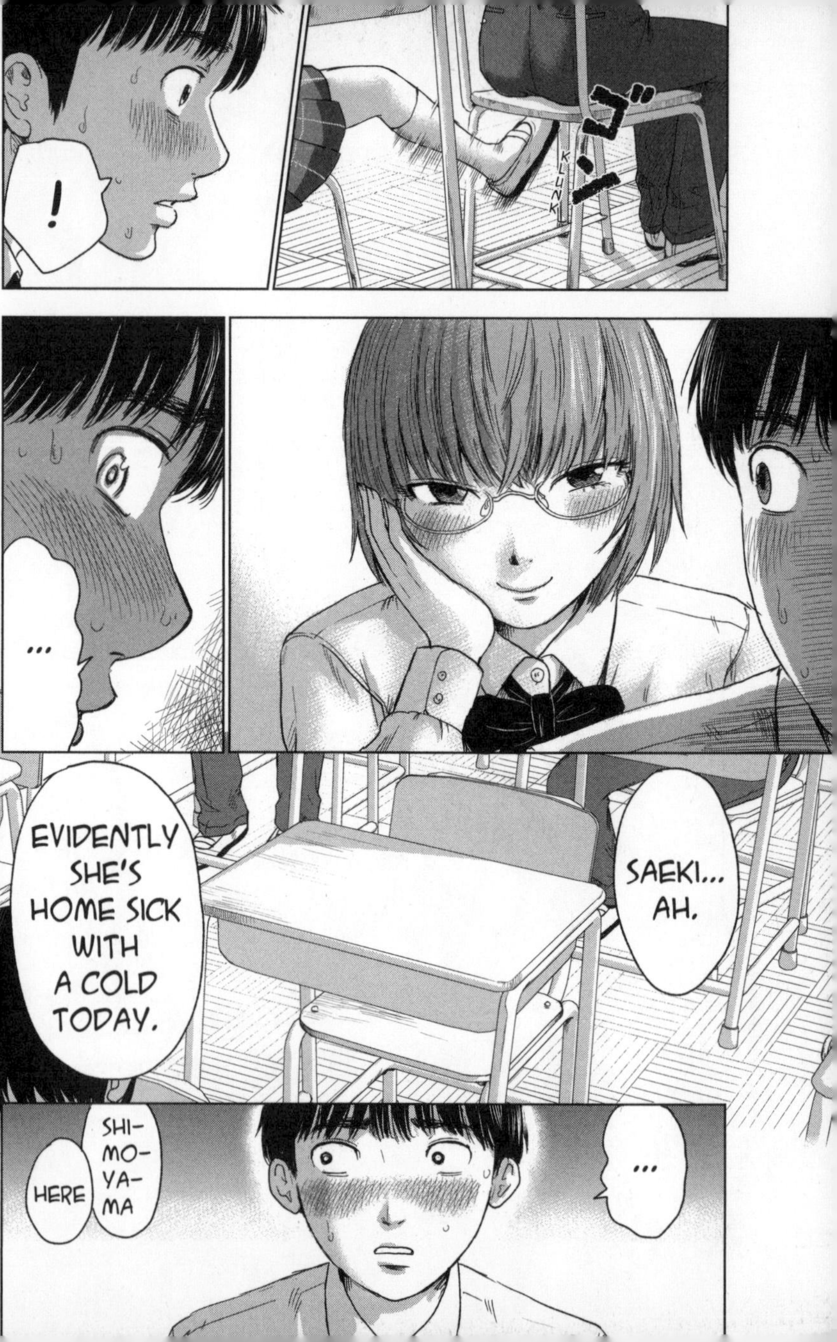
ゴッ
KLUNK
!
...
SAEKI... AH.
EVIDENTLY SHE'S HOME SICK WITH A COLD TODAY.
...
SHI-MO-YA-MA
HERE

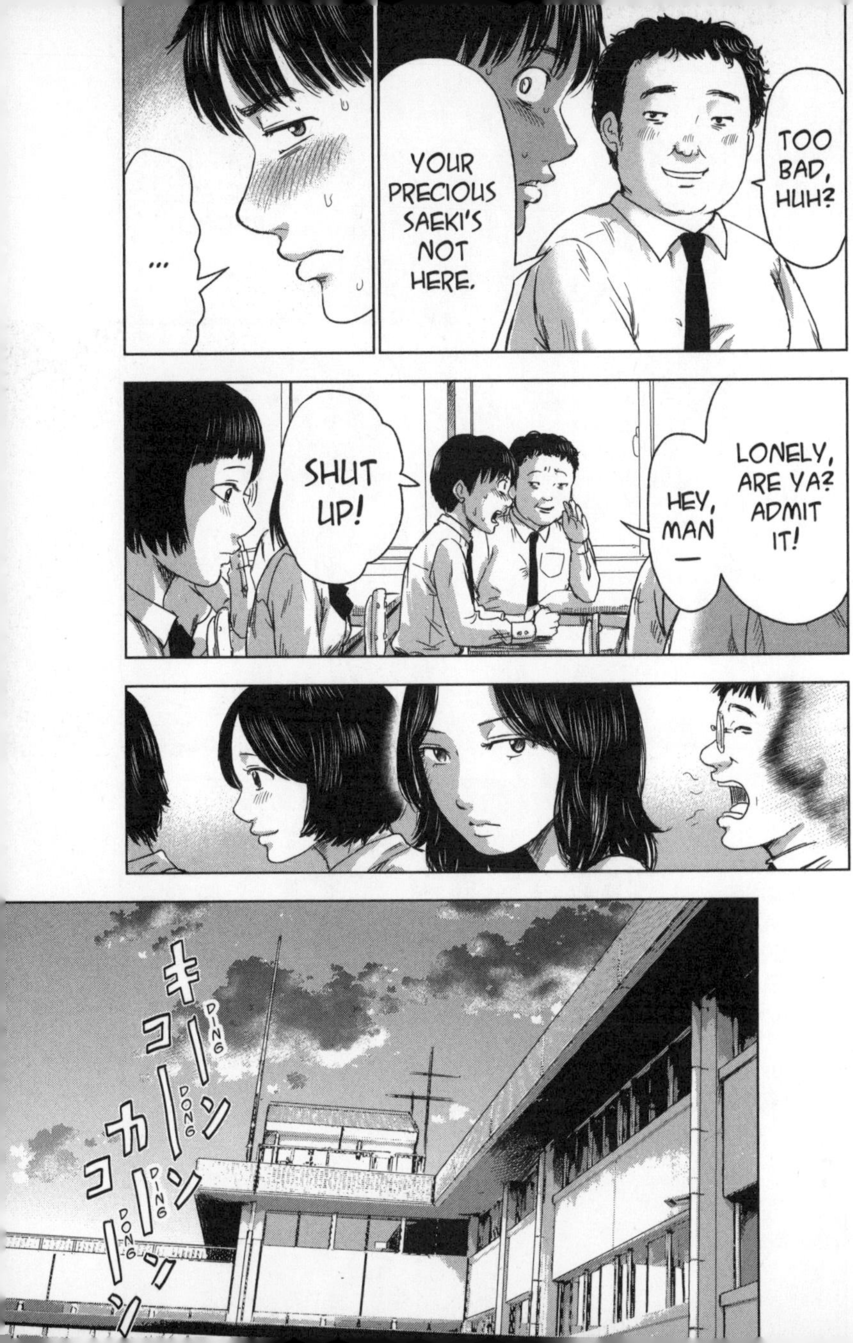
TOO BAD, HUH?
YOUR PRECIOUS SAEKI'S NOT HERE.
...
HEY, MAN —
LONELY, ARE YA? ADMIT IT!
SHUT UP!
キーンコーンカーンコーン
DING DONG DING DONG

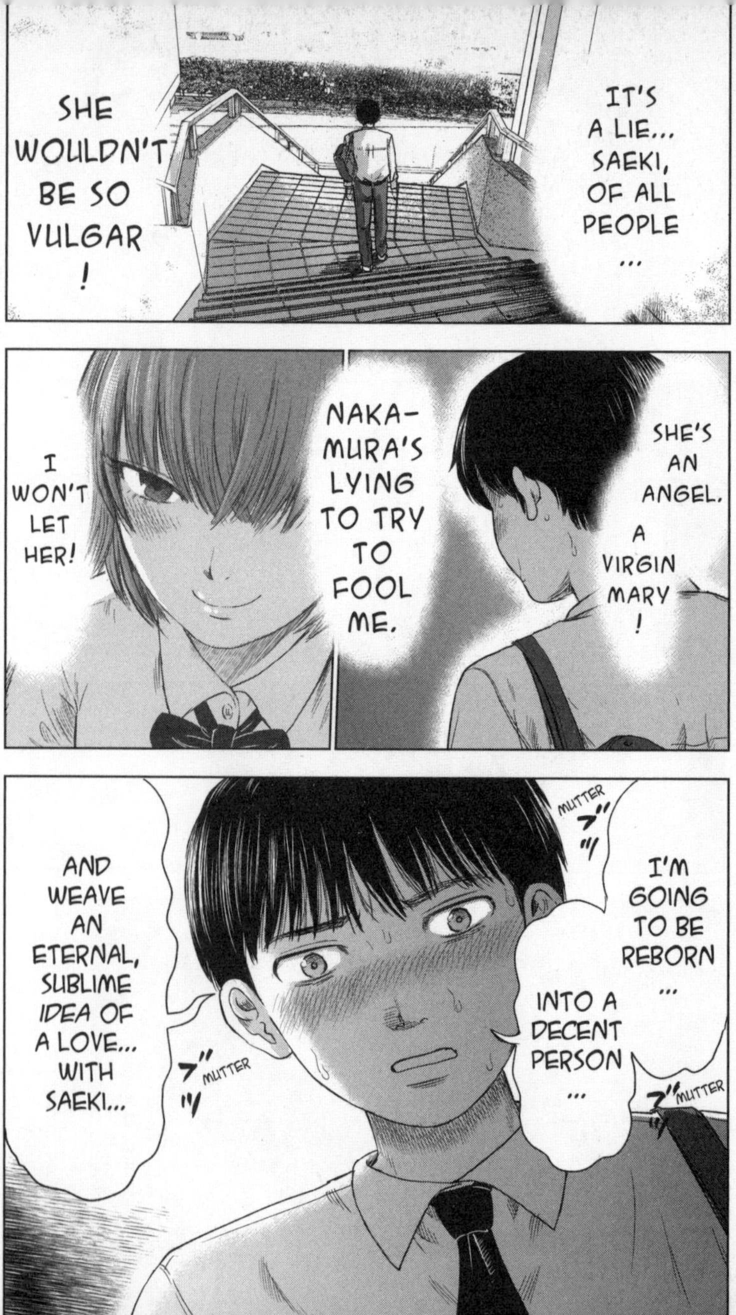
IT'S A LIE... SAEKI, OF ALL PEOPLE ...
SHE WOULDN'T BE SO VULGAR!
SHE'S AN ANGEL. A VIRGIN MARY!
NAKAMURA'S LYING TO TRY TO FOOL ME.
I WON'T LET HER!
MUTTER
I'M GOING TO BE REBORN ...
INTO A DECENT PERSON ...
MUTTER
AND WEAVE AN ETERNAL, SUBLIME IDEA OF A LOVE... WITH SAEKI...
MUTTER

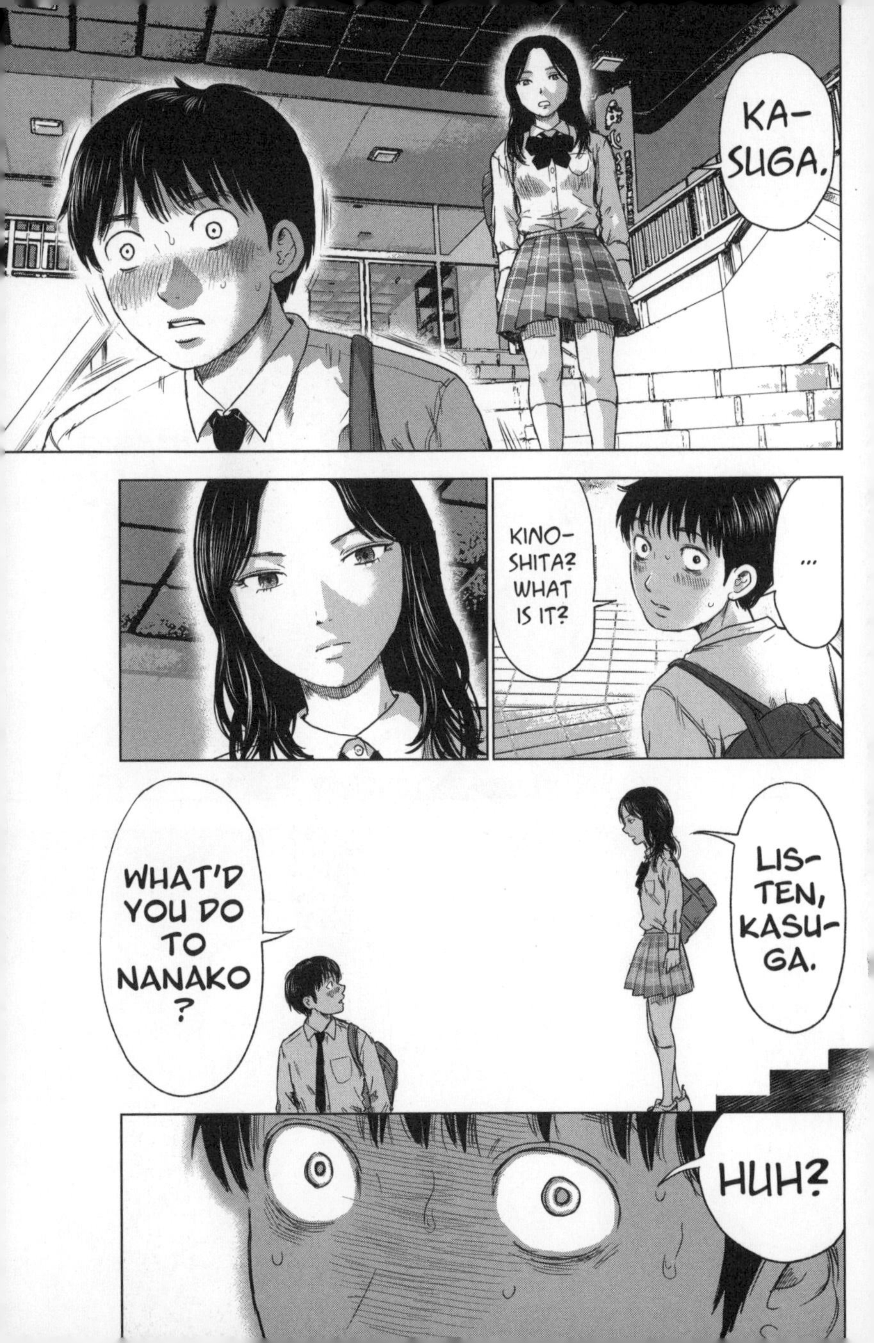
KA-SUGA.
...
KINO-SHITA? WHAT IS IT?
LIS-TEN, KASU-GA.
WHAT'D YOU DO TO NANAKO?
HUH?

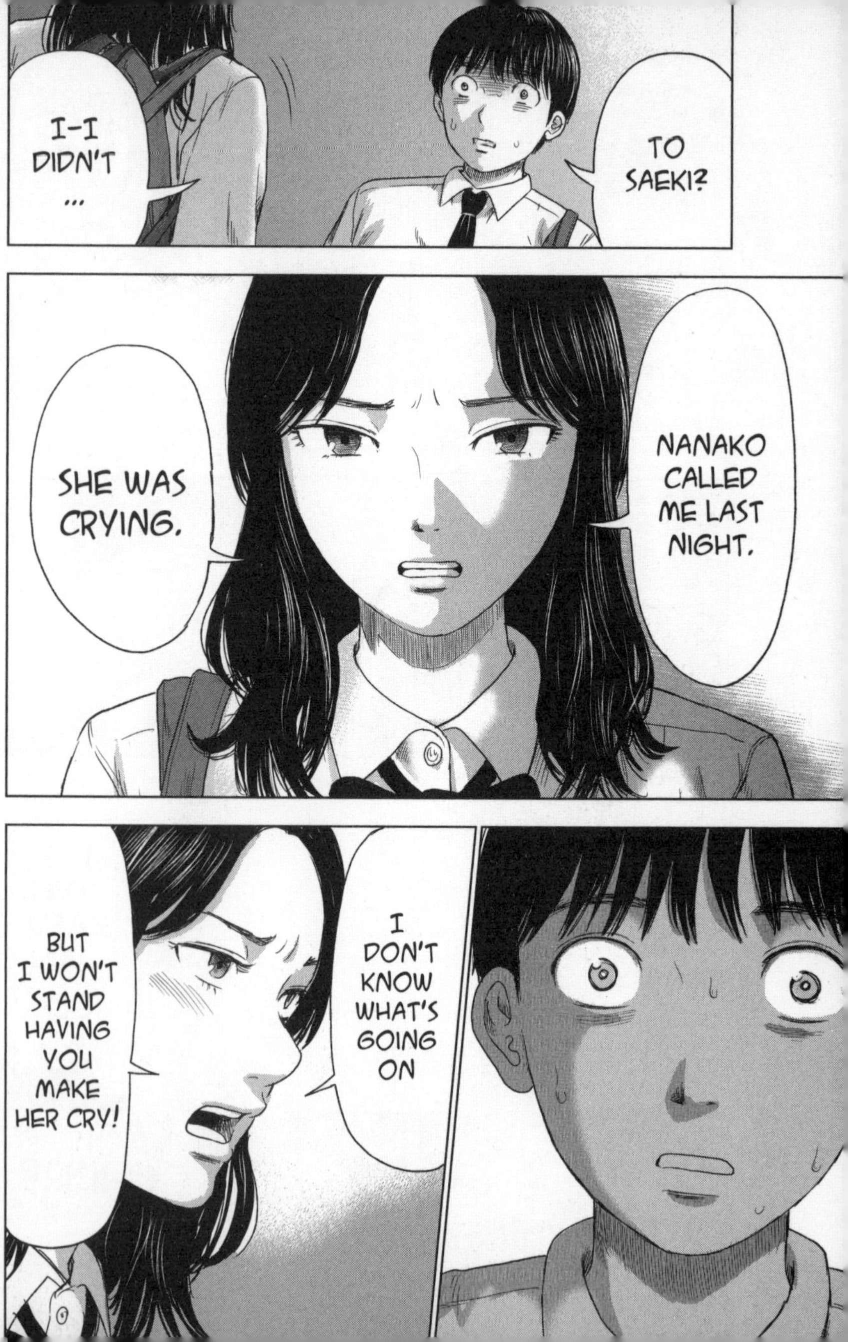
TO SAEKI?
I-I DIDN'T ...
NANAKO CALLED ME LAST NIGHT.
SHE WAS CRYING.
I DON'T KNOW WHAT'S GOING ON
BUT I WON'T STAND HAVING YOU MAKE HER CRY!

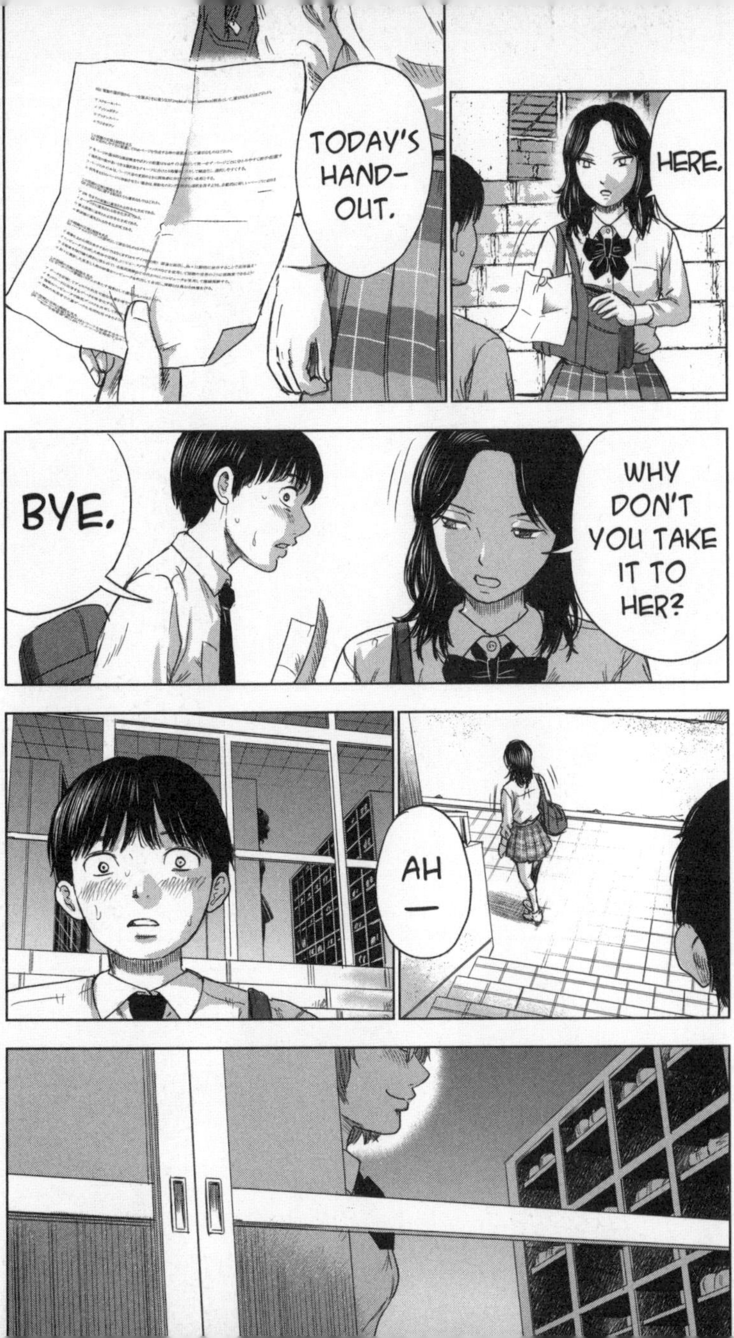
HERE.
TODAY'S HAND-OUT.
WHY DON'T YOU TAKE IT TO HER?
BYE.
AH —

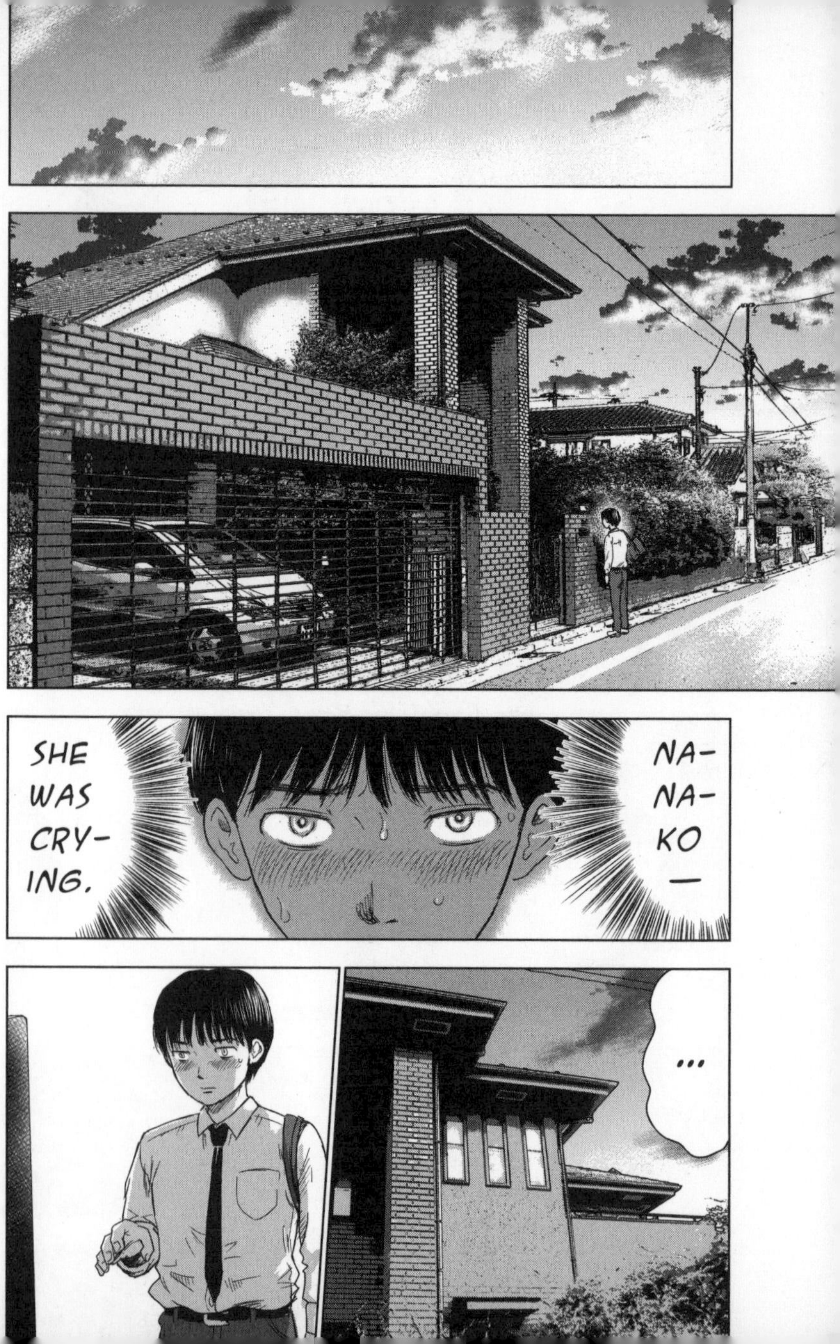
NA-NA-KO —
SHE WAS CRY-ING.
...

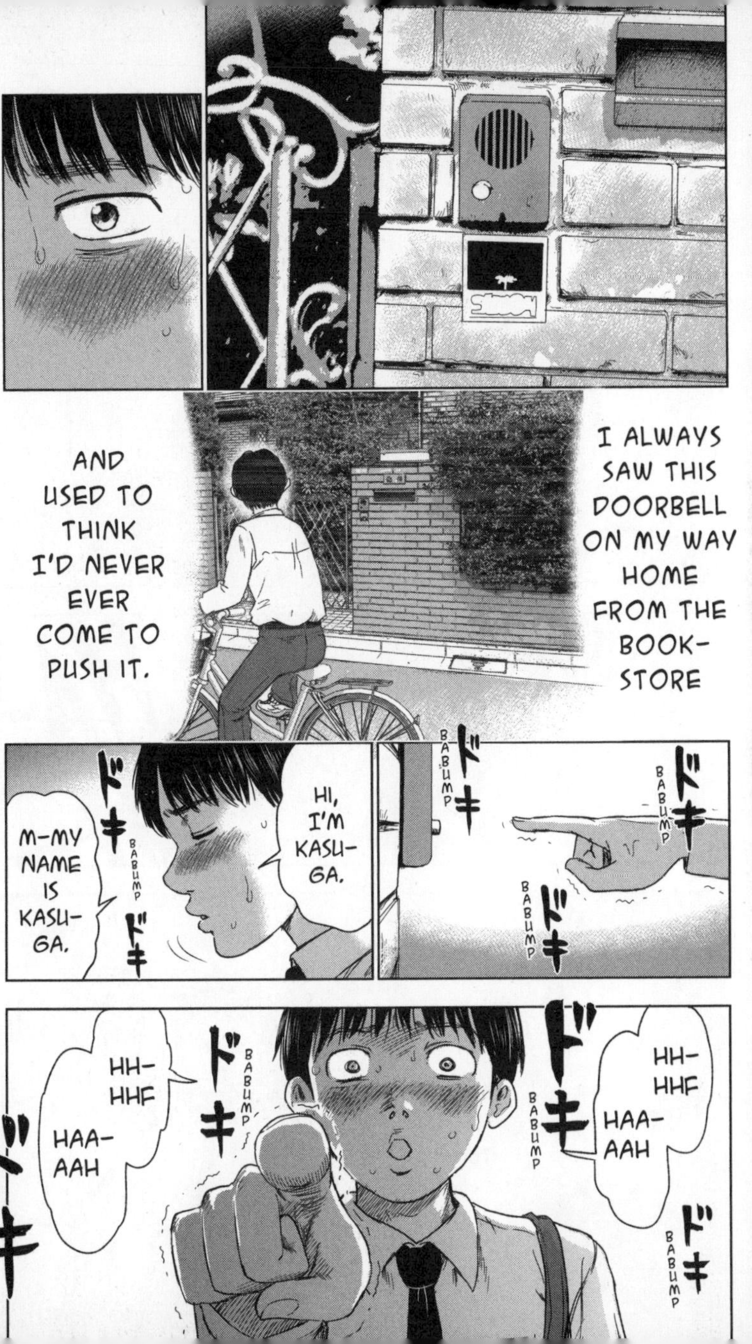
I ALWAYS SAW THIS DOORBELL ON MY WAY HOME FROM THE BOOK-STORE
AND USED TO THINK I'D NEVER EVER COME TO PUSH IT.
ドキ BABUMP
ドキ BABUMP
ドキ BABUMP
HI, I'M KASU-GA.
ドキ BABUMP
M-MY NAME IS KASU-GA.
ドキ
ドキ BABUMP
HH-HHF
HAAA-AAH
ドキ BABUMP
ドキ BABUMP
HH-HHF
HAAA-AAH
ドキ BABUMP

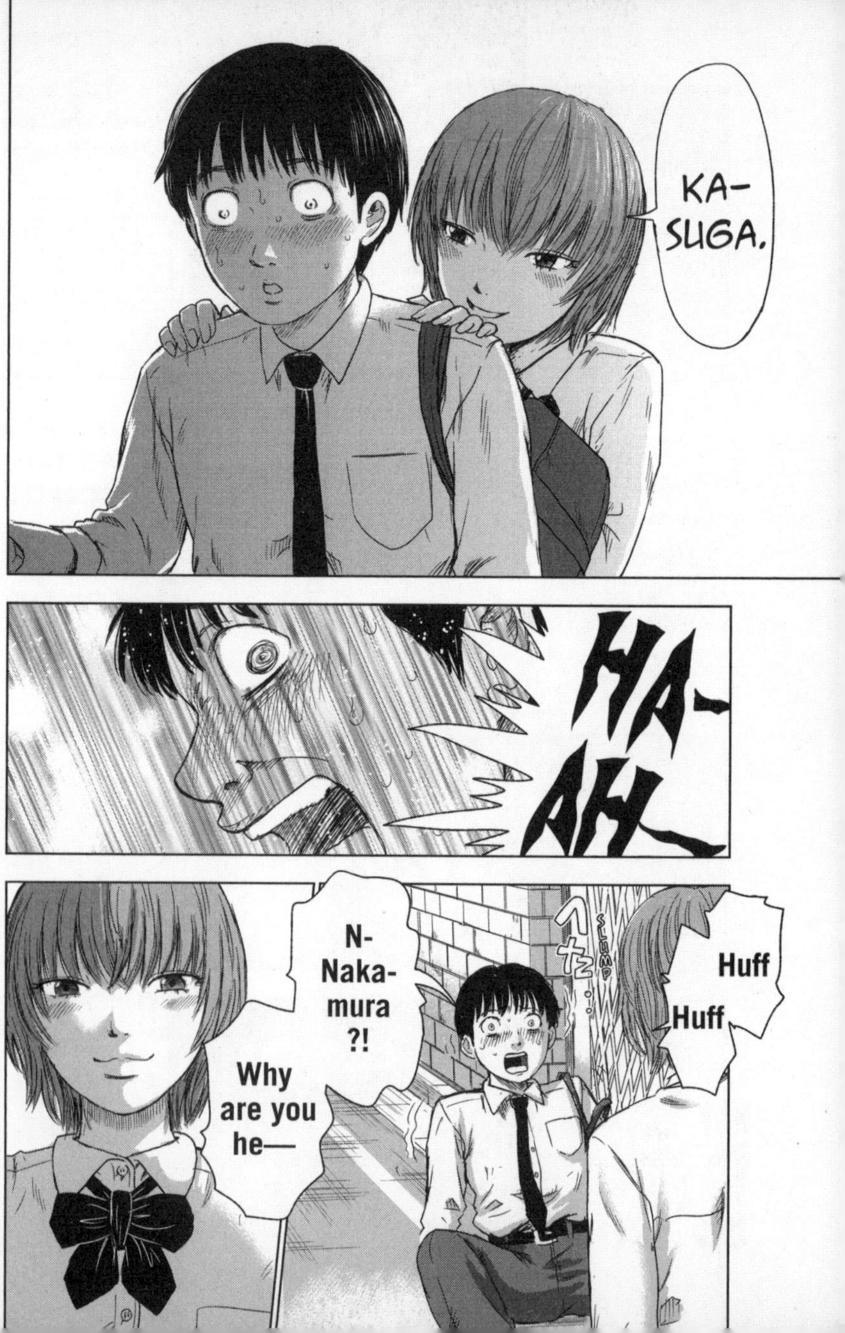

KA-SUGA.
HA-AH—
Huff
Huff
SLUMP
N-Nakamura?!
Why are you he—

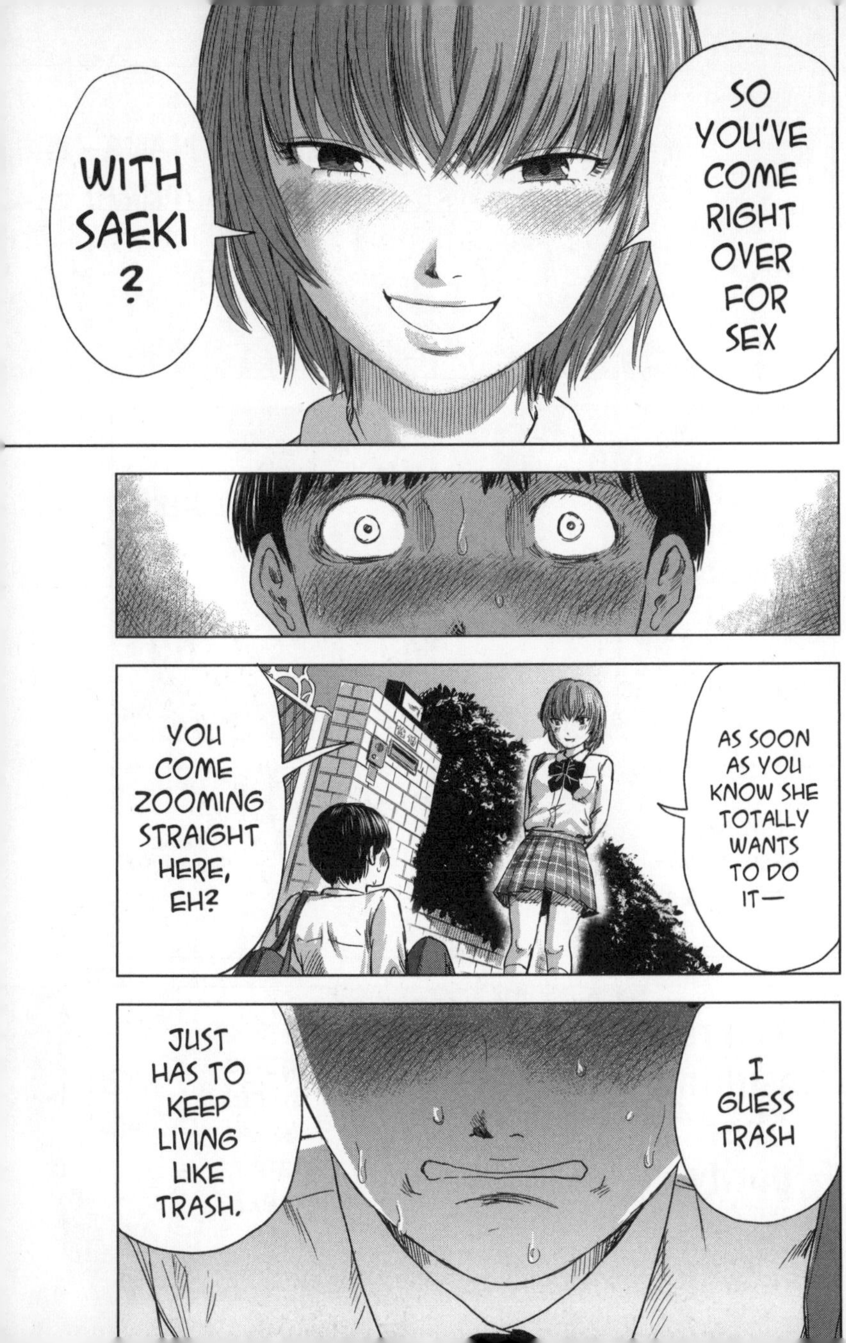
SO YOU'VE COME RIGHT OVER FOR SEX
WITH SAEKI?
AS SOON AS YOU KNOW SHE TOTALLY WANTS TO DO IT—
YOU COME ZOOMING STRAIGHT HERE, EH?
I GUESS TRASH
JUST HAS TO KEEP LIVING LIKE TRASH.

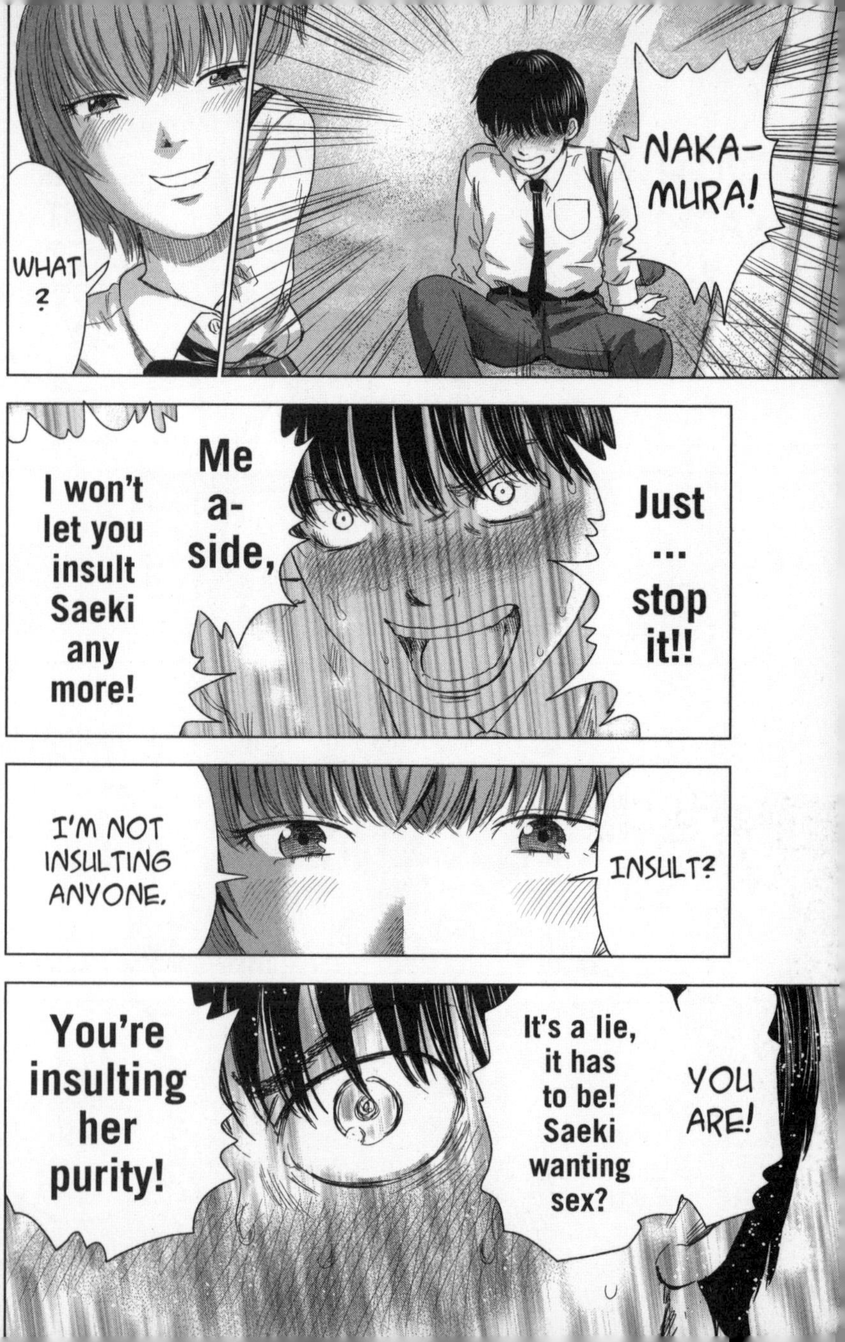
NAKA-MURA!
WHAT?
Just ... stop it!!
Me a-side,
I won't let you insult Saeki any more!
INSULT?
I'M NOT INSULTING ANYONE.
YOU ARE!
It's a lie, it has to be! Saeki wanting sex?
You're insulting her purity!

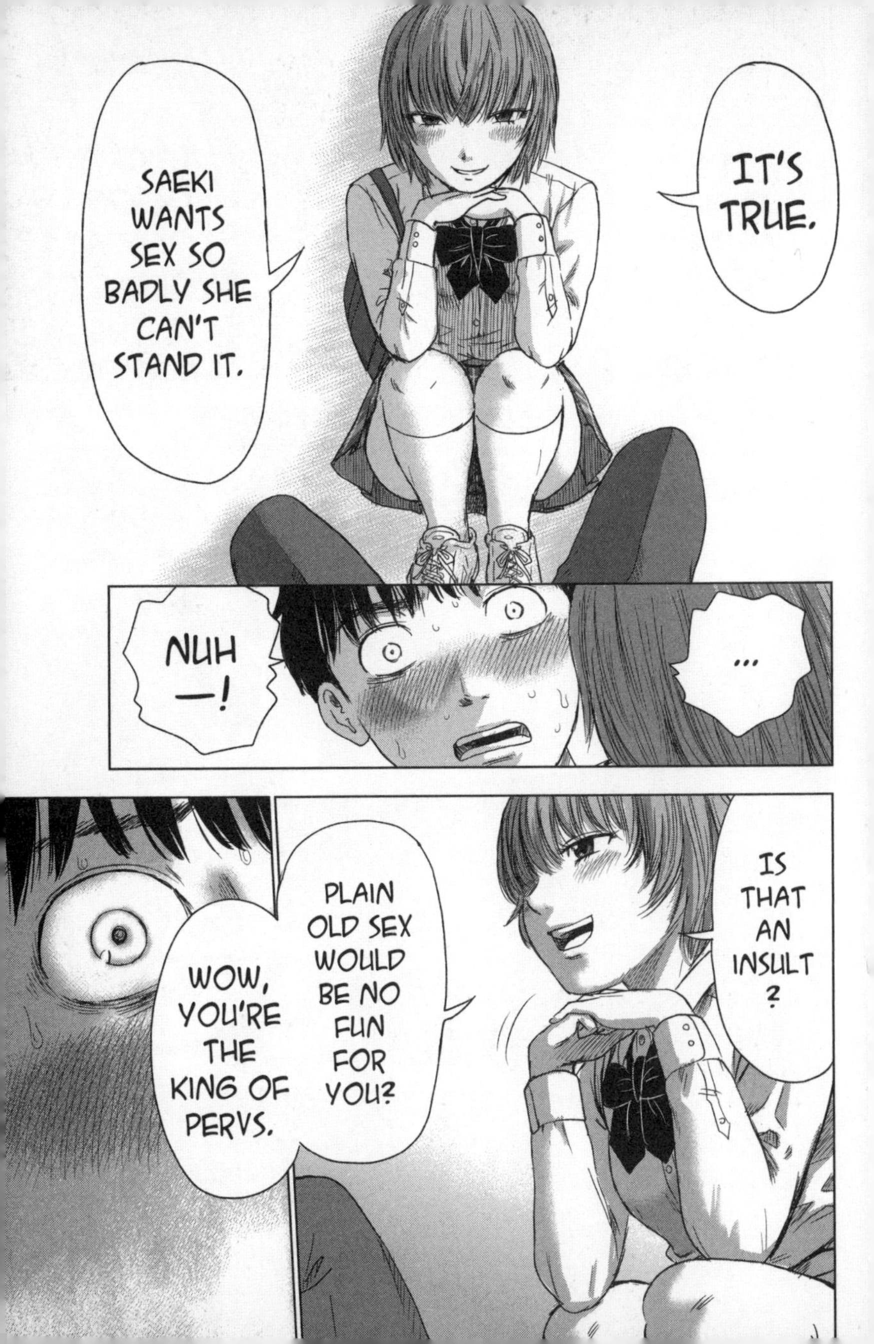
IT'S TRUE.
SAEKI WANTS SEX SO BADLY SHE CAN'T STAND IT.
...
NUH—!
IS THAT AN INSULT?
PLAIN OLD SEX WOULD BE NO FUN FOR YOU?
WOW, YOU'RE THE KING OF PERVS.

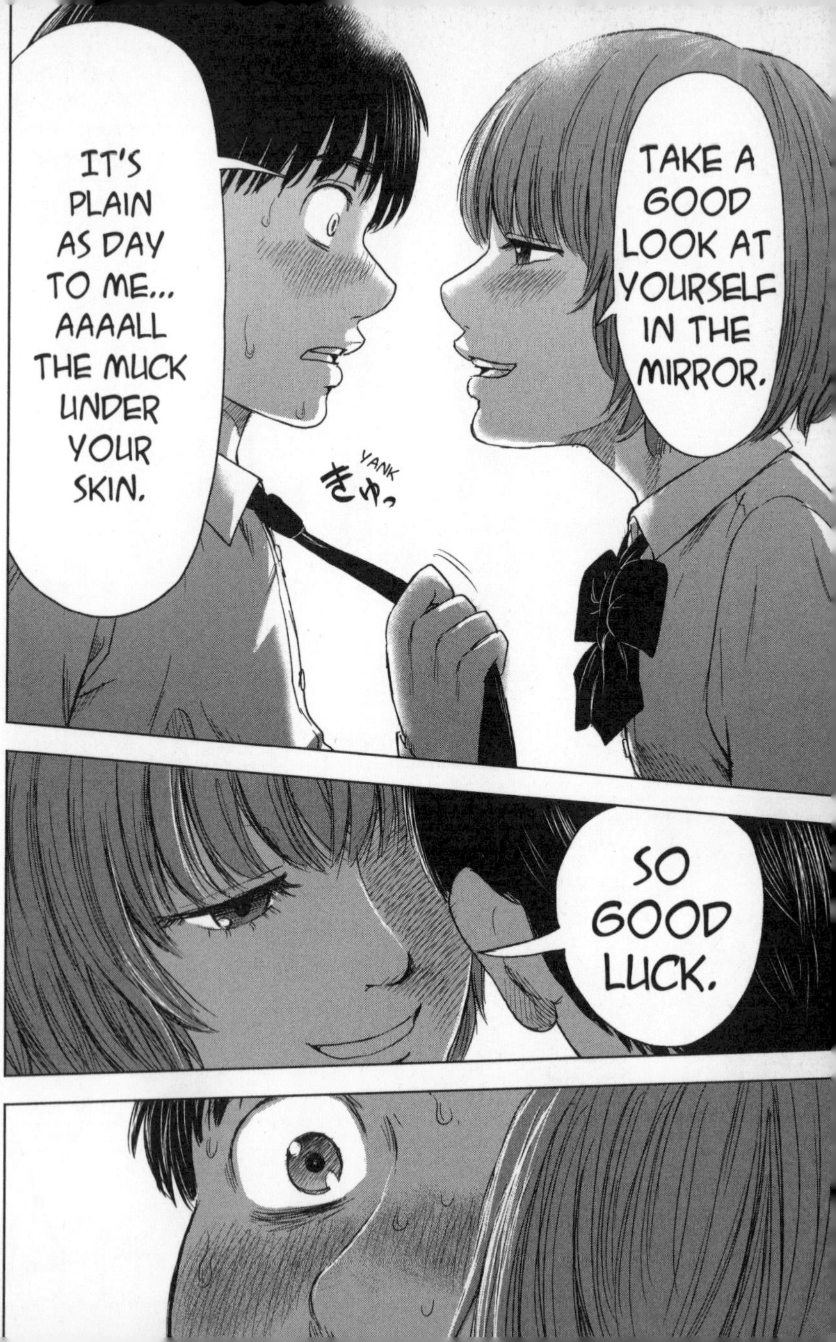
TAKE A GOOD LOOK AT YOURSELF IN THE MIRROR.
IT'S PLAIN AS DAY TO ME... AAAALL THE MUCK UNDER YOUR SKIN.
きゅっ
YANK
SO GOOD LUCK.

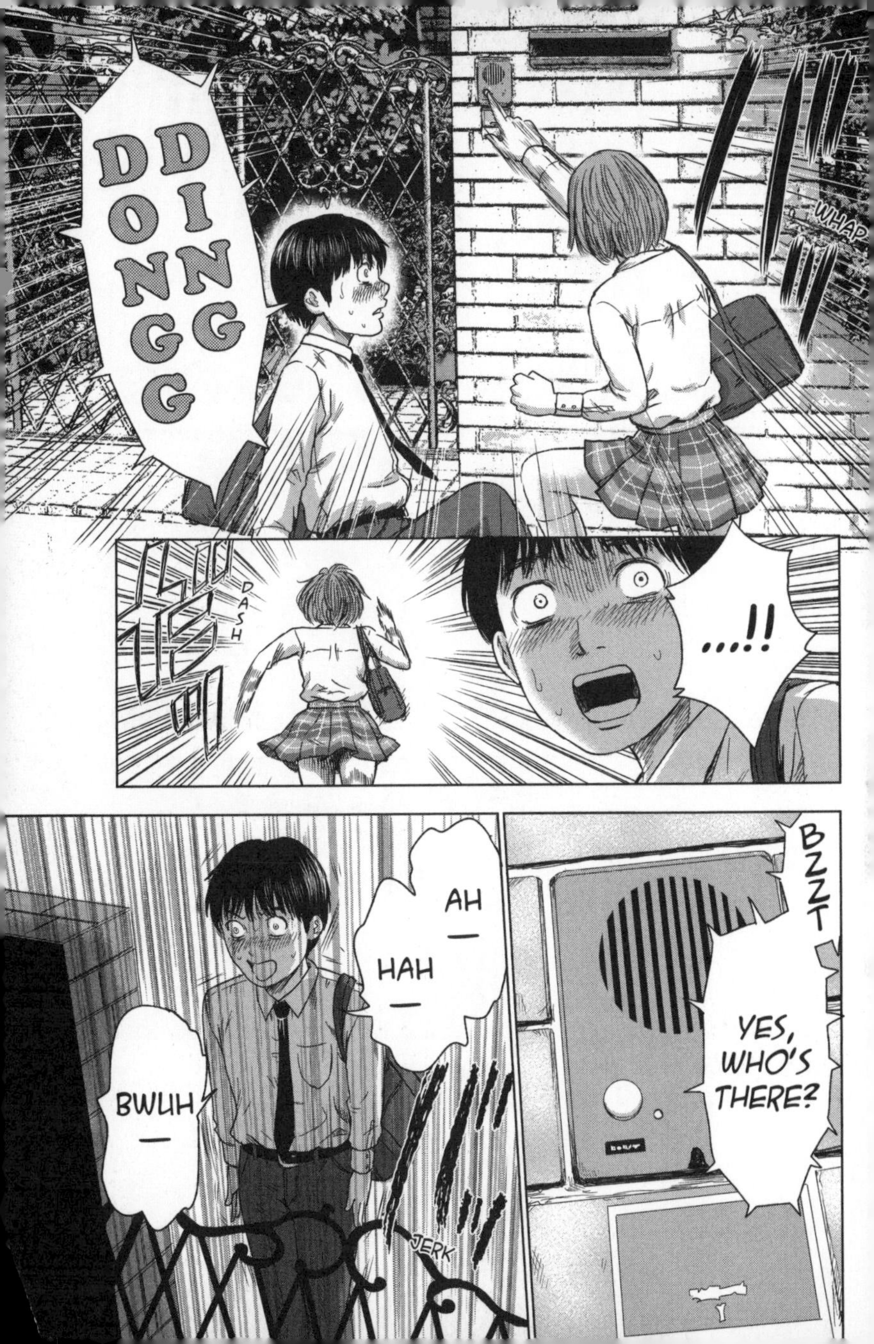
WHAP
DING
DONGG
...!!
DASH
BZZT
YES, WHO'S THERE?
AH— HAH—
BWUH—
JERK

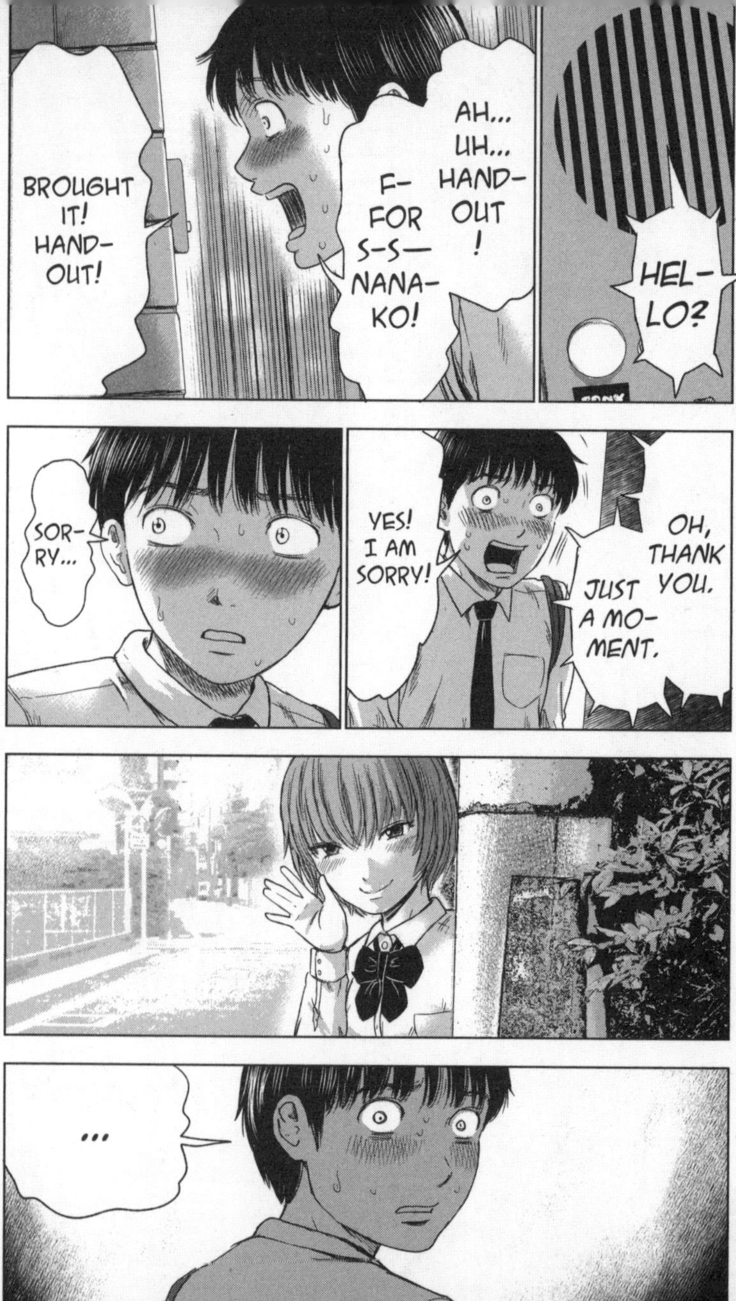
HEL-LO?
AH... UH... HAND-OUT!
F-FOR S-S— NANAKO!
BROUGHT IT! HAND-OUT!
OH, THANK YOU.
JUST A MO-MENT.
YES! I AM SORRY!
SOR-RY...
...

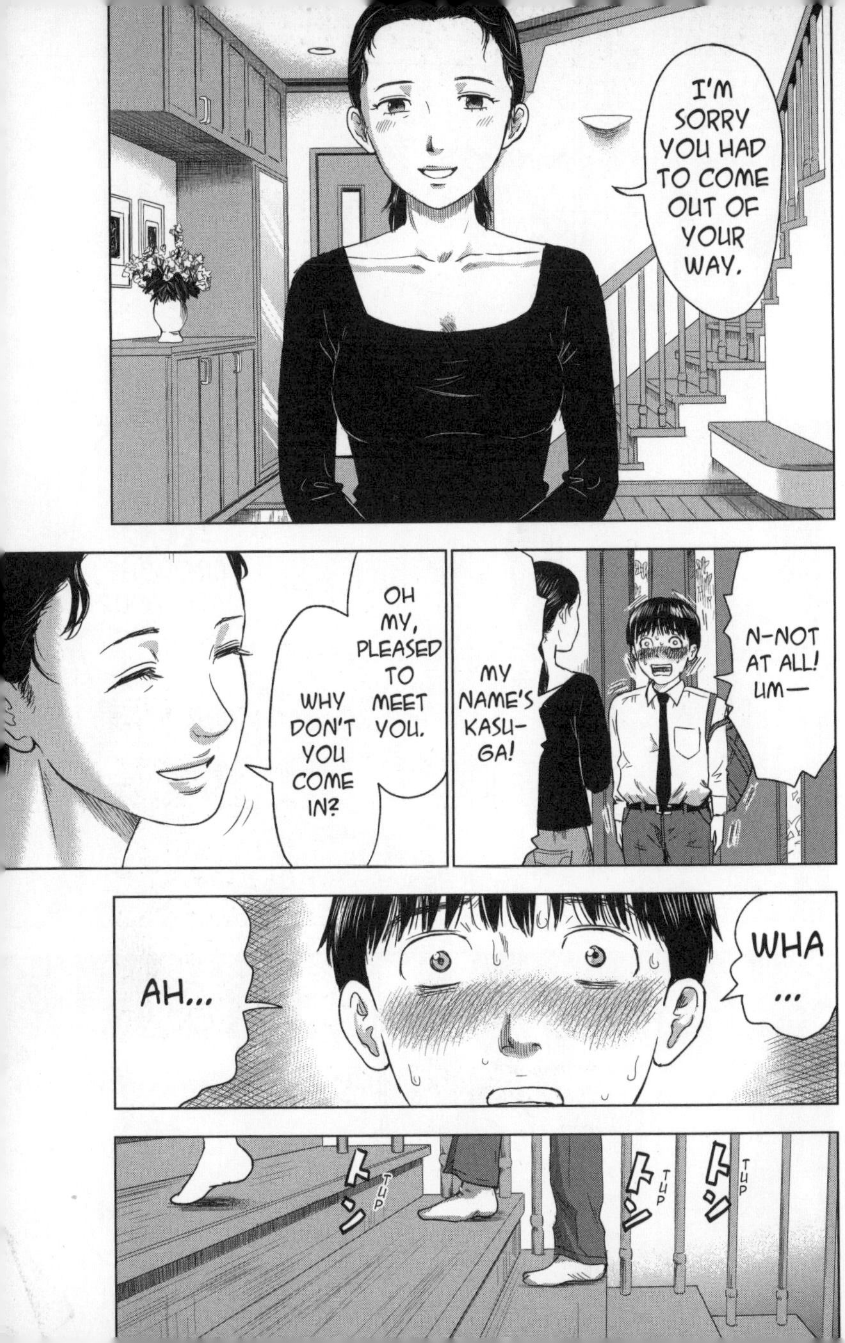
I'M SORRY YOU HAD TO COME OUT OF YOUR WAY.
N-NOT AT ALL! UM—
MY NAME'S KASU-GA!
OH MY, PLEASED TO MEET YOU.
WHY DON'T YOU COME IN?
WHA...
AH...
TUP
TUP
TUP

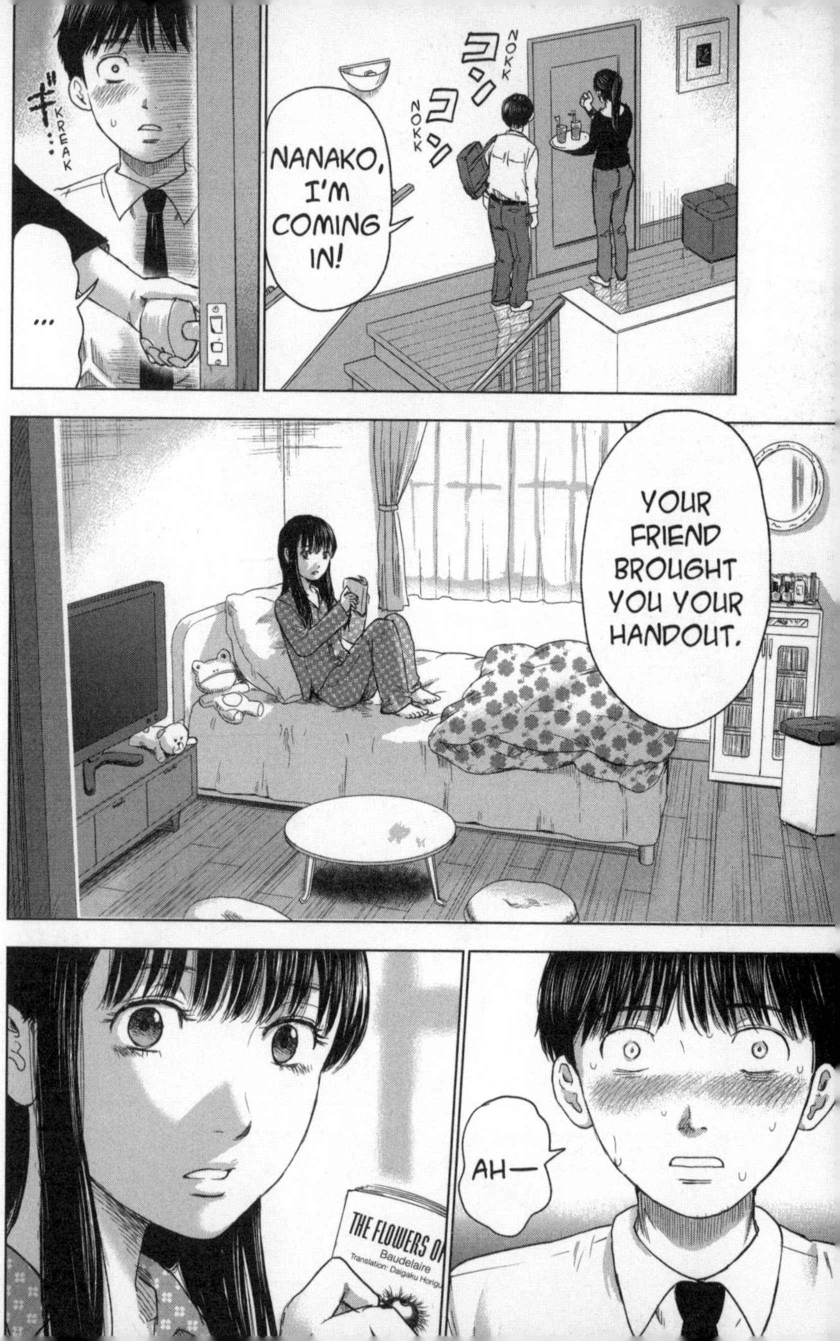
NOKK
NOKK
NANAKO, I'M COMING IN!
KREAK
...
YOUR FRIEND BROUGHT YOU YOUR HANDOUT.
AH—
THE FLOWERS
Baudelaire

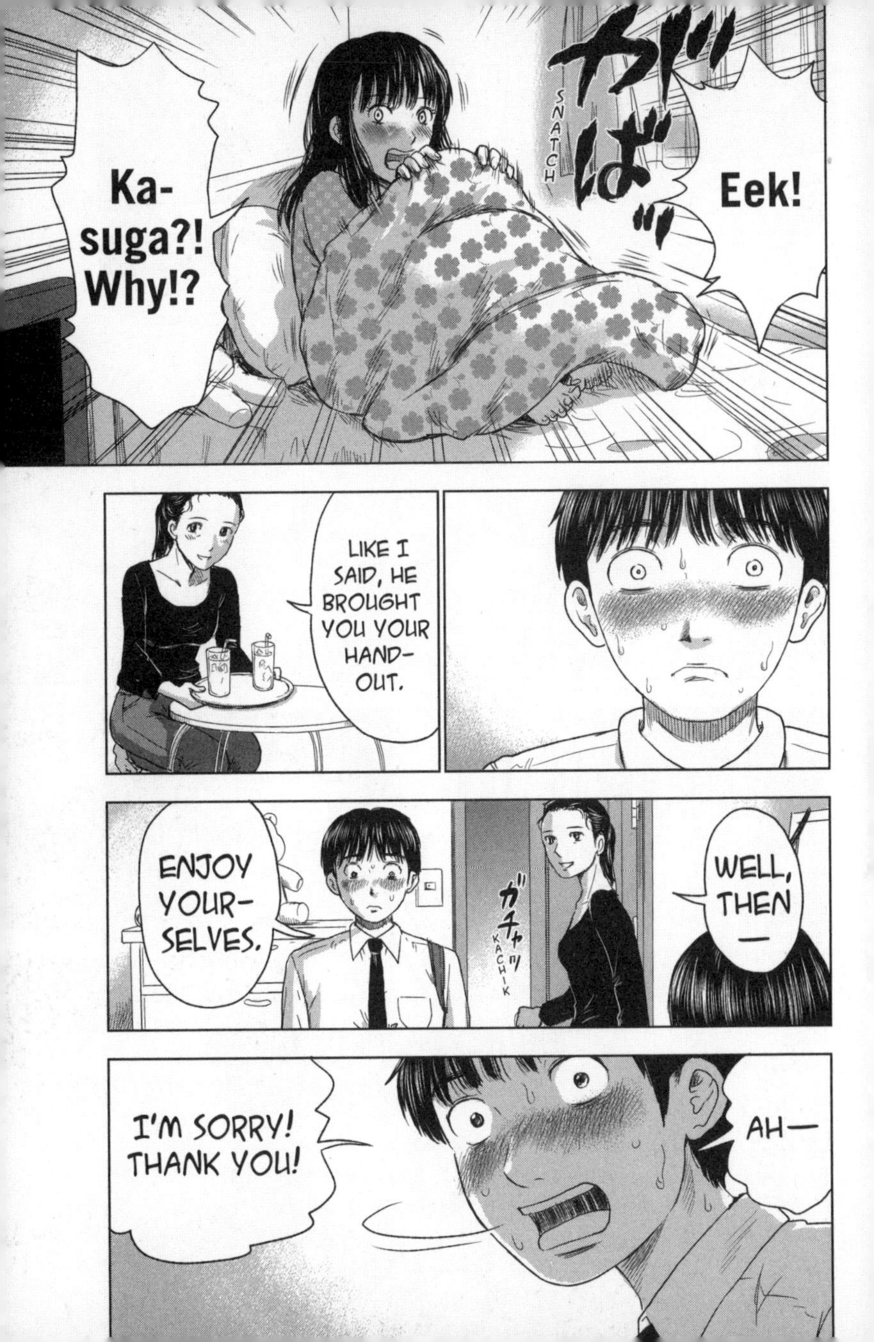
Eek!
がばっ
SNATCH
Ka-suga?! Why!?
LIKE I SAID, HE BROUGHT YOU YOUR HAND-OUT.
WELL, THEN —
ガチャッ
KACHIK
ENJOY YOUR-SELVES.
AH—
I'M SORRY! THANK YOU!

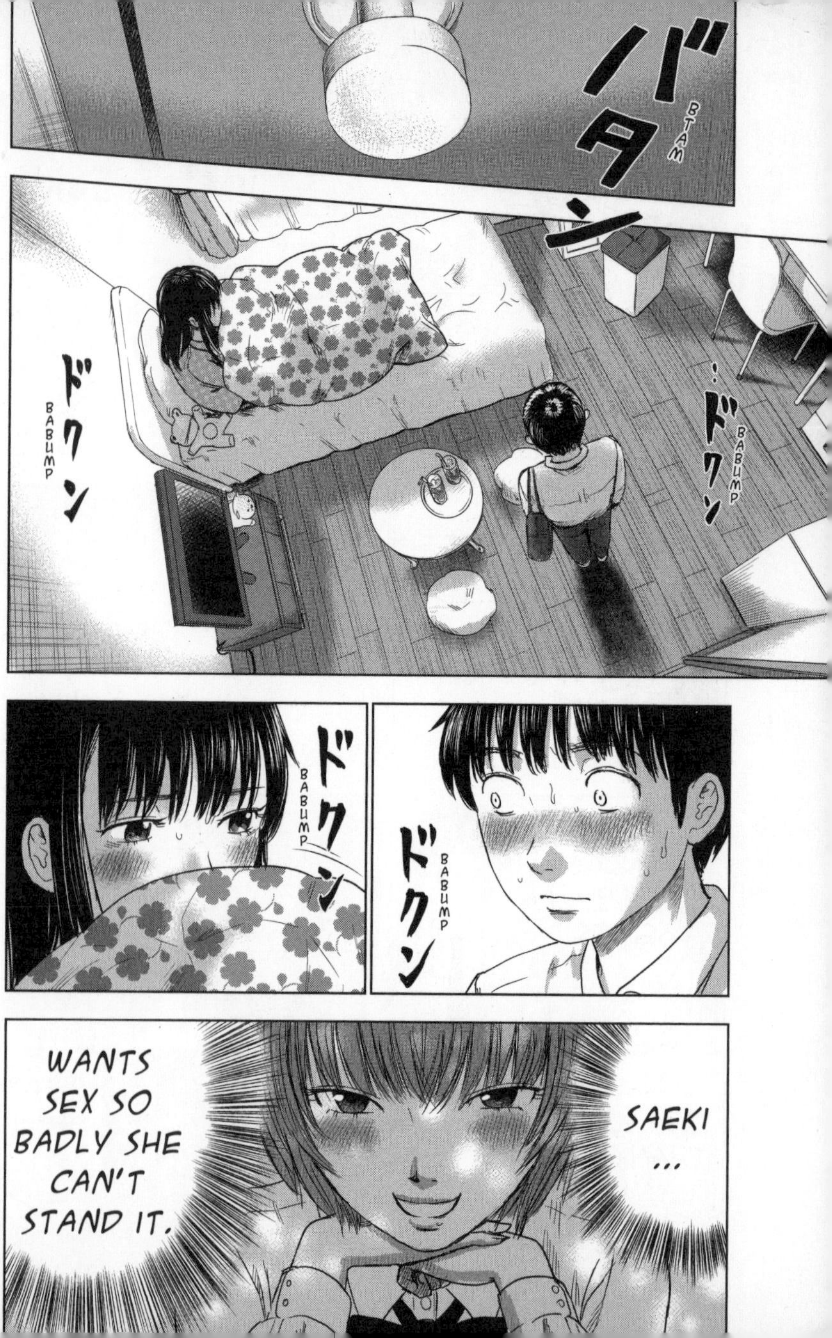

バタン
BTAM
ドクン
BABUMP
ドクン
BABUMP
ドクン
BABUMP
ドクン
BABUMP
SAEKI ...
WANTS SEX SO BADLY SHE CAN'T STAND IT.

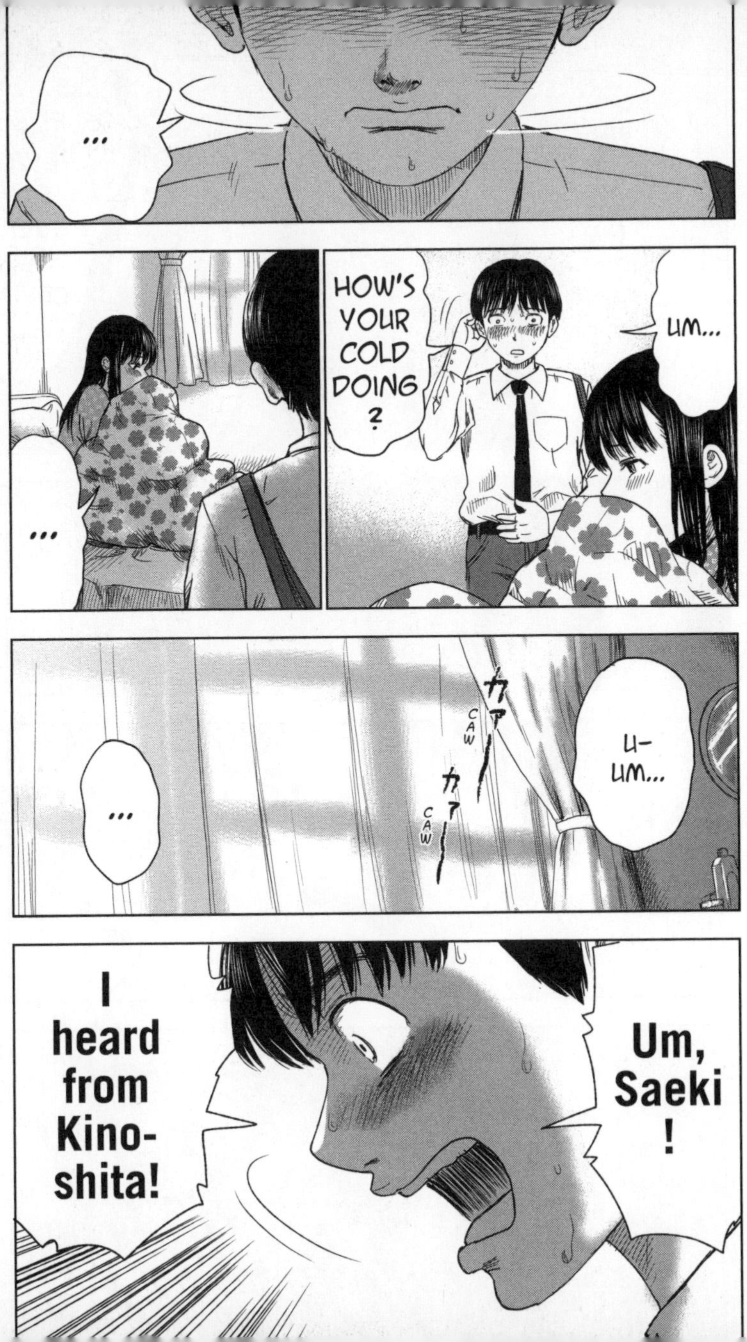
...
UM...
HOW'S YOUR COLD DOING?
...
U-UM...
カァー CAW
カァー CAW
...
Um, Saeki!
I heard from Kino-shita!

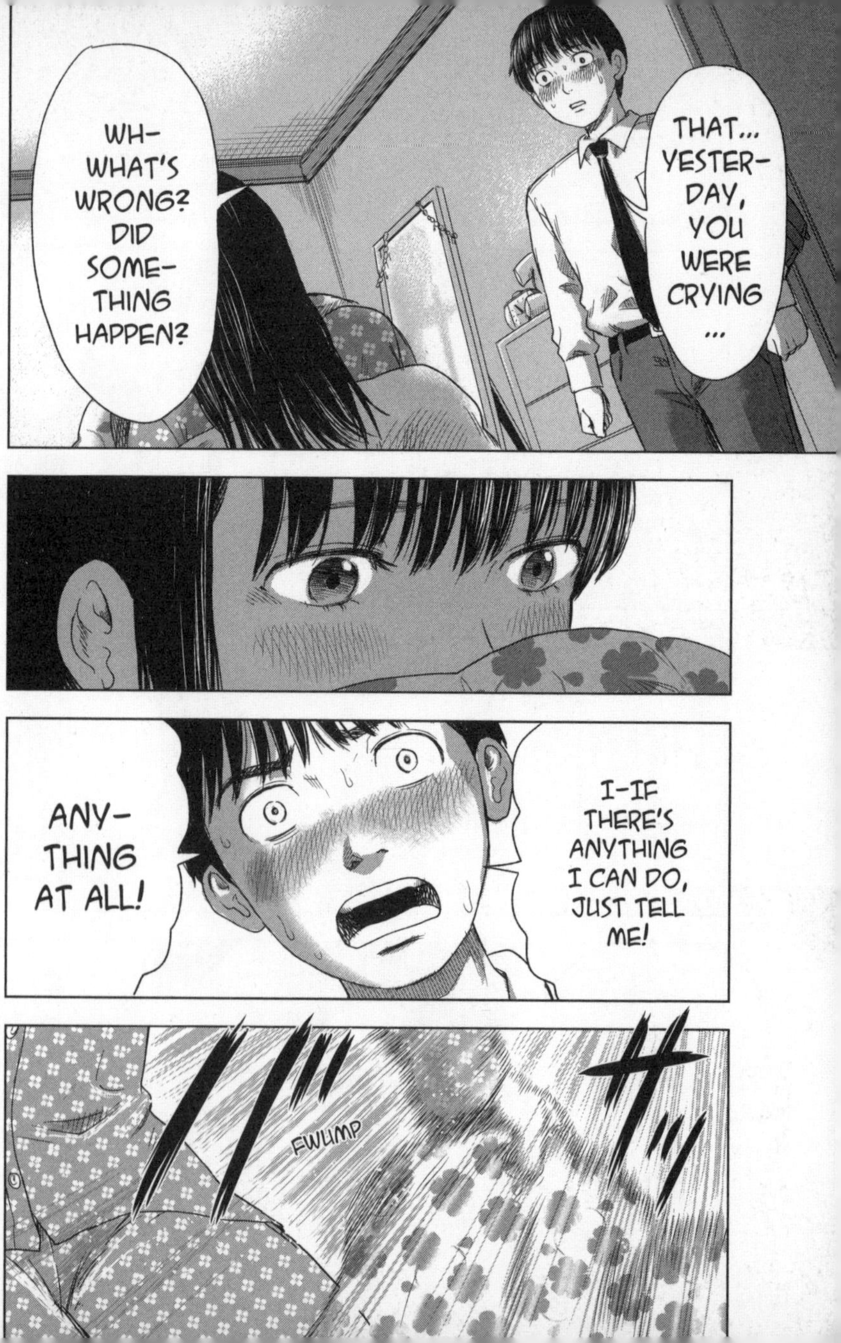
THAT... YESTER-DAY, YOU WERE CRYING ...
WH-WHAT'S WRONG? DID SOME-THING HAPPEN?
I-IF THERE'S ANYTHING I CAN DO, JUST TELL ME!
ANY-THING AT ALL!
FWUMP

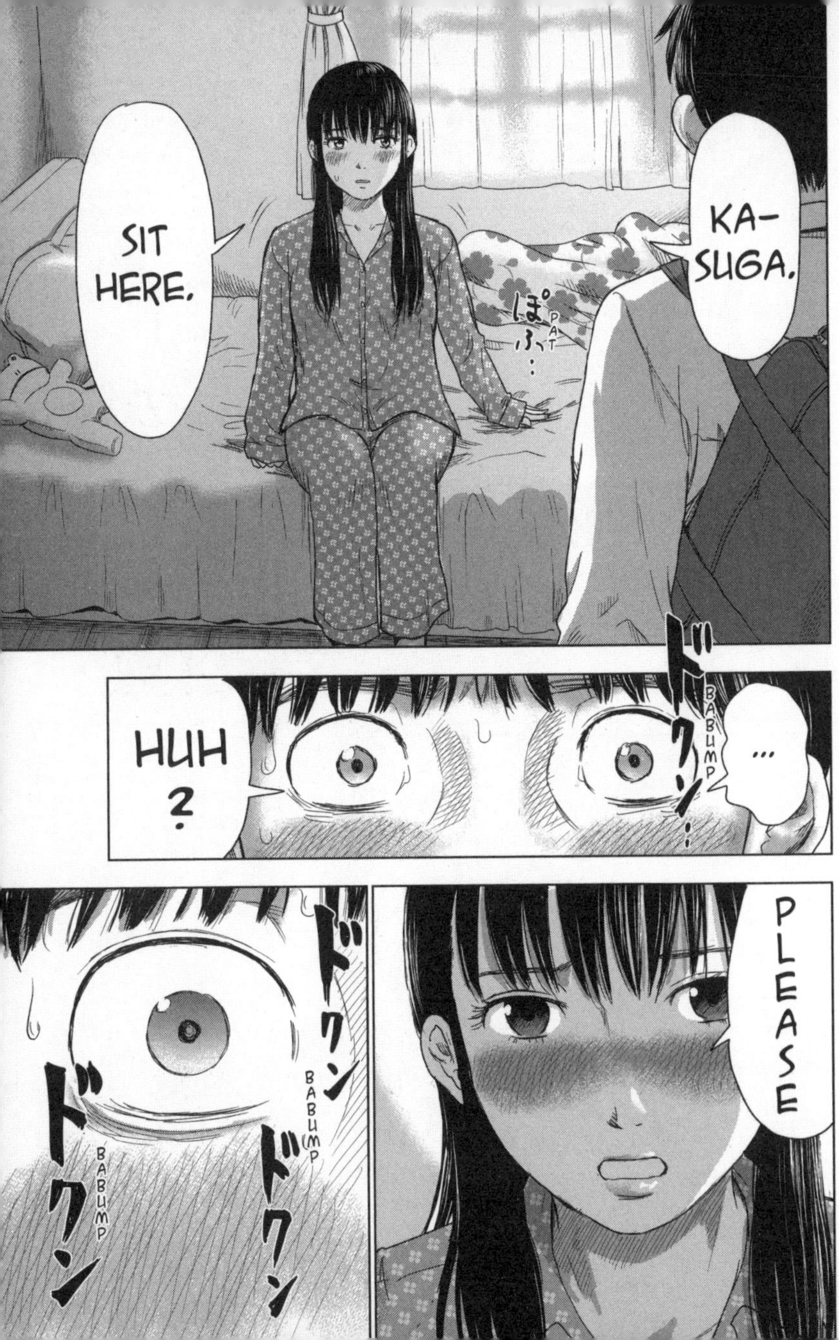
KA-SUGA.
ぽふ…
PAT
SIT HERE.
ドクン!!…
BABUMP
…
HUH?
PLEASE
ドクン
BABUMP
ドクン
BABUMP
ドクン

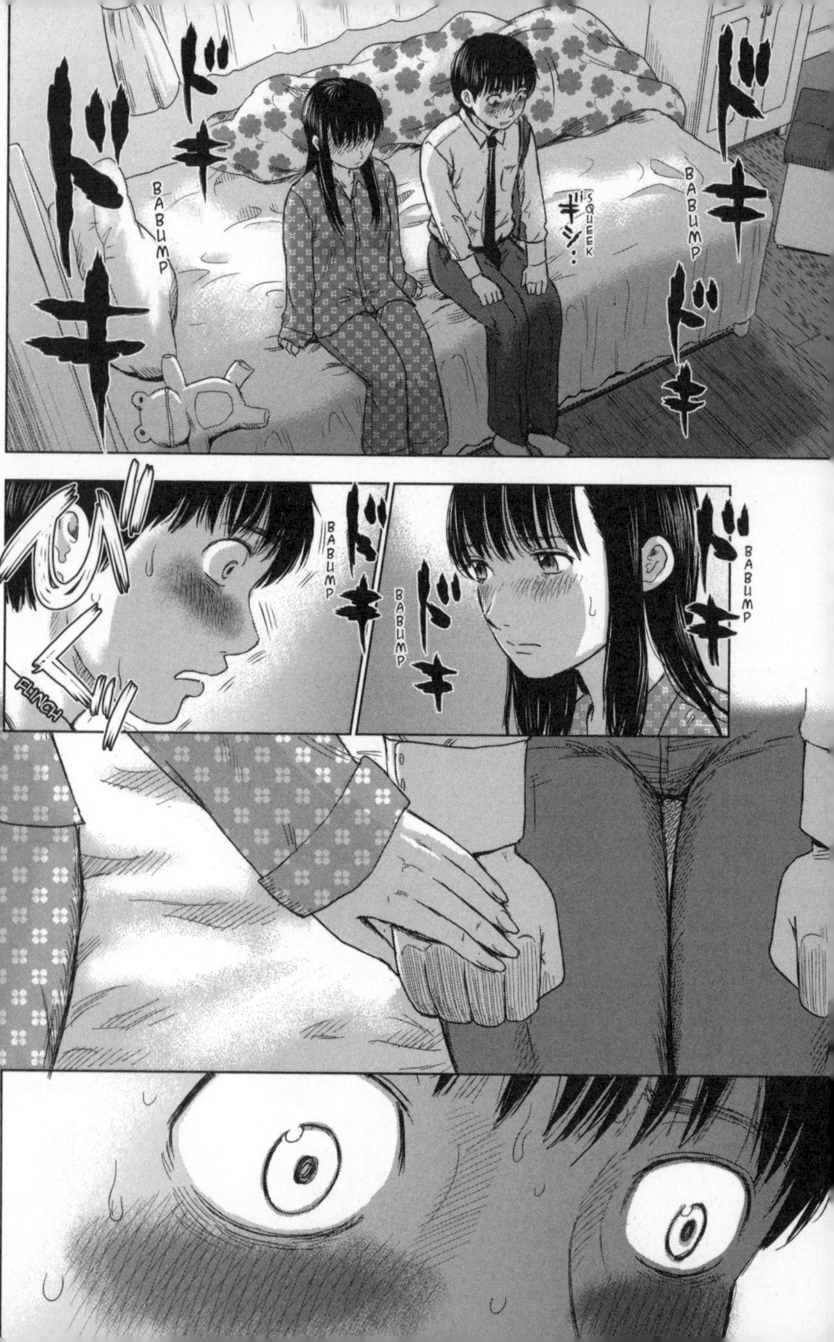

ドキ
BABUMP
ドキ
ギシ…
SQUEEK
ドキ
BABUMP
ドキ
ドキ
BABUMP
ドキ
BABUMP
ドキ
BABUMP
FLINCH

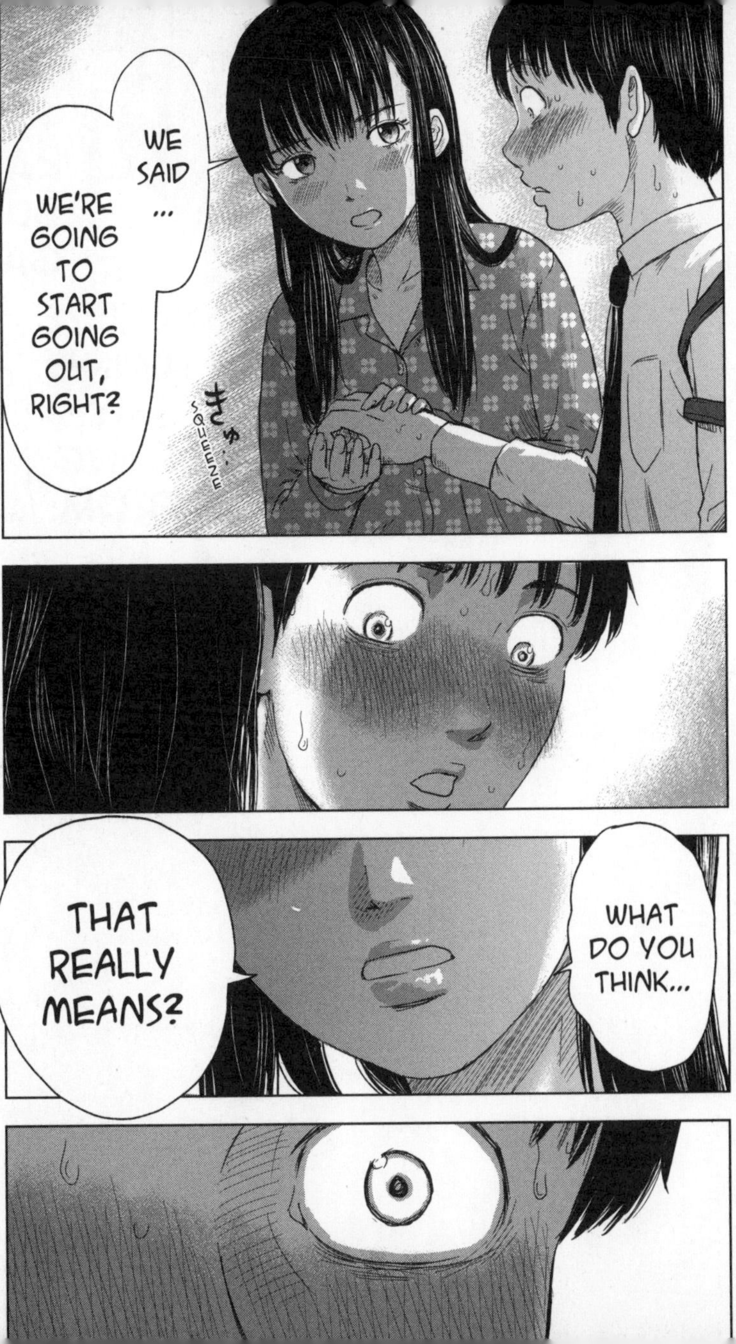
WE SAID ...
WE'RE GOING TO START GOING OUT, RIGHT?
きゅ SQUEEZE
WHAT DO YOU THINK...
THAT REALLY MEANS?

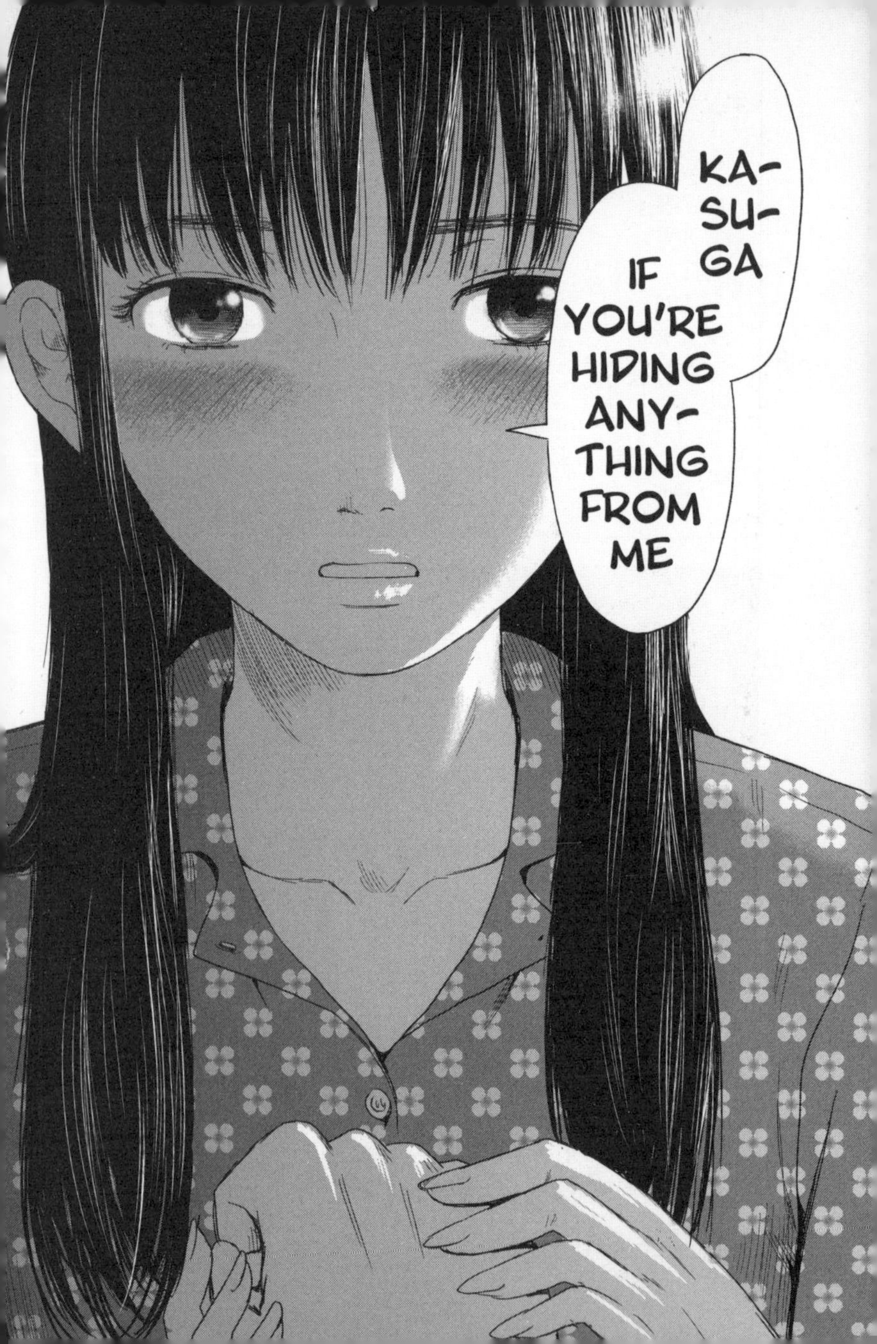
KA-SU-GA
IF YOU'RE HIDING ANY-THING FROM ME

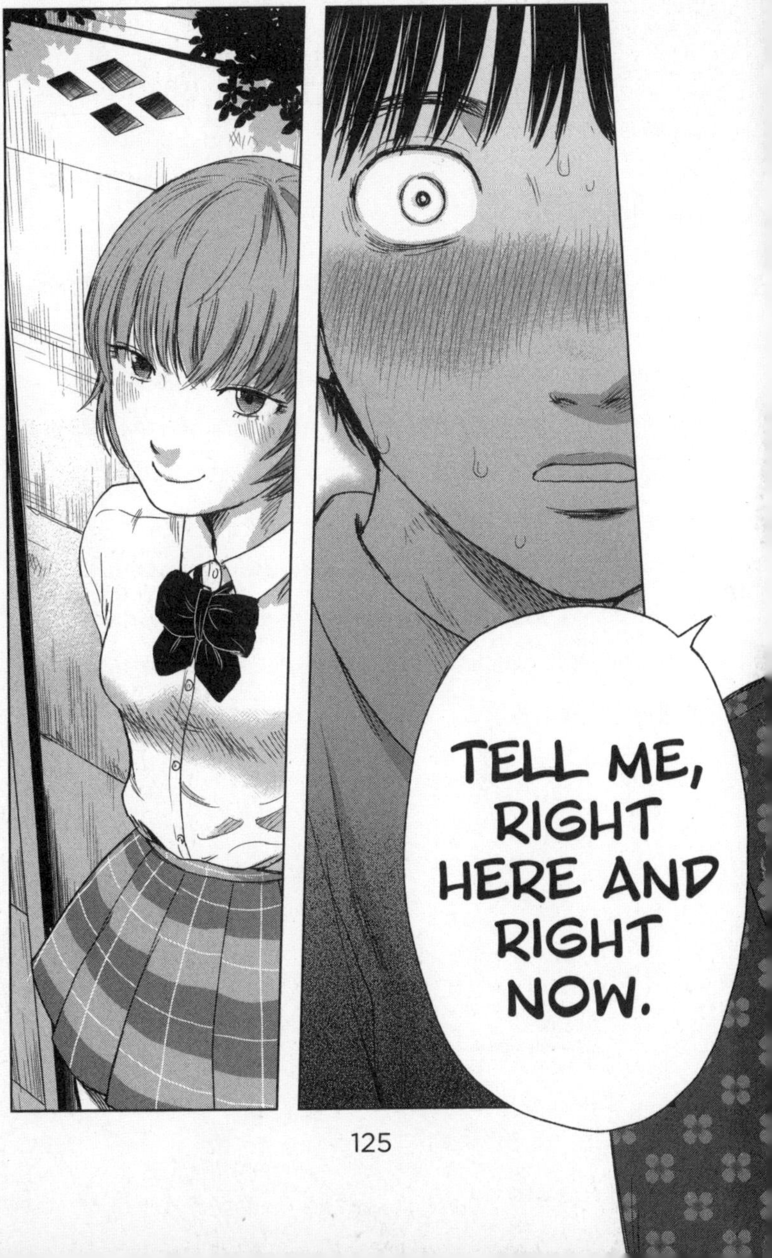
TELL ME, RIGHT HERE AND RIGHT NOW.

Afterword

Chapter 11

When you live in Tokyo, you realize that even in the dead of
night, there are lights everywhere. I've lived here for over
ten years and I'd forgotten all about it, but back in the
countryside there are only a few lights. When the sun sets
and dusk covers the town, it gets so dark you can hardly
see anything. With nowhere to go I'd ride my bike around
the outskirts of town, and as the darkness deepened I'd
feel a helpless despair. I don't want to forget the feelings I
had then, as I watched the lights of distant cars speeding
through the blackness.

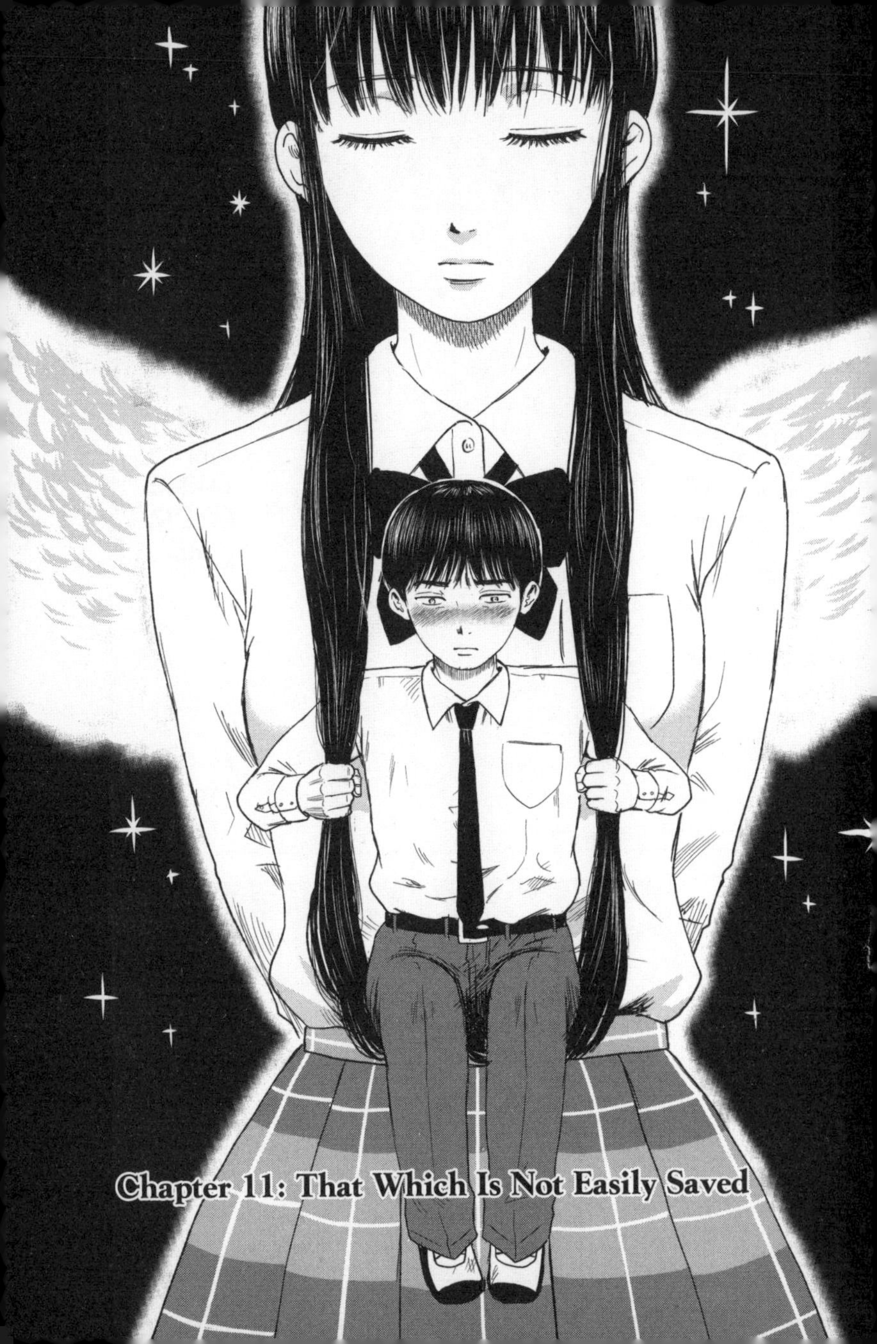
Chapter 11: That Which Is Not Easily Saved

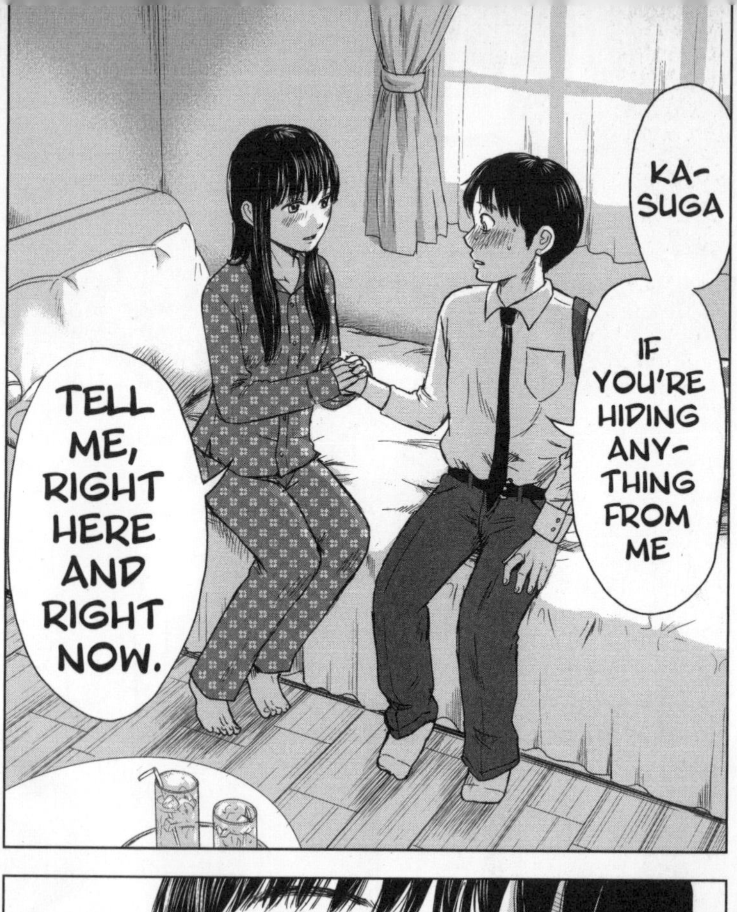
KA-SUGA
IF YOU'RE HIDING ANY-THING FROM ME
TELL ME, RIGHT HERE AND RIGHT NOW.
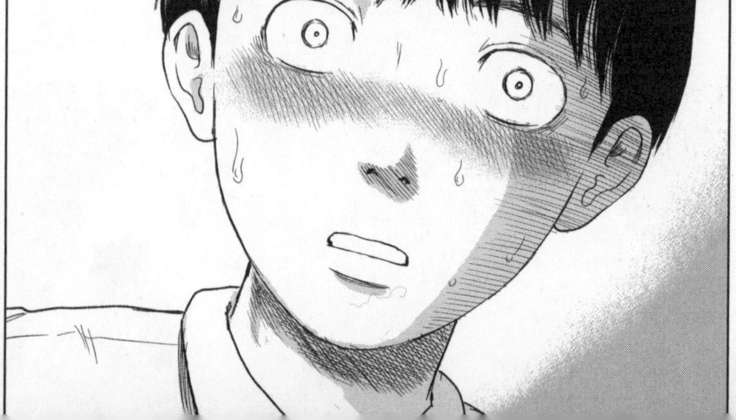

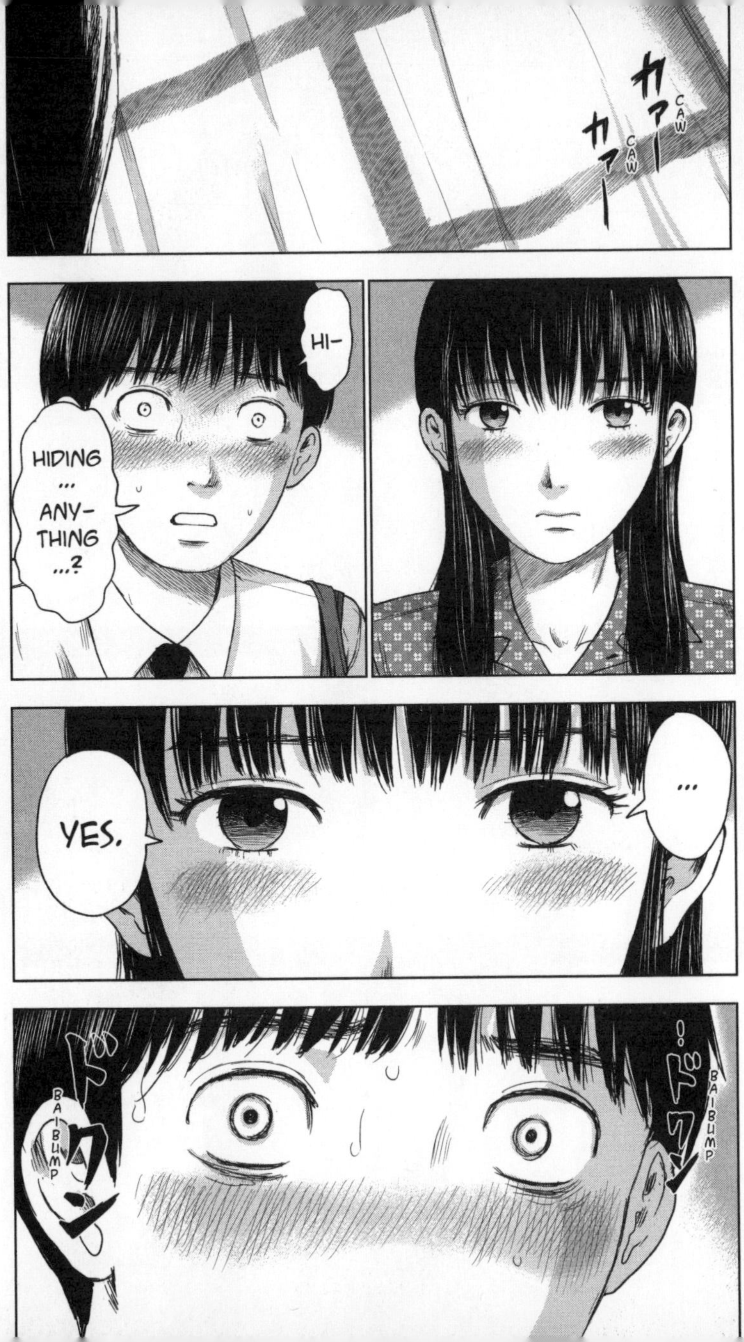
カァー
CAW
カァー
CAW
HI-
HIDING ... ANY-THING ...?
...
YES.
BABUMP
ドクン
BABUMP

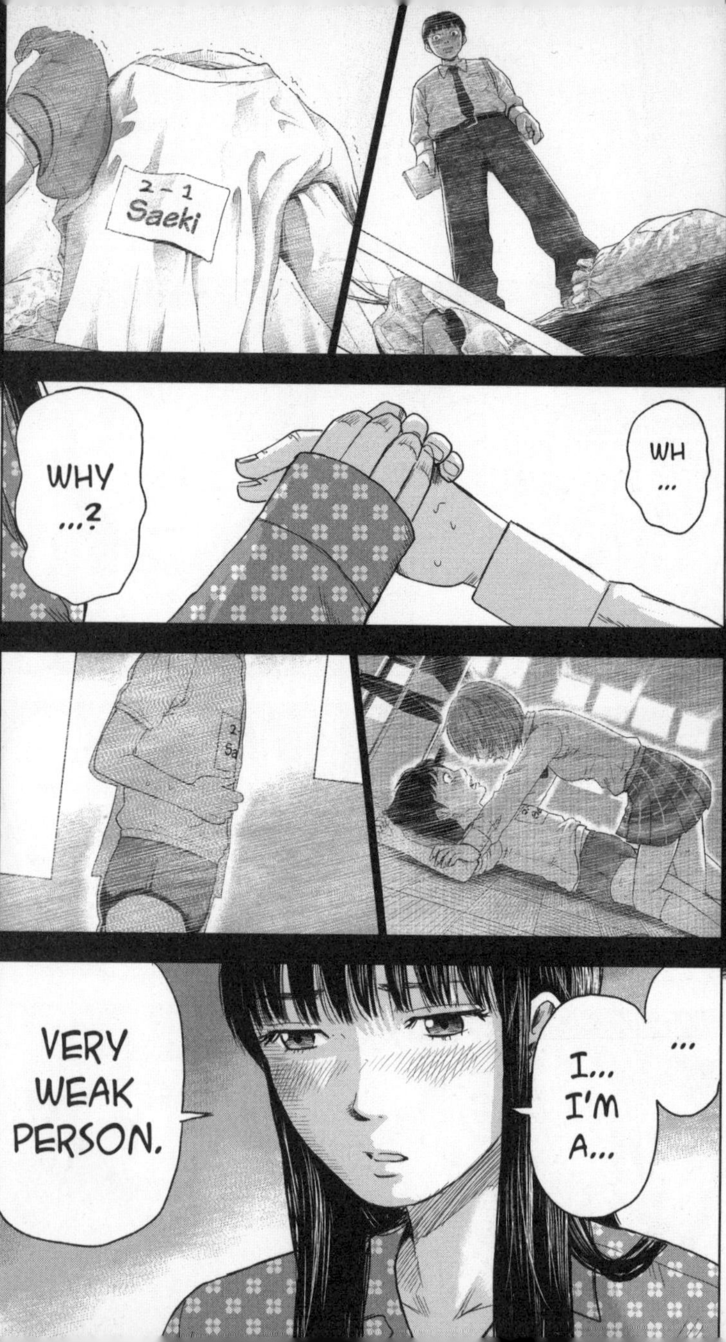
2 – 1
Saeki
WH ...
WHY ...?
... I... I'M A...
VERY WEAK PERSON.

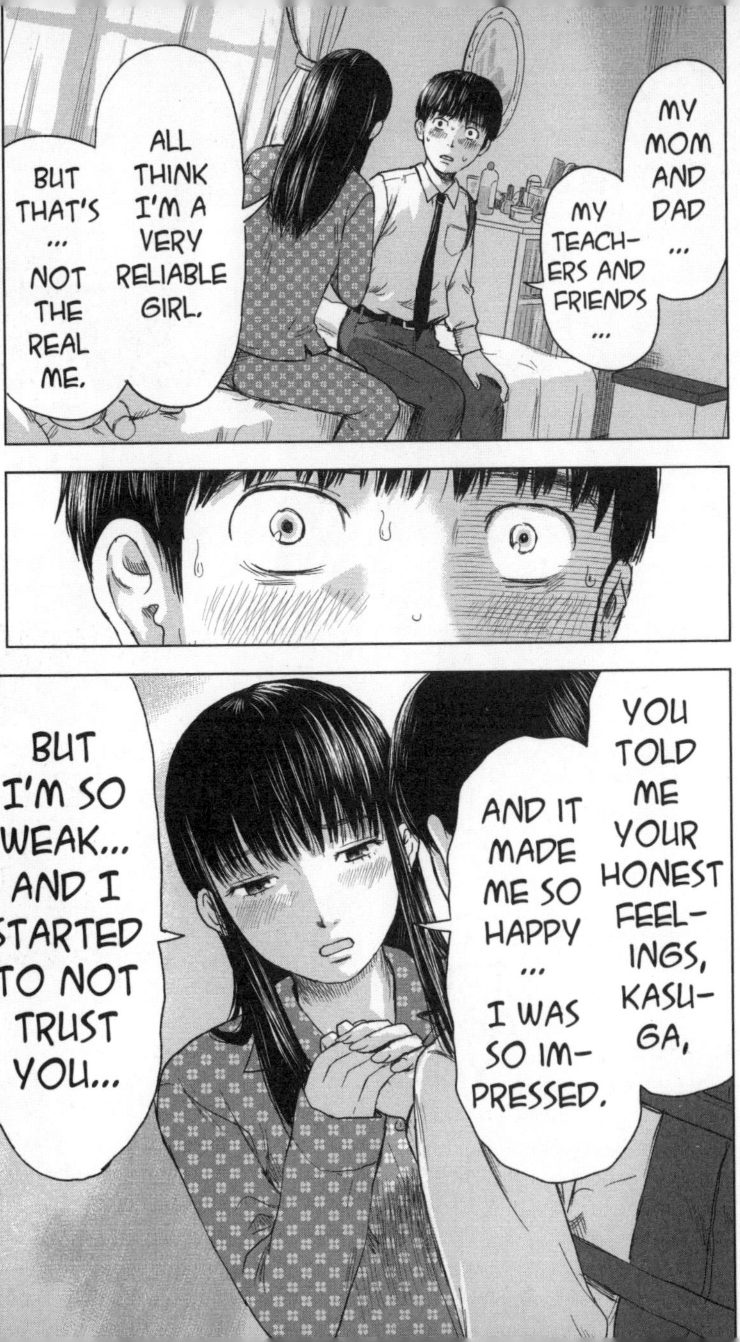
MY MOM AND DAD ...
MY TEACHERS AND FRIENDS ...
ALL THINK I'M A VERY RELIABLE GIRL.
BUT THAT'S ... NOT THE REAL ME.
YOU TOLD ME YOUR HONEST FEELINGS, KASUGA,
AND IT MADE ME SO HAPPY ... I WAS SO IMPRESSED.
BUT I'M SO WEAK... AND I STARTED TO NOT TRUST YOU...

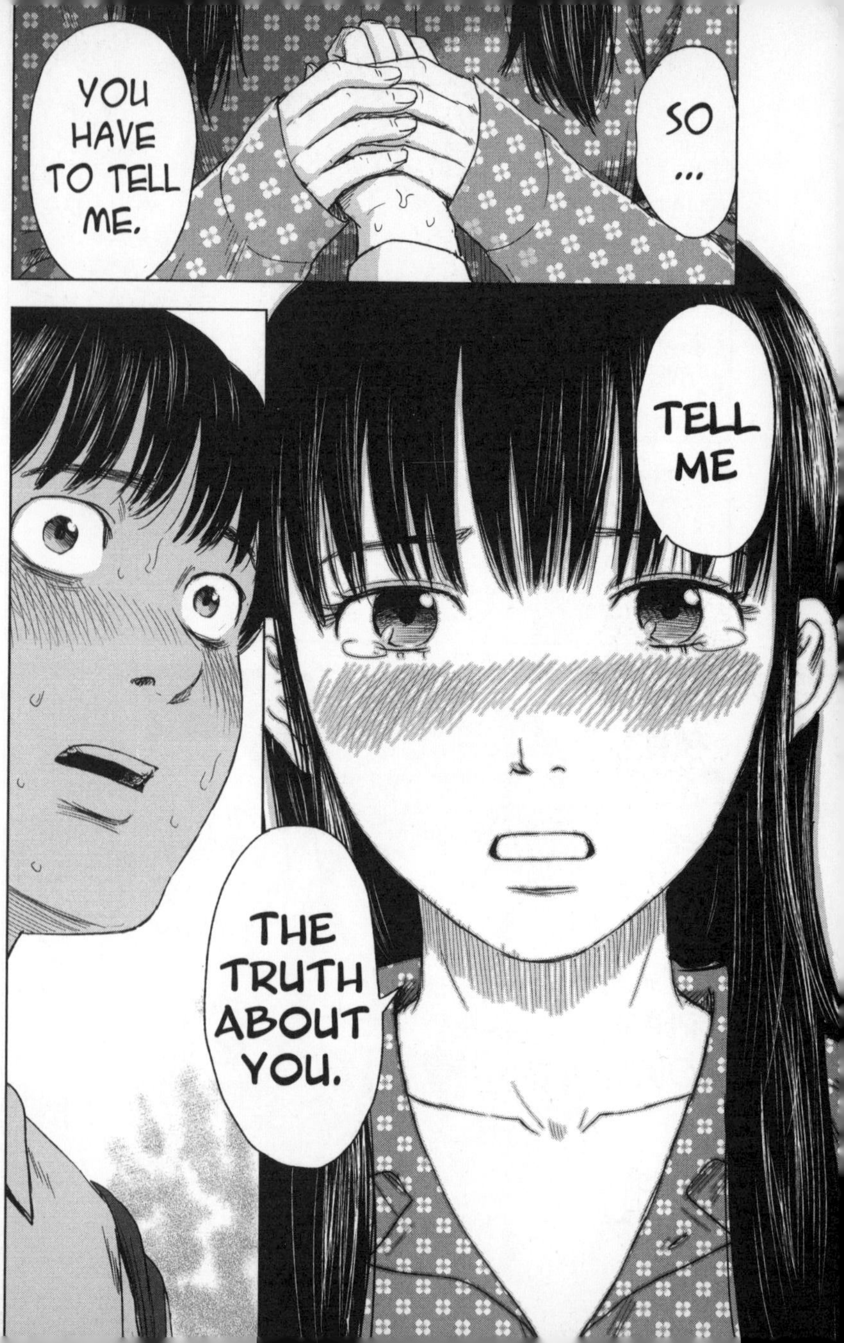
SO ...
YOU HAVE TO TELL ME.
TELL ME
THE TRUTH ABOUT YOU.

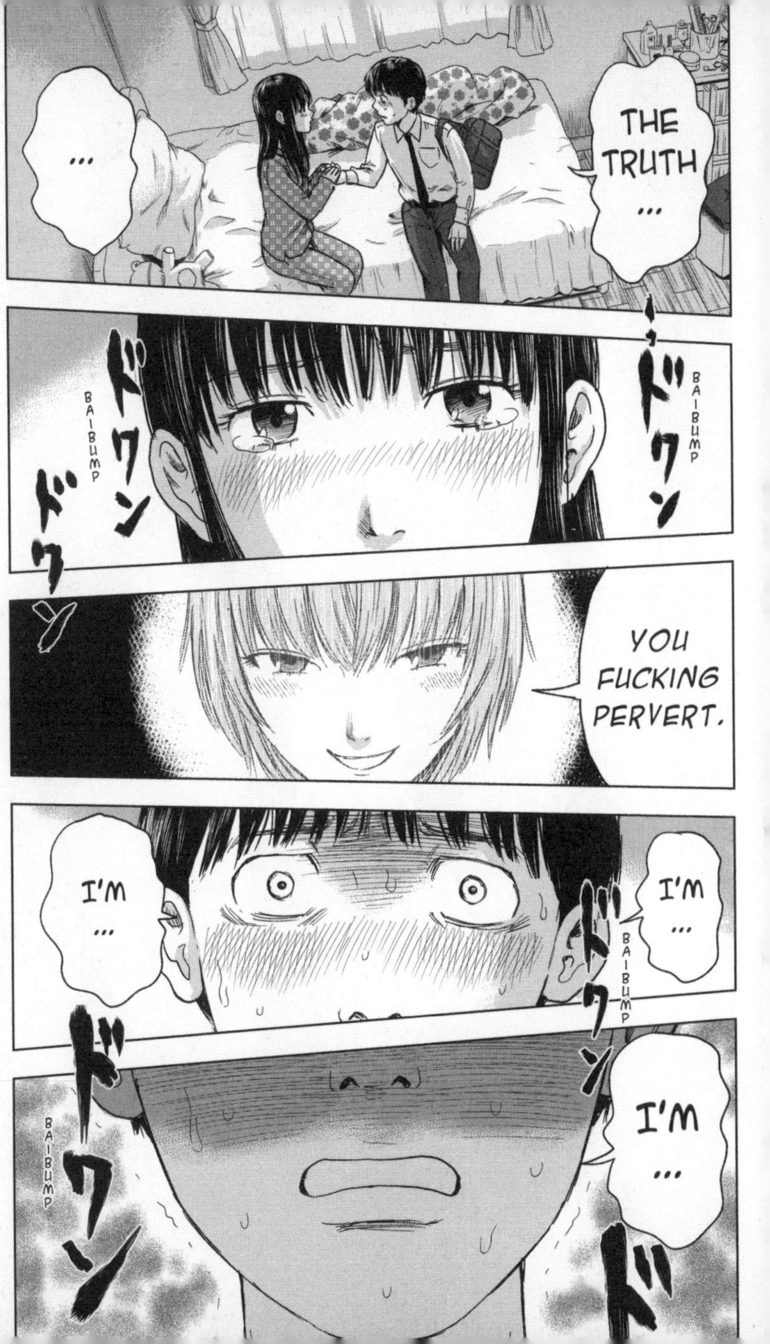
THE TRUTH ...
...
ドクン
BAIBUMP
ドクン
BAIBUMP
ドクン
YOU FUCKING PERVERT.
I'M ...
ドクン
BAIBUMP
I'M ...
I'M ...
ド
ドクン
BAIBUMP

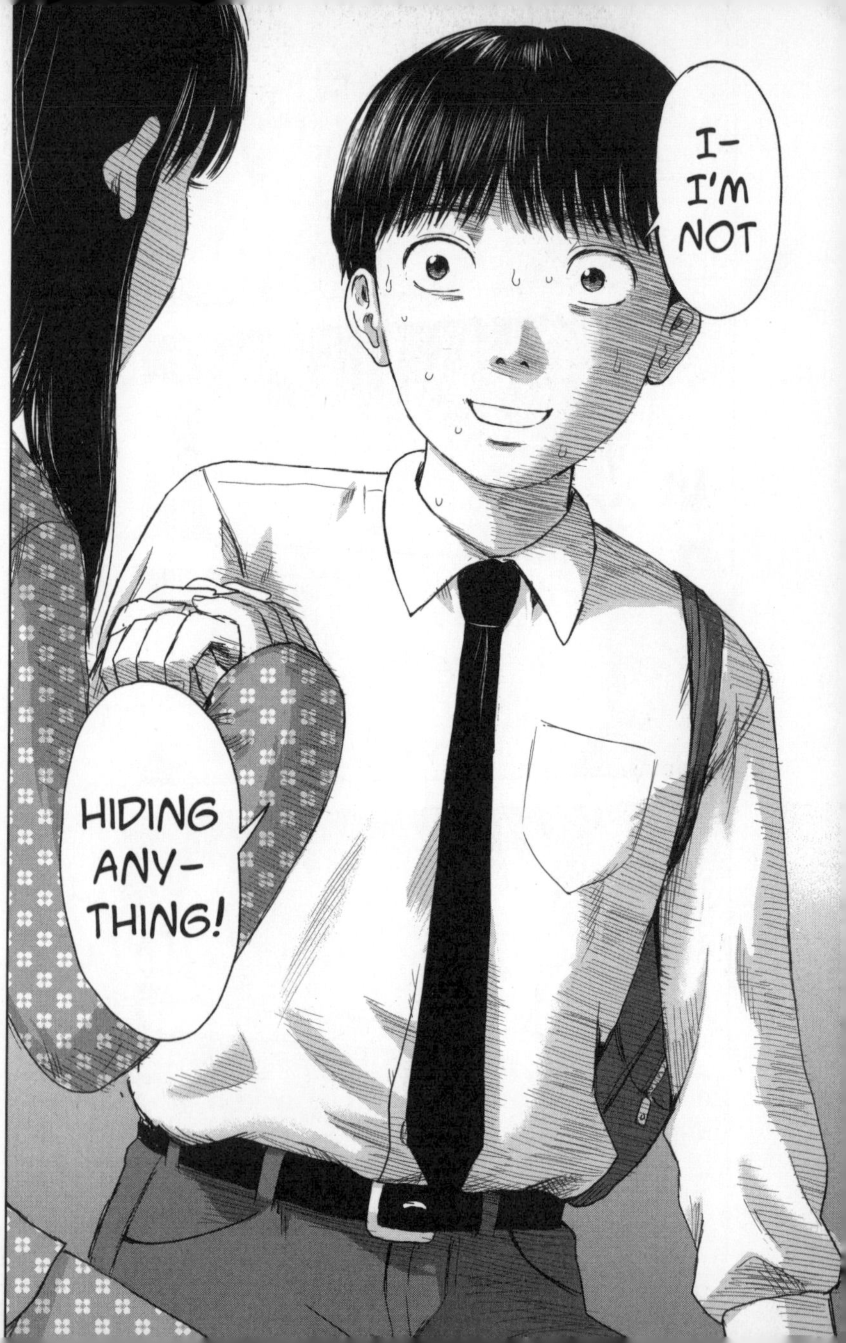
I- I'M NOT
HIDING ANY- THING!

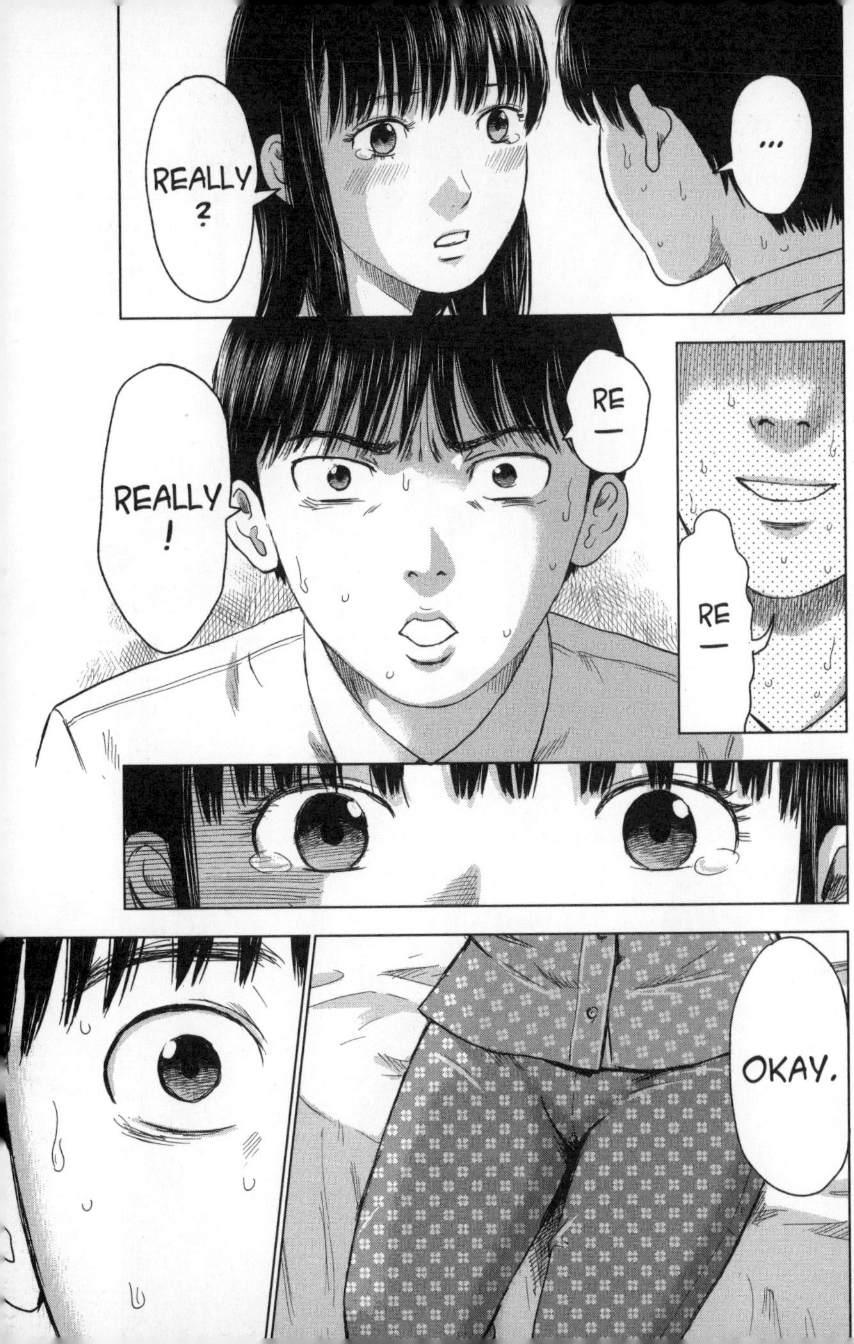
...
REALLY ?
RE —
RE —
REALLY !
OKAY.

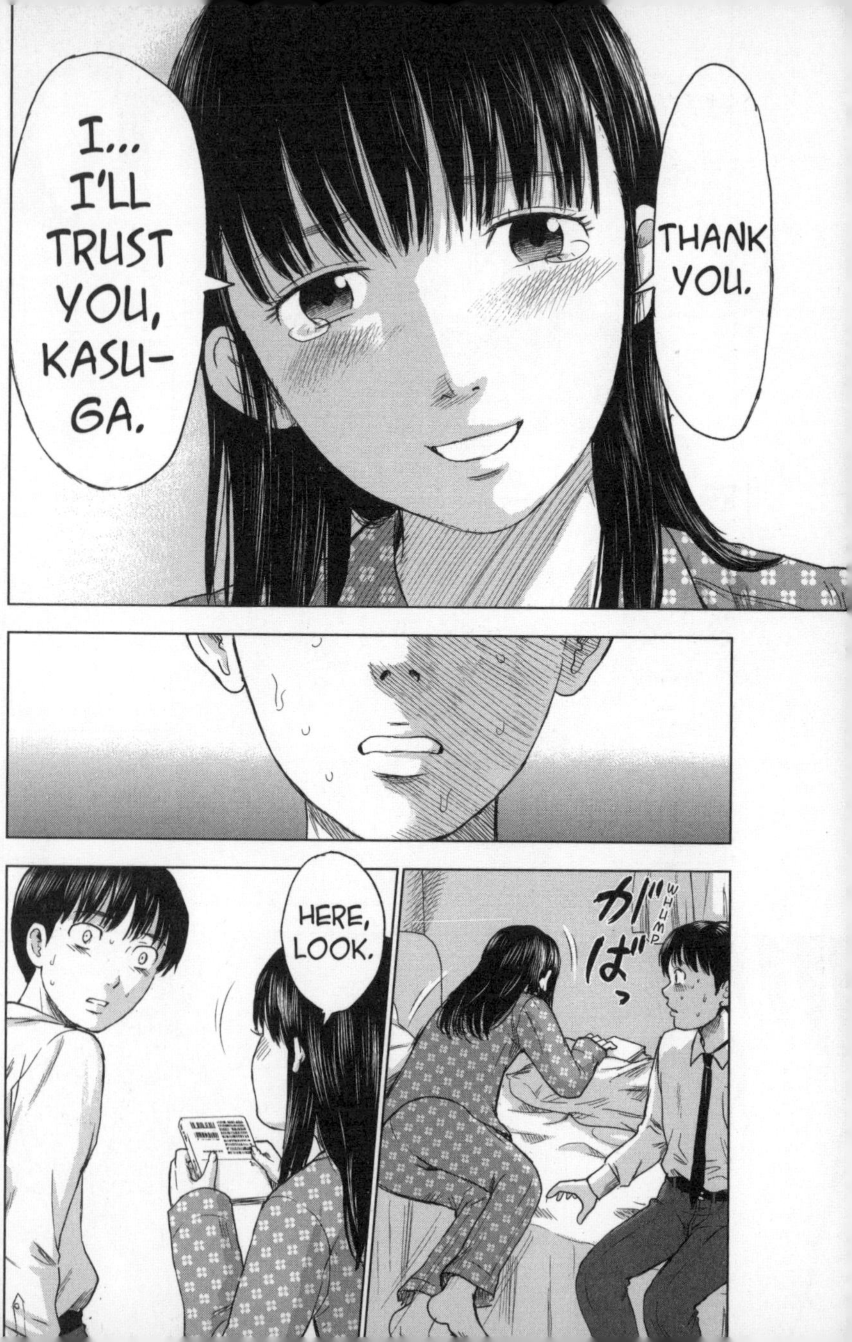
THANK YOU.
I... I'LL TRUST YOU, KASUGA.
がばっ
WHUMP
HERE, LOOK.

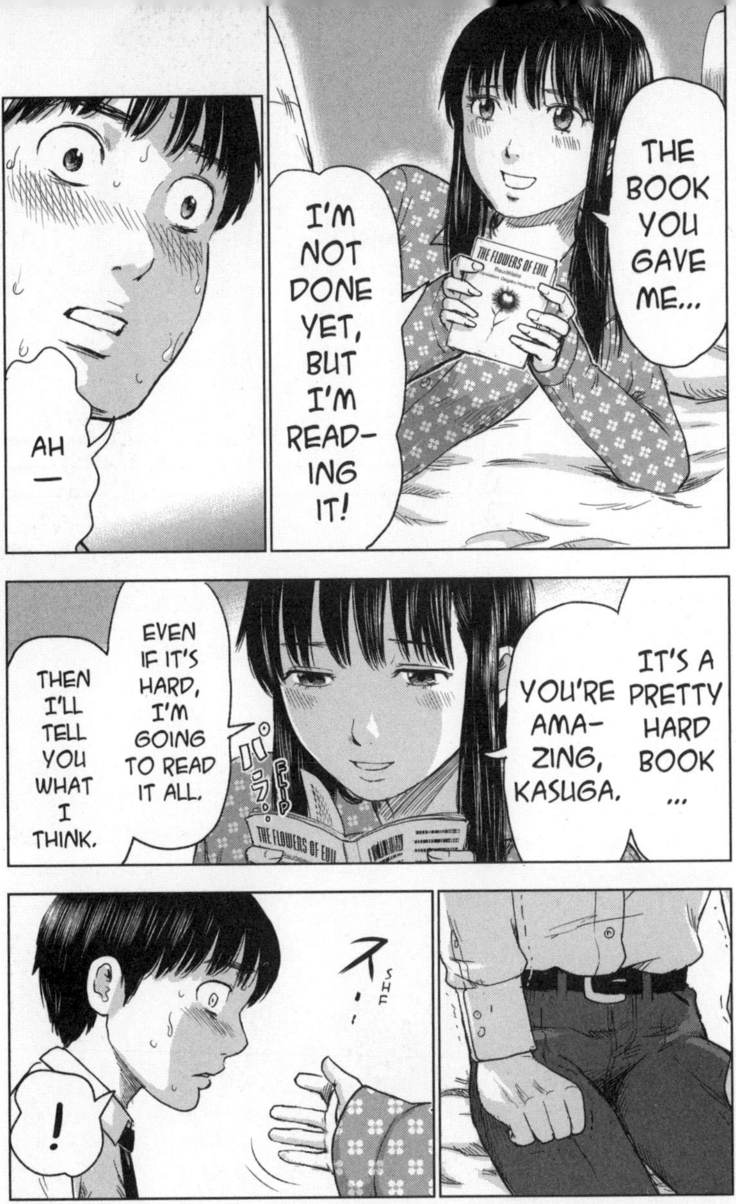
THE BOOK YOU GAVE ME...
THE FLOWERS OF EVIL
I'M NOT DONE YET, BUT I'M READING IT!
AH —
IT'S A PRETTY HARD BOOK ...
YOU'RE AMAZING, KASUGA.
パラ FLIP
THE FLOWERS OF EVIL
EVEN IF IT'S HARD, I'M GOING TO READ IT ALL.
THEN I'LL TELL YOU WHAT I THINK.
スッ SHF
!

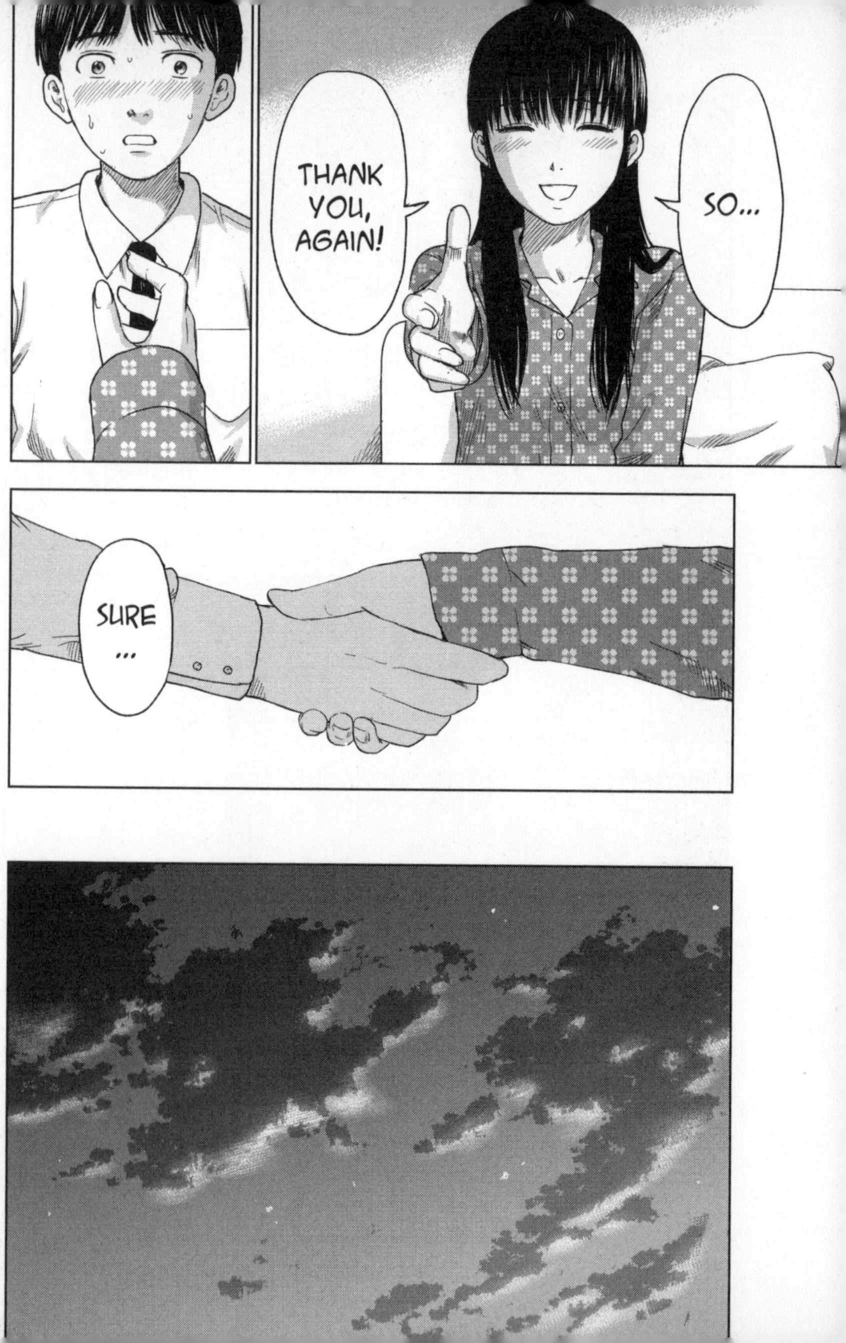
SO...
THANK YOU, AGAIN!
SURE ...

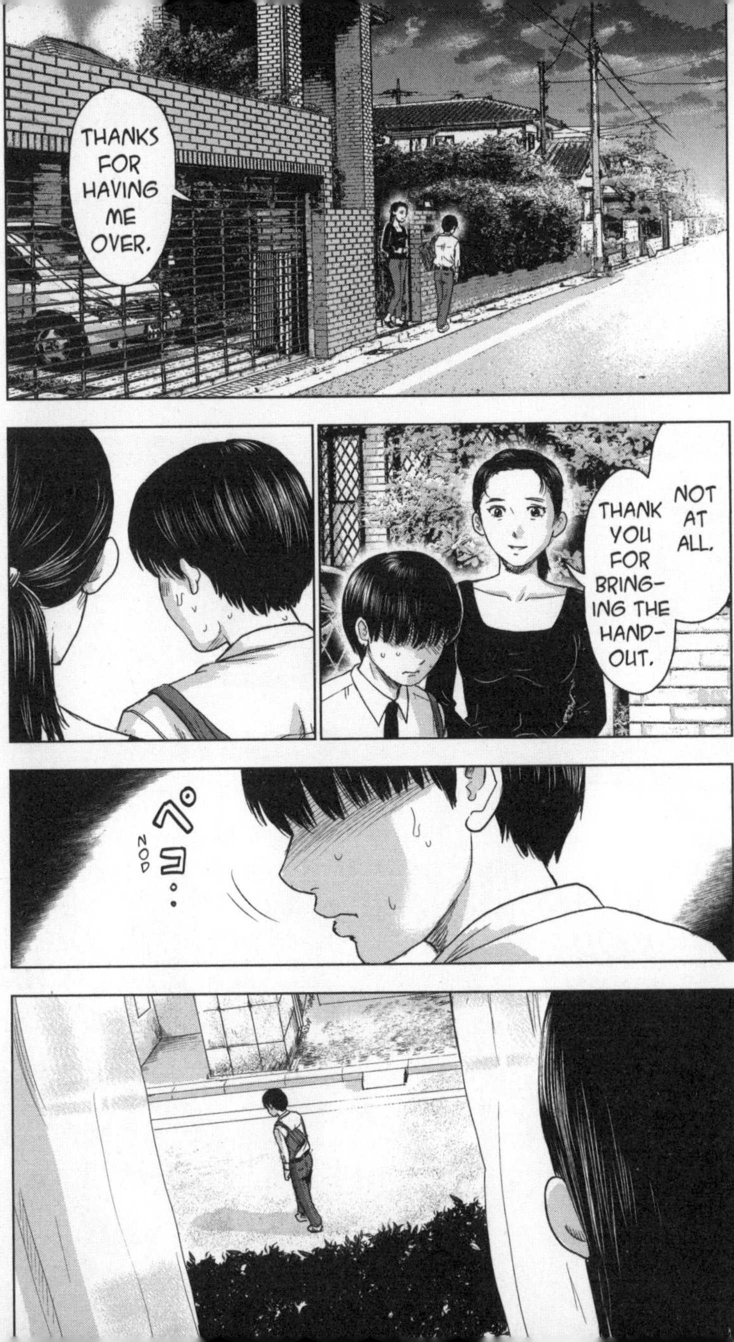
THANKS FOR HAVING ME OVER.
NOT AT ALL.
THANK YOU FOR BRING-ING THE HAND-OUT.
ペコ
NOD

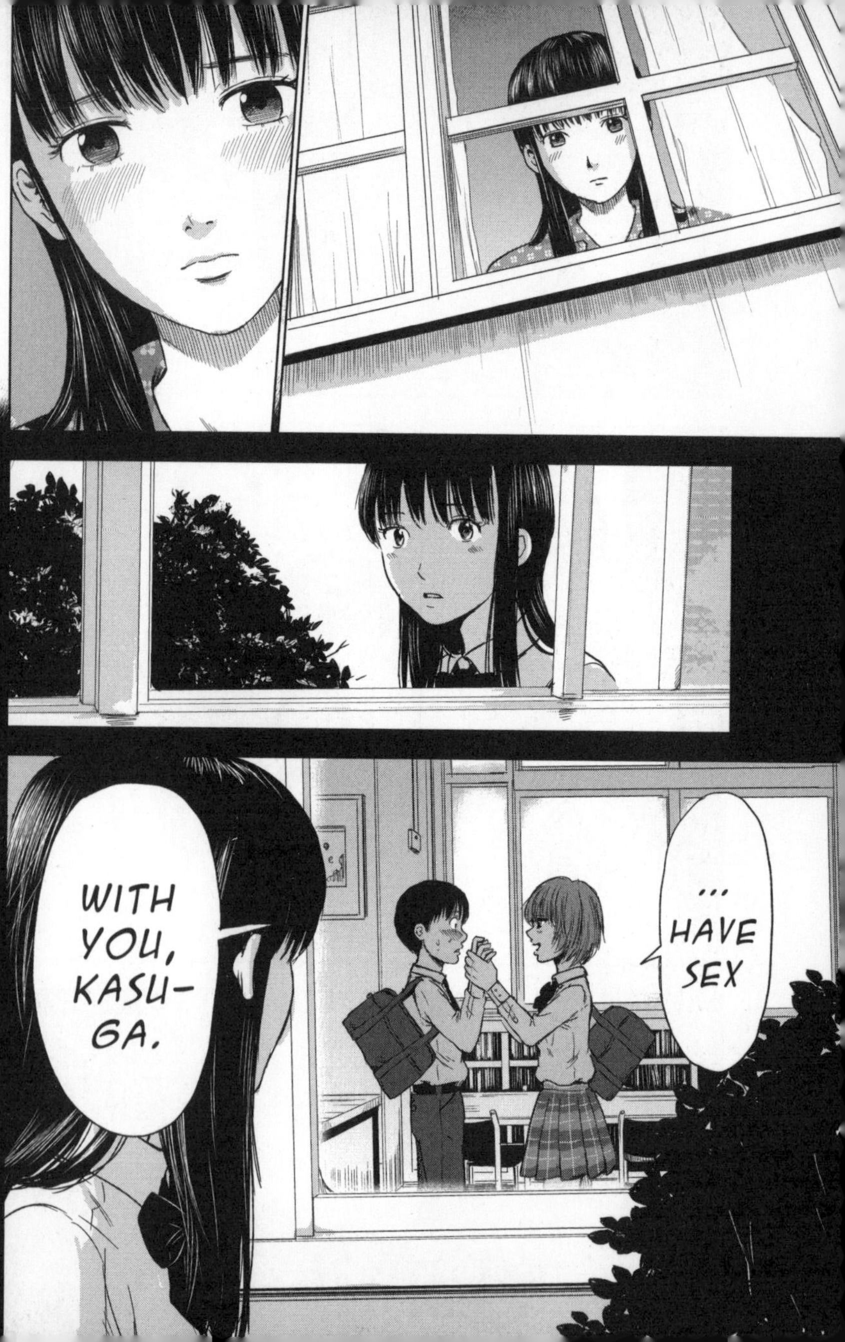
... HAVE SEX
WITH YOU, KASU-GA.

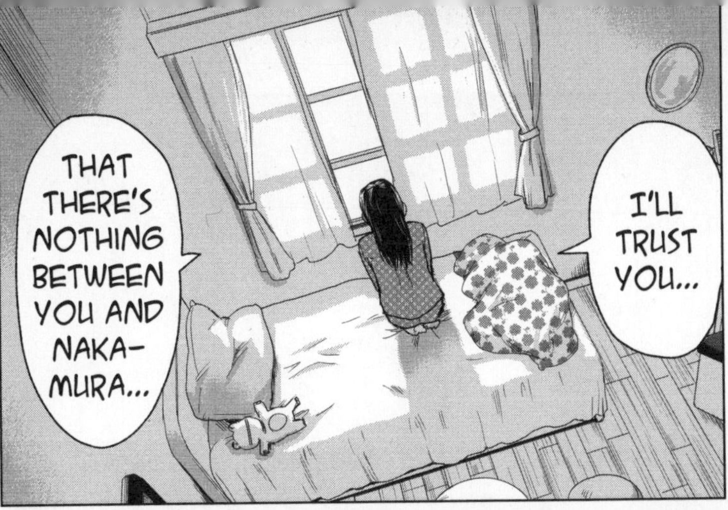
I'LL TRUST YOU...
THAT THERE'S NOTHING BETWEEN YOU AND NAKA-MURA...
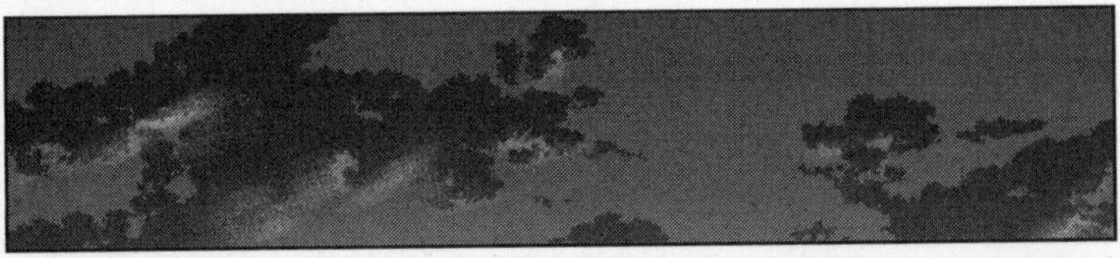
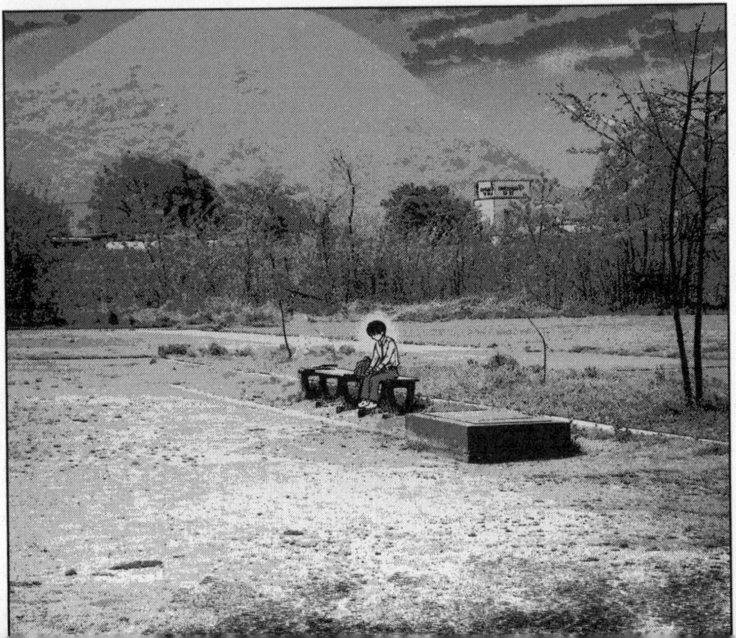

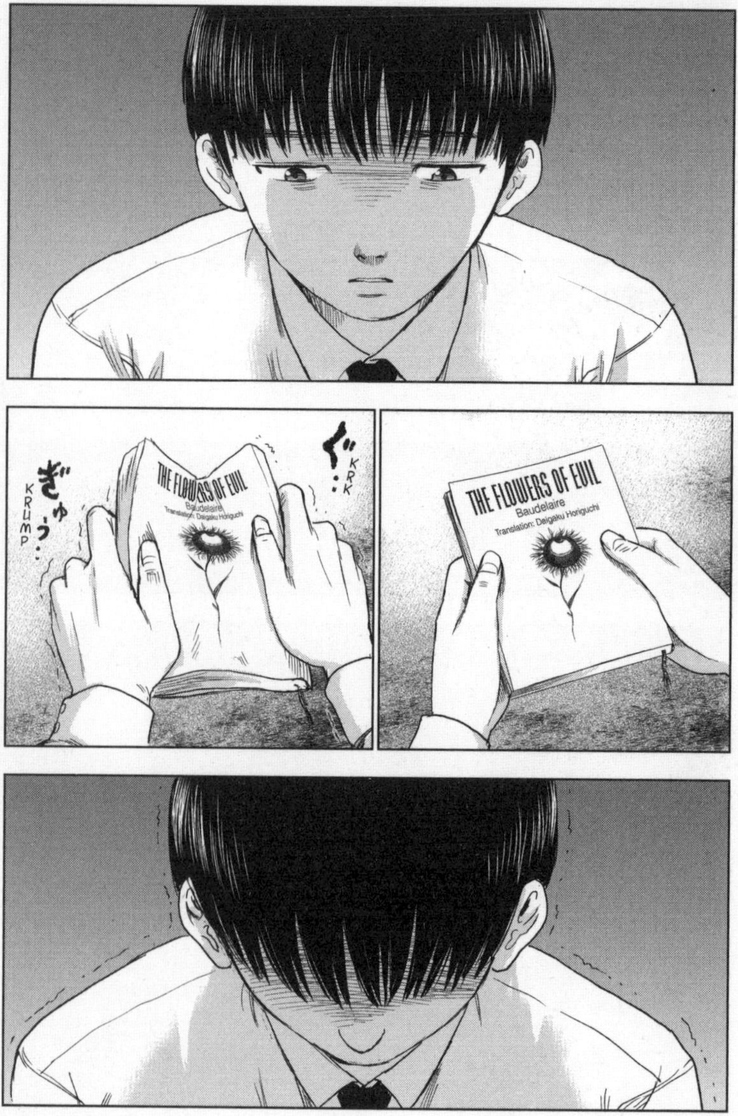
THE FLOWERS OF EVIL
Baudelaire
Translation: Daigaku Horiguchi
ぐ…
KRK
ぎゅう…
KRUMP
THE FLOWERS OF EVIL
Baudelaire
Translation: Daigaku Horiguchi

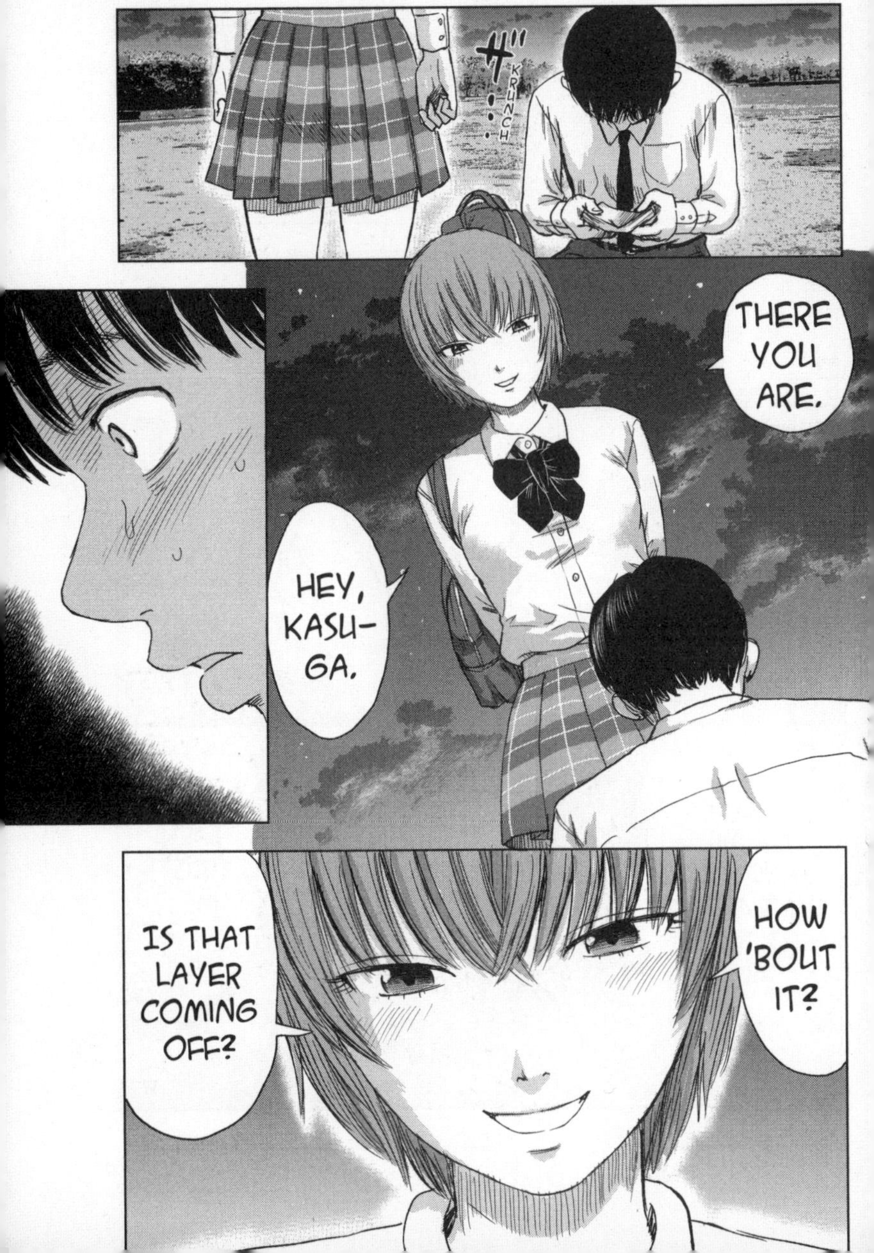
ザッ
KRUNCH
THERE YOU ARE.
HEY, KASU-GA.
HOW 'BOUT IT?
IS THAT LAYER COMING OFF?

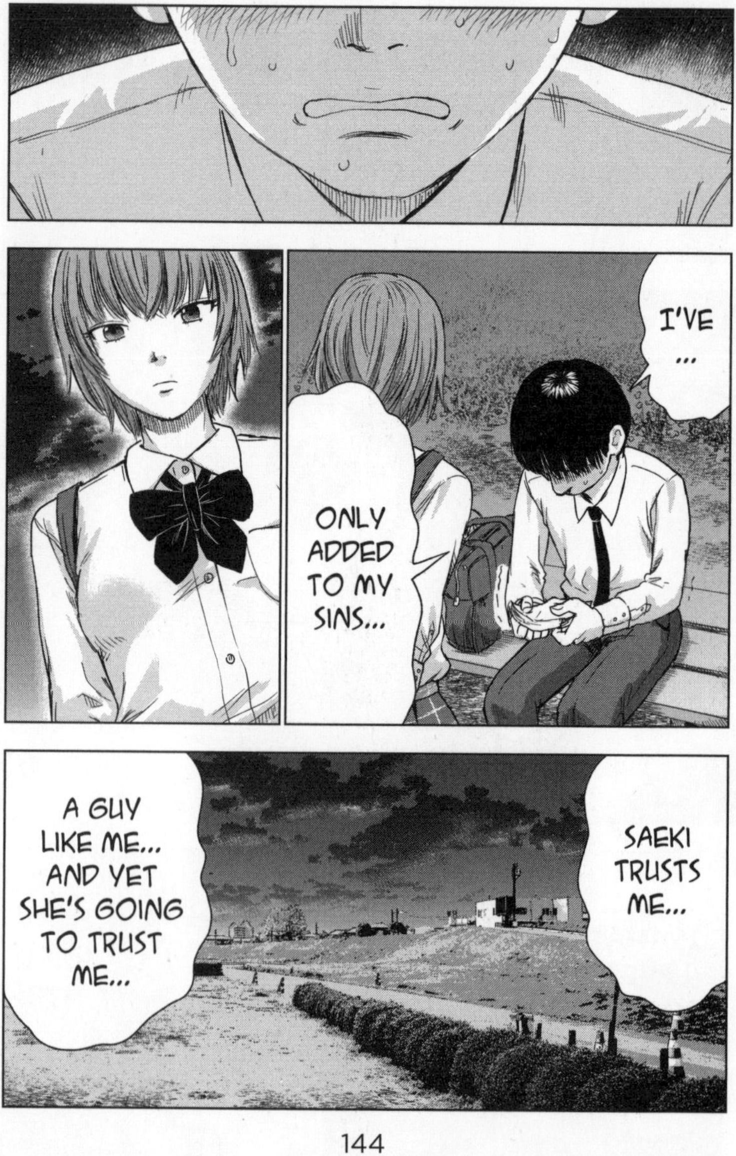
I'VE ...
ONLY ADDED TO MY SINS...
SAEKI TRUSTS ME...
A GUY LIKE ME... AND YET SHE'S GOING TO TRUST ME...

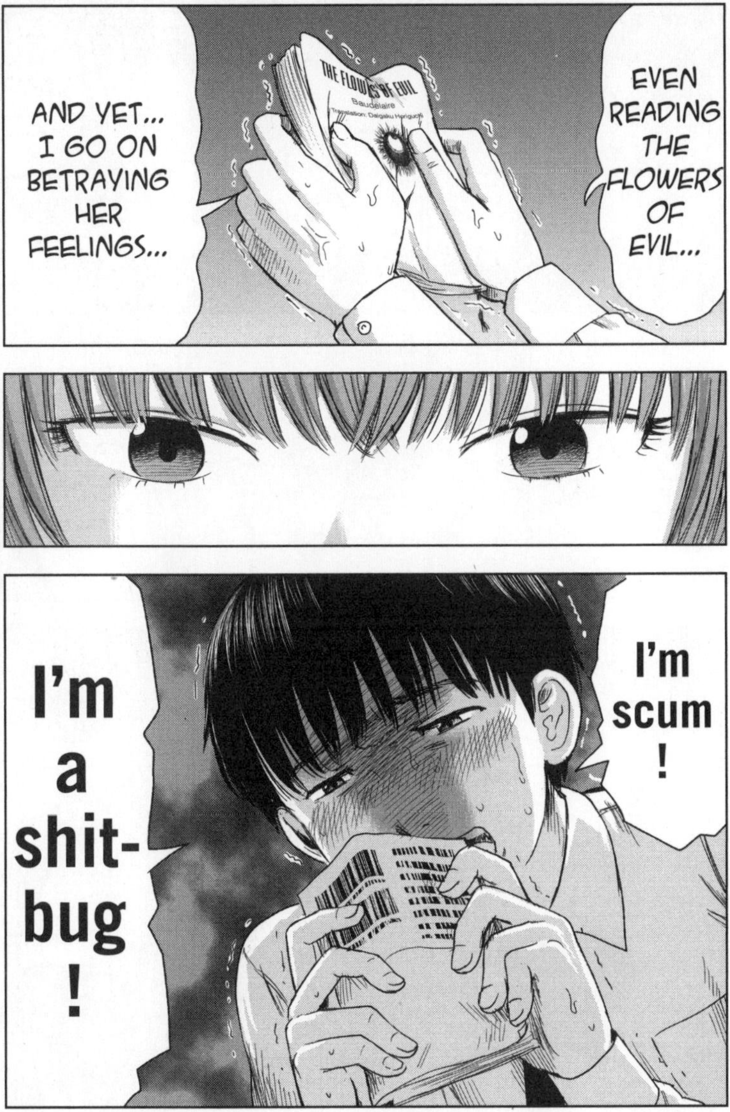
THE FLOWERS OF EVIL
Baudelaire
Translation: Daigaku Horiguchi
EVEN READING THE FLOWERS OF EVIL...
AND YET... I GO ON BETRAYING HER FEELINGS...
I'm scum!
I'm a shit-bug!

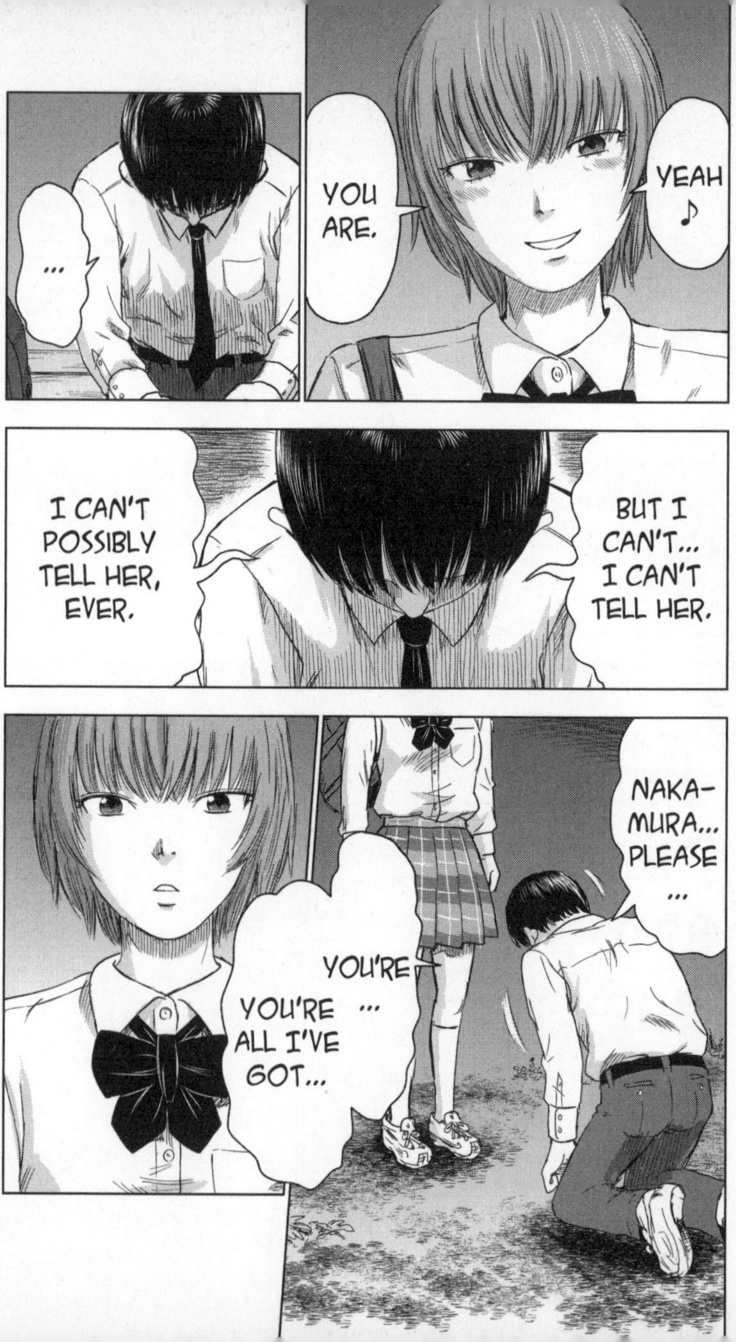
YEAH ♪
YOU ARE.
...
BUT I CAN'T... I CAN'T TELL HER.
I CAN'T POSSIBLY TELL HER, EVER.
NAKA-MURA... PLEASE ...
YOU'RE ...
YOU'RE ALL I'VE GOT...

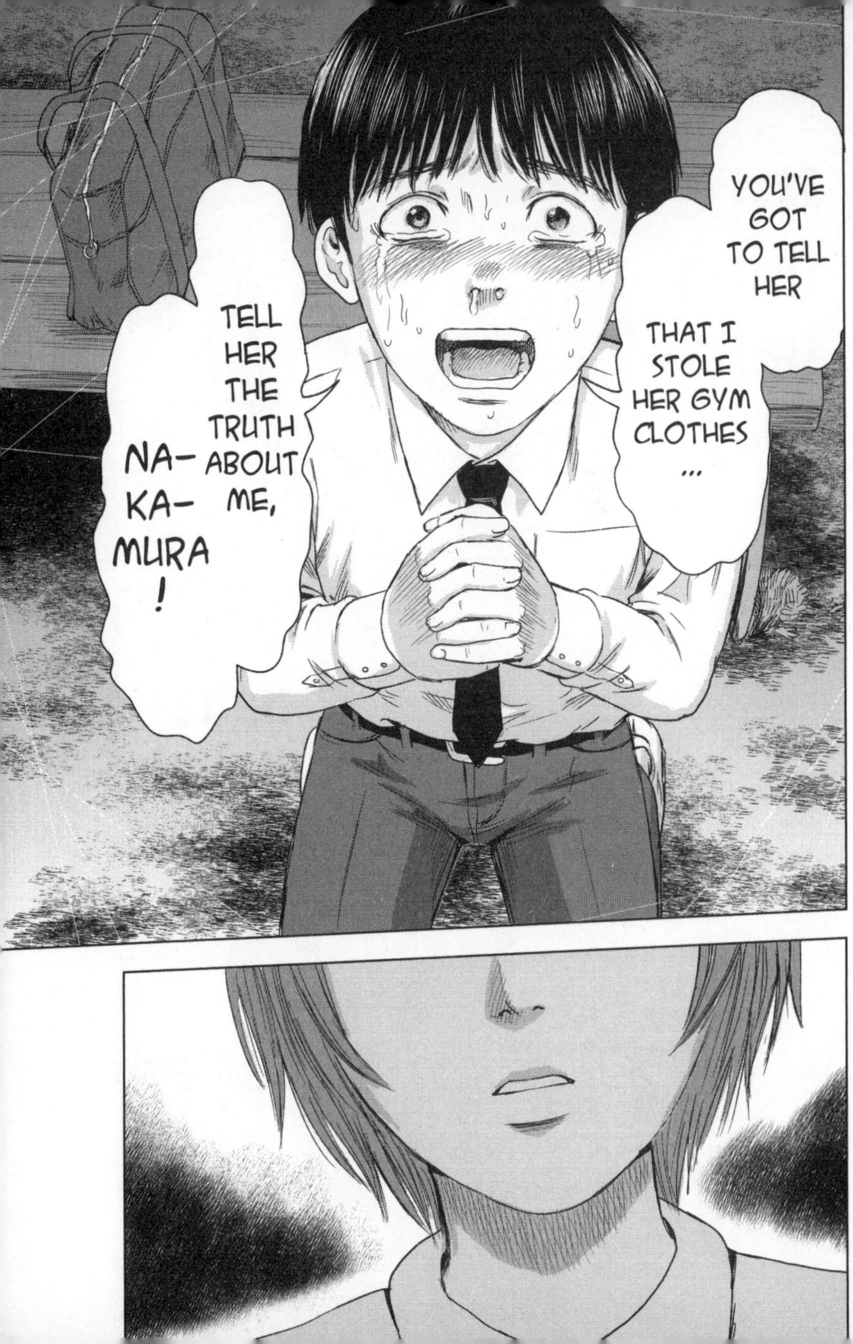
YOU'VE GOT TO TELL HER
THAT I STOLE HER GYM CLOTHES ...
TELL HER THE TRUTH ABOUT ME, NA-KA-MURA!

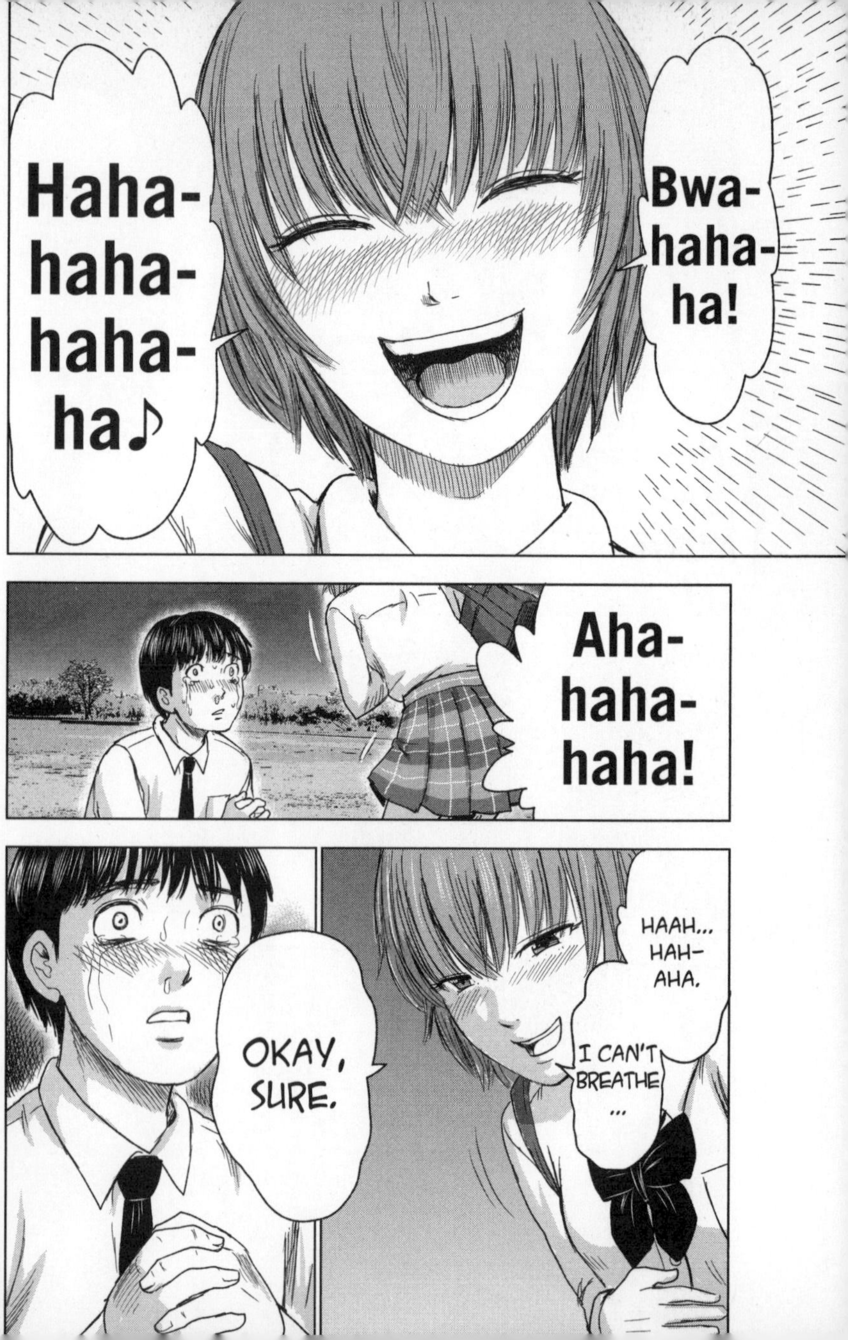
Bwa-haha-ha!
Haha-haha-haha-ha♪
Aha-haha-haha!
HAAH... HAH-AHA.
I CAN'T BREATHE ...
OKAY, SURE.

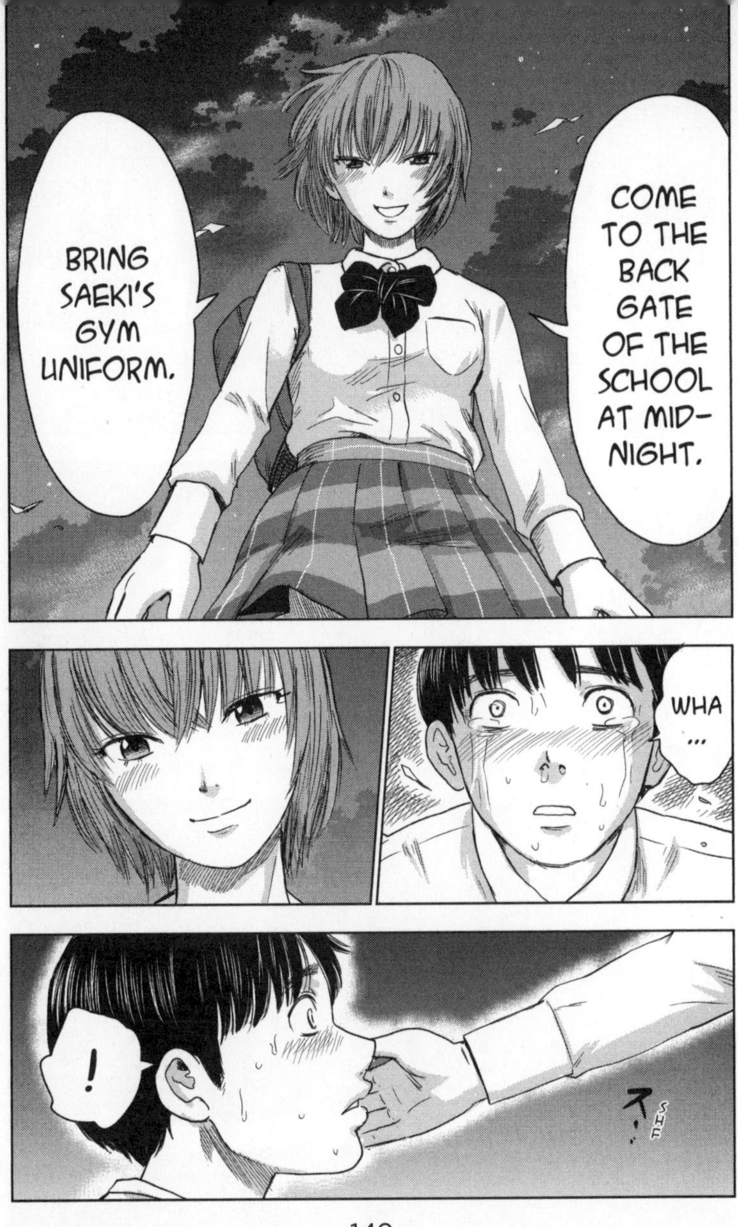
COME TO THE BACK GATE OF THE SCHOOL AT MID-NIGHT.
BRING SAEKI'S GYM UNIFORM.
WHA ...
ス..
SHH
!

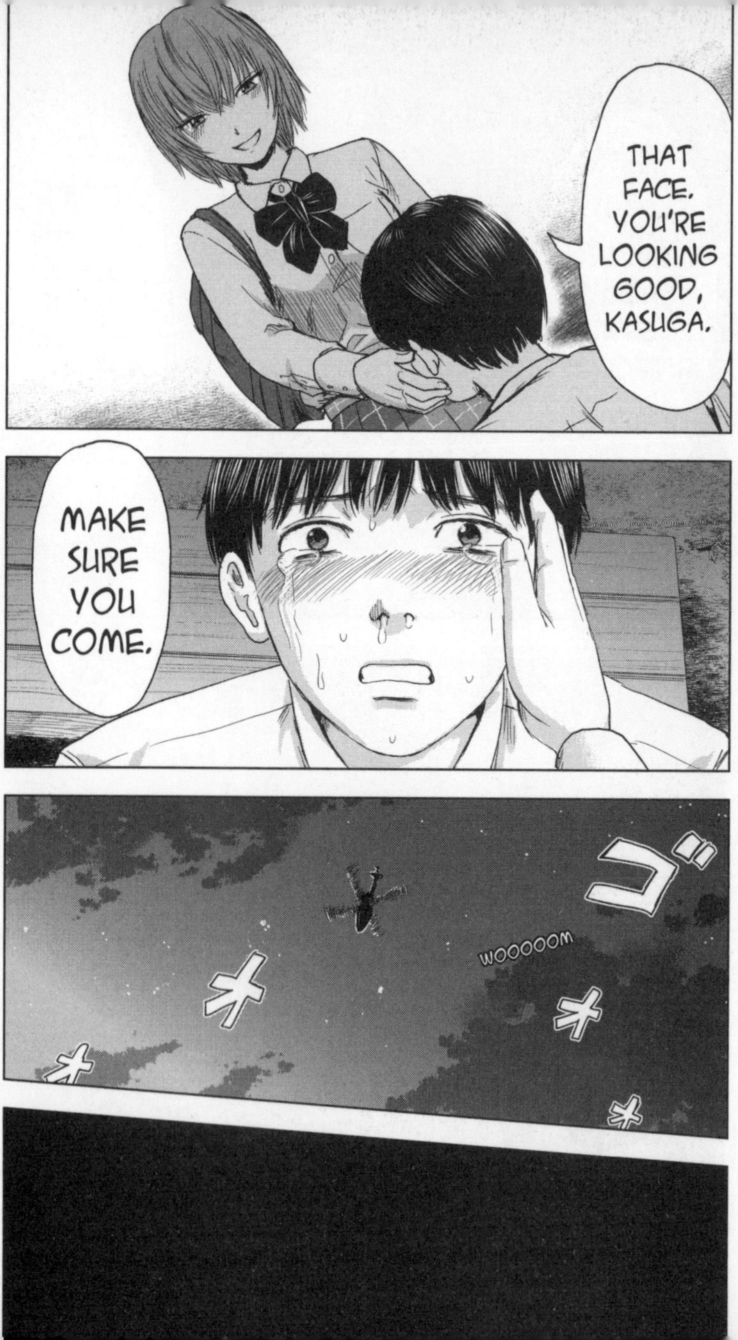
THAT FACE. YOU'RE LOOKING GOOD, KASUGA.
MAKE SURE YOU COME.
ゴオオオオ
WOOOOOM

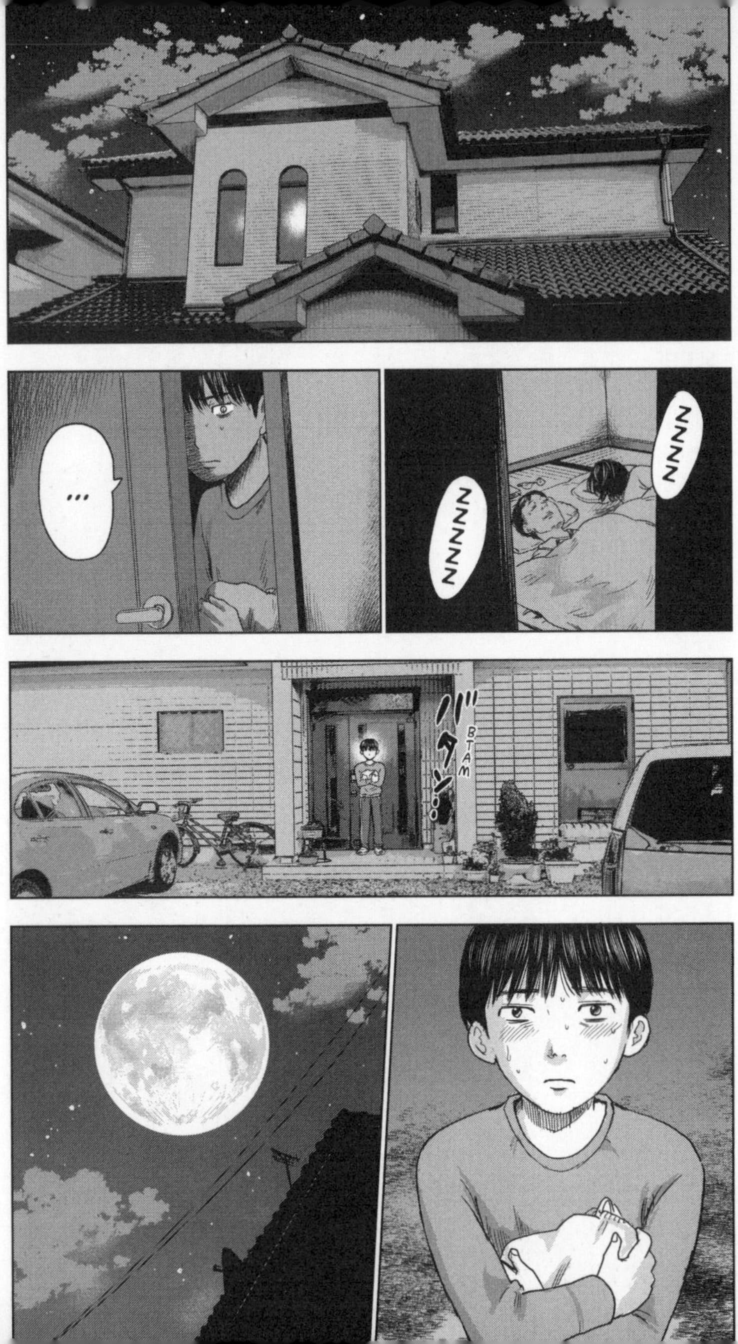
ZZZZ
ZZZZZ
...
バタン
BTAM

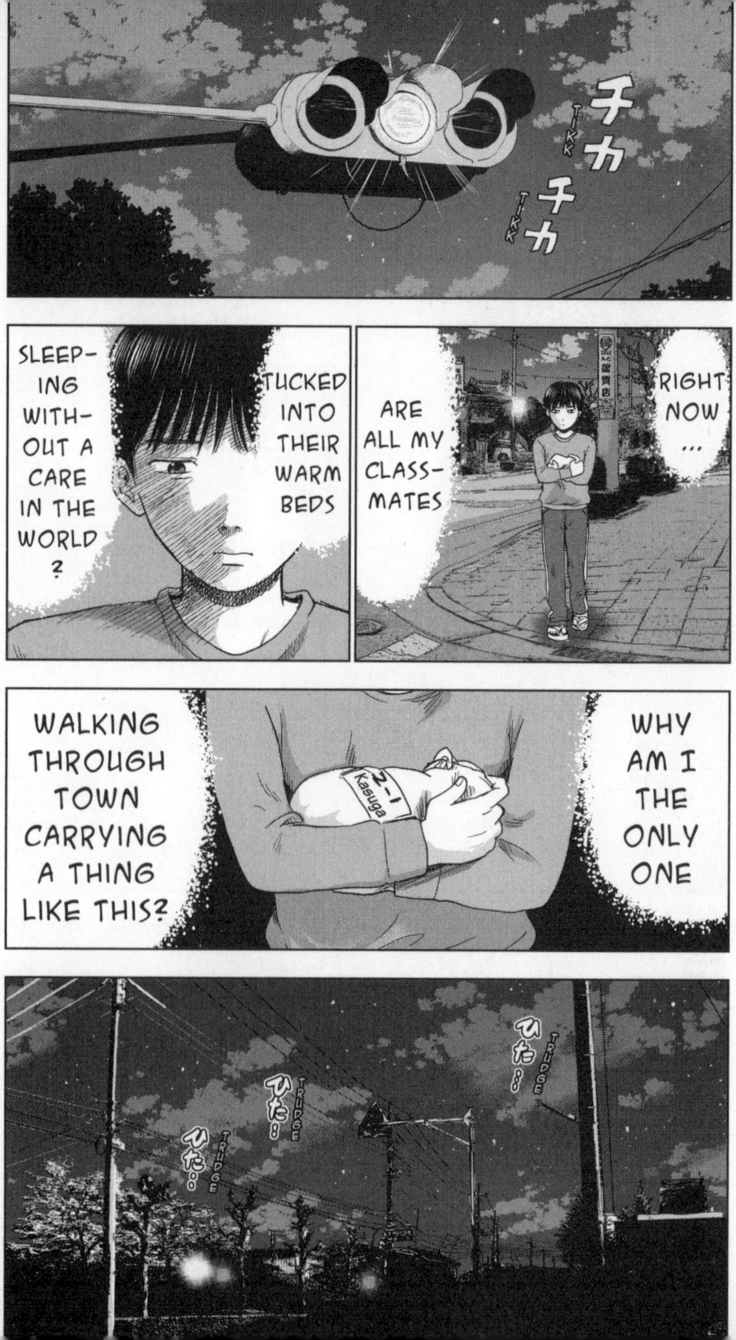
チカ
TIKK
チカ
TIKK
RIGHT NOW ...
ARE ALL MY CLASS-MATES
TUCKED INTO THEIR WARM BEDS
SLEEP-ING WITH-OUT A CARE IN THE WORLD?
WHY AM I THE ONLY ONE
2-1
Kasuga
WALKING THROUGH TOWN CARRYING A THING LIKE THIS?
ひた..
TRUDGE
ひた..
TRUDGE
ひた..
TRUDGE

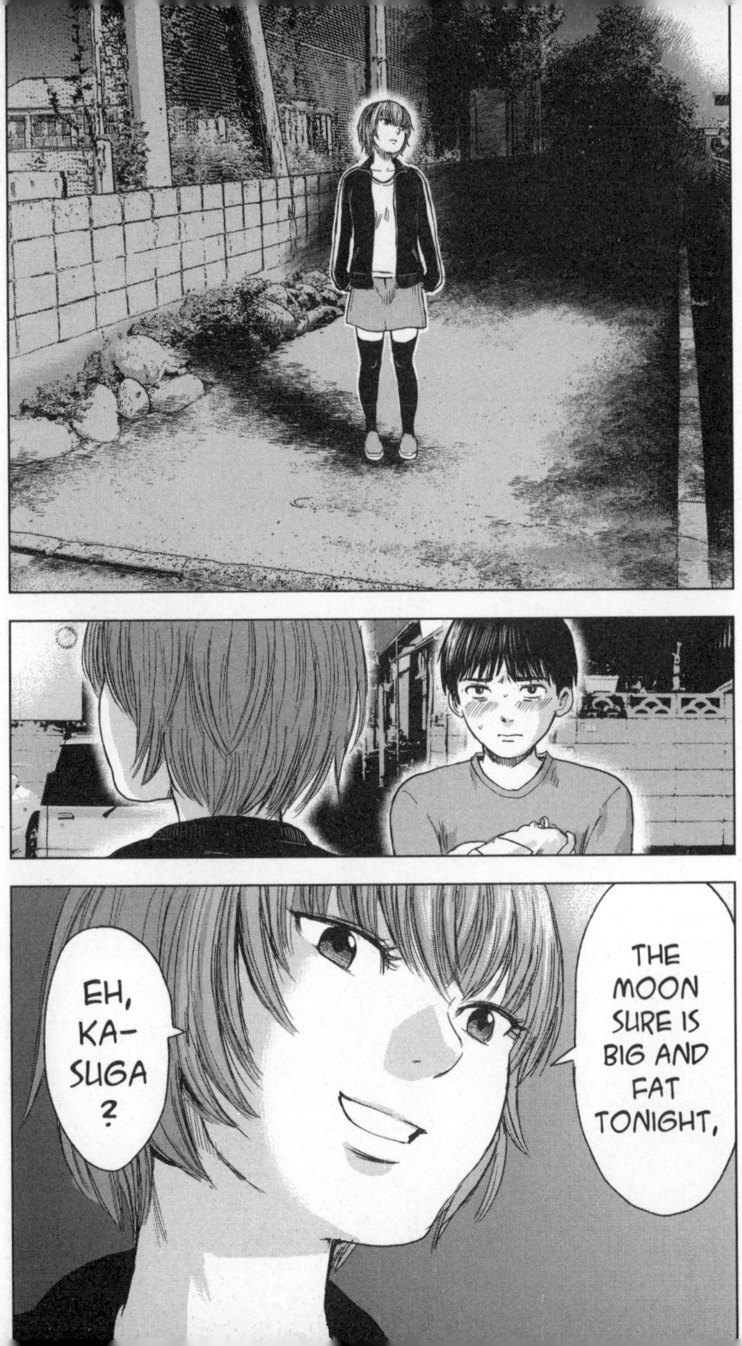
THE MOON SURE IS BIG AND FAT TONIGHT,
EH, KA-SUGA?

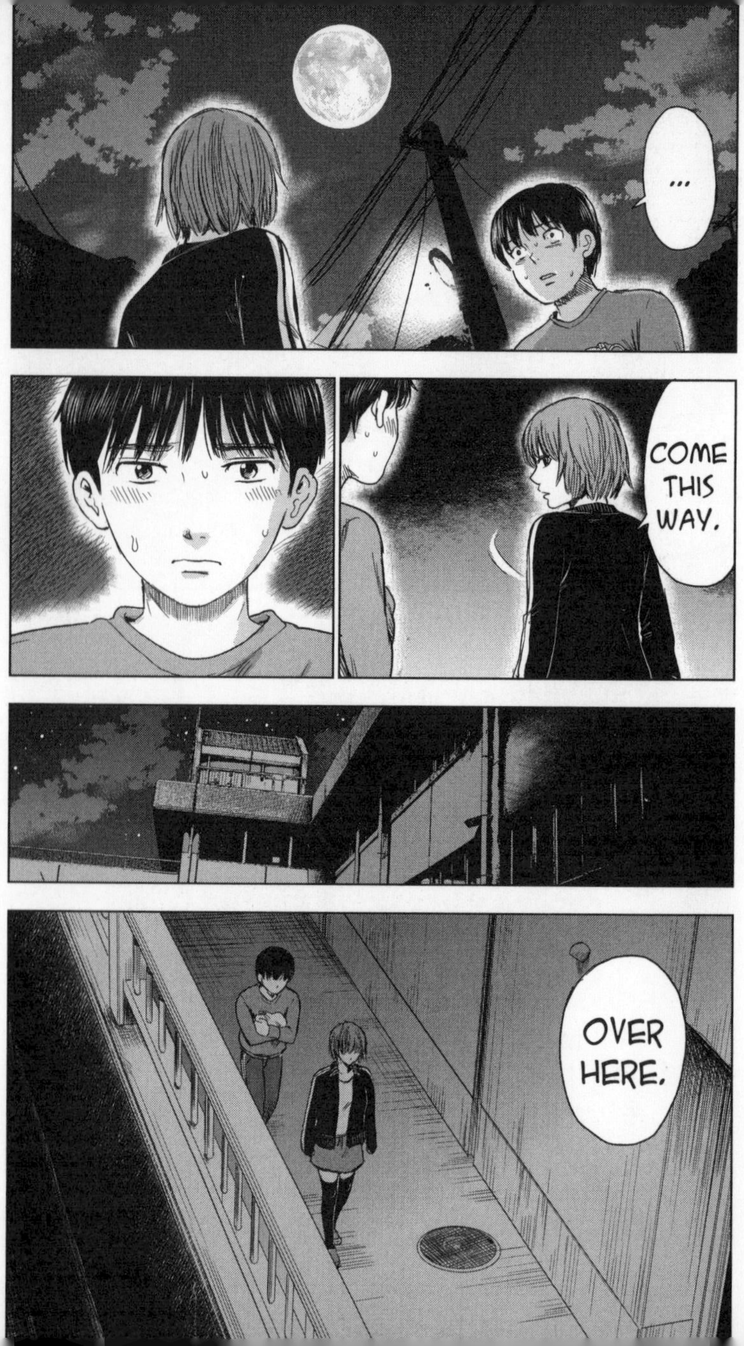
...
COME THIS WAY.
OVER HERE.

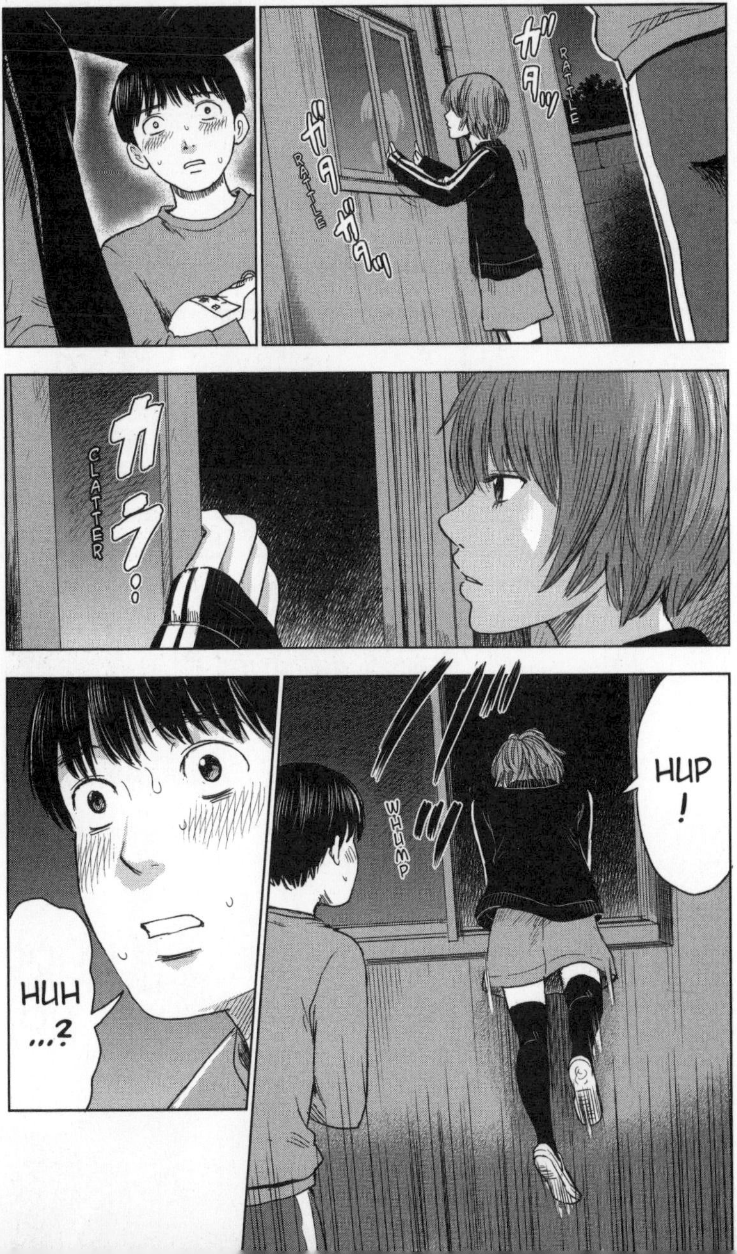

ガタッ
RATTLE
ガタガタッ
RATTLE
カラ..
CLATTER
HUP!
WHUMP
HUH ...?

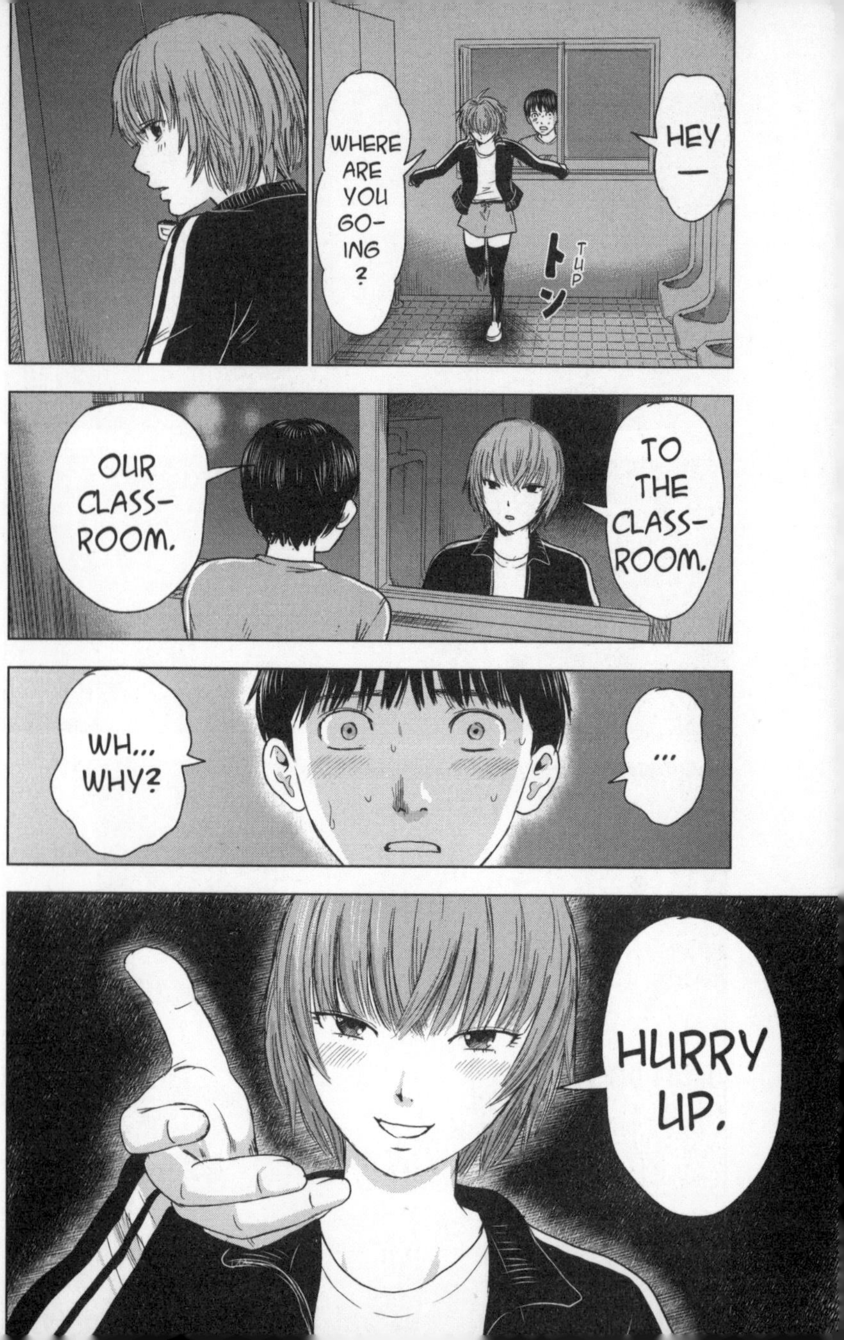
HEY —
WHERE ARE YOU GO-ING?
トン
TUP
TO THE CLASS-ROOM.
OUR CLASS-ROOM.
...
WH... WHY?
HURRY UP.

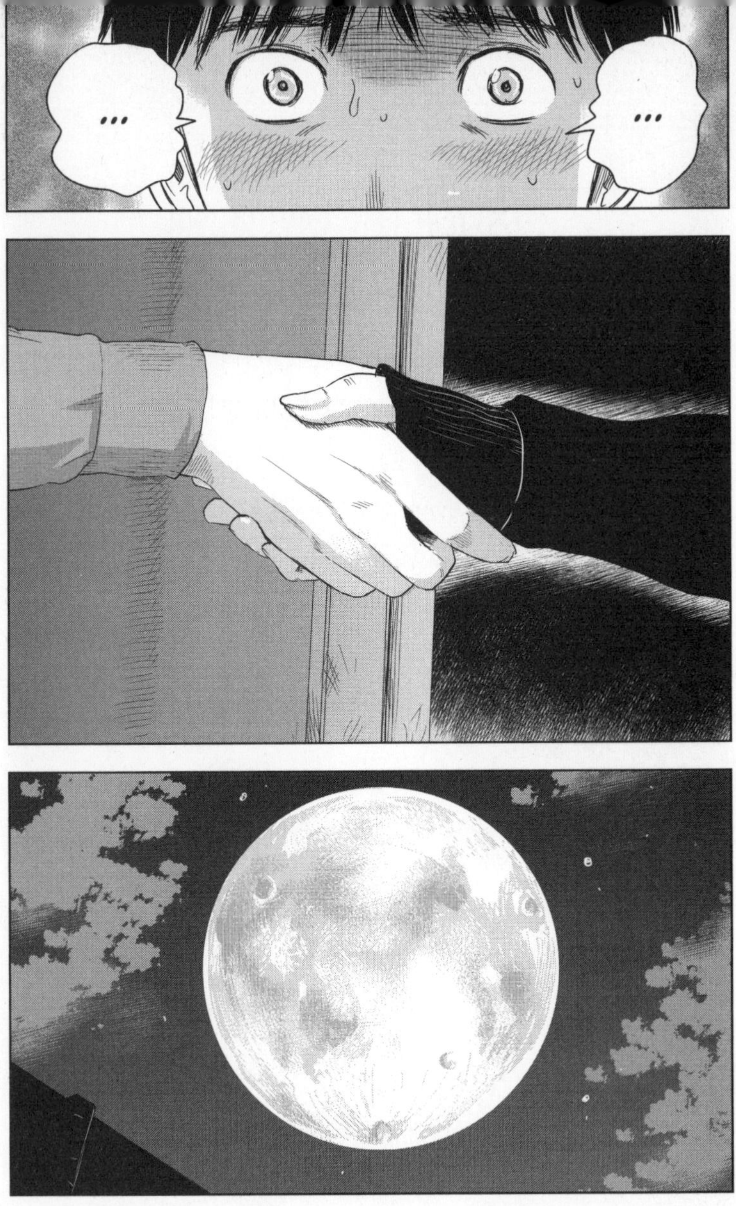
...
...

Afterword

Chapter 12

Back when I was in junior high, when I was done with cram school I'd often go back to the school at night for no reason, and hang out on the emergency stairs. Nowadays I kill time at pubs, karaoke, or manga cafes, but back then the only places I could go were pretty much the riverbank, the school stairs, and the bookstore. I'd go there, and feel endless angst.

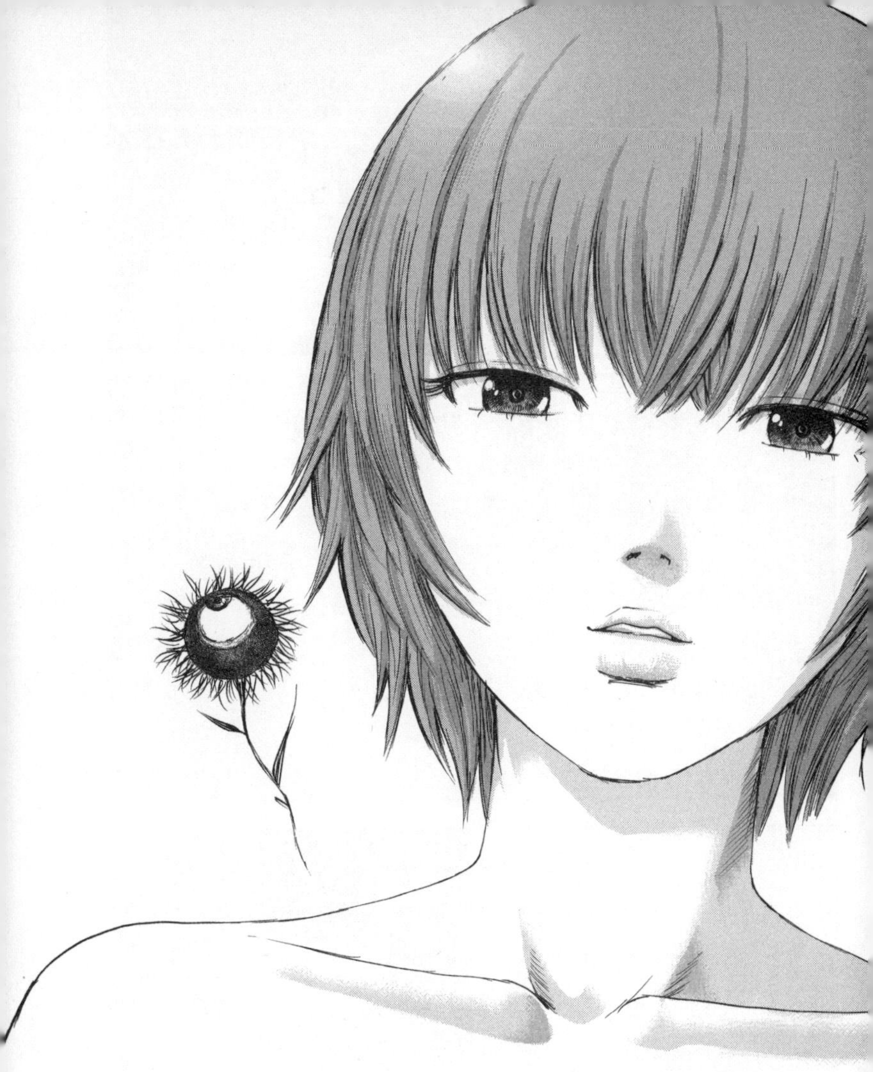

Chapter 12: That Which Punishes Self and Soul

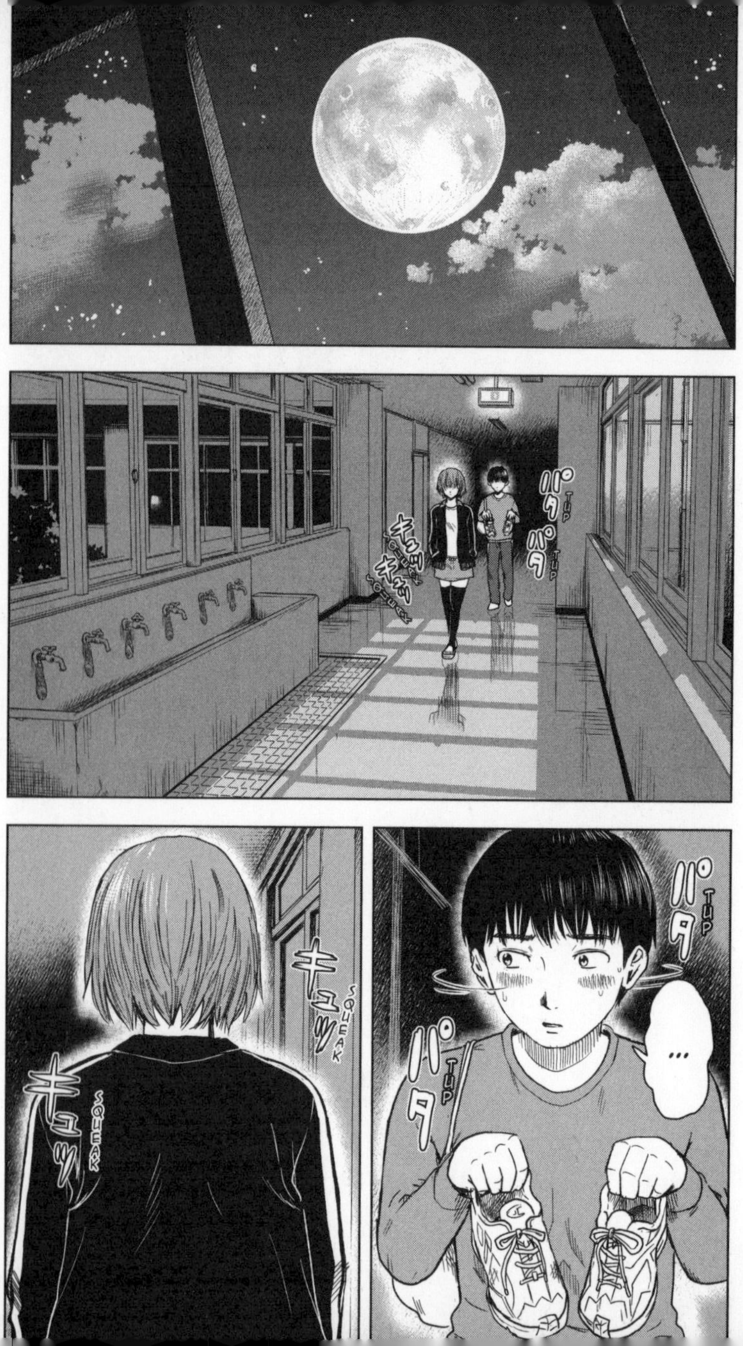
パタ
TUP
パタ
TUP
キュッ
SQUEAK
キュッ
SQUEAK
パタ
TUP
パタ
TUP
...
キュッ
SQUEAK
キュッ
SQUEAK

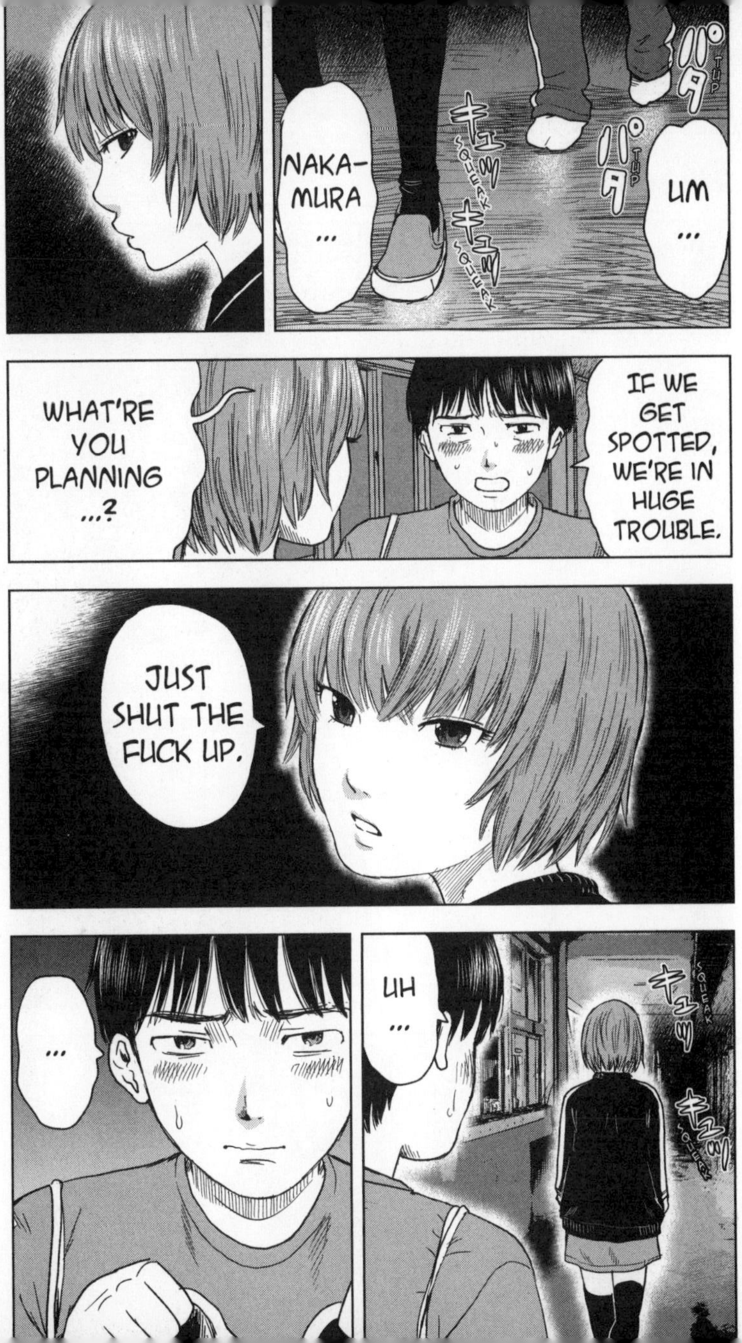
TUP
TUP
UM ...
SQUEAK
SQUEAK
NAKA-MURA ...
IF WE GET SPOTTED, WE'RE IN HUGE TROUBLE.
WHAT'RE YOU PLANNING ...?
JUST SHUT THE FUCK UP.
SQUEAK
SQUEAK
UH ...
...

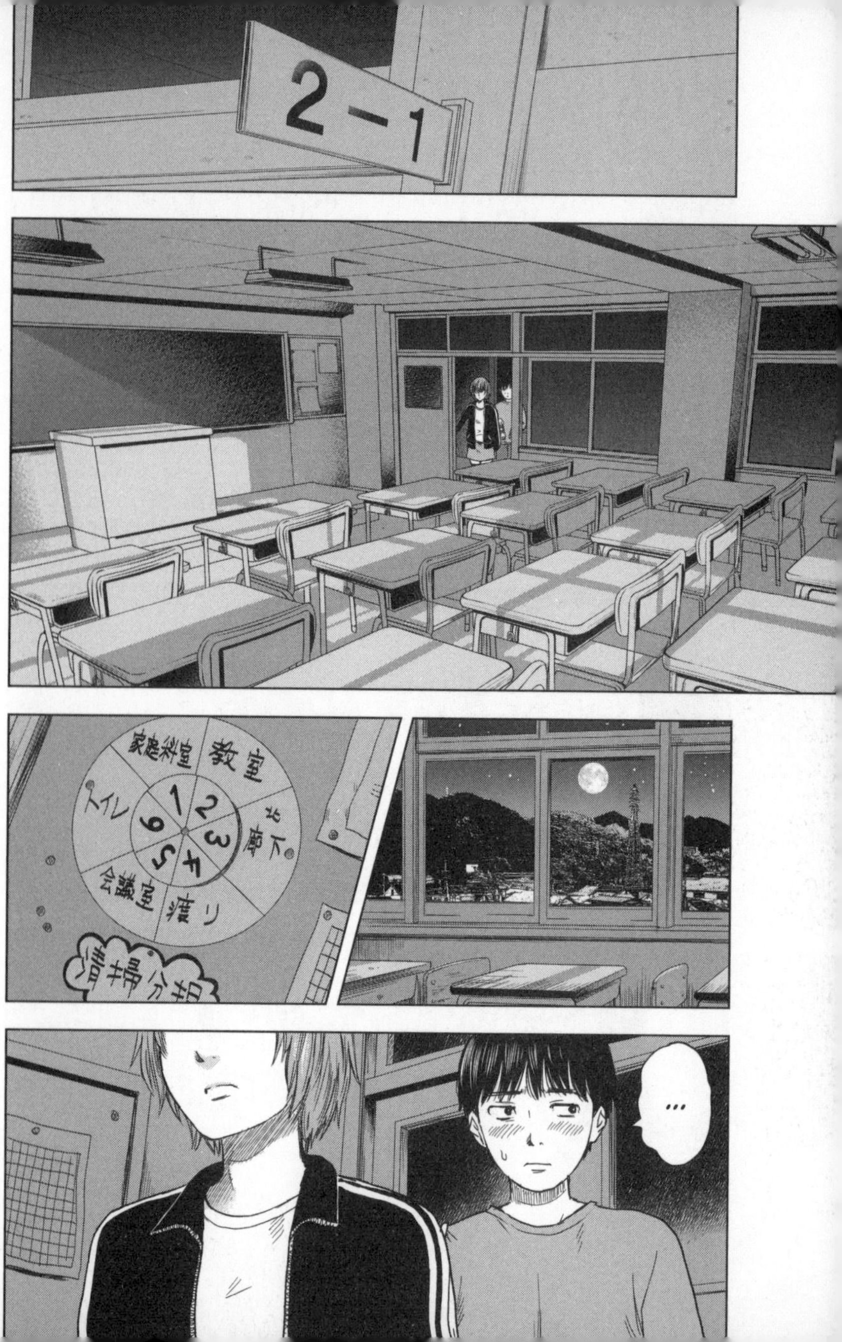
2-1
清掃分担
教室
廊下
渡り
会議室
トイレ
家庭科室
…

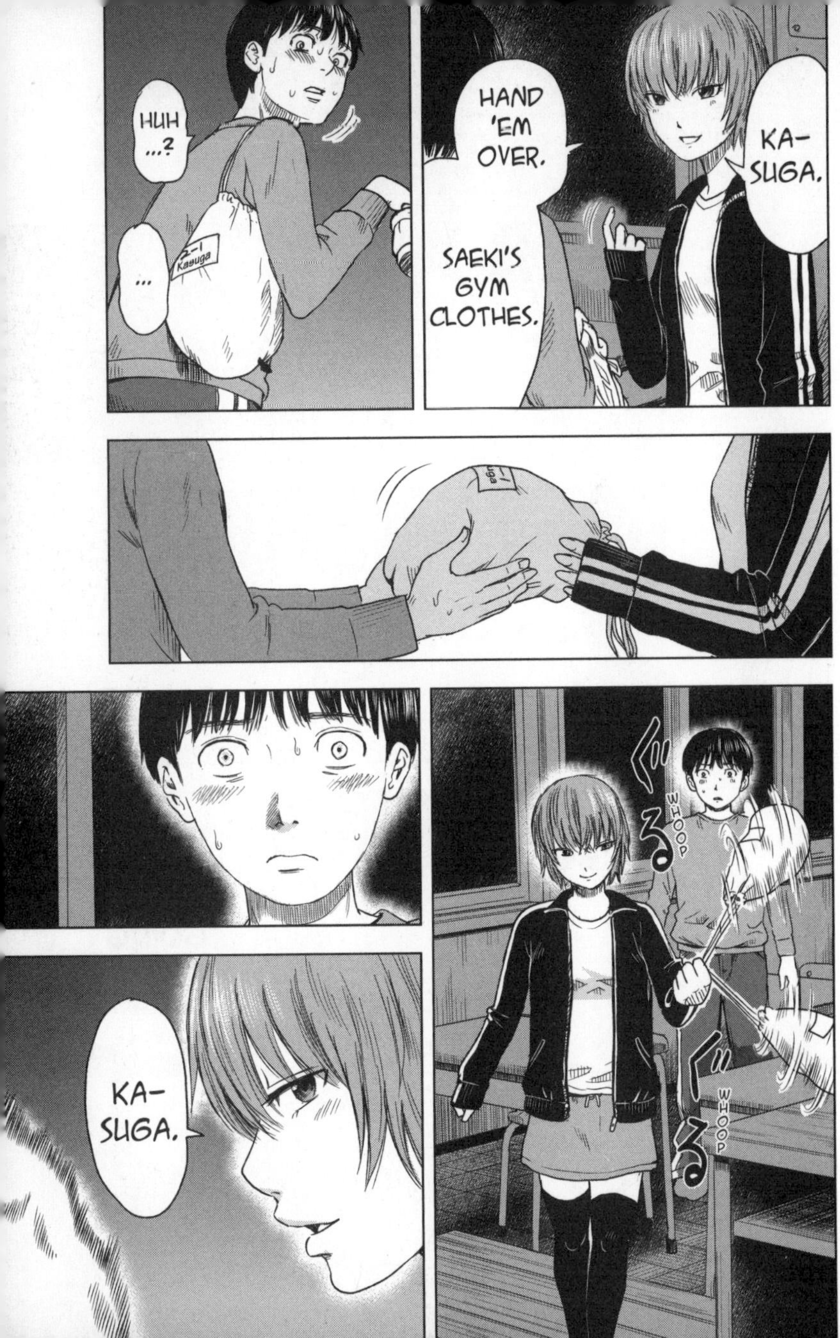
KA-SUGA.
HAND 'EM OVER.
SAEKI'S GYM CLOTHES.
HUH ...?
...
2-1 Kasuga
WHOOP
WHOOP
KA-SUGA.

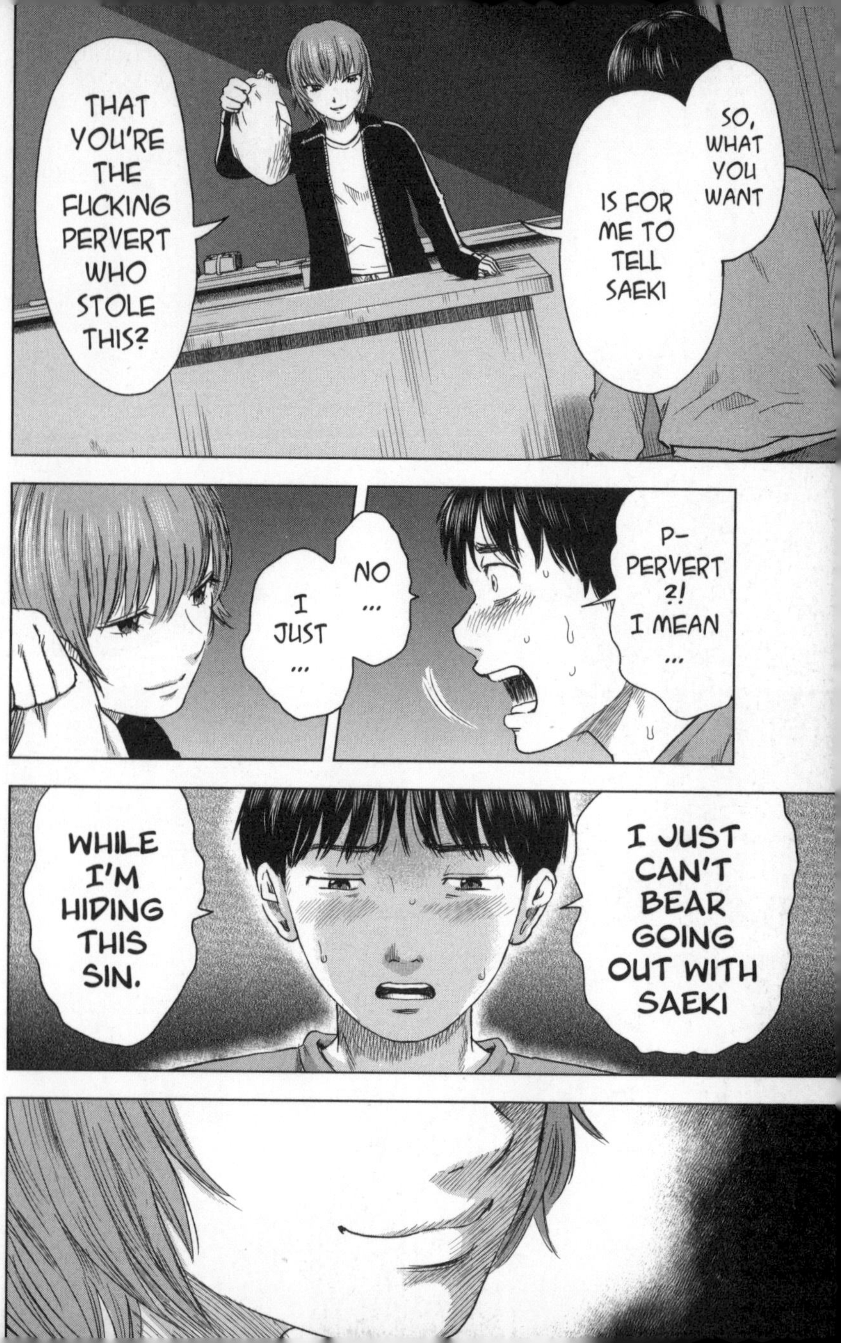
SO, WHAT YOU WANT IS FOR ME TO TELL SAEKI
THAT YOU'RE THE FUCKING PERVERT WHO STOLE THIS?
P-PERVERT?! I MEAN ...
NO ... I JUST ...
I JUST CAN'T BEAR GOING OUT WITH SAEKI
WHILE I'M HIDING THIS SIN.

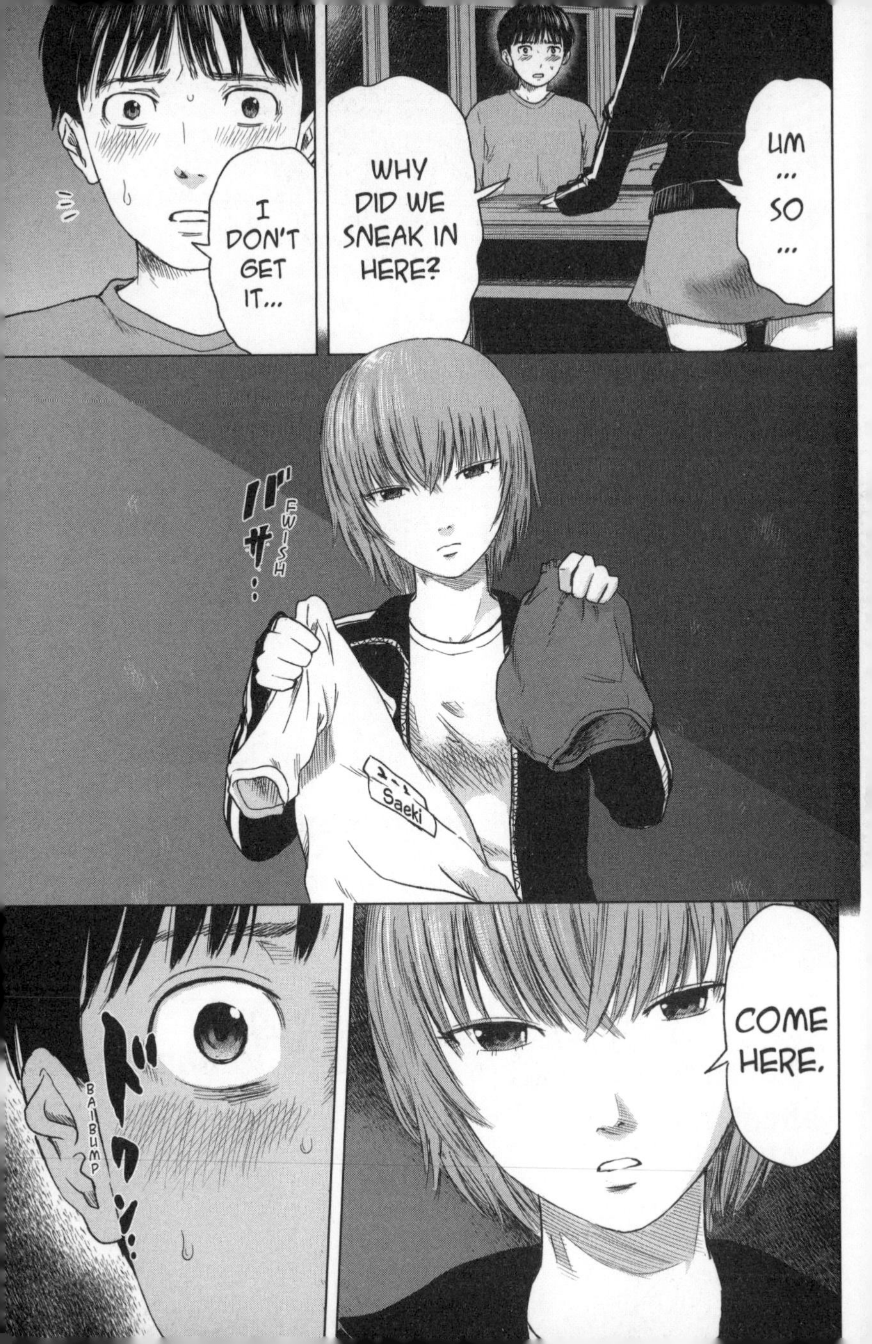
UM ... SO ...
WHY DID WE SNEAK IN HERE?
I DON'T GET IT...
FWISH
Saeki
COME HERE.
BAIBUMP

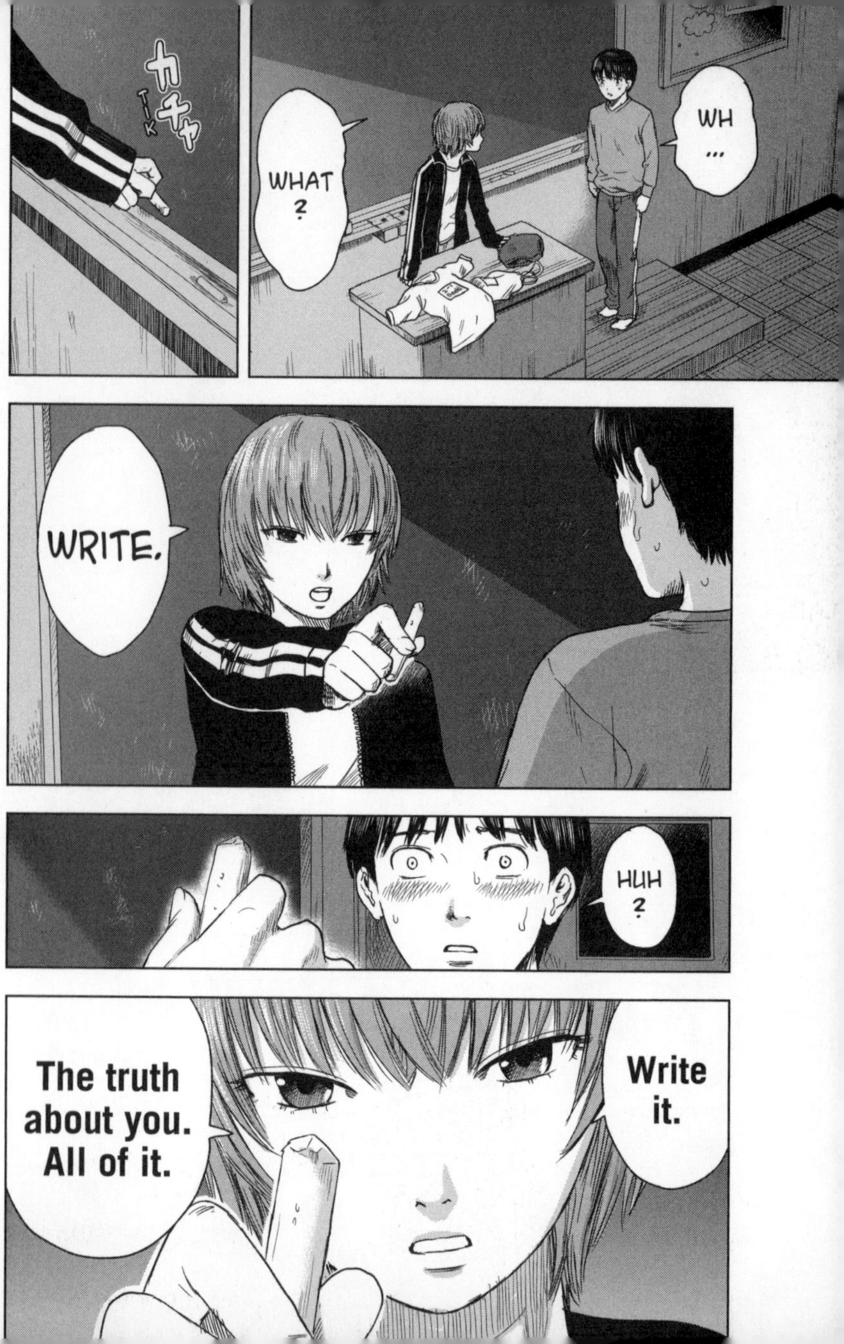
WH ...
WHAT?
カチャ
TIK
WRITE.
HUH?
Write it.
The truth about you. All of it.

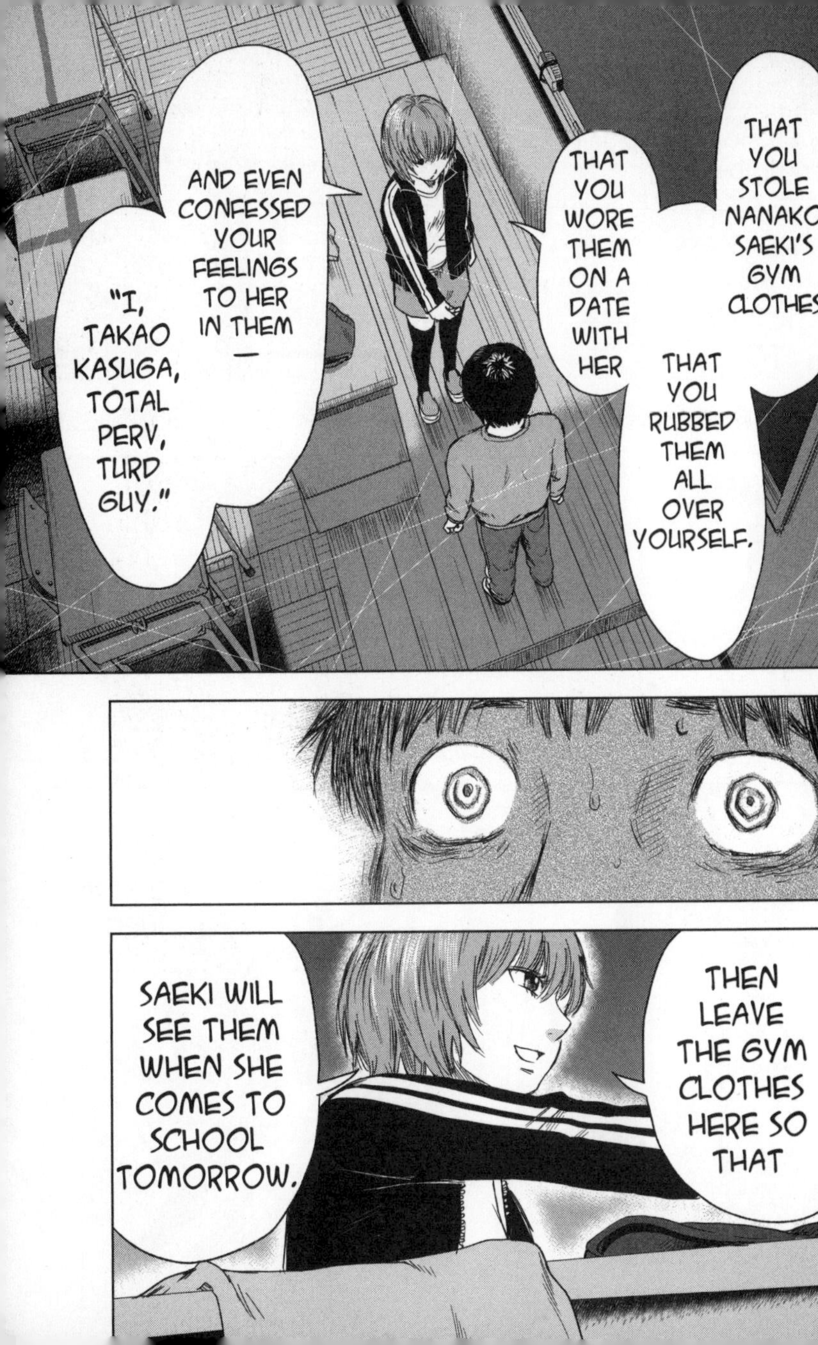
THAT YOU STOLE NANAKO SAEKI'S GYM CLOTHES.
THAT YOU RUBBED THEM ALL OVER YOURSELF.
THAT YOU WORE THEM ON A DATE WITH HER
AND EVEN CONFESSED YOUR FEELINGS TO HER IN THEM —
"I, TAKAO KASUGA, TOTAL PERV, TURD GUY."
THEN LEAVE THE GYM CLOTHES HERE SO THAT
SAEKI WILL SEE THEM WHEN SHE COMES TO SCHOOL TOMORROW.

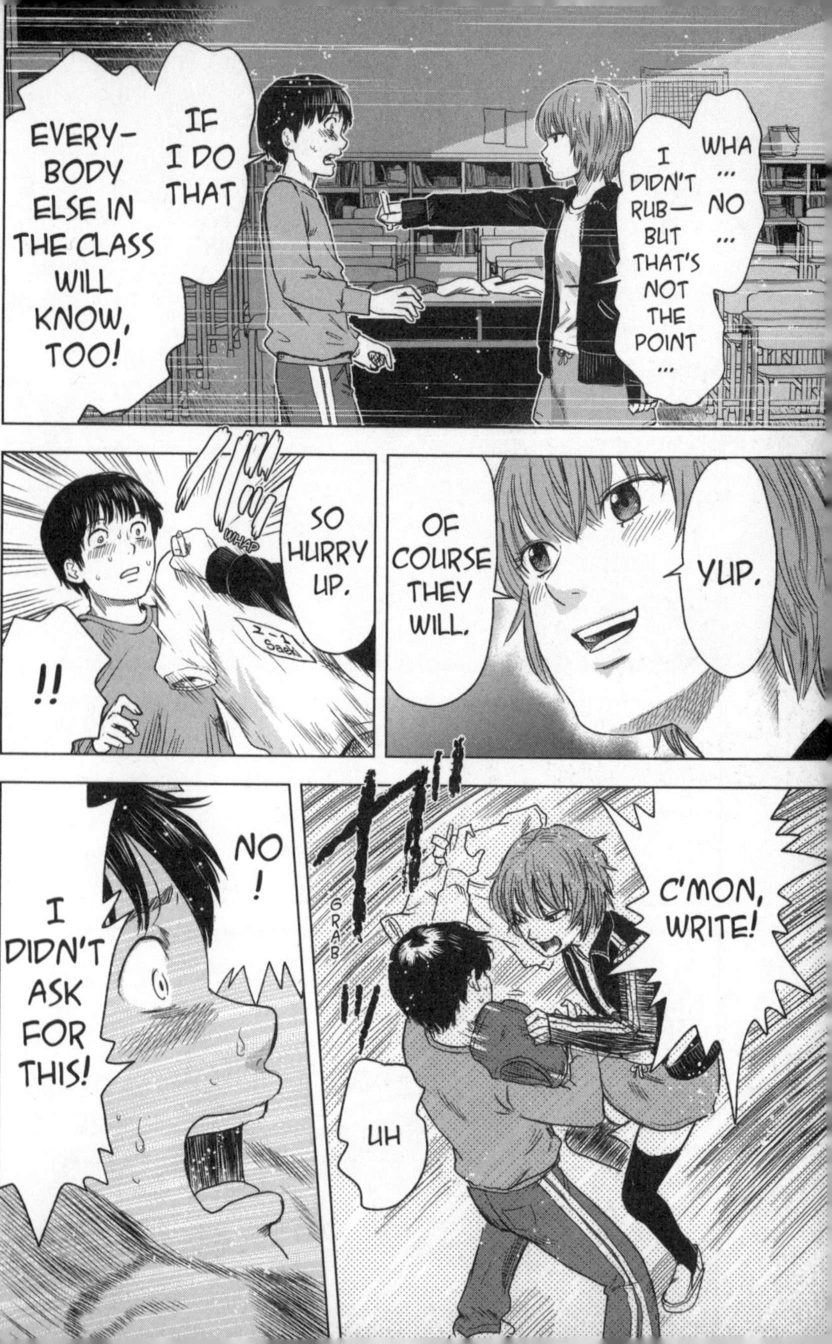
WHA... NO...
I DIDN'T RUB— BUT THAT'S NOT THE POINT...
IF I DO THAT
EVERYBODY ELSE IN THE CLASS WILL KNOW, TOO!
YUP.
OF COURSE THEY WILL.
SO HURRY UP.
WHAP
2-1 Saeki
!!
C'MON, WRITE!
GRAB
UH
NO!
I DIDN'T ASK FOR THIS!

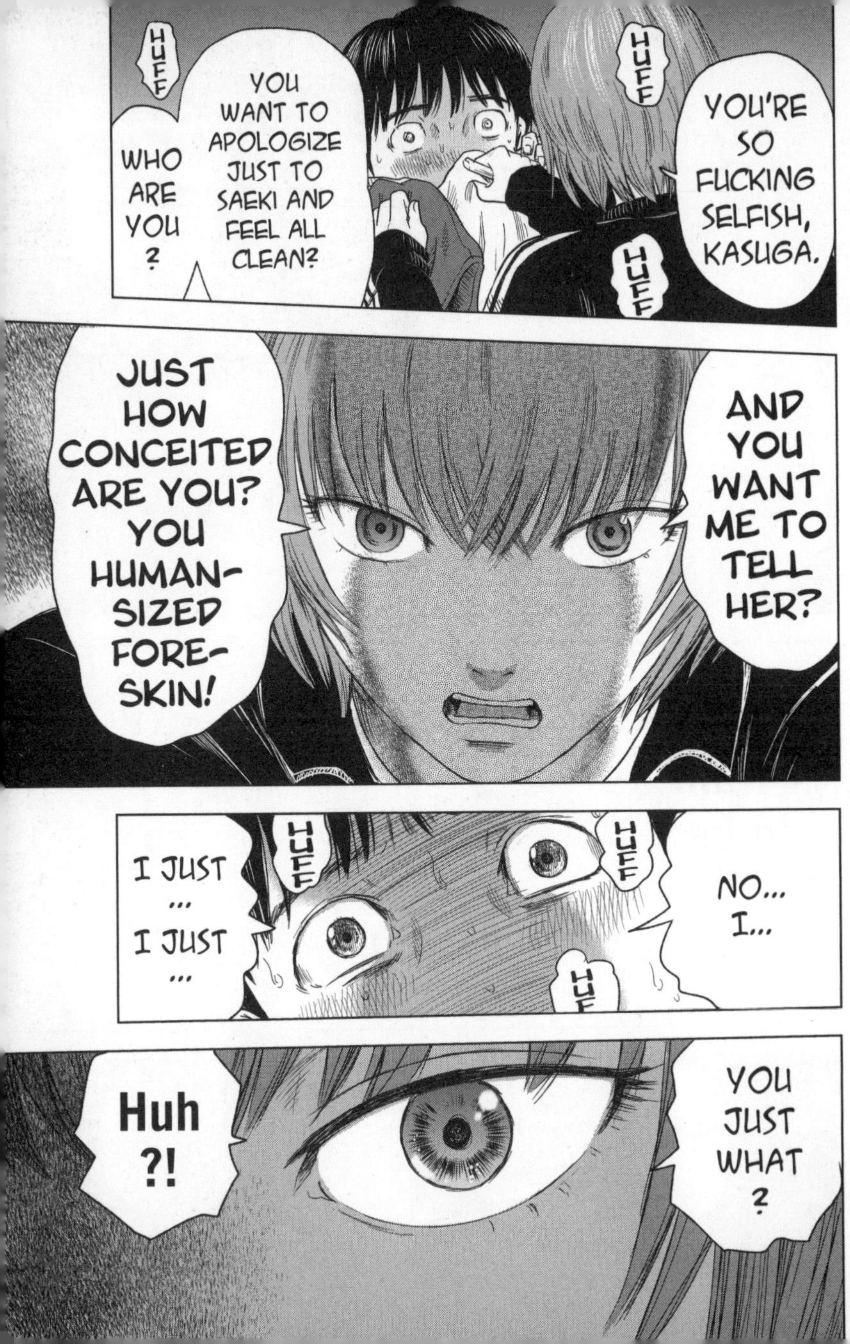
HUFF
YOU'RE SO FUCKING SELFISH, KASUGA.
HUFF
YOU WANT TO APOLOGIZE JUST TO SAEKI AND FEEL ALL CLEAN?
HUFF
WHO ARE YOU?
AND YOU WANT ME TO TELL HER?
JUST HOW CONCEITED ARE YOU? YOU HUMAN-SIZED FORE-SKIN!
NO... I...
HUFF
HUFF
I JUST... I JUST...
HUFF
YOU JUST WHAT?
Huh?!

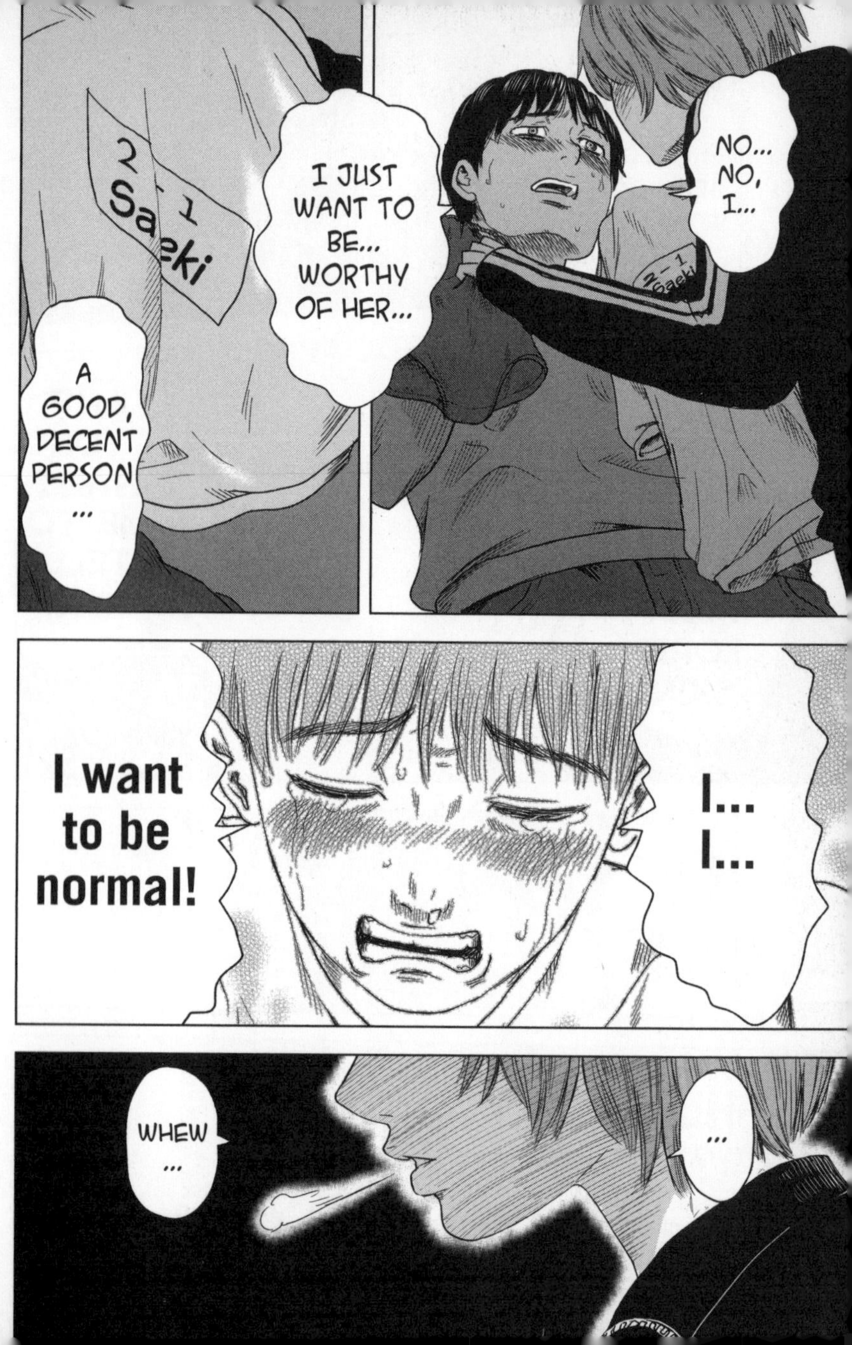
NO... NO, I...
2-1 Saeki
I JUST WANT TO BE... WORTHY OF HER...
2-1 Saeki
A GOOD, DECENT PERSON ...
I... I...
I want to be normal!
...
WHEW ...

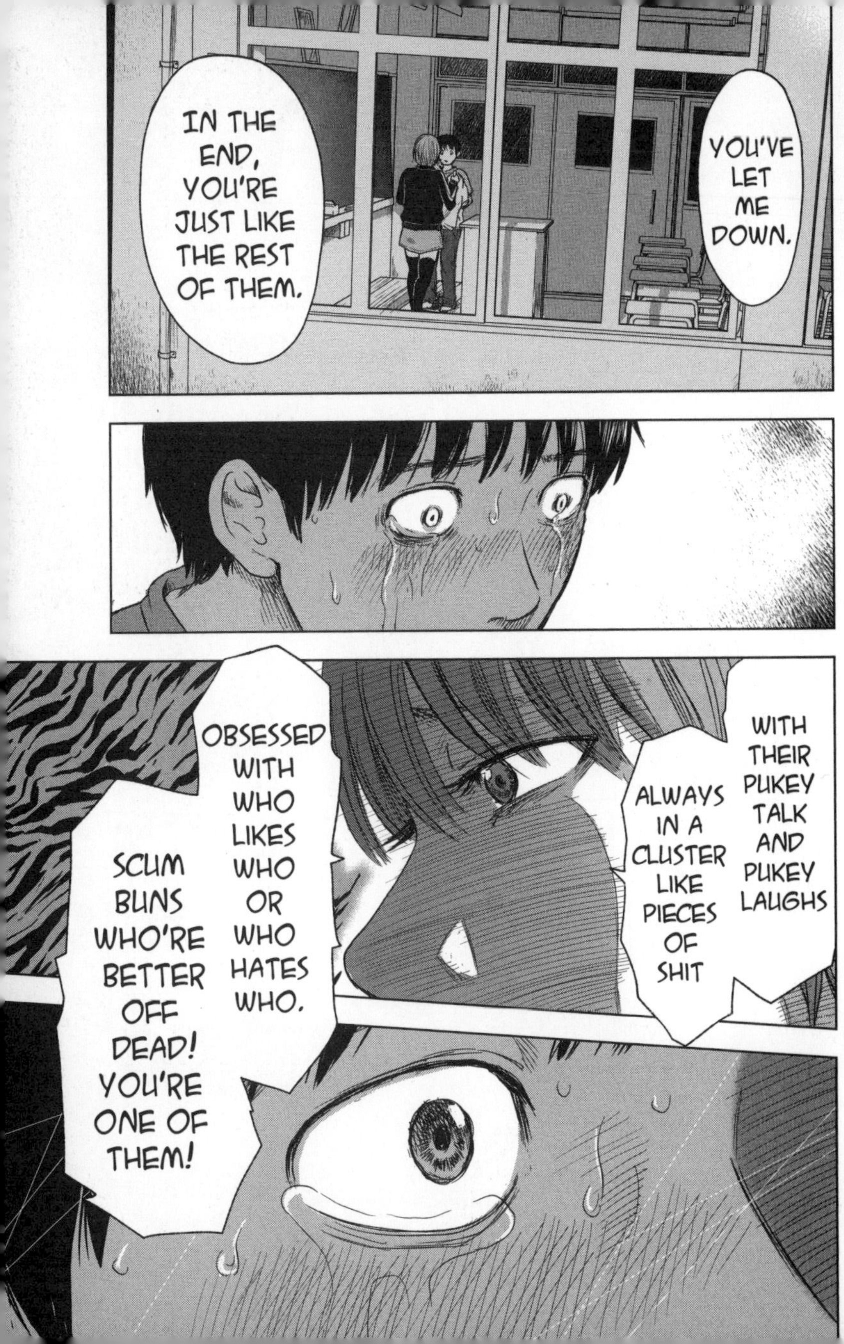
YOU'VE LET ME DOWN.
IN THE END, YOU'RE JUST LIKE THE REST OF THEM.
WITH THEIR PUKEY TALK AND PUKEY LAUGHS
ALWAYS IN A CLUSTER LIKE PIECES OF SHIT
OBSESSED WITH WHO LIKES WHO OR WHO HATES WHO.
SCUM BUNS WHO'RE BETTER OFF DEAD! YOU'RE ONE OF THEM!

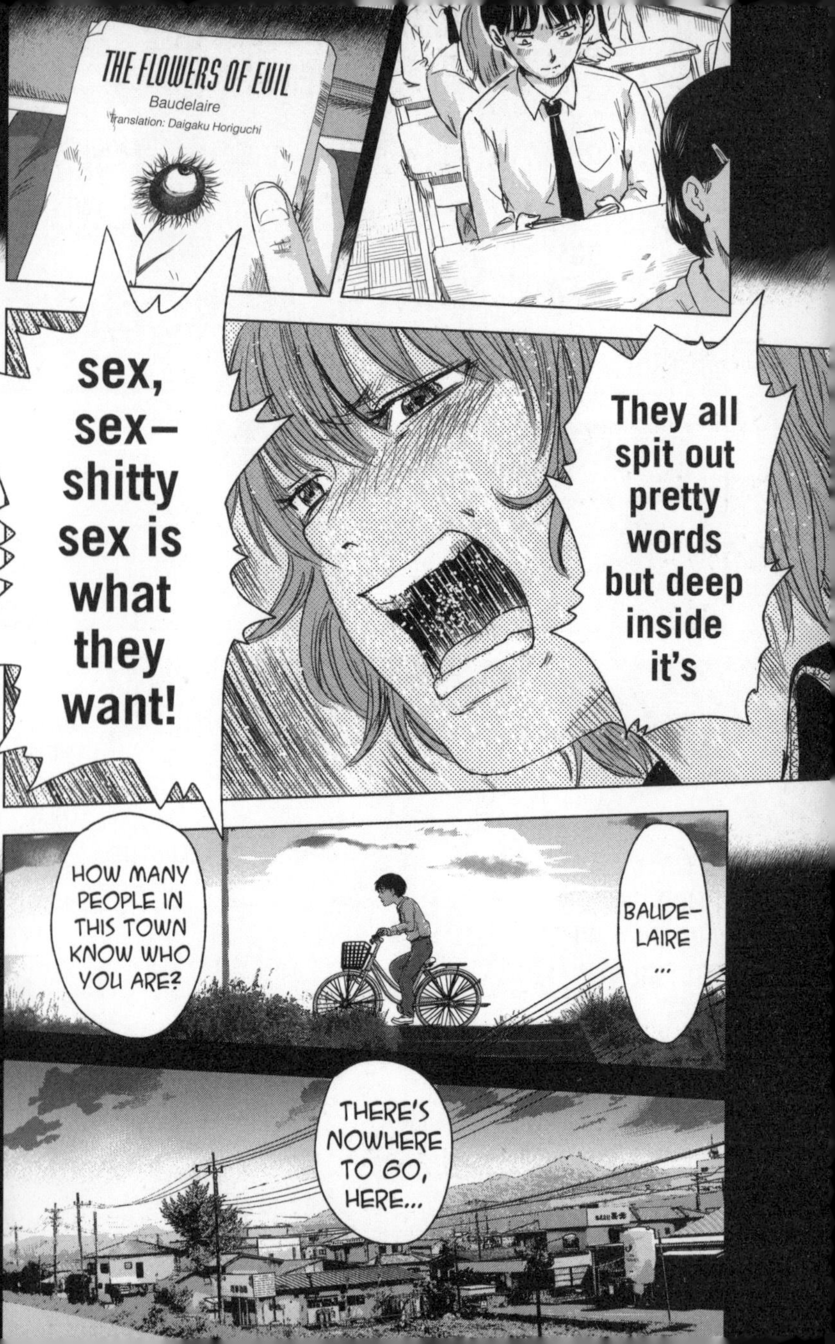
THE FLOWERS OF EVIL
Baudelaire
Translation: Daigaku Horiguchi
They all spit out pretty words but deep inside it's
sex, sex– shitty sex is what they want!
BAUDE-LAIRE ...
HOW MANY PEOPLE IN THIS TOWN KNOW WHO YOU ARE?
THERE'S NOWHERE TO GO, HERE...

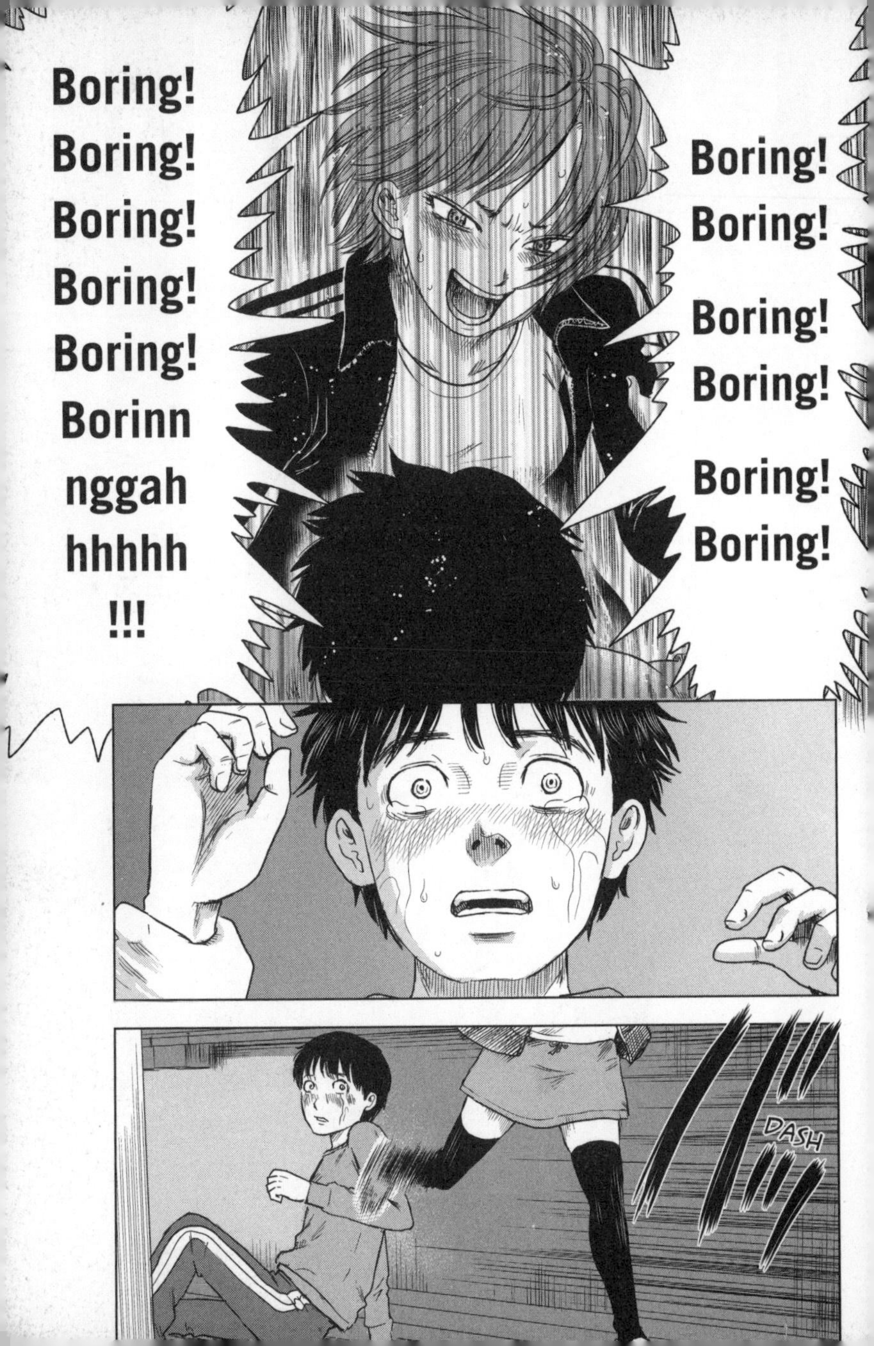
Boring! Boring!
Boring! Boring!
Boring! Boring!
Boring! Boring! Boring! Boring! Boring! Borinnnggahhhhhh!!!
DASH

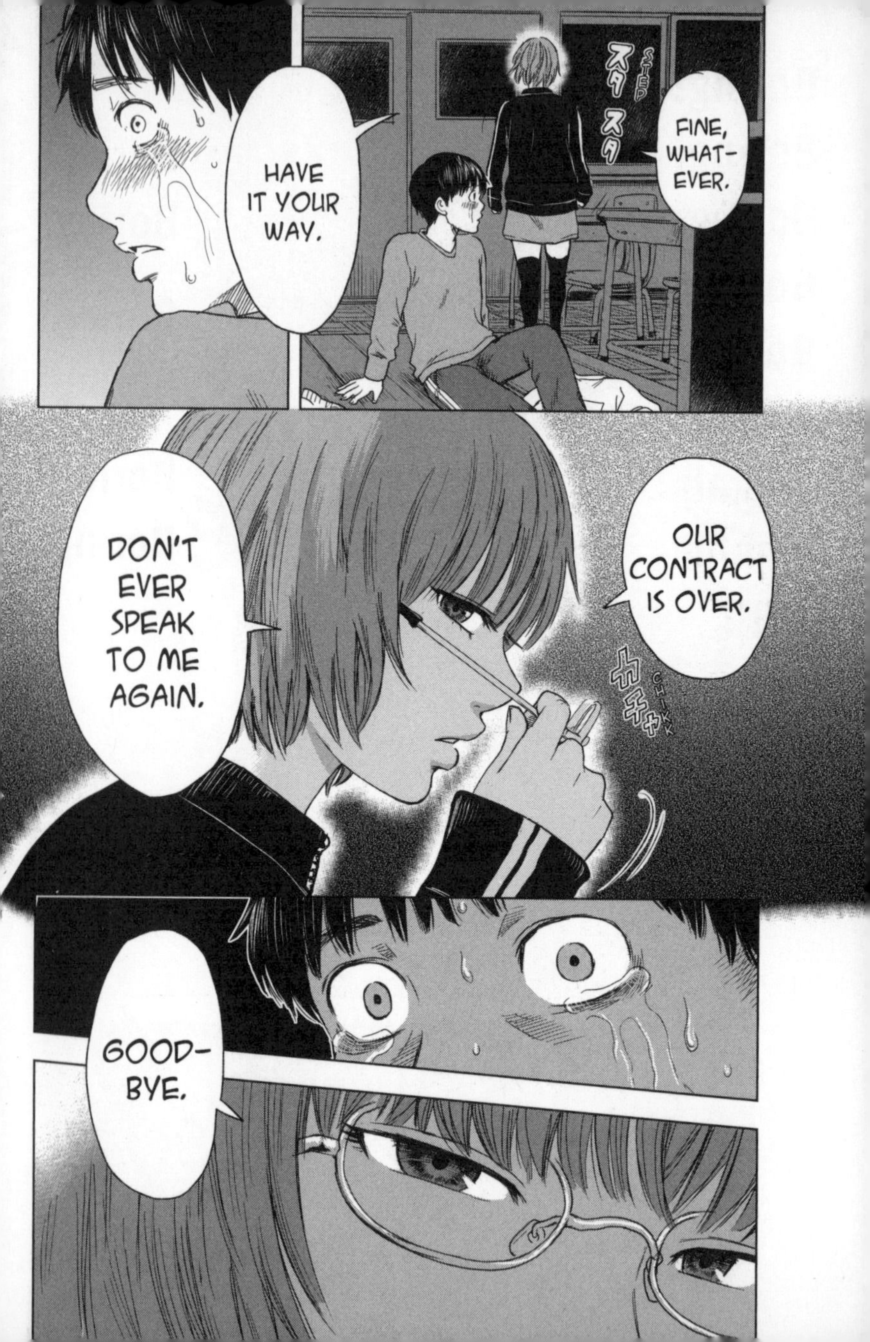
スタスタ
STEP
FINE, WHAT-EVER.
HAVE IT YOUR WAY.
OUR CONTRACT IS OVER.
カチャ
CHIKK
DON'T EVER SPEAK TO ME AGAIN.
GOOD-BYE.

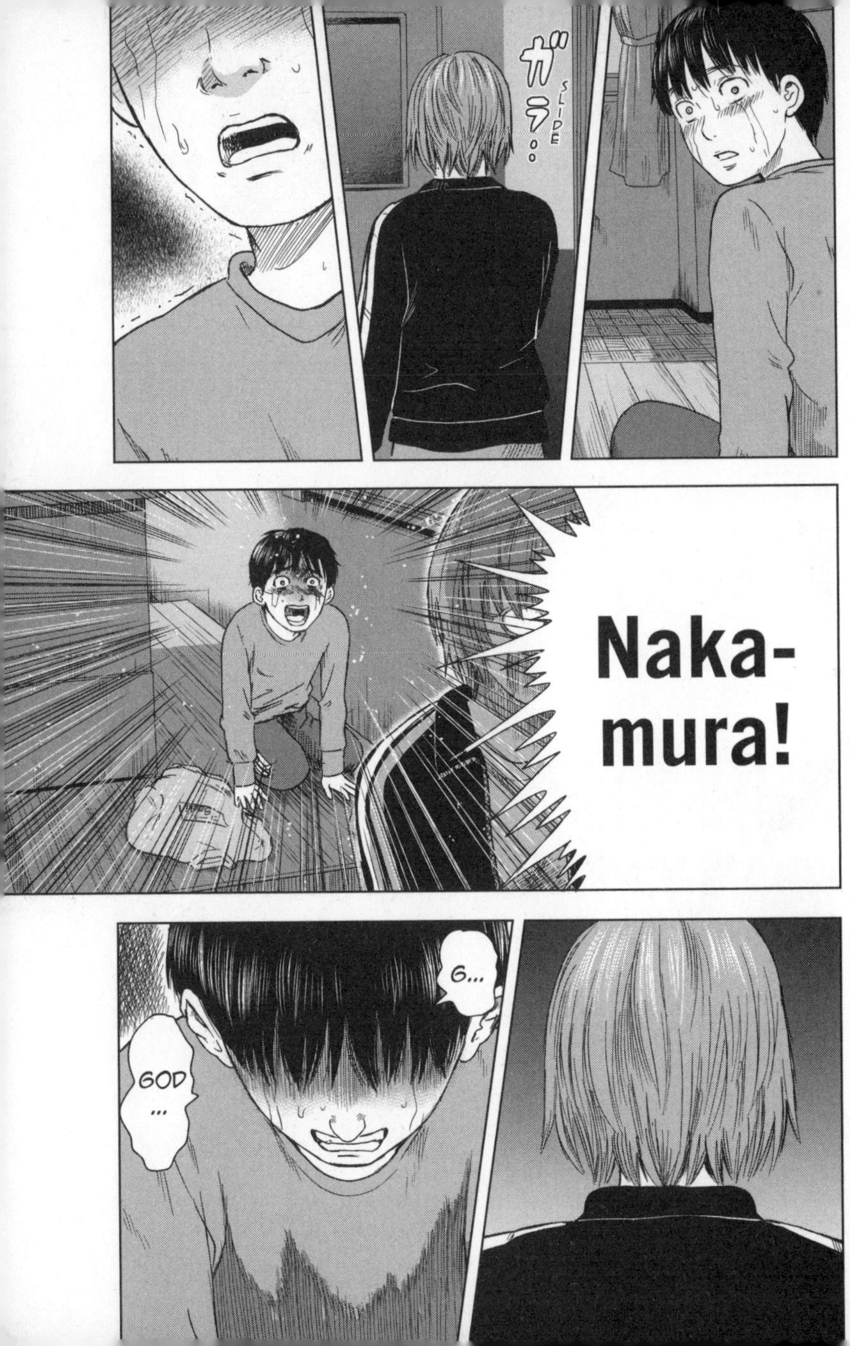

ガラ。。
SLIDE
Naka-mura!
G...
GOD ...

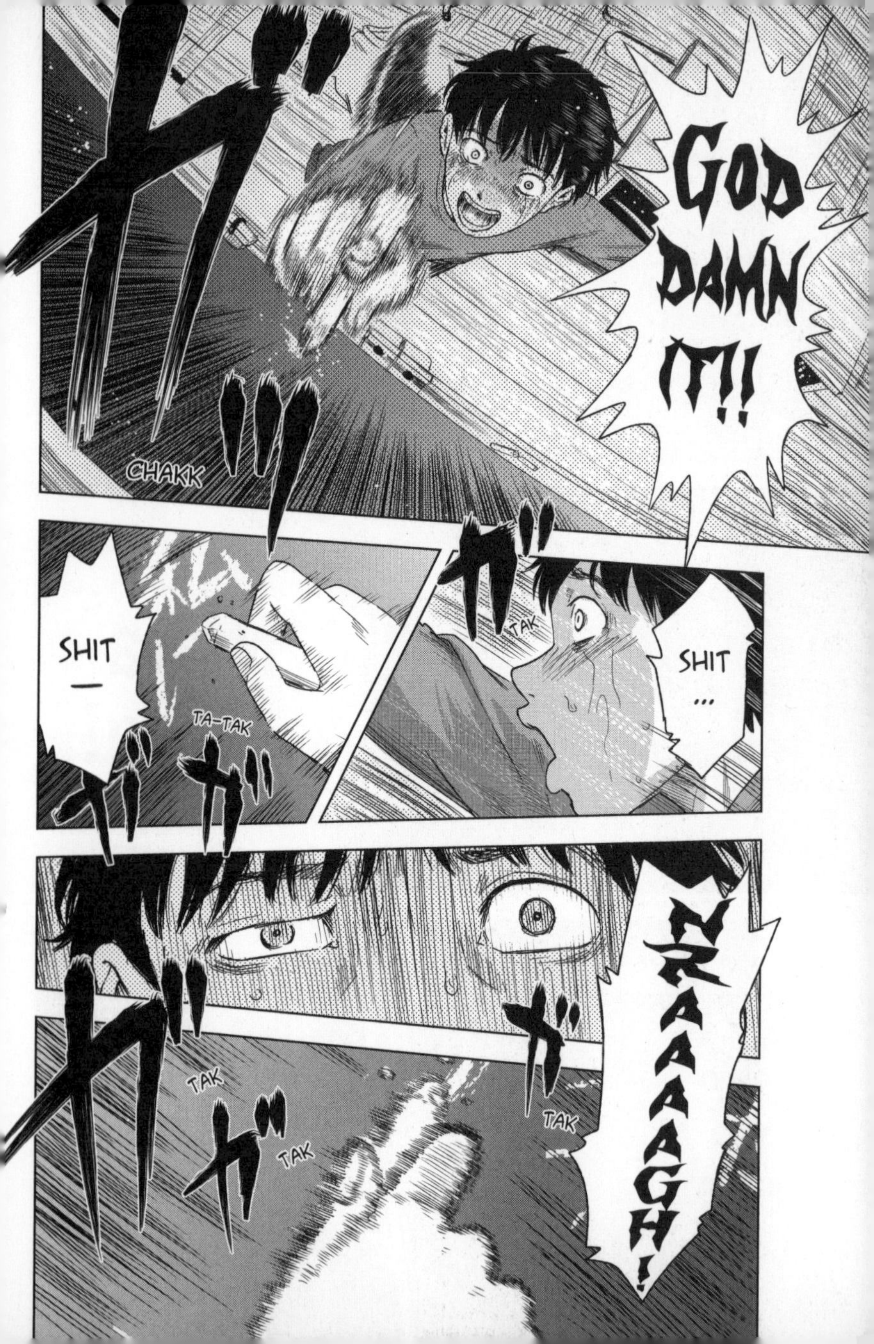
GOD DAMN IT!!
CHAKK
SHIT ...
TAK
SHIT —
TA-TAK
NRAAAAAGH!
TAK
TAK
TAK

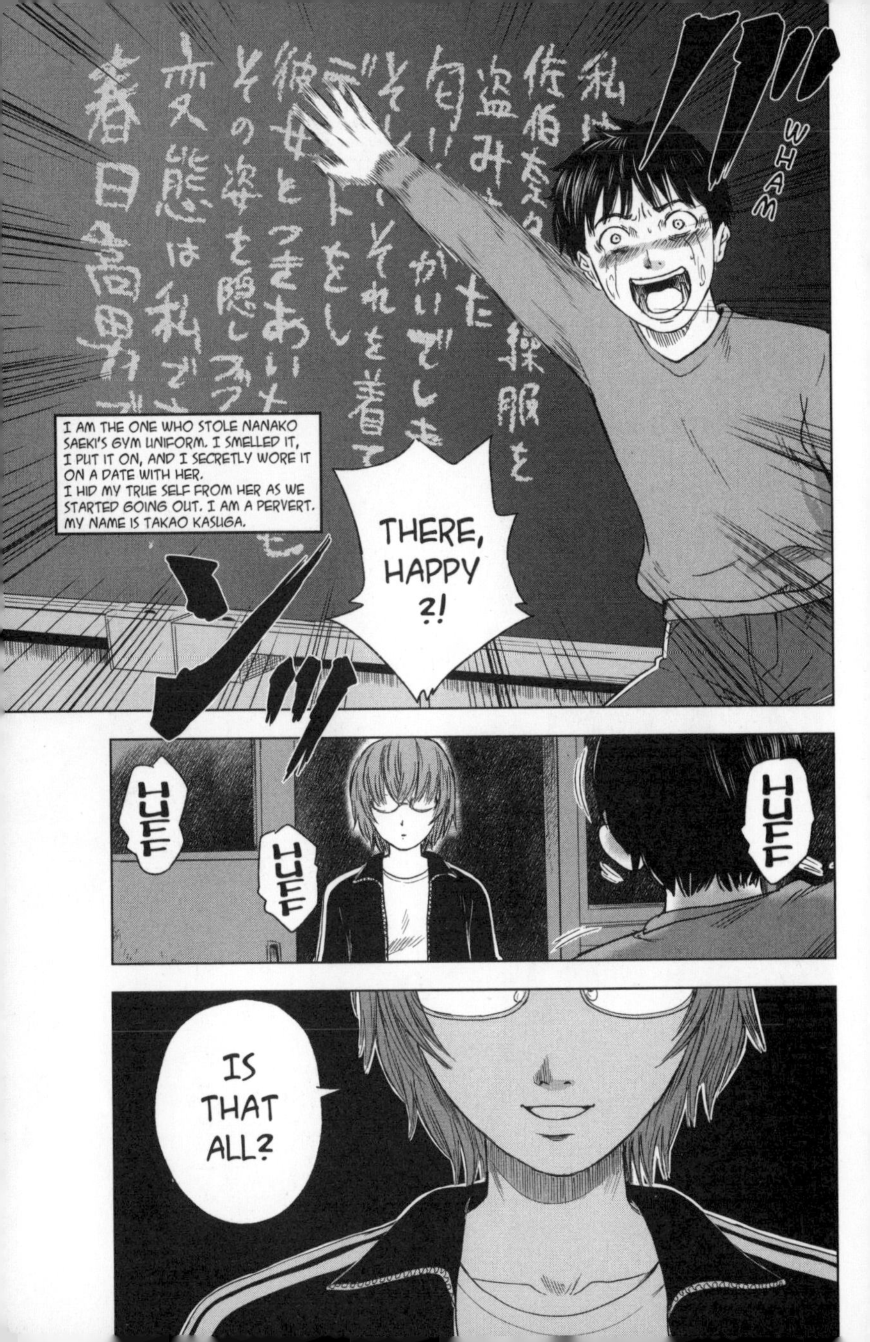
WHAM
I AM THE ONE WHO STOLE NANAKO SAEKI'S GYM UNIFORM. I SMELLED IT, I PUT IT ON, AND I SECRETLY WORE IT ON A DATE WITH HER.
I HID MY TRUE SELF FROM HER AS WE STARTED GOING OUT. I AM A PERVERT. MY NAME IS TAKAO KASUGA.
THERE, HAPPY ?!
HUFF
HUFF
HUFF
IS THAT ALL?

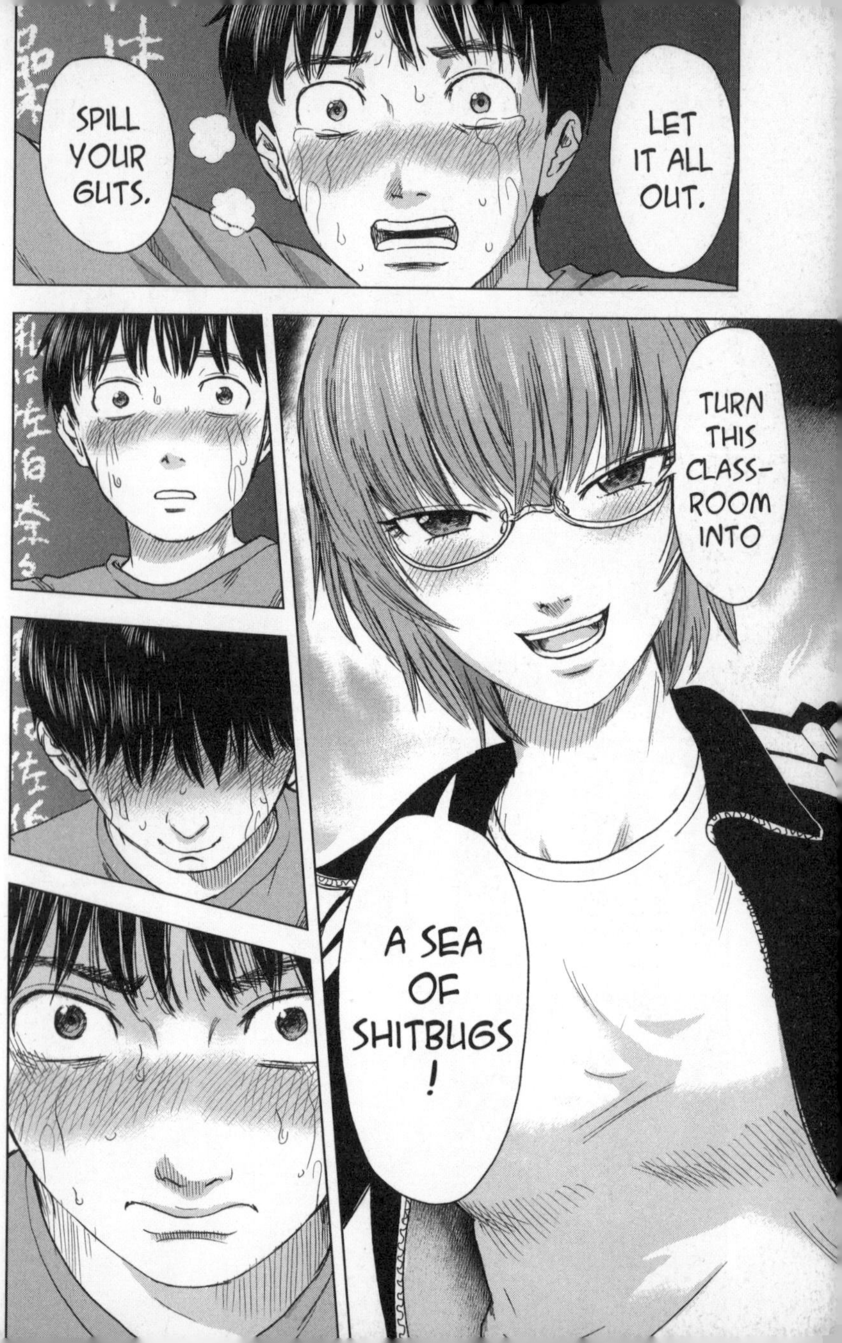
LET IT ALL OUT.
SPILL YOUR GUTS.
TURN THIS CLASS-ROOM INTO
A SEA OF SHITBUGS!

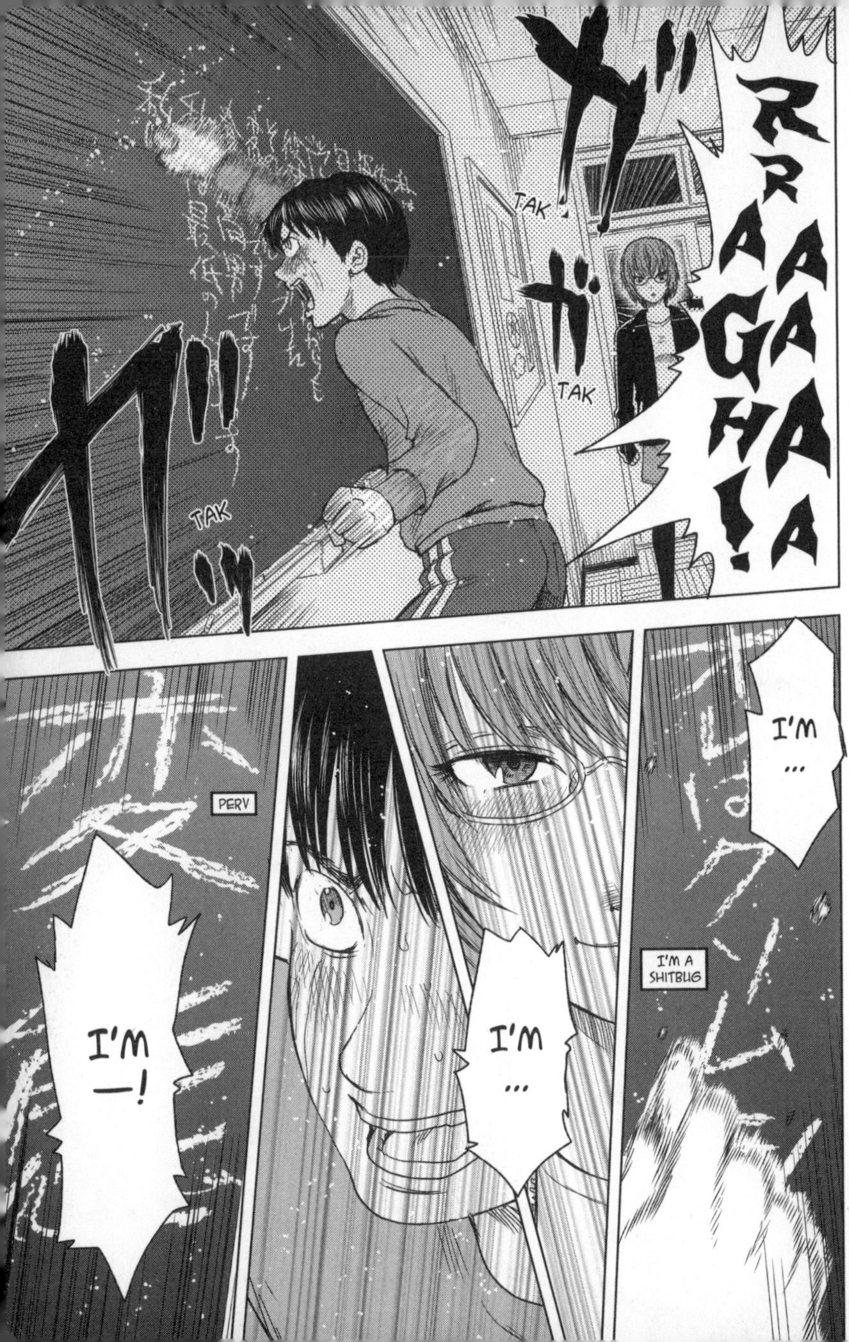
RRAGAHA!
AAAA
TAK
TAK
TAK
I'M ...
I'M A SHITBUG
I'M ...
PERV
I'M —!

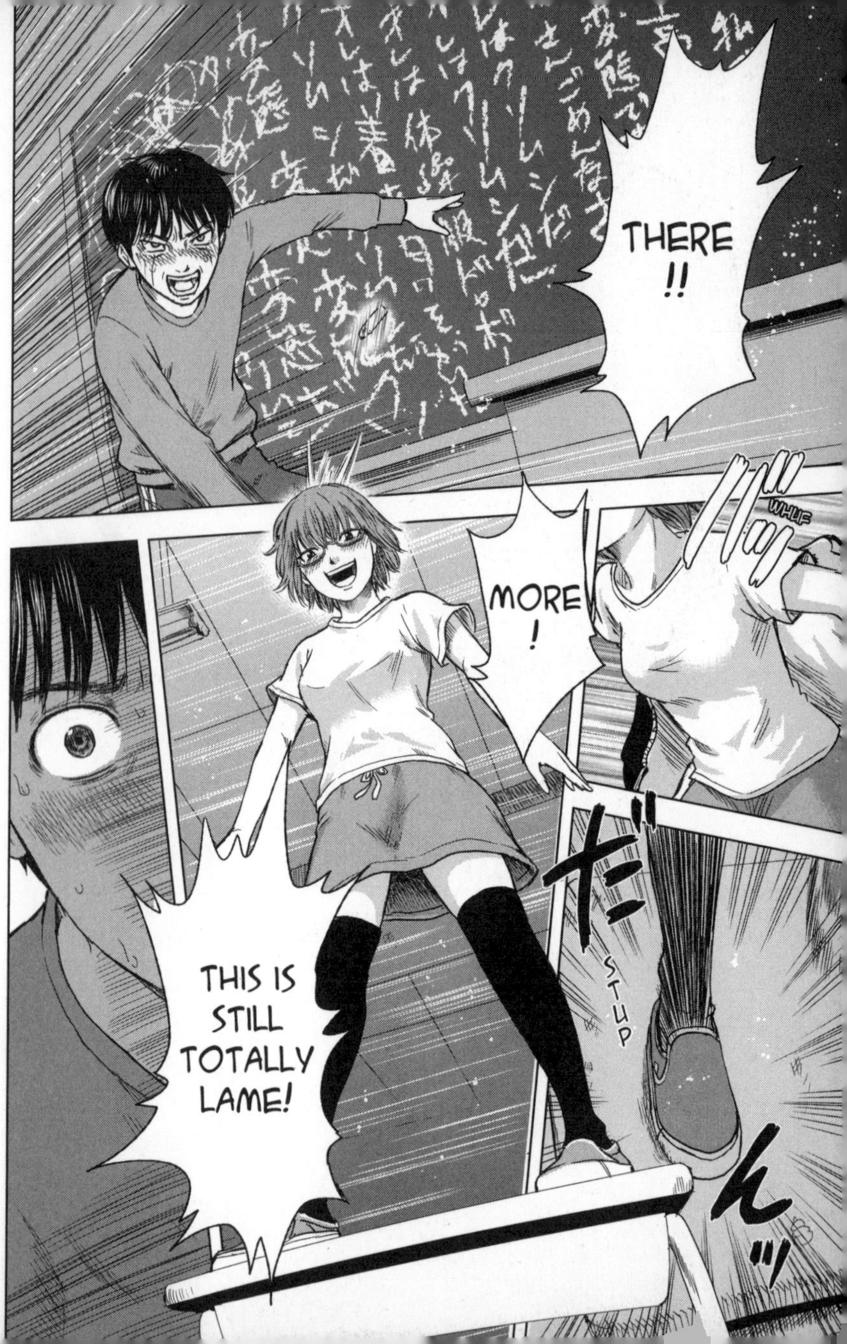
THERE !!
WHUF
STUP
MORE!
THIS IS STILL TOTALLY LAME!

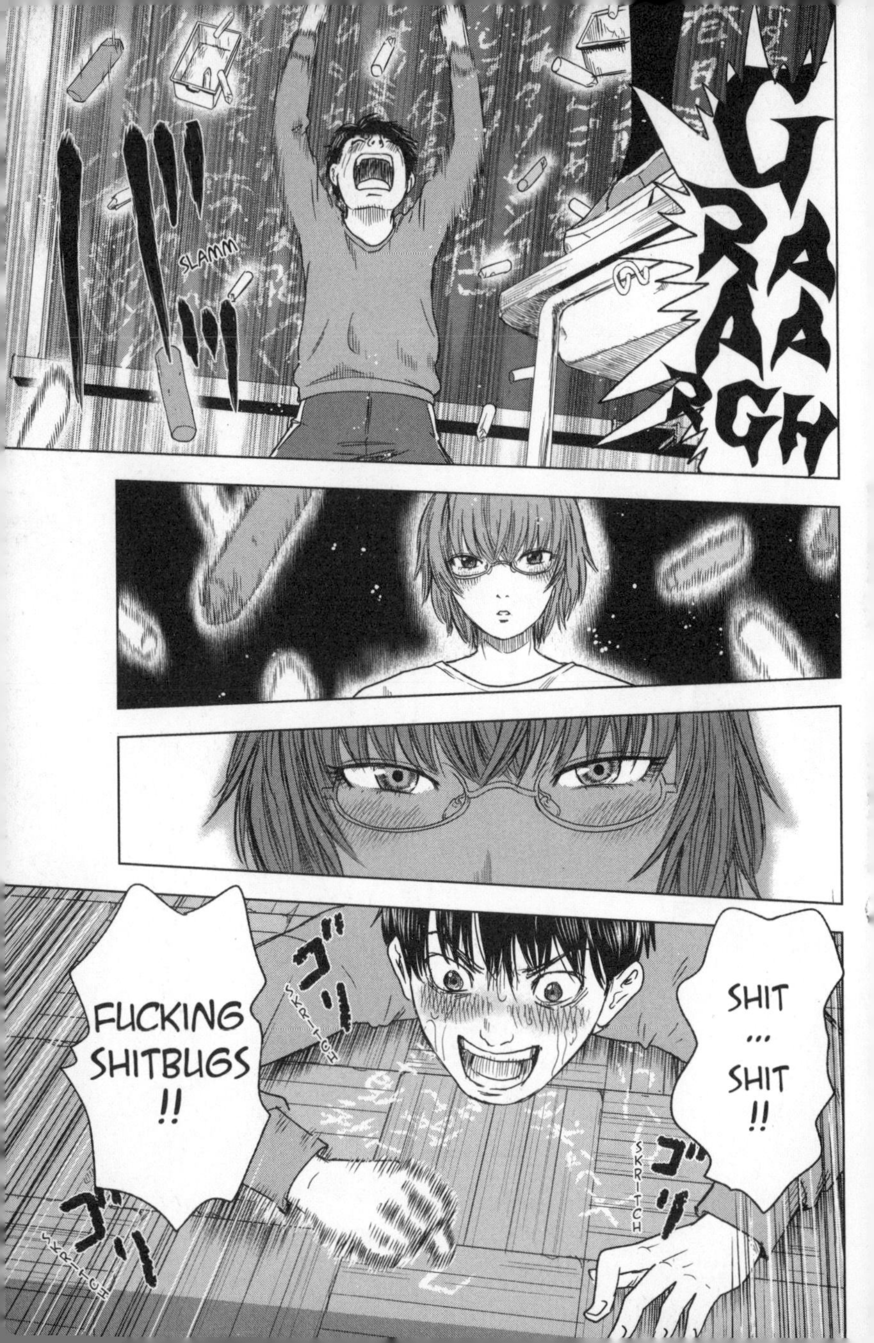
GYRAAARGH
SLAMM
SHIT ... SHIT !!
SKRITCH
SKRITCH
FUCKING SHITBUGS !!
SKRITCH

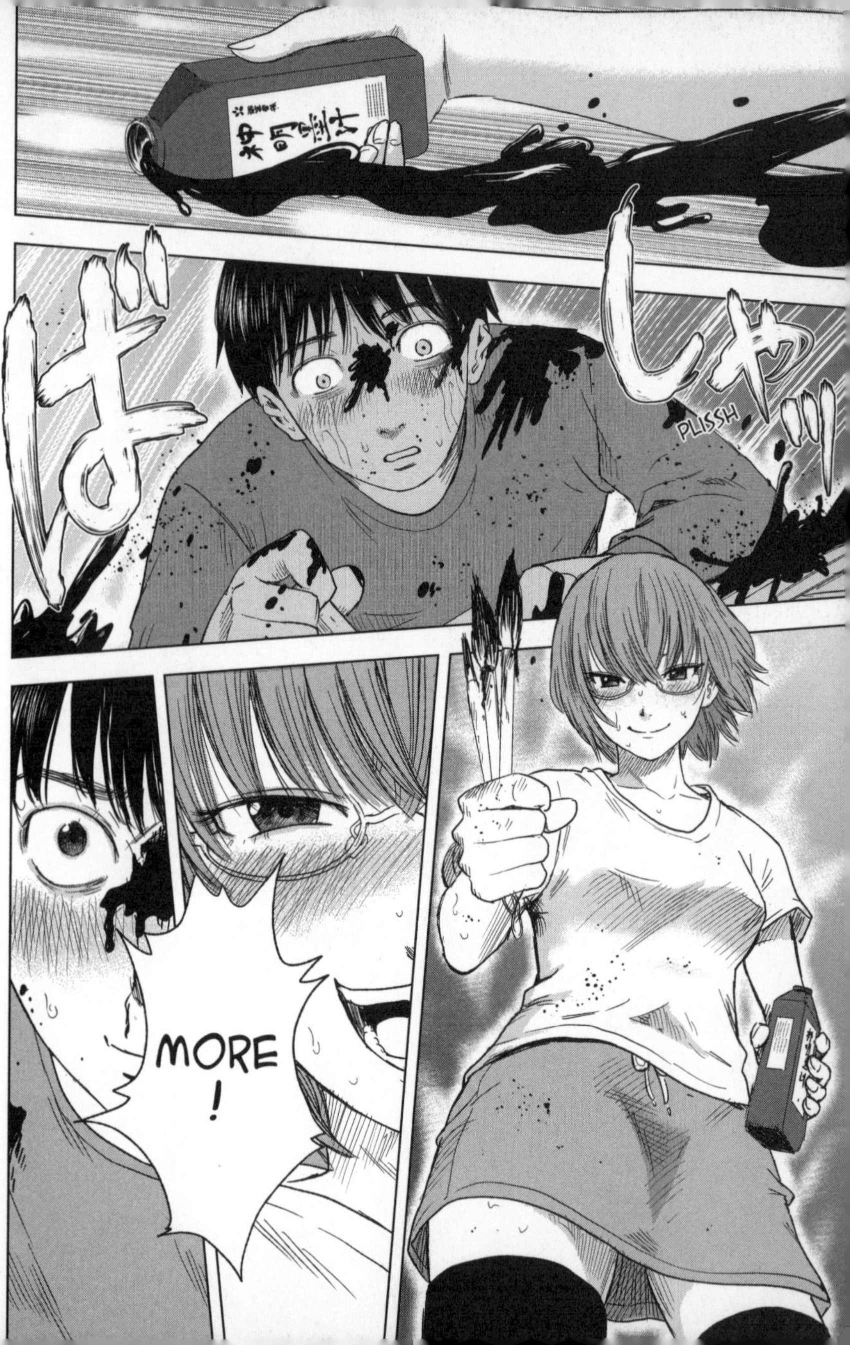
PLISSH
MORE
!

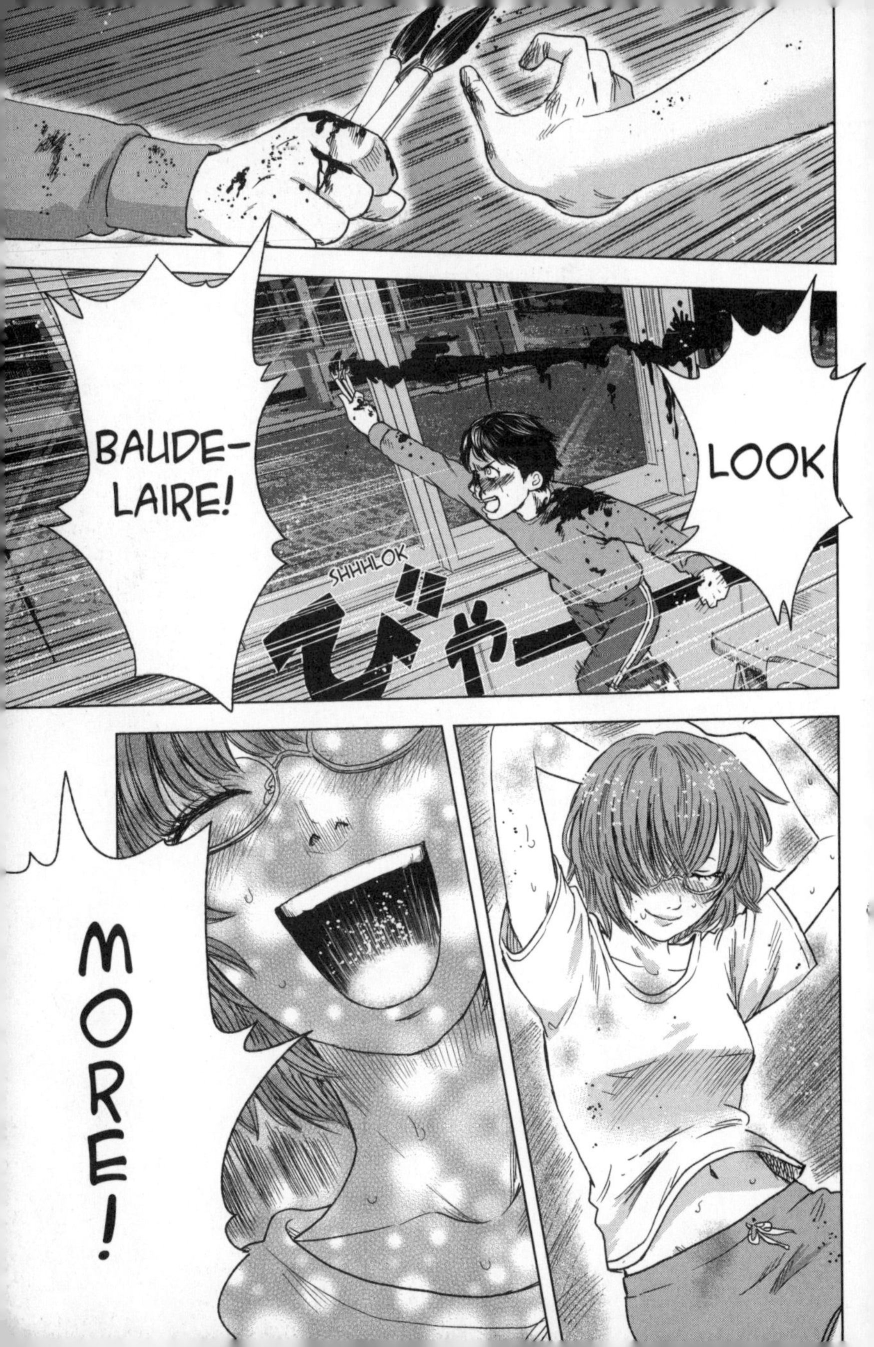
LOOK
BAUDE-LAIRE!
SHHHLOK
びゃー
MORE!

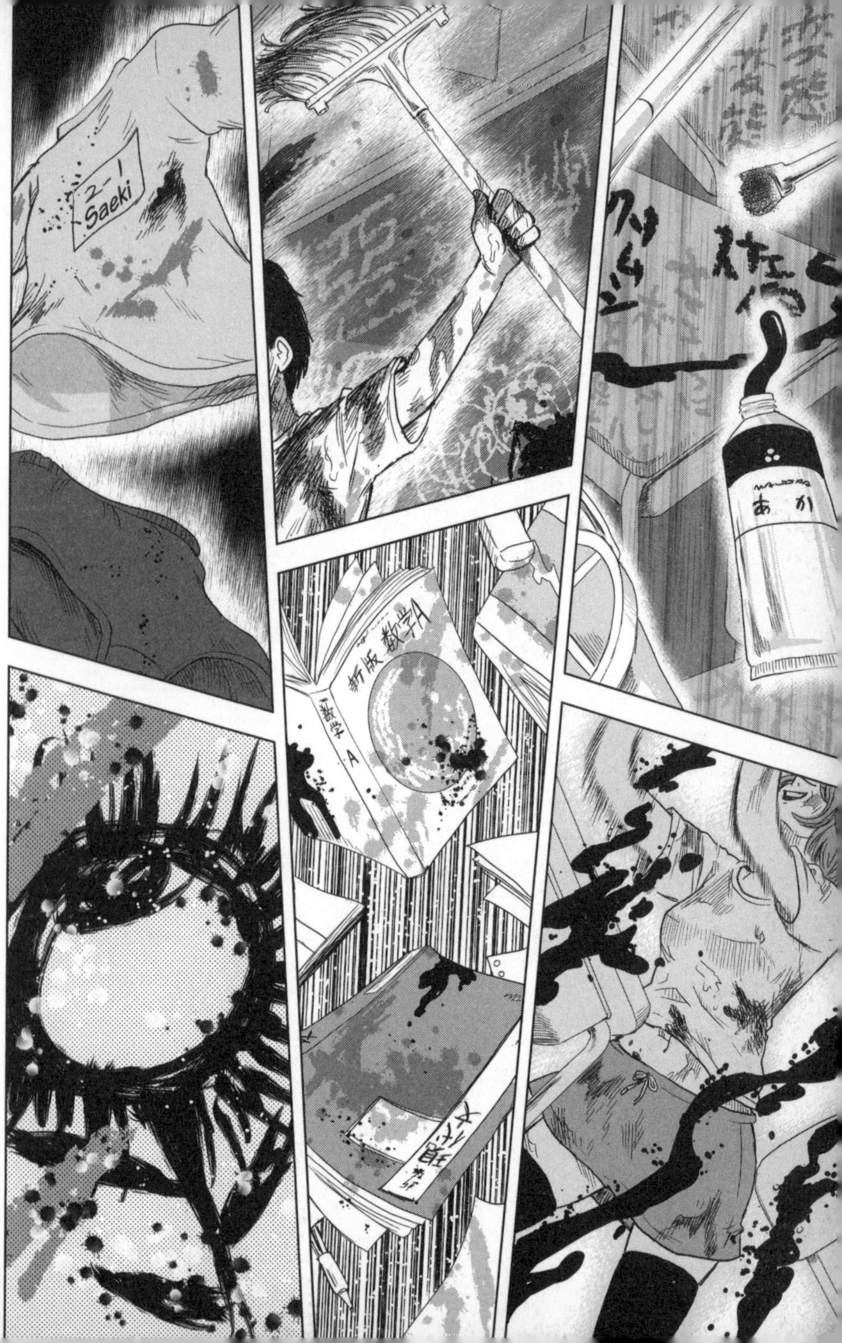
あか
新版 数学A
数学 A
2-1
Saeki

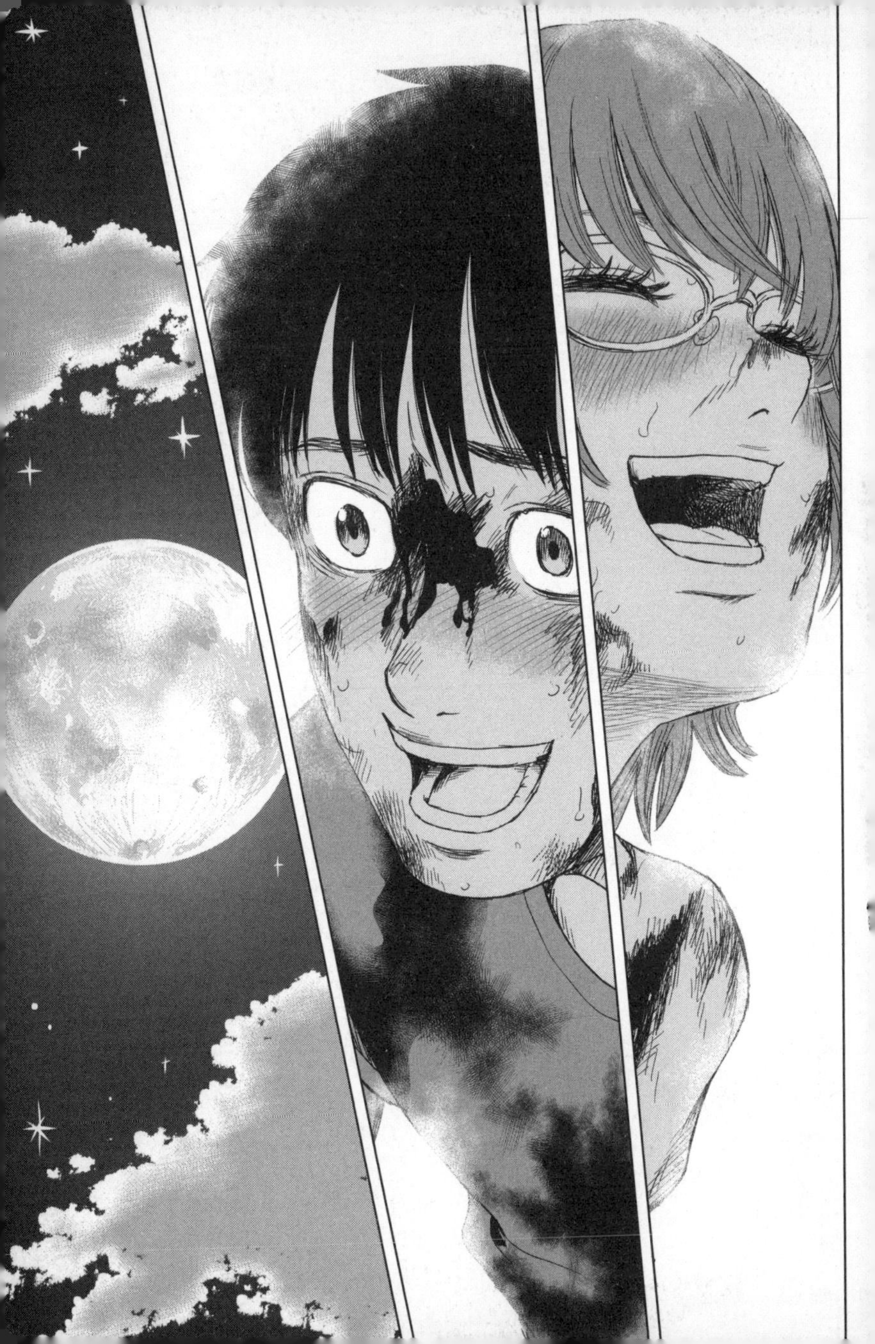

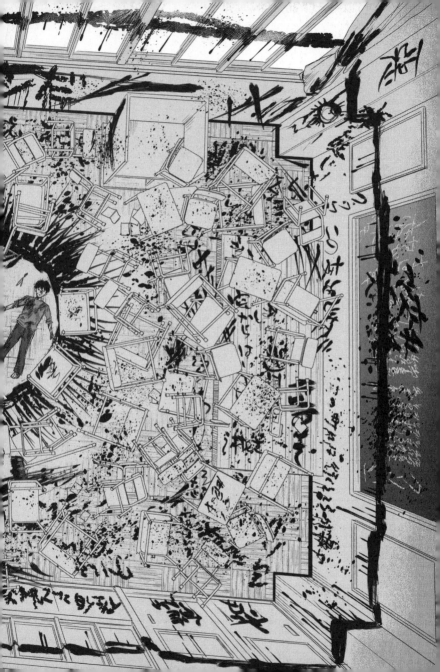

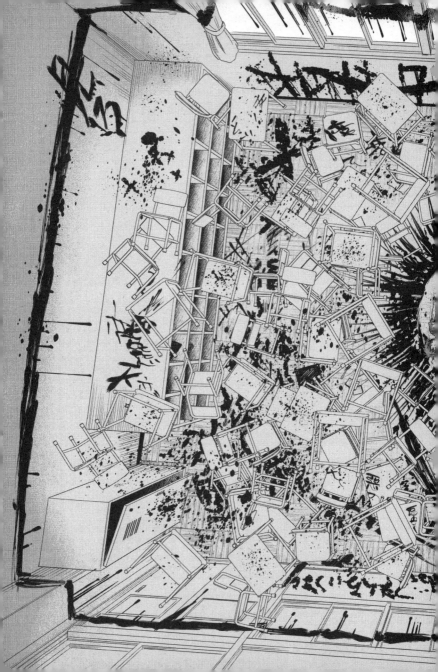

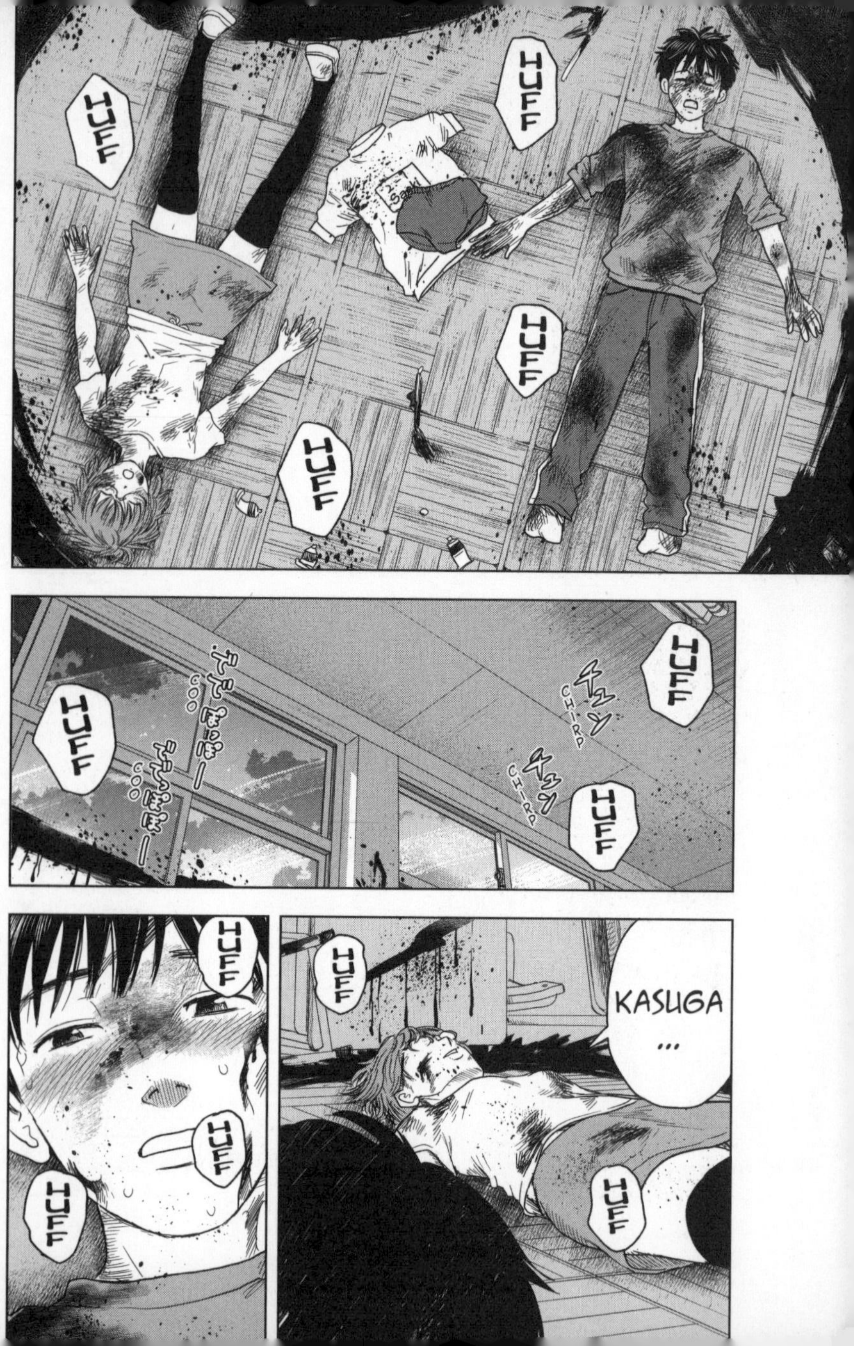
HUFF
HUFF
HUFF
HUFF
HUFF
チュン CHIRP
チュン CHIRP
HUFF
でででぽっぽー COO
でででぽっぽー COO
HUFF
KASUGA ...
HUFF
HUFF
HUFF
HUFF
HUFF

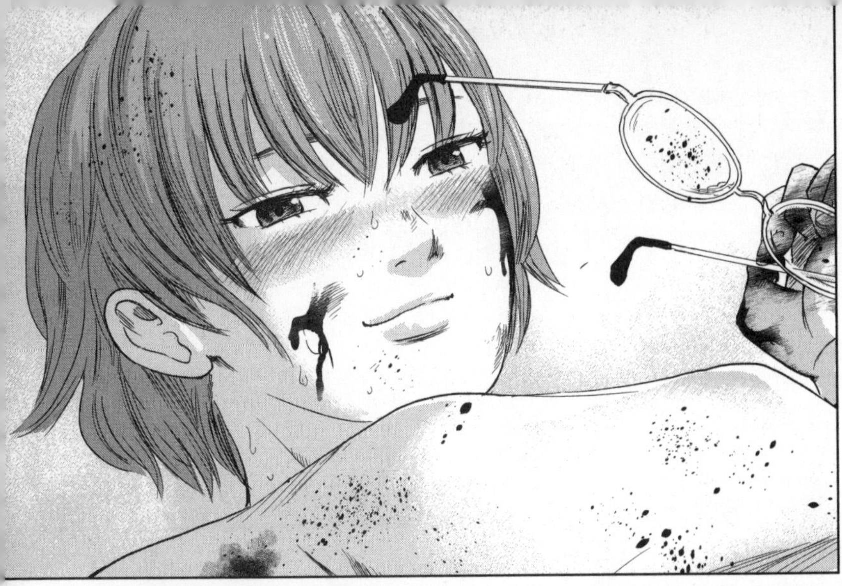

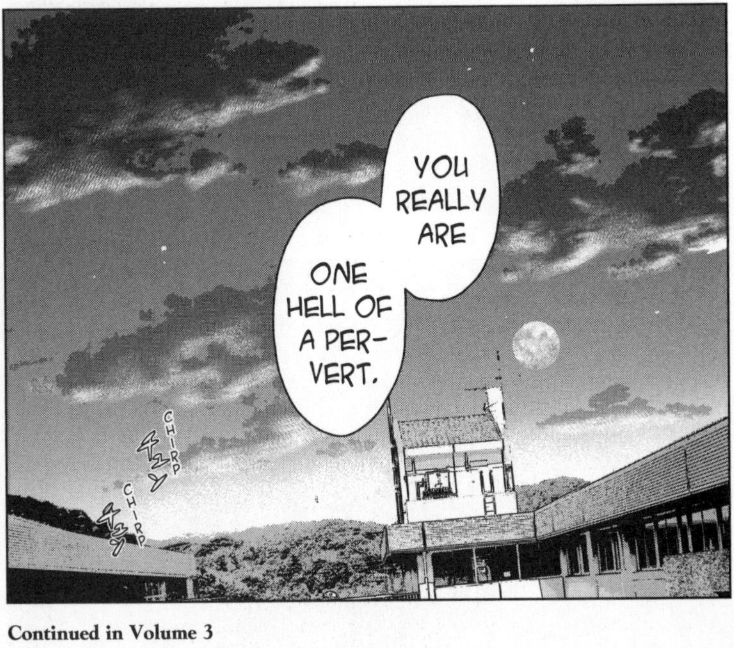
YOU REALLY ARE
ONE HELL OF A PER-VERT.
CHIRP
CHIRP

Continued in Volume 3

"It's clearly a comedy, but when it takes a turn into drama, it doesn't feel unnatural. *14 Days in Shonan* looks like one of those series that can be brutally funny when it wants to be." —*Comics Alliance*

"I loved it... The most surprising thing about *14 Days in Shonan* is its ability to address serious social problems without devolving into an Afterschool Special." —*The Manga Critic*

"Suffice to say, the first chapter grabbed me almost immediately. It was the same *Great Teacher Onizuka* humor I remember, and most importantly, I reacted the same to it as I had when I was stuck in my college dorm on those long Syracuse winter nights." —*Japanator*

"Established fans will definitely get more out of it, but there's enough fun here to 'open the doors of all hearts,' as Onizuka himself would put it." —*Otaku USA*

GTO
GREAT TEACHER ONIZUKA
14 DAYS in SHONAN
by TORU FUJISAWA

Completed only last year, this new arc in the saga of the most badass teacher ever requires no prior schooling in the franchise to move you (when you aren't laughing your head off).

VOLUMES 1 TO 3 AVAILABLE NOW!

200 pages, $10.95 each

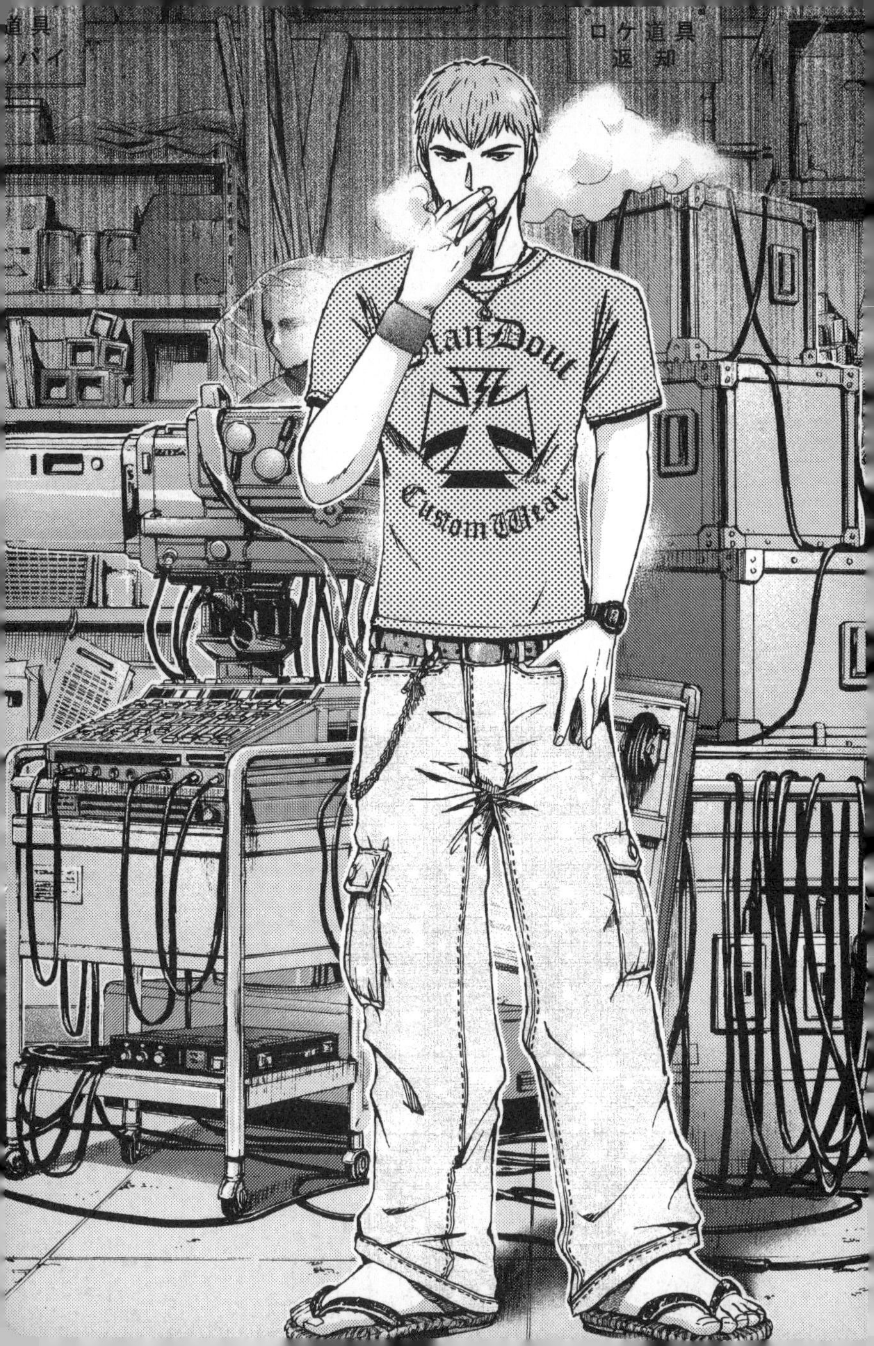
ロケ道具
返知
Custom Wear

The Flowers of Evil, volume 2

Translation: Paul Starr
Production: Hiroko Mizuno
          Tomoe Tsutsumi
          Nicole Dochych

Copyright © 2012 Shuzo Oshimi. All rights reserved.
First published in Japan in 2010 by Kodansha, Ltd., Tokyo
Publication for this English edition arranged through Kodansha, Ltd., Tokyo
English language version produced by Vertical, Inc.

Translation provided by Vertical, Inc., 2012
Published by Vertical, Inc., New York

Originally published in Japanese as *Aku no Hana* by Kodansha, Ltd., 2010
Aku no Hana first serialized in *Bessatsu Shonen Magazine*, Kodansha, Ltd., 2009.

This is a work of fiction.

ISBN: 978-1-935654-47-6

Manufactured in Canada

First Edition

Second Printing

Vertical, Inc.
451 Park Avenue South
7th Floor
New York, NY 10016
www.vertical-inc.com